Advancing Empire

In this book, L. H. Roper explores the origins and early development of English overseas expansion. Roper focuses on the networks of aristocrats, merchants, and colonial-imperialists who worked to control the transport and production of exotic commodities, such as tobacco and sugar, as well as the labor required to produce them. Roper focuses in particular on the relationship between the English state and the people it governed, the role of that state in imperial development, the sociopolitical character of English colonies, and English relations with Asians, Africans, American Indians, and other Europeans overseas. The activities stimulated the expansion and integration of global territorial and commercial interests that became the British Empire in the eighteenth century. In exploring these activities from a wider perspective, Roper offers a novel conclusion that revises popular analyses of the English Empire and of Anglo-America.

L.H. ROPER is Professor of History at the State University of New York at New Paltz and the author of *Conceiving Carolina* (2004) and *The English Empire in America, 1602–1658* (2009). He has edited several books of essays and published numerous articles on early American history. He is also Co-General Editor of *The Journal of Early American History*.

Advancing Empire

English Interests and Overseas Expansion, 1613–1688

L. H. ROPER

State University of New York at New Paltz

CAMBRIDGE
UNIVERSITY PRESS

CAMBRIDGE
UNIVERSITY PRESS

One Liberty Plaza, 20th Floor, New York, NY 10006, USA

Cambridge University Press is part of the University of Cambridge.

It furthers the University's mission by disseminating knowledge in the pursuit of education, learning, and research at the highest international levels of excellence.

www.cambridge.org
Information on this title: www.cambridge.org/9781107545052
DOI: 10.1017/9781316340493

© L. H. Roper 2017

First published 2017

Printed in the United States of America by Sheridan Books, Inc.

A catalogue record for this publication is available from the British Library.

Library of Congress Cataloging-in-Publication Data
NAMES: Roper, L. H. (Louis H.), author.
TITLE: Advancing empire : English interests and overseas expansion, 1613-1688 / L. H. Roper.
DESCRIPTION: New York, NY : Cambridge University Press, 2017.
IDENTIFIERS: LCCN 2017009161| ISBN 9781107118911 (Hardback) |
ISBN 9781107545052 (Paperback)
SUBJECTS: LCSH: Great Britain–Colonies–History–17th century. | Great Britain–Foreign relations. | Imperialism. | BISAC: HISTORY / United States / Colonial Period (1600-1775).
CLASSIFICATION: LCC DA16 .R58 2017 | DDC 909/.097124106–dc23
LC record available at https://lccn.loc.gov/2017009161

ISBN 978-1-107-11891-1 Hardback
ISBN 978-1-107-54505-2 Paperback

Contents

Acknowledgments and Note on Sources

The completion of this book enables me to express my deep gratitude to those who have helped make it possible. Staff at the National Archives at Kew, the British Library, the Bodleian Library, London Metropolitan Archives, the John Carter Brown Library, and the National Archives (Riksarkivet) of Sweden were exceedingly helpful in producing documents and handling my enquiries. Trinity College (Dublin) Library and the Huntington Library kindly provided copies of documents electronically, and the Interlibrary Loan staff at the Sojourner Truth Library of the State University of New York at New Paltz provided consistently effective service in obtaining materials from afar.

The Office of the Provost/Vice President for Academic Affairs at SUNY New Paltz granted me Research and Creative Project Awards in 2013 and 2015 and United University Professions granted a Professional Development and Quality of Working Life Award in 2015 that helped to defray the costs of conducting research in England. The Dean of the College of Liberal Arts and Sciences and the Department of History also kindly provided funds to support my research. My home institution also granted me a term of sabbatical leave that enabled me to finish free of other obligations. Martha Teck went well beyond the call of duty in providing assistance in acquiring documents.

Martine van Ittersum and Jaap Jacobs have rendered consistent and consistently valuable assistance with the Dutch sources, and I have bene-fited immensely from our discussions of Anglo-Dutch issues. My former pupils, Melissa Franson, Kirk McLeod, Nikki Parker, and Shaun Sayres, have also offered helpful suggestions. Enrique Hernández continues to provide me with insights into the nature of British involvement in South

America and, thus, the nature of empire, from his own work on the independence of Uruguay, while Erik Gøbel kindly advised me on seventeenth-century Danish overseas activity and on Anglo-Danish relations from Copenhagen's perspective.

I presented parts of this work at the History of Empire Seminar at Uppsala University, the Atlantic World Workshop at New York University, the British Group in Early American History, the Annual Meeting of the Southern Historical Association, and the Medieval and Early Modern Studies Colloquium at SUNY New Paltz, and the comments I received from these audiences greatly assisted my thinking. Max Edling and Karen Kupperman extended kind invitations to appear at Uppsala and New York University, respectively.

I would also like to thank Debbie Gershenowitz, my editor at Cambridge, for her immediate enthusiasm for this project and for steering my proposal through acceptance by the Press. Debbie, her assistant Kris Deusch, content manager Josh Penney, and Catherine Kuruvilla then oversaw the process of turning the manuscript into a book; anonymous readers offered excellent critiques and Stephanie Sakson did a splendid copy-editing job.

Finally, but certainly not least, my deepest thanks go to Rosemarie Frisone for her constant patience and the grounding she has provided.

All references from the sources, unless otherwise noted, are dated Old Style in accordance with the Julian calendar that was in effect in the Anglophone world until 1752 and in which the new year began on 25 March.

Abbreviations

Ag. HR	*The Agricultural History Review*
AHR	*The American Historical Review*
AOI	C.H. Firth and R.S. Rait (eds.), *Acts and Ordinances of the Interregnum, 1642–1660*, 3 vols. (London: H.M.S.O., 1911)
APC	W.L. Grant and James Munro (eds.), *Acts of the Privy Council, Colonial Series, Vol. 1, 1613–1680* (London: H.M.S.O., 1908)
BL	British Library
Bodl.	Bodleian Library, University of Oxford
CCMEIC	Ethel B. Sainsbury (ed.), *A Calendar of Court Minutes, etc., of the East India Company, 1635–1639 to 1677–1679*, 11 vols., with introductions by Sir William Foster (Oxford: Oxford University Press, 1907–38)
CJ	*Journal of the House of Commons*, 267 vols. (London: H.M.S.O., 1802 to present)
CMHS	*Collections of the Massachusetts Historical Society* (Boston: For the Society)
CNYHS	*Collections of the New-York Historical Society* (New York: For the Society)
CO	Records of the Colonial Office, TNA
CRNC	William L. Saunders (ed.), *The Colonial Records of North Carolina*, 10 vols. (Raleigh: State of North Carolina, 1886–90)

CSPC AWI	W. Noel Sainsbury et al. (eds.), *Calendar of State Papers, Colonial Series, America and West Indies*, 44 vols. (London: H.M.S.O., 1860–1963)
CSPC EI	W. Noel Sainsbury et al. (eds.), *Calendar of State Papers, Colonial Series, East Indies, China and Japan*, 5 vols. (London: H.M.S.O., 1862–92)
CSPD	Mary A.E. Green et al. (eds.), *Calendar of State Papers, Domestic Series* (London: Longman, Brown, Green, Longmans & Roberts, 1856–1947)
Ct. Recs.	J. Hammond Trumbull and Charles J. Hoadly (eds.), *The Public Records of the Colony of Connecticut*, 15 vols. (Hartford: Brown & Parsons, 1850–90)
DIHSTA	Elizabeth Donnan (ed.), *Documents Illustrative of the History of the Slave Trade to America*, 4 vols. (Washington, D.C.: Carnegie, Institution of Washington, 1930–5)
DRCHNY	E.B. O'Callaghan and B. Fernow (eds.), *Documents Related to the Colonial History of the State of New York*, 15 vols. (Albany: Weed, Parsons, and Co., 1853–87)
Econ. HR	*The Economic History Review*, new series
EHR	*The English Historical Review*
FP	Furley Papers, Balme Library, University of Ghana, available online at http://ugspace.ug.edu.gh/handle/123456789/3
HCA	High Court of Admiralty records series, TNA
HJ	*The Historical Journal*
HMC	*Historical Manuscripts Commission*
IOR	India Office Records, BL
JAS	*The Journal of Asian Studies*
JBS	*The Journal of British Studies*
JEH	*The Journal of Economic History*
JICH	*The Journal of Imperial and Commonwealth History*
JIH	*The Journal of Interdisciplinary History*
LJ	*Journal of the House of Lords*, 243 vols. (H.M.S.O., 1767 to present)
LMA	London Metropolitan Archives
MAS	*Modern Asian Studies*
NEQ	*The New England Quarterly*
PC	Records of the Privy Council and other records collected by the Privy Council Office, TNA
P&P	*Past & Present*

RVC	Susan Myra Kingsbury (ed.), *Records of the Virginia Company*, 4 vols. (Washington, D.C.: Government Printing Office, 1906–33)
T	Records created or inherited by HM Treasury, TNA
TGC	Margaret Makepeace (ed.), *Trade on the Gold Coast, 1657–1666: The Correspondence of the English East India Company* (Madison: University of Wisconsin–Madison, African Studies Program African Primary Texts, 4, ed. David Henige)
TNA	The National Archives, Kew, Richmond, Surrey
TSP	Thomas Birch (ed.), *A Collection of the State Papers of John Thurloe*, 7 vols. (London, 1742)
VMHB	*The Virginia Magazine of History and Biography*
WMQ	*The William and Mary Quarterly*, 3rd series
WP	Worthington C. Ford, Stewart Mitchell, Allyn Bailey Forbes, and Malcolm Freiberg (eds.), *The Winthrop Papers*, 6 vols. (Boston: Massachusetts Historical Society, 1925–92)

Introduction

In 1613, the English overseas presence, while geographically extensive, had little to commend it in terms of substance, consisting as it did of the bedraggled six-year-old Jamestown colony on the North American mainland, the newly established trading factories of the East India Company at Surat on the Arabian Sea and at Bantam (modern Bandung) in western Java, the small island of Bermuda in the Atlantic Ocean, a clutch of fishing stations in Newfoundland, and a scattering of Asian trading outposts that stretched as far east as Japan. By 1688, that presence had become much more economically and politically vigorous, although its geographical scope had receded. It now included a chain of colonies that extended along the Atlantic coast of North America from Maine to South Carolina; plantations on the islands of the Bahamas, Barbados, Jamaica, Antigua, St. Christopher's (St. Kitts), Montserrat, and Nevis; the Newfoundland trading outpost; and another post on Hudson's Bay in northern Canada. In the Eastern Hemisphere, the English possessed a colony on the Atlantic island of St. Helena and governed Bombay (Mumbai) and Madras (Chennai) as well as Bencoolen (Bengkulu) in Sumatra. They also pursued commercial relations along the Hooghly River in Bengal and at other Indian locations as well as in the South China Sea. In West Africa, they maintained trading factories on the Gambia River, the Gold Coast, and the Bight of Benin.

Who assumed responsibility for directing these endeavors and to what ends? To what degree did this direction constitute coordinated, integrated oversight? What role did the English state have in the progress of matters outside Europe before 1689 and the Glorious Revolution? What geographic, social, and cultural effects did the pursuit of English overseas trade and colonization generate and why?[1]

In addressing these questions, the book you are about to read first clarifies who assumed the primary responsibility for advancing seventeenth-century English commercial and territorial activities: a cohort of aristocrats and merchants, a significant number of whom held heterodox Protestant religious beliefs; the context in which their careers unfolded is set forth in Chapter 1. This series of London-based operators developed and bequeathed to successors in interest an array of overseas initiatives, as set forth in Chapters 2, 3, and 4. Their participation in the mid-century takeover of the English state involved that state closely and more deeply in these matters, as Chapter 5 details. Yet even through 1688 (and thereafter), these private interests retained the initiative in promoting and maintaining the English Empire. The study of their activities also illuminates the inherent connections between English social and political history and the history of English overseas affairs.

In recreating the seventeenth-century English imperial world, we need to address the nature of the historical record of seventeenth-century English overseas trade and colonization: it consists primarily of state papers; account books, minutes, and official correspondence of chartered companies; public records of various colonies; court records; and pamphlets created by supporters and opponents of various stripes related to overseas activities. Some unofficial correspondence and rather less of the personal record of certain traders and colonizers have survived but none of the records of unofficial enterprises. This record was created largely to further political and economic positions, and it conveys the highly charged atmosphere in which the pursuit of advantage via overseas ventures took place. This continuous jockeying for position invariably entailed complaints and polemical denunciations rather than detached observations on empire.

The political and social connections formed by these people furthered English commercial and territorial situations, the administrative and cultural integration of English overseas interests, and the social and political development of English colonies that constituted the basis of the English Empire in the seventeenth century and provided the platform for the post-1707 British Empire. Accordingly, any comprehension of

---

[1] There was no British Empire in any legal or formal sense prior to the Act of Union that created the Kingdom of Great Britain (incorporating Scotland with England and Wales) in 1707.

imperial history must start with a proper appreciation of the consistently reactive role played by the English state in the conduct of overseas trade and colonization during the period under study. In the first instance, the continuing fiscal limits under which the state operated prevented it from taking a lead; none of its various incarnations initiated any undertaking outside the British Isles that might be styled as imperial prior to 1689. Only the state, however, could legitimize overseas operations and grant the authority that these endeavors entailed. It did so by granting charters, which customarily invoked the authority granted to the medieval Bishops of Durham, whose remote and extensive see bordered an unfriendly Scotland. Under the terms of these documents, which it invariably issued at the behest of their recipients, the Crown delegated extraordinary powers that transformed the grantees into conductors of royal authority with the power to, inter alia, engage in diplomacy, recruit and transport migrants, establish laws and governments, manage trade, grant land, and construct forts.

Even when overseas affairs required state intervention, as in the case of the first Navigation Act and the captures of Jamaica and New Netherland, the state had to be prodded to make that intervention. Securing governmental approval for these plans, accordingly, always required the articulation of public purposes such as increasing the employment of mariners, the extension of dominions, the propagation of religion, and the increase of trade, sometimes in competition with other Europeans, especially the Dutch. To speak of the seventeenth-century English Empire, then, means to conceive of it, perhaps counterintuitively, as an entity that resulted from territorial and commercial agendas of often competing private individuals and groups, such as the Courteen Association and the East India Company or the Royal African Company and its rivals, which directed state behavior rather than because the state directed individuals and groups to effect policies that government officials pursued; the power and capabilities of the English state and the extent of the English overseas presence – "state formation" – increased in the seventeenth century primarily – and ironically – due to the behavior of people outside the state and even in spite of the state.[2]

Rather than diminishing the importance of the center of the English-speaking world to the propulsion of overseas trade and colonization, however, these circumstances underscore its overriding significance

---

[2] For "state formation," see Bliesemann de Guevara, "State Formation."

to the development of wider English interests. Working within an economy that was already commercialized, London-based patrons partnered with their clients to undertake trading, plundering, and settlement ventures on a steadily increasing scale after 1613. These groups had the economic and political wherewithal that enabled them to absorb the exceptional costs and risks inherent in their pursuits, and they used their experience, as well as their networks and the wealth that their pursuits generated, to construct their personal empires. In doing so, they also advanced the general condition of English overseas matters thanks to their control over the production and transportation of an array of commodities from around the world for which demand increased – or was encouraged to increase: Canary wines, Swedish iron, Levant currants, silk, chintzes, calicoes, cowrie shells, ivory, fish, cinnamon, pepper, tobacco, sugar, beaver pelts, and human beings. As sociopolitical leaders, they drew on their connections with the lower social orders to put their plans into effect: mariners handled the transporting of goods and people, while agents with mercantile or gentry backgrounds served as overseas trading factors, recruited migrants for colonies, and became colonial leaders themselves.[3]

In this vein, investors intended to benefit from the successful establishment of plantation colonies, which they recognized, first, required securing a labor supply, then securing a reliable stream of necessary commodities to support the inhabitants that would be exchanged for export crops. In actuality, though, it was preferable in terms of costs and convenience to recruit in situ local workers who possessed the requisite skills. Thus, the East India Company sought to attract Indian weavers and other cloth producers to its factories. Accordingly, the population of places like Madras, the establishment of which in 1639 began a reorientation of South Asian economic and political realities, consisted of a handful of customarily transient Englishmen overseeing a much more substantial population of Asians, as set forth particularly in Chapters 4 and 9.[4]

---

[3] Bailey, "Historiographical Essay." Pointedly, "feudal" did not appear as a description of any society until the seventeenth century, while "feudalism" is a nineteenth-century characterization of earlier societies; Brown, "The Tyranny of a Construct."

[4] Subsequently, the plantation system, with labor secured on long-term indentures rather than as slaves, spread with the expansion of British territorial claims into the twentieth century in, for instance, the Indian subcontinent, East Africa, and Fiji; Sturman, "Indian Indentured Labor and the History of International Rights Regimes"; Roy, "Sardars, Jobbers, Kanganies"; Amrith, "Tamil Diasporas across the Bay of Bengal"; Okia, "The

On the other hand, in the Americas, such entities, as well as the social and cultural relations required to govern them, had to be constructed de novo, at least in English terms, since the nature of the indigenous economies was fundamentally different, and no equivalent of Madras existed. The populations of Anglo-American colonies accordingly developed demographic and, therefore, social characteristics different from their Asian counterparts, while, customarily, the directors of plantation endeavors had to import labor either via contract or via the trans-Atlantic slave trade or to enslave indigenous people.

The immediate demand for plantation labor also meant that it was no coincidence that English involvement in Africa, as tracked especially in Chapters 3, 8, and 9, increased almost exactly contemporaneously with the expansion of English interests in America. Correspondingly, the "Guinea trade" became the nexus of seventeenth-century English overseas activities and imperial comprehension. In conjunction with the success that African-oriented initiatives achieved, English trade between Gambia and Gabon prompted an increased state interest and direct participation not evident elsewhere.

Those in charge of such pursuits naturally transported contemporary sociopolitical mechanisms and the contemporary political culture in order to govern those operations on the ground. In the first instance, this meant securing and employing the chartered powers noted above. The sponsorship of such extraordinary projects exceeded the fiscal and institutional capacity of the pre-1689 incarnations of the notoriously cash-strapped English state, although governments did involve themselves in overseas affairs, especially in their quest for revenue, albeit intermittently. Moreover, the greater distances between the metropolis and the locales of overseas projects aggravated costs and risks and placed management of these matter even further beyond governmental reach.

The perennial weakness of state authority and the delegation mechanisms that were devised to propel overseas projects meshed with the time-honored English sensibility, as manifested in concepts such as trial by jury, that local people should have primary responsibility for local affairs; interventions by the center, without invitation, were frequently regarded with distrust. The tumults that fractured the state in the 1640s, however, eroded that sensibility, as the actions of those responsible for the demise

Northey Forced Labor Crisis"; Wenzlhuemer, "Indian Labour Immigration and British Labour Policy in Nineteenth-Century Ceylon"; Baak, "About Ex-Slaves, Uncaptured Contract Coolies and Unfreed Freedmen."

of the government of Charles I (reigned 1625–49) resulted in a paradoxical increase in the capacity for the exercise of state power. Most particularly, the parliamentary success in ratifying and levying the hated excise devised in 1643 after the outbreak of the Civil Wars provided a relatively secure basis for paying the parliamentary army. This device provided the clearest means for ensuring victory – although what this would entail remained unclear – over the King even as English governments continued to incur new obligations of a variety and scale previously unknown.[5]

In considering these developments, *Advancing Empire* strives to consider the record in accordance with the political and religious views of the times. Unfortunately, while the often heated character of these documents has considerable importance for our understanding of the world in which seventeenth-century overseas trade and colonization took place, the friction that permeates the evidence can aggravate the temptation to identify certain seventeenth-century views as the precursors of modern sentiments.

From the perspective of those, especially historians of the United States, who seek the origins of modern phenomena, the seventeenth century constitutes an especially pivotal phase of the "early modern period" in which, sometime between the Reformation and the French Revolution, new ways of thinking and behaving ruptured longstanding social and economic systems and the ways of thinking that underpinned them and replaced them with new comprehensions of society, government, and economics. England, which witnessed the trial and execution of Charles I followed by the abolition of the House of Lords in 1649, has been frequently identified as the harbinger of modernity where the fundamentally distinctive characteristics of modern society first developed: individual liberties, state formation, the relatively easy widespread movement of people, ideas, and commodities, as well as the rise of capitalism, industrialization, and globalization, for better or for worse. These characteristics spread around the world in conjunction with the expansion of English overseas interests.[6]

Accordingly, we have been instructed to think that these phenomena gave rise to all sorts of corresponding novelties: new societies founded in

---

[5] For early Stuart attempts to solve the perennial revenue problem, see Hollis, "The Crown Lands and the Financial Dilemma in Stuart England." Austin Woolrych has observed that the monthly assessment of the excise "was fixed at about double the total regular revenue that Charles [I] had at his accession, and it was levied upon a much higher proportion of the population than the old parliamentary subsidies," *Britain in Revolution*, 276.

[6] Randolph Starn, "Review Article," offers helpful cautions about modernity and historiographical periodization.

America, new forms of labor employed to wring wealth from those societies, new traffic in new commodities (including human beings), new sociopolitical forms, including increased centralization of state power, all propelled by a novel sense of opportunity, improvement, restlessness, and freedom. For an increasing number of modern observers, however, this conception of freedom is deeply and fatally paradoxical given its grounding in slavery and the other, perhaps related, forms of coerced labor practiced by contemporaries.

Although all of these phenomena arose within European contexts, the formation of what has come to be called Colonial British America entailed, according to an entrenched vision of reality, a distinctively, if not uniquely, American strain of modernity. Thus, those who seek the origins of various aspects of modern American society and culture inevitably have found the creation and formation of Anglo-American societies to be fruitful areas in which to conduct their inquiries; after all, twelve of the thirteen colonies that broke away from the British Empire and became the United States were founded before 1688. These societies incorporated migrants of various socioeconomic and religious stripes from England and, to a lesser but palpable extent, other parts of Europe. They also became the unwanted new homes of millions of enslaved Africans and the scenes of bitter conflicts between Native American people and settlers. The search for the origins of modernity has also incorporated, albeit from different perspectives, the view that its green shoots emerged contemporaneously with stirrings of the early Anglo-American sensibility of human rights.[7]

Recent attempts to correct triumphalist tendencies in the historiography of the United States have spread further confusion despite recognizing that seventeenth-century states did not operate as their nineteenth-century counterparts did. For the study of the seventeenth century, this determination to

---

[7] It is unclear why the origins and character of the United States, especially when framed in terms of the migration of Anglophone people, should distinguish that nation from others: Australia, Canada, Kenya, New Zealand, the Republic of South Africa, and Rhodesia (now Zambia and Zimbabwe) were all constituted through similar migration streams and the experiences (including the perceptions thereof) of those migrants, especially in terms of their relations with indigenous societies; Okoye, "Dingane and the Voortrekkers"; Shadle, *The Souls of White Folk*; Gough, "Maori and Pakeha in New Zealand Historiography"; Bonello, "The Development of Early Settler Identity in Southern Rhodesia"; Madley, "From Terror to Genocide." The same phenomena that preoccupy today's historians of the United States also preoccupy today's historians of the modern British Empire; Kennedy, "The Imperial History Wars"; Howe, "British Worlds, Settler Worlds, World Systems, and Killing Fields."

deemphasize national histories has led to a reconsideration of the role of
the state in imperial development under the now-fashionable rubric of
Atlantic History. This school of thought operates in conjunction with a
conception of European overseas trade and colonization as hallmarks of a
distinctive, if not unique, Atlantic World in which the movement of people,
ideas, and commodities transcended national and imperial boundaries to
incorporate the four continents that encompass the Atlantic Ocean. Yet,
notwithstanding its seemingly new approach to the colonial American past,
the Atlantic perspective shares a similar conception of the history of European expansion and its effects, even with the important inclusion of Africans and American Indians in its analyses, with the nineteenth-century
vision of reality: as "the English mingled with other Europeans, clashed
at times savagely with the indigenous peoples whose worlds they exploited
but did not understand, and formed networks of association stretching
from the Appalachian Mountains to Western Europe, Latin America, the
Caribbean, and Africa," they contributed to the formation "of the immense
socioeconomic structure of Atlantic civilization."[8]

Atlantic historians have also provided a frame for the rehearsal of
characterizations of the history of the English Empire that regard the
restoration of the monarchy in May 1660 as a benchmark of English
imperial history. The return of kingly government, according to this
comprehension, enabled Charles II (reigned 1660–85) and James II
(reigned 1685–8) to extend their absolutist vision of state and empire
over their dominions. This imperial conception of the royal brothers,
which built on the approach of their predecessor, Oliver Cromwell
(Lord Protector 1653–8), involved a greater practice of mercantilism –
state direction of imperial economic policy to imperial ends – and of
central control in general over colonial affairs.

This interpretative scheme has identified the third quarter of the seventeenth century, during which the first Navigation Act was enacted (1651)
and then revamped (1660, 1663) and the English captured Jamaica
(1655–60) and New Netherland (1664), as the crucial period here; also
at this time the imperial administration was reconfigured and seemingly
strengthened, and a governmental intention to become increasingly
involved in overseas matters became more evident. Governmental encouragement of trade in Africa and Asia after 1660 bred conflicts in the form
of unlicensed trading, parliamentary inquiries, and public outcry against

---

[8] Bailyn, *The Barbarous Years*, xiv.

the chartered corporations and triggered colonial resistance to late Stuart plans for state building and imperial expansion. The Atlantic School links these disputes to ideological debates, invariably connected to partisans of chartered parties and interlopers on their patents, over the nature of empire that reflected the divisions within the English political nation in the last quarter of the seventeenth century and the first decades of the eighteenth. A related recent trend has sought to link the expansion of overseas interests with English "state formation" during the seventeenth century, a time when the central government assumed greater direct oversight over local matters.[9]

Without questioning the historical outcome, however, this focus on the increasing function and power of the central government overlooks the consistent centrality of the operators noted above to the progress of state and empire during the seventeenth century. They took the lead in securing legitimacy for their undertakings, in considering locations for colonization and from which to conduct commerce, in recruiting the labor required for the success of plantations and trade, and even in devising the institutions for administering the crazy quilt of colonies and other overseas interests. In doing so, they curried favor with powerful people with whom they shared social and confessional affinities as they maneuvered to improve their positions. These pursuits generated endless internecine and international conflicts.

Since self-interest propelled these activities, it propelled the creation of the record of their history. This makes it tricky to discern the nature of an English "ideology of empire" in this period. A cluster of English people with overseas ambitions continued to identify Spain as a major threat to Protestant interests and accordingly couched their behavior in religious terms through the middle of the century.[10] Yet from the second decade of the seventeenth century the very Protestant Dutch, whose representatives competed with the English from to Surinam to Sumatra, were increasingly identified as England's chief rivals through 1675. For all of the attention that has been paid to seventeenth-century Anglo-Spanish and Anglo-French relations, the first and foremost occasions of the English government engaging in diplomacy and war over overseas interests concerned

---

[9] Recent treatments include Swingen, *Competing Visions of Empire*; Pincus et al., "Forum: Rethinking Mercantilism." For "state formation" and empire, see Braddick, *State Formation in Early Modern England*, 397–419.

[10] E.g., "Sir Benjamin Rudyerds Speech in Parliament, 21 January concerning America," in Castell, *A Short Discoverie of the Coasts and Continents of America*, 14–16.

the Dutch at this time, and a Dutch "Black Legend" as profound for contemporaries, if not as enduring, as its Spanish counterpart, held corresponding sway.[11]

The enduring historiographical tendency to frame the seventeenth century in terms of "how did we get to now?" rather than "how did they go from then?" has been encouraged by the reality that seventeenth-century English overseas trade and colonization occurred in conjunction with the deep mid-century convulsions that occurred within England itself. These upheavals also involved the formulation of written constitutions, as an array of novel views on the nature of society was propagated, and substantial subsequent scholarly debate, sometimes as fierce in its way as the battles fought by Parliamentarians and Royalists, over the nature of this reconfiguration.

The torturous seventeenth-century history of the English state makes it difficult to accept recent characterizations of the seventeenth-century English Empire that adopt a state-centered perspective. One influential study has marveled at this "remarkable period" during which "England had transformed itself from a kingdom on the European margins to one well-positioned to take advantage of new opportunities all around the world," while the English state metamorphosed from one "too weak to intrude effectively in European affairs in 1560" into one that had become an "empire," a "powerful kingdom with global reach by 1660." "If a regime is labeled imperial when it relies on territorial conquest and is militaristic and brutalizing to its subjects," seconds a recent analysis, "then England's early modern exploits in the Atlantic World were absolutely imperial." As we shall see, though, at no point prior to 1689 did the English state exhibit "a global reach" or a reliance on territorial conquest, nor was it especially "militaristic and brutalizing" to its subjects."[12]

The continuing focus on the state has also meant that the various entities that had actual charge of imperial matters, whether through charters or otherwise, have generally received short shrift. Yet although the corporate form of proprietorship lost favor for a time after 1641 and despite continuing allegations that ventures of this sort were impractical monopolies, experienced and knowledgeable English people continued to involve themselves in proprietary ventures: Carolina (1663), East and West Jersey (1664), New York (albeit to the

---

[11] Nocentelli, "The Dutch Black Legend"; e.g., [Worsley], *The Advocate*; cf. Armitage, *The Ideological Origins of the British Empire*; Pestana, *Protestant Empire*.

[12] Games, *The Web of Empire*, 7; Swingen, *Competing Visions of Empire*, 3.

Duke of York, 1664), Pennsylvania (1682), and Georgia (1732) as well various incarnations of the trading companies.[13]

The delegation of such extensive powers may also give rise to the perception that their recipients operated as "free states" – although, of course, they were not sovereign as the metropolitan government could withdraw what it had bestowed. This situation continued even through the development of the increasingly formal empire that developed after 1688, but especially after 1763 when the capacity of the state to take initiatives expanded, when governmental willingness to employ – and to increase – that capacity increased, and when, correspondingly, an imperial administration fledged. Later technological advances, most notably the steamship and in artillery, enabled British ambitions to paint the globe pink by seeing off resistance by both indigenous people and imperial rivals from Canada to the Sudan to Nyasaland (Malawi) to Mysore (Mysuru).

Yet even the state's new ability to conceptualize imperial policy, to direct territorial and commercial expansion, and to coordinate overseas interests more centrally became apparent thanks largely to the recourse to state power employed by those with governmental access who sought control over long-range economic scenarios. Thus, imperial development followed the earlier pattern, as in the cases of Cecil Rhodes's British South African Company chartered as late as 1889, in the colonization of Australia and New Zealand, and in the cases of British companies that enjoyed economic – and, therefore, political – preeminence in South America after the collapse of the Spanish Empire there in the 1820s.[14]

As these ventures provided new avenues for opportunity they also provided natural venues for replicating the struggles between factions that plagued English political culture. Since any prospect for the success of overseas colonizing and commercial activities required reliable managers on the ground, they provided opportunities for social and political

---

[13] Malcolm Gaskill professes his disdain for "impracticable" private colonizing ventures on five occasions in *Between Two Worlds*, xvii, xxi, 75, 91, and 138.

[14] The classic statement of the nature of nineteenth-century British imperial expansion and the nature of imperial policy and the accompanying conception of "informal empire" remains Gallagher and Robinson, "The Imperialism of Free Trade," but with, of course, reconsiderations of their conception of the degree to which the Victorian state led the pursuit of empire; e.g., Thompson, "Informal Empire?"; Lewis, "Britain, the Argentine and Informal Empire." For the activities of nineteenth-century colonizing companies, see Hudson, "English Emigration to New Zealand, 1839–1850"; Broeze, "Private Enterprise and the Peopling of Australasia"; Ndlovu-Gatsheni, "Mapping Cultural and Colonial Encounters."

advancement through office-holding as well as, more usually, through the acquisition of estates, also the bases for achieving prominence in the metropolis, for migrants. The pursuit of these opportunities brought status, power, and wealth for some individuals, who laid the foundation for imperial expansion yet to come, and failure for many others again following the nature of society and politics in England. The character of these relationships, however, remained manifestly fluid in the seventeenth century as did that of the English state itself at this time. Conflicts over overseas interests that brought appeals for state intervention also contributed to the course that the developing empire took, and these were exacerbated by the conflicting sensibilities of the time: one that continued to privilege local control of local affairs and another that advocated increased central control.[15]

This situation was evident from Maine to Surinam. Those involved in colonization at both ends replicated the factional behavior inherent in the sociopolitical frame that linked the center of the state with the localities – although, by definition, overseas colonies stretched those attachments across oceans. Moreover, individuals who had no official position cultivated ties with those who held such positions in order to further their personal interests – as well as those of the state, as they saw it. In doing so, they extended Anglo-American territorial claims often without the knowledge of the state, as with, for instance, Plymouth (1620), Connecticut (1636), Rhode Island (1636), New Haven (1638), and the Bahamas (1649). In Asia and Africa, a parade of unauthorized parties carried on trade with scant regard for the privileges of chartered companies either on the ground or at Whitehall. Even the two seeming exceptions to the rule that the state followed where unofficial interests led – the seizures of Jamaica and of New Netherland – actually demonstrate it: in both cases the impetus for the attacks originated outside the government. This private direction of overseas affairs resulted in a number of cases in which the Crown granted overlapping patents to competitors, thereby generating years of fierce dispute over who had which rights in the Indian Ocean, Maryland, and the West Indies.[16]

---

[15] I readily accept Natasha Glaisyer's suggestion that an investigation of networks should prove useful to our understanding of empire. Her attention, though, focuses on the eighteenth century; Glaisyer, "Networking."

[16] Such activities might be styled "settler colonialism," but they were customarily managed by Anglo-Americans who did not necessarily intend to relocate to the target area of colonization; cf. Veracini, "Settler Colonialism"; Wolfe, "History and Imperialism."

Moreover, the advance of the English Empire stuttered as these ventures incurred a litany of failures and false starts in the Amazon and Orinoco basins, Ambon in the East Indies, Roanoke, Saghedoc (Maine), Madagascar, Providence Island, the Bahamas, St. Lucia, Surinam, Tobago, and Tangier. In imperial terms, these wrecks were generally abandoned. The only exception – another one that proves the rule – was Virginia where the colony had achieved sufficient importance by 1625 that the Crown could not countenance the squabbling within the Virginia Company that threatened its future and so intervened to place it under direct royal administration. Then as with Virginia, as colonial populations grew, their success attracted the attention of a state increasingly conscious of potential revenue streams.[17]

Thus, even the increased capacity of the English state to exercise power arose from initiatives from individuals outside the state. The downfall of the monarchy erased the lines between these initiators and the state and left the latter with a capacity to exercise greater power after the restoration of kingly government. The ability of the Interregnum governments (1649–60), despite the considerable unpopularity of both the exactions and those who enacted them, to levy and collect taxes translated into unprecedented military might: the Commonwealth was the first English government to subjugate both Scotland and Ireland, an English dream since the reign of Edward I (1272–1307). It also imposed heavy losses on the Dutch Republic and achieved the first victories for English arms outside the British Isles since 1544, thereby raising the nation's esteem in European eyes to a level not seen since the reign of Henry VIII (1509–47).

The capacity of the restored monarchy to build on these achievements, though, remained limited, notwithstanding the widespread acclaim with which the Restoration was greeted. The demands of the various incarnations of the Commonwealth and the Protectorate outstripped even the greater revenues those governments enjoyed relative to their predecessors; Charles II had to pay off much of the army that had engineered his coming to power as one of his first acts. Accordingly, the King generally continued to delegate responsibility for overseas affairs to various private entities such as William Penn and the Hudson's Bay Company as his father had done. The Exclusion Crisis and Popish Plot (1677–82), however, incorporated an even greater concern over the

---

[17] Farnell, "The Navigation Act of 1651, the First Dutch War, and the London Merchant Community."

increasing revenue derived from overseas commerce and brought increased Crown involvement into local government, as Chapter 9 discusses. Fears of a return to the 1640s, perhaps tinged with a desire for revenge, led Charles and his brother to take a keener interest in overseeing their subjects both across the oceans and closer to home. This interest, though, did not necessarily translate into substantially greater state power after 1660; the English abandoned Tangier and lost their Jambi trading post in the face of superior local enemies in the 1680s. They also fought three wars (1652–4, 1664–7, and 1672–4) with the Dutch Republic. The first two of these conflicts were manifestly imperial, and all three constituted eruptions in the global Anglo-Dutch competition that ended only when England itself was invaded and its government overthrown by the invading army of William of Orange in 1688–9. This "Glorious Revolution" also confirmed the France of Louis XIV as the new primary overseas competitor, which correspondingly intensified the formal involvement of the English state in overseas matters. Even so, the manner by which the English actually conducted those matters remained essentially the same.[18]

---

[18] Slack, "The Politics of Consumption and England's Happiness in the Later Seventeenth Century"; Slack, "Material Progress and the Challenge of Affluence in Seventeenth-Century England."

I

Foundations

Anyone with an interest in the seventeenth-century English Empire should be aware of the name of Maurice Thompson. This London merchant rose to preeminence among the figures who drove seventeenth-century English overseas trade and colonization and whose behavior must therefore constitute the touchstone of any inquiry related to those interests. In addition, he and his associates, such as Thomas Andrews, Samuel Moyer, William Pennoyer, Rowland Wilson, and John Wood, who shared his ardently Calvinist religious views, played central roles in the rebellion against Charles I and became deeply involved in government between 1642 and 1660. The emergence of Thompson and others like him, regardless of individual confessional orientation, occurred in conjunction with the increasing importance of the wider world to English society, politics, and economics. The centrality of their association, which included one of the most prominent of the godly peers, Robert Rich, Earl of Warwick, to overseas ventures demonstrates the importance of networking and also helps to repair further the anachronistic separation that has developed between the religious views of contemporaries and the continuing quest to provide labor, especially slaves, for the colonies. Yet their careers have rarely received the attention they warrant outside of Robert Brenner's mammoth study, now over twenty years old.[1]

---

[1] Brenner, *Merchants and Revolution*, for a discussion of which see Chapter 5 herein. Parliament passed a series of statutes between 1661 and 1665 that barred those who did not conform to the Church of England from local office and deprived clerics who would not subscribe to the Thirty-nine Articles of their livings. Thompson verified his dissenting religious views by providing twenty shillings each to "one hundred poore silenced Ministers" in his will; Will of Maurice Thomson of Haversham, Buckinghamshire, 9 May 1676,

A tendency to focus on results has contributed to this neglect and the sketchy historical record has not helped our understanding of these imperial movers and shakers. Yet notwithstanding the ultimately extensive global influence of the English, failure constitutes the primary result of their activities, and it is only through the study of the many failures they incurred that we can obtain a comprehensive sense of the history of the English Empire.

In the grandest sense, we have the singular instance of a vision of global empire that was conceived and pursued by the Anglo-Dutch merchant Sir William Courteen. Sir William sponsored plantations in the West Indies as well as Asian and African trading ventures that he sought to link via West Africa before his death in 1636. Maurice Thompson and his partners inherited and revamped the Courteen plan over the next two decades. Their Assada Adventure, however, ran afoul of indigenous resistance to the settlement of this island in the Indian Ocean and then of the interests of the restored monarchy in the Guinea trade in the early 1660s. Even so, the scheme provided the basis for extending the English presence in the Eastern Hemisphere and for establishing the connection between Africa and Anglo-America.

The cases of Thompson and his counterparts also provide clear illustrations of how their pursuit of overseas trade and colonization fit into the changing circumstances in which these activities took place as well as how those changes affected the conduct of those ventures. As English people, such as Thompson, sought – or were obliged to seek – new situations, their understanding of the nature of society and government remained essentially the same – with the vital exceptions that emanated from the creation of the Church of England and accompanying dissolution of the monasteries in the 1530s. Prior to the 1640s, England remained very much a monarchy in which the sovereign ruled over a hierarchical society of orders in accordance with an "ancient constitution," a hodge-podge of the common law, parliamentary statute, and royal prerogative. Justices of the peace, sheriffs, bailiffs, and a plethora of lower officials connected the localities to the central government, while municipal and other corporations, such as universities, conducted their affairs in accordance with the charters that had been granted by monarchs over the centuries. Meanwhile landlords governed

PROB 11/353/63, www.marinelives.org/wiki/Tools:_PROB_11/351/63_Will_of_Maur ice_Thomson_of_Haversham,_Buckinghamshire_09_May_1676.

their estates under a manorial system that included courts that provided the customary means of resolving the grievances of "subordinates."[2]

Important elements of this system became entrenched in faraway places. Among the most important of these was the belief that an individual's landed income or "estate" constituted the barometer of social and political status. Reciprocity between the social orders constituted the ligaments of the body politic that served as the sociopolitical ideal throughout Western Europe and beyond. In its ideal form, tenants, servants, and other "inferiors" rendered deference to gentry and aristocrats, who, in their turn, condescended to provide order through their service as justices of the peace, members of parliament, sheriffs, and other offices. Notwithstanding the socioeconomic changes that England experienced during the seventeenth century, landed income continued, as readers of Jane Austen know, to constitute the English sociopolitical barometer of status at least through the time of the Battle of Waterloo even as England continued to experience novel socioeconomic phenomena, of which intensifying overseas trade and colonization were manifest examples.[3]

In addition, this system entailed the development of a metropolitan-style political culture that was based on the cultivation of patronage networks usually headed by aristocrats. These partnerships undertook the common political, social, and economic interests of their memberships, including activities in distant locations. Inevitably, the formation of these associations fostered rivalries, sometimes fierce, between them as they maneuvered for advantage at the expense of their opponents. By definition, this behavior incorporated a substantial political element. Thus, it clouded – or was clouded by – the degree to which other elements, such as religion most profoundly in the seventeenth-century, played a part in politics.[4]

By the 1610s, certain figures had worked out that overseas trade and colonization could boost both their incomes and their political prominence. Carrying out such long-range agendas, however, not only required

---

[2] Hindle, "Persuasion and Protest in the Caddington Common Enclosure Dispute," illustrates how the system worked – and was worked – in a Hertfordshire parish, while Hindle, "Hierarchy and Community in the Elizabethan Parish," discusses a case in which local people regarding themselves as governmentally vulnerable with respect to existing institutions sought to establish their own, in accordance with ancient custom.

[3] Zagorin, *Rebels and Rulers*, 1: 61–86.

[4] Shephard, "Court Factions in Early Modern England." For the emergence of ideology, which arose from the confessional differences of the Reformation, see Kelley, *The Beginning of Ideology*.

substantial capital, in both fiscal and mental terms, to absorb the myriad risks and extensive costs. The most successful of these individuals formed the links that enabled them to transcend the distances that aggravated the ordinary issues involved in conducting business and in governing people thousands of miles away. Reciprocity was again at the heart of these interactions as manifested in the identification of prospective patron–client relationships that sustained the political and economic wherewithal necessary for undertaking such ventures, to recruit migrants, and to sound out further opportunities. The upper echelons of these networks also used their positions to secure state approval for these initiatives. In pursuing their designs, then, those involved in overseas schemes invariably stressed the public purposes involved: the extension of trade, the augmentation of customs revenue, and increased employment.

The significance of this culture to the settlement vein of seventeenth-century English overseas expansion appears in several ways, although crucial differences existed between the metropolitan theme and its colonial variations, especially the absence of a hereditary aristocracy since people with titles tended not to migrate certainly on a permanent basis. Prior to 1613, the goals of those English people interested in the Western Hemisphere had focused on trade, primarily for animal pelts, with American Indians; the search for mines containing seams of ores that could be processed into precious metals; bases for conducting piracy; the search for a passage around or through America to Asia; and fishing.

These pursuits remained in play after 1613, but two events occurred in that year that marked a permanent shift in the raison d'être of Anglo-American colonization efforts to the construction of plantations. The first of these was the chartering of Robert Harcourt's settlement venture for Guiana, and the other was the successful introduction of the cultivation of Varinas, or "sweet-smelling," tobacco to Bermuda and Virginia. Harcourt's venture followed a series of English failures on the South American mainland including one of his own four years previously. As evidenced by the pamphlet he published to promote his venture, Harcourt had already developed an awareness of the suitability of America for plantations in general and of which commodities worked well in Guiana in particular. Thus, he identified sugar as the "first and principal commodity in these parts" where the canes "doe there grow to great bignesse in a short time" so that "by erecting convenient works for the boyling and making of Sugers (which at the first will require som charge & expence) may be yearly returned great benefit and wealth: the long experience of the Portugals, and Spaniards, in Brasill, and the Islands of the Canaries;

and of the Moores in Barbary, may give us certain assurance." Other likely commodities included cotton, drugs, and dyestuffs. Guiana already produced tobacco to the extent that leaf reportedly worth £60,000 had been imported into England in 1610. As it was also in high demand in the Netherlands, Germany, Ireland, and "all the Easterly Countries," Harcourt observed, its price "is great, the benefit our Merchants gaine thereby is infinite, and the Kings rent for the custome thereof is not a little."[5]

Harcourt's initiative came to nothing, however. Thus, it might have been lumped with prior English expeditions to Guiana, which sought El Dorado and other chimera, as manifestations of English foolhardiness in the attempt to duplicate in the Orinoco jungles what Hernan Cortes and the Pizarro brothers had achieved in Mexico and Peru.[6] Yet unlike the epiphenomenal efforts of Sir Walter Ralegh and other gold-blinded explorers, it ignited English interest in colonization in the West Indies. In the broader sense, Harcourt's investigation of Guiana reflected the sensibility that colonizers should back plantation agriculture as the likeliest way of promoting national and personal interests. Tobacco of the variety produced in South America became the best immediate prospect for achieving those ends. Within three decades, however, sugar, in accordance with Harcourt's analysis, began to replace it in Barbados.

The belief that Virginia should devote itself to plantation agriculture manifested itself coincidentally. We do not know whose idea it was to bring tobacco from Venezuela to Jamestown. We do know, though, that John Rolfe played an integral role in extending cultivation of the weed to Virginia by conducting the first trial of Venezuelan tobacco there. Rolfe provided another boost to the previously ill-starred colony when, after her kidnaping, he famously married Pocahontas, daughter of the Powhatan sachem Wahunsonacock, thereby ending the First Anglo-Powhatan War that had beset Virginia since its founding. Less famously but no less importantly, he and his new wife then ventured to England where they served as the faces of a promotional campaign that yielded both successful recapitalization of and new management for the Virginia Company and the "tobacco boom" of 1618–22. As the colony's future seemed to be now secured, the new officers of the company devised a plan for governing it and for providing access to labor to planters, which provided the model for the subsequent sociopolitical nature of English overseas colonization.[7]

[5] Harcourt, *A Relation of a Voyage to Guiana*, 31–2 (on sugar), 36–7 (on tobacco).
[6] Davies, *The North Atlantic World in the Seventeenth Century*, 3–23.
[7] Roper, *English Empire in America*, 69–71.

The overhaul of the administration of the Virginia Company that accompanied the introduction of tobacco cultivation involved the removal of Sir Thomas Smythe, sometime Lord Mayor of London and leading English overseas merchant prior to 1625, who had led the company since its founding in 1606, and his replacement by a group led by Henry Wriothesley, Earl of Southampton, in 1616. Southampton's clients, Sir Edwin Sandys and the merchant Ferrar brothers, John and Nicholas, put into effect several plans, all of which were employed in Anglo-America as it expanded, while Pocahontas and Rolfe publicized Virginia's new prospects.

First, the Sandys–Ferrar directorate sought to attract migrants who had a socioeconomic position that would enable them to oversee Virginia's progress and who would have a stake in the future of the colony. Thus, they developed the practice of granting headrights that granted allocations of land to free migrants that were substantially augmented according to the number of additional migrants the original grantee brought with them. They also devised a House of Burgesses as a local governmental institution, the membership of which was chosen by local planters. This institution provided the main point of contact between metropolis and colony, ensured local oversight over local affairs, and thus provided protection for the estates of planters in conformity with the seventeenth-century English comprehension of social structure.[8]

Last, but by no means least, they devised the practice of indentured servitude in 1618 as a modification of the crucial norm in any preindustrial society: the employment of bound labor in agricultural production. Servitude remained a familiar mechanism of ensuring that an agricultural labor force was in place throughout the year as well as, by dint of the customary practice of providing servants with room and board over the course of their term (customarily one year in England), an avenue for conducting reciprocity between servants and masters.[9]

The Sandys–Ferrar modification of the familiar master–servant relationship also included the cost of transportation in an indenture by which migrants who lacked the wherewithal (£6 usually) to transport themselves to America contracted with the Virginia Company (and its assigns) to

---

[8] Roper, *English Empire in America*, 79–80.
[9] Woodward, "Early Modern Servants Revisited"; Gritt, "The 'Survival' of Service in the English Agricultural Labour Force"; Wallace, "Governing England through the Manor Courts." For the creation of the indentured version of servitude, see Virginia Company, Instructions to Sir George Yeardley, 18 November 1618, *RVC* 3: 98–109 at 100–1.

provide labor for a term of years to recover that cost. In addition to their diet, accommodation, and whatever other terms they negotiated, servants in Anglo-America were customarily rewarded with "freedom dues" after they completed their obligations: a land grant along with seed, tools, and other items necessary to make their way. This device facilitated the creation of a stunted, but nevertheless quite recognizable, version of the metropolitan sociopolitical hierarchy, but one, thanks to the use of indentures, which provided the means – at least theoretically – for servants to move up the social pyramid that did not exist in England. The promise of tobacco-producing estates brought a wave of migrants to Virginia sufficient, on the one hand, to ensure its survival, and, on the other, to nearly bring it to its knees, and indentures remained an important element of migration to the Americas into the nineteenth century.[10]

Yet the requirement of a written contract to enforce the respective obligations of the parties, due to the unfamiliarity of those involved with each other due to the nature of long-range migration, marked a deviation from custom as people could now trade in, and even speculate in, these contracts. By 1640, it had become the general practice of those trading in the Caribbean "to get servants bound to them and send them to the West Indies and there to sell them for tobacco or such like commodity," while "sundry prisoners" taken at the surrender of Colchester to parliamentary forces in 1648 "did freely tender themselves & did sign and seal indentures" to be transported to Barbados "as is usual in such cases." Even so, reports emanated that "a great many were not appareled as they ought to have been" (with the cost of clothing, transport and diet for a servant reported "at the last seven pounds" sterling per migrant). These incidents dampened enthusiasm for America among prospective servants; some individuals, having signed on to migrate, changed their minds before crossing the Atlantic. Furthermore, even if a servant had the same master for the whole of their term, the contractual tie, along with the unprecedented control that colonial planters exercised over the governmental institutions of their small ponds, undoubtedly enabled American masters to take greater liberties in the treatment of their servants than their English counterparts.[11]

---

[10] Galenson, *White Servitude in Colonial America*; Fogleman, "From Slaves, Convicts, and Servants to Free Passengers."

[11] For trafficking in indentures, see Deposition of Thomas Silver, 4 October 1639, HCA 13/55, f. 268; deposition of Samuel Leigh, 30 January 1639/40, HCA 13/55, ff. 420r–421r; for the indenture of the Colchester prisoners, Deposition of Samuel Mott, 23 December 1648, CLA/024/06/002 (unfoliated), Depositions in Mayor's Court of

Meanwhile, significant changes did take place, some of which resounded very deeply, if temporarily, within the familiar sociopolitical frame. In the first instance, England's population continued on the steep upward trajectory that had commenced at the very end of the fifteenth century and continued into the middle of the seventeenth. This demographic increase necessarily placed a greater general strain on the ability of the society to feed itself and to provide other essentials of life to its members, already susceptible to the vagaries of climate, while the government routinely failed to acquire sufficient revenues to meet its needs. Perhaps not coincidentally, religious fervor and sociopolitical disaffection became more pronounced during this time of recurring dearth amid profound climate fluctuations, while bread riots and objections to attempts by the Crown to attract revenue, always referencing the kingdom's ancient constitution, appeared more frequently and more stridently during the economizing Personal Rule of Charles I (1629–40).[12]

The increasing scale of commerce accompanied and then transcended the demographic rise. At least one-half of the population of England were wage workers in 1613. The export of raw wool, which had been an English economic bellwether from at least the late thirteenth century, collapsed in the third quarter of the sixteenth century, but the woolen

London 1647–8, LMA. For lack of enthusiasm of servants for American opportunities, see, e.g., Joseph West to Anthony Lord Ashley, 10 September 1669, Cheves, *Shaftesbury Papers*, 153–4. The perennial – and for social leaders, perennially vexing – issue of the movement of people in and around England had already eroded the ideal (to the degree that it ever existed) even as it gave rise to the device of indentured servitude; Souden, "'Rogues, Whores, and Vagabonds'."

[12] Precise population figures for seventeenth-century England are, of course, impossible to recover with precision, but the accepted approximations remain some 4.11 million in 1610 rising to 5.28 million in 1656; see Wrigley and Schofield, *The Population History of England*, 207–10, despite serious concerns that have been raised about the methodology employed; Hatcher, "Understanding the Population History of England." The period under consideration began with harvests "about average as a whole," in terms of yields between 1480 and 1619, but the 1610s included "two deficient harvests (1613, 1617) and two good harvests (1618–19) to end the decade," before a "really bad harvest" in 1622; Hoskins, "Harvest Fluctuations and English Economic History, 1480–1619," 39–40. Between 1619 and 1689, England experienced eighteen "deficient" harvests and twenty-seven "good" ones, but the 1630s saw just one "good harvest in ten years, instead of the usual four" (with accompanying high prices for grain), while "five bad harvests in a row" occurred between 1646 and 1650 and again between 1657 and 1661; Hoskins, "Harvest Fluctuations and English Economic History, 1620–1759," 17–20. For agrarian revolt, see Zagorin, *Rebels and Rulers*, 1: 122–39.

cloth trade, both domestic and export, increased dramatically during the 1500s. Accordingly, the manorial system – and the tenants and copyholders to whom this extended some legal protection – that served as a primary means of ordering local society continued to erode through the practice of engrossment. This practice, whereby larger farms absorbed smaller ones, as well as that of enclosing formerly common lands by landlords, became increasingly apparent from the fourteenth century as "agrarian capitalism" spread, particularly in the southern and eastern parts of the country.[13]

The combination of shrinking smallholdings and tenancies along with the rising population, even with checks placed on it by recurring epidemics of plague, smallpox, "sweating sickness," and typhoid fever, caused a movement of people of a scope sufficient to create a perception that lawlessness and brigandage beckoned unless something was done, especially since the medieval framework for caring for the poor had been shattered by the Reformation. And something was done: the parliaments of Elizabeth I (reigned 1558–1603) passed a series of statutes, building on previous local practices and culminating in the Poor Laws of 1597 and 1601, which provided a relatively substantial measure of poor relief by the standards of the time but was accompanied by provision for whippings for "sturdy beggars" who had moved from their parish of origin. Local corporations, assigned the responsibility for providing the relief that would stem vagrancy, employed various measures. Godly people had a particular desire to reform the indigent by putting them to work that control of the locality enabled; the approach of many towns, though, came to focus on a desire to improve the recipients of relief, as opposed to the mere "popish" provision of charity. This attitude severed the reciprocity inherent in the medieval system and may have cut many impoverished people adrift from the society of orders. Dorchester, where the Reverend John White, an early promoter of godly colonization, was a community leader, established a brewery to employ its indigent population.[14]

Overseas colonization became an obvious remedy for these issues in the minds of the Elizabethan promoter of colonization, Ralegh, and his

---

[13] Rorke, "English and Scottish Overseas Trade"; Shaw-Taylor, "The Rise of Agrarian Capitalism and the Decline of Family Farming in England."
[14] Although the extent to which this happened varied from town to town even from parish to parish; Fideler, "Impressions of a Century of Historiography." For Dorchester, see Underdown, *Fire from Heaven*, 113–29.

mouthpiece, Richard Hakluyt. In 1584, when Ralegh solicited additional Crown support for his American plantation schemes, Hakluyt identified the revival of trade and employment for vagrants and beggars as foremost public purposes of "western planting." Despite Hakuyt's urgings, the schemes of Ralegh and his contemporaries had no lasting impact outside of memory. Later promoters of colonization, however, invariably included among the reasons for pursuing their ventures the removal of the impoverished and convicts from unproductive circumstances – and parish charge – to productive labor on plantations.[15]

At the same time, overseas ventures contributed to the exploding demographics of seventeenth-century London. Even at the end of Elizabeth's reign, when the notion of an English Empire did not even rate the proverbial glimmer in a paternal eye, a district of docks, warehouses, shipyards, and trades catering to maritime industry had begun to teem with an increasing number of mariners, masters, merchants, and their wives (or widows) and families. The contemporary historian-geographer, John Stow, born in the 1520s, recalled that the first building ("a fayre free school") was constructed in the hamlet of Ratcliffe in the large parish of Stepney, just east of the city's walls, "in my youth." But "of late yeares," when Stow wrote his *Survey of London*, "ship-wrights and (for the most part) other marine men, haue builded many large and strong houses for themselues, and smaller for Saylers, from thence almost to Poplar, and so to Blake wal. Now for Tower hil, the plaine there is likewise greatly diminished by Merchants, for building of small tenements: from thence towards Aldgate."[16]

One study suggests that Stepney, which stretched north from the Thames to include, in addition to Ratcliffe, the riverside hamlets of Wapping, Limehouse, Shadwell, Poplar, and Blackwall, contained 12,000 to 13,000 inhabitants between 1606 and 1610. A careful, if necessarily crude, estimate speculates that the parish's demographics burgeoned from some 21,000 to over 91,000 during the course of the seventeenth century, notwithstanding several plague outbreaks that underscored the precariousness of urban life in this period: it was the continuing flow of migrants to the capital that propelled its continuing population increase as deaths outpaced baptisms throughout the period

---

[15] Deane, *A Discourse concerning Western Planting Written in the Year 1584 by Richard Hakluyt*, 19–35, 36–44.
[16] Stow, "The Suburbs without the walls," in Kingsford, *A Survey of London*, 69–91.

under study and that fueled the accompanying eastwardly spread of housing and commercial construction along the river.[17]

Ledgers and other business records that would have provided evidence of the increasing scope of trade and corresponding expansion of accommodation of the lading and unlading of commodities does not survive in significant numbers, unfortunately. Happily for the historian, however, these endeavors often resulted in disappointment and disaster and, thus, court cases. The survival of the records of these disputes does allow shafts of light to penetrate this world; they reveal that the geographic scale of English overseas interests expanded remarkably and rapidly from the late 1620s. They also reveal that it was the leaders of Stepney, now the economic locus of England, who set the agendas, provided the resources, and laid the groundwork for further overseas ventures even as the kingdom recovered from an extended period of "trade depression" that followed the Spanish siege and sack of Antwerp (1576–85) during the Dutch Revolt. The wool trade, staple of the English export economy since the Middle Ages, never recovered from the loss of access to what had been its primary Continental entrepôt. Currency debasements in Germany that devalued the price of English cloth there as well as the pursuit of costly and ineffective war waged by Charles I against France and Spain from 1625 to 1629, not to mention the wider Thirty Years War (1618–48), along with the predations of corsairs from the Barbary Coast and Dunkirk in the Spanish Netherlands, aggravated this decline.

The attempts of the Crown to reverse this trend – while simultaneously trying to promote the customs revenue generated by these trades – generally yielded negligible results. Its overhaul of the impositions placed on imports such as currants was ratified by the courts but resented by merchants, while the implementation of the "New Draperies" plan devised by the merchant and London official William Cockayne in 1614, the most dramatic instance of government intervention, proved disastrous. These circumstances reinforced the painful reality that the Dutch, who produced their cloth and other exports at lower cost, kept their English competitors for Continental markets at a disadvantage in the early seventeenth century. The resumption of the Dutch war with Spain in 1621 did provide somewhat better opportunities for English traders engaged in the Baltic Sea carrying trade from the 1630s in which iron

---

[17] East London History Group, Population Studies Group, "The Population of Stepney in the Early Seventeenth Century," 40–1; Power, "East London Housing in the Seventeenth Century," 237.

importation coincidentally played an increasingly important role. This commodity was in great demand in West Africa where, along with Asian and European cloth, guns, and gunpowder, it was exchanged for "elephants teeth," gold, and "Negroes."[18]

Unfortunately for the Sandys–Ferrar management of the Virginia Company, their own experience clearly illustrates the pitfalls that were entailed in overseas matters. In a bitter irony, their plan for reviving Virginia proved to be too successful: more migrants arrived there than the colony could accommodate comfortably. By all accounts – although the political heat that the "tobacco boom" touched off obliges us to be particularly wary of the claims made therein – Virginia lacked sufficient food, housing, and other necessities to support the sudden influx of people, resulting in considerable misery. Moreover, the sudden population influx had alarmed the Powhatans, whose sachem Opechancanough harbored a longstanding enmity toward the English. On Easter 1622, the Indians carried out a devastating attack, killing over one-quarter of the settlers and destroying plantations, crops, and livestock, which might have destroyed Virginia if the English had not had some advance warning. The Powhatan attack gave Virginia a severe scorching, but the persons and attitudes of the corps of metropolitan backers of overseas trade and colonization were joined by survivors of the "massacre" who had the ambition and the experience to carry on these efforts and to assume, accordingly, leading roles in such successes as were achieved after 1622.[19]

The Virginia Company's efforts also ran afoul of seventeenth-century English political culture. Warwick may have been the most prominent proponent of expanding English overseas interests during the first half of the seventeenth century; he certainly was one of the leading politicians of the period prior to the breakdown of the government in 1642. This aristocrat had his fingers in all of the proverbial overseas pies: he was a

---

[18] E.g., Deposition of William Coppin, 3 March 1648/9, HCA 13/61, ff. 237r–238r; "Voyage to Gambo" of the *Henrietta, Sophia, Amity, Griffin,* and *Kinsale,* 30 April 1662, T 70/309, ff. 1v–2v; Cormontine to Right Worshipful Company, 18 February 1661/2, IOR E/3/27, ff. 106r–107r. The "Guinea trade" receives fuller attention in Chapters 3 and 6 through 9 below. For the situation of the English export trade at this time, see, e.g., Gould, "The Trade Depression of the 1620s," 87–90; Federowicz, *England's Baltic Trade in the Seventeenth Century,* 90–131, esp. 124–6. For grievances against impositions, which received judicial approval in *Bates' Case* (4 Mich., 4 Jac. 1), see, e.g., Journal of the House of Commons, 12 May 1614, in Jansson, *Proceedings in Parliament,* 210–18 at 211–14.

[19] Hecht, "The Virginia Muster of 1624/5 as a Source for Demographic History."

leading member of the first English company, chartered in 1618, to trade with Africa; he was an early supporter of attacks on Spanish shipping – he commanded such a voyage himself in 1627; and he was a patron of colonization ventures from the Caribbean to New England. After he assumed his earldom in 1619, Warwick assembled an extensive web of mercantile, clerical, and political clients that he used, in conjunction with like-minded aristocrats, such as his brother, Henry Rich, Earl of Holland, and William Fiennes, Viscount Saye and Sele, to promote his fiercely anti-Spanish views, the legacy of his maternal grandfather, the Elizabethan Robert Devereux, Earl of Essex.[20]

Warwick joined the Virginia Company in 1617 and allied with South-ampton in the battle to end Sir Thomas Smythe's leadership of its venture. While he had been content initially with the management of Sandys and the Ferrars, problems arose with Warwick's enthusiasm for piracy, which extended to the Indian Ocean where to the deep irritation of the East India Company one of his crews seized a vessel carrying the mother of the Mughal Emperor and £100,000 worth of cargo. In the Western Hemi-sphere, the Earl invested in the Somers Island Company, which governed Virginia's sister colony, Bermuda; that island's location made it an ideal base for Daniel Elfrith and other skippers affiliated with Warwick that they used in their attacks against the Spanish; these privateers also called at Virginia. Prior to 1623, however, this sort of activity ran afoul of the peace policy of James I (reigned 1603–25). It therefore exposed the charters of colonies that harbored pirates to the threat of annulment for violating their corporate privileges. Thus, Sandys solicited Warwick to cease and desist in order to avoid royal wrath. The Earl responded to this overture, however, by forming a new alliance with Smythe that attacked Sandys's oversight of Virginia, pointing to the admittedly compelling evidence of the calamities suffered by the overflow of servants punctuated by the disaster of the Powhatan attack. The resulting campaign of denun-ciation and counterdenunciation created such distractions that the Crown had to step in reluctantly, dissolve the Virginia Company in June 1624, and place the colony under royal administration.[21]

The creation of this first Crown Colony in English imperial history was supposed to have been a temporary expedient, but James died the

---

[20] For the political effects of Essex and his circle, see Hammer, *The Polarization of English Politics*.

[21] For Warwick and "privateering," see Bard, "The Earl of Warwick's Voyage of 1627"; Craven, "The Earl of Warwick, a Speculator in Piracy."

following March, and although the idea of the recreation of the Virginia Company was mooted on subsequent occasions, it never gained currency as the colonists were concerned about their land titles if the company was revived. In practical terms, however, the administration of the province remained under the guidance of men, such as Edward Sackville, Earl of Dorset, Sir John Danvers, Sir John Wolstoneholme, Sir Francis Wyatt, and Abraham Jacob, who had amassed extensive Virginia experience during the company era that they carried with them after 1624. Dorset headed the eponymous but temporary Commission for Foreign Plantations, created in 1631, which provided Charles I with advice on Virginia (and recommended a return to corporate government for the colony).[22]

Meanwhile, Warwick and his associates turned their attention more closely to the Caribbean. In 1619, he joined Roger North, a veteran of Ralegh's last expedition, in a new Guiana or Amazon Company, but the patent for this venture was suspended at the behest of Diego Sarmiento de Acuña, Count Gondomar, the Spanish Ambassador, and North was sent to the Tower when he returned to London with a cargo of Venezuelan tobacco. A consideration of the case by the Privy Council, though, resulted in the reinstatement of the grant to a new company headed by the Earl, who recruited Harcourt for a resumption of colonization efforts in Guiana. This venture lasted from 1625 to 1629 while England and Spain were at war after which it became bankrupt and Harcourt was killed by Indians in 1631. This failed effort seems to have prompted Warwick to abandon the mainland and focus his West Indian agenda on the islands.[23]

The Earl's circle by no means, however, constituted the only group of English people interested in the Caribbean in the early 1620s, and it is interesting that so many prominent individuals and their clients became involved in the West Indies at this time. The region had been officially off limits to English overseas operators after the Anglo-Spanish Treaty of London of 1604. This restriction, which memorialized the pacific policies preferred by James I, deeply annoyed his more militant subjects. This irritation turned to alarm as Europe became engulfed in a seemingly confessional struggle in which the Austrian cousins of the Spanish Habsburgs had driven the King's daughter, Elizabeth of Bohemia, and

---

[22] MacMillan, *The Atlantic Imperial Constitution*, 150–1; Roper, *English Empire in America*, 73–92.

[23] Andrews, *Trade, Plunder and Settlement*, 298–300; MacMillan, *Sovereignty and Possession in the English New World*, 86–9.

her unfortunate husband, Frederick, the Elector Palatine, from their Bohemian throne as well as their Rhineland principality.

This situation turned in 1623 when the plans for the "Spanish Match" between Prince Charles and the Infanta Maria Anna collapsed into humiliating farce. Charles and the all-powerful royal favorite, George Villiers, Duke of Buckingham, controversially traveled incognito to Madrid hoping to finalize a marriage agreement but suffered a series of rebuffs. The pair returned to England in October determined to seek revenge for the treatment the Spanish had afforded them, and their indignation overwhelmed the King's preference for continued negotiation. A clamor for renewed hostilities with the old enemy meant that traders and colonizers could now frequent the Caribbean without risking incarceration in the Tower.[24]

Sir William Courteen was the most active of the backers of overseas ventures outside Warwick's circle. Born around 1568, Sir William, along with his Zeeland-based brother, Sir Peter Courteen, inherited their father's highly successful silk and linen tailoring firm; then, utilizing their Dutch associations, they expanded into whaling and the salt trade. Their immense operation extended its sphere of interest to the Wild Coast of Guiana adjacent to the Venezuelan salt pans by the 1610s. As the overseer of the English side of things, Sir William cultivated patronage, frequently lending substantial sums of money to the Crown, which owed him a reported £200,000 by the 1630s, and to various aristocrats.

The Zeeland port of Vlissingen (Flushing), which the English held until 1616 as security for loans extended to the United Provinces during the Dutch Revolt, provided a ready point of collaboration. From there, Sir William's group began shipping English, Irish, and Dutch settlers to the Essequibo River on the Wild Coast of Guiana after James I returned the town to Zeeland's control. By 1623, these settlements were producing a reported 800,000 pounds of tobacco per annum. The Courteen involvement in America spread after one of their captains, John Powell, called at Barbados on his return from the Dutch expedition that had seized Bahia from the Portuguese. His favorable report convinced Sir William to secure a patent to the island through the offices of William Herbert, Earl of Pembroke; he then invested upward of £10,000 in establishing a colony there. The first settlers immediately and naturally

[24] Cogswell, "England and the Spanish Match"; Lake, "Constitutional Consensus and the Puritan Opposition in the 1620s."

turned their hands to planting tobacco, following the examples of Virginia and St. Christopher's.[25]

This undertaking, however, ran afoul of the unfortunate practice, whether due to oversight, ministerial inefficiency, disinterest, dissimulation, or confusion, of Charles I of granting multiple patents to similar rights to conduct overseas trade and colonization. In addition to granting a proprietorship for Barbados to Pembroke, the King made grants to the island to James Ley, Earl of Marlborough, and James Hay, Earl of Carlisle. While Marlborough accepted a settlement and relinquished his claims, Carlisle insisted his agents had established a prior settlement to the Courteen colony. To make a long story short, violence and suits ensued that prevented the colony's political situation from stabilizing for the first decade or more of its existence and, happily for the historian, continued to produce documents related to the founding of the English colonies in the West Indies into the 1640s.[26]

As these colonizers knew well, plantations required bound labor to succeed. Indentured servitude certainly offered one feasible means of addressing this issue, yet it never brought migrants in sufficient numbers. It is quite conceivable, given the chronology of events, that some of those involved in early Anglo-American settlement found the indenture process less than optimum for meeting colonial labor requirements fully from its inception, although we lack direct evidence of the thinking of the colonizers and merchants concerned.

Slaves presented an obvious alternative despite the emphasis that has been placed on the absence of slavery from England and the relatively late arrival of the English to the trans-Atlantic slave trade. Notwithstanding these realities, we can certainly say that the introduction of African slavery into Anglo-America actually preceded that of indentured servitude. The first recorded mention of Africans at Virginia occurred in 1619/20 when Rolfe reported to Sandys that a Dutch privateer had brought "20. and odd Negroes" whom its crew had seized from a Portuguese slaver to the colony, but enslaved Africans were cultivating tobacco, as well as scouring shipwrecks for salvage on Bermuda

---

[25] Handler, "Father Antoine Biet's Visit to Barbados," 69; Davis, "Papers Relating to the Early History of Barbados and St. Kitts," 328; Mijers, "A Natural Partnership," 245–50; Klooster, "Anglo-Dutch Trade in the Seventeenth Century," 263–5; Sheridan, *Sugar and Slavery*, 81–2.

[26] E.g., Papers Relating to the Barbadoes and the Caribbean Islands, MS 736, Trinity College Library, Dublin.

first African slaves ✓

(founded in 1612) by 1616, and they constituted 5 to 10 percent of that colony's population by 1619.[27]

Michael Jarvis and others have suggested that the overlapping involvement of Warwick and his circle of merchants and mariners in the plantation trade, Guinea, and piracy triggered English involvement in the trans-Atlantic slave trade. This group had developed a substantial awareness of the scope of the European demand for tobacco, of the management of Spanish tobacco production in Venezuela, and of how the slave trade in America worked by circa 1615. It is quite conceivable also that Courteen's group shared this awareness given their familiarity with Dutch plantations in Essequibo. Certainly, as Caroline Arena has recently demonstrated, Courteen's agents used their knowledge and mainland contacts to introduce Indian slavery, with natives they brought from Guiana to Barbados, directly after the English began settling that island.[28]

The Warwick group certainly translated this system to Bermuda where they held sway, and the disasters that befell Virginia in the early 1620s seem to have encouraged a turn toward islands in English colonization. St. Christopher's might well occupy a place on anyone's favored list of places to recuperate from a nasty shock, but it might be regarded as an unlikely location for what proved to be the permanent rejuvenation of English long-range commercial and colonizing initiatives. Nevertheless, the establishment of a tobacco colony there, in conjunction with the slow recovery of Virginia after the tumults it had endured, provided both the platform for the further expansion of English overseas interests and a sense that these interests required better oversight.

The English settlement of St. Christopher's began, according to Captain John Smith's account, as an offshoot of Roger North's Amazon forays, with the first colonists arriving in January 1624 led by Captain Thomas Warner. The Englishmen found three Frenchmen already residing there with whom they divided the island, the English occupying the central part and the French the two ends. The new arrivals set to planting tobacco as well as provision crops and engaging in trade with the Indians. Smith's narrative details the tribulations of the early colonists, which included hurricanes, Indian and French plots, and excessive duties placed

---

[27] John Rolfe to Sir Edwin Sandys, January 1619/20, *RVC* 3: 241–8; Bernhard, *Slaves and Slaveholders in Bermuda*, 17–26.

[28] Arena, "Indian Slaves from Guiana in Seventeenth-Century Barbados," 74–7; she notes that Indian slaves constituted a significant, albeit secondary, element in what became "the juggernaut of sugar production" on the island (81). For Jarvis's argument, see *In the Eye of All Trade*, 26–32.

by the Crown on tobacco. In 1629, Smith reported that almost three thousand people lived in the English zones of the island. Although in that same year the Spanish sacked the colony, the five years that had elapsed had proven sufficient to enable the English to extend their Caribbean presence and the socioeconomic sensibility that had developed to the much larger and less vulnerable Barbados.[29]

During this same period, Maurice Thompson began to work his way into the role in the supplying of colonies that enabled him to rise to a commanding prominence in the direction of seventeenth-century English overseas endeavors. Thompson actually lived in Virginia for four or five years when he was a young man, conceivably as a servant, although we have no evidence on this point. Born in 1604, he was among those who came to Virginia at the onset of the "tobacco boom"; according to his own evidence, he arrived in the colony in 1618 at the age of fourteen. Thompson's subsequent career, however, manifestly does not jibe with that of the stereotypical Anglo-American settler. In the first instance, having survived the Powhatan attack of 1622, Thompson returned to England, never to cross the Atlantic again, although his name appears among those, including William Claiborne, Ralph Hamor, Samuel Mathews, George Sandys, William Tucker, and the new governor, Sir Francis Wyatt, who received land patents in the aftermath of the disaster wrought by Opechancanough and his warriors; Thompson received a relatively middling 150 acres. He also was among the sixteen subscribers to "The Answer of divers Planters that have long lived in Virginia [to the] unmasquing" of the Virginia Company's management by Warwick's client, the privateer and former Governor of Bermuda, Nathaniel Butler, one of the key documents of the record in the dispute over the colony between the Southampton–Sandys and Warwick groups.

Thompson's involvement in this struggle constitutes the first apparent opportunity for him to have come to the attention of Warwick, with whom he formed a close partnership through their shared interest in promoting overseas trade and colonization and their opposition to the religious policies of Charles I. Thompson's Virginia experience would certainly have made him aware of how a colony operated as well as the pitfalls involved. It would also have provided him with the opportunity to study how to take advantage of the opportunities entailed in supplying

---

[29] Smith, *The True Travels, Adventurers, and Observations of Captain John Smith, in Europe, Asia, Affrica, and America, from* Anno Domini *1593, to 1629* [London, 1630], in Horn, *Captain John Smith*, 671–770 at 753–62.

the commodities and bound labor Anglo-American planters required and acquiring, in turn, colonial produce for resale in the metropolis or elsewhere.[30]

Was it a coincidence then that the slave trade became entrenched in Anglo-America at this time? In 1626, within three years of subscribing to "The Answer to the unmasquing" and just two years after the founding of the colony at St. Christopher's, Thompson shipped "about sixty slaves" to that island, the first recorded English slaving voyage ever made to an English settlement. Thompson did not report on the origins of that voyage, but its occurrence indicates that he (and probably other English people) had an awareness of how the trans-Atlantic slave trade worked. A year later, the early settler of Barbados Henry Winthrop reported that 40 of the 100 inhabitants of that island, directly after the colony's founding, were enslaved people.[31]

The cases of Virginia and St. Christopher's set the precedent whereby tobacco provided the economic lifeline to the metropolis, but this frequently snarled: planters relied on imports for practically everything and the resulting debts required repaying; the shortage of regular money as well as of nonagricultural economic activity made the staple the currency of these places; and the need to pay for imports addicted the planters to cultivation of the weed to an extent that inevitably caused its price to plunge in the 1630s. The initial success of tobacco also brought unwanted

---

[30] For his subscription, see List of Subscribers and Subscriptions for the Relief of the Colony, [4] July 1623, *RVC* 4: 245–6 at 245. For Thompson's land, see Extracts of all the Titles and Estates of Land, sent home by Sir Francis Wyatt, May 1625, *RVC* 4: 551–9 at 557. For the extent of his tenure in Virginia, see "The Answer of diuers Planters that haue long lived in Virginia and alsoe of sundry Marriners and other persons yt haue bene often at Virginia vnto a paper intituled The Vnmasked face of our Colony in Virginia as it was in ye Winter of ye yeare 1622," 30 April 1623, *RVC* 2: 381–9 at 386; for his age, see HCA 13/54, f. 137. For Warwick's politico-religious network, see Donagan, "The Clerical Patronage of Robert Rich, Second Earl of Warwick"; Hunt, *The Puritan Moment*, 160–82, 202–18, 251–78.

[31] Examination of Mr. Morris Thompson in Brief Collection of the Depositions of Witnesses and Pleadings of Counsellors at Law in a difference depending in Parliament between the Merchants Inhabitants and Planters in Barbados on the one part, and the Earl of Carlisle Lord Willoughby &c on the other part, 15, 17, 19, and 26 March and 19 April 1647, MS Rawlinson C 94, f. 7v, Bodl. Thirty-two Africans reportedly lived in Virginia in 1620, see Thorndale, "The Virginia Census of 1619"; McCartney, "An Early Virginia Census Reprised," 178–96. For Thompson and the colonial provision trade, see, e.g., Deposition of Thomas Weston, Saunders v. Weston, 1638, HCA 13/54, f. 83; Governor Harvey to the Virginia Commissioners, 27 May 1632, *CSPC AWI* 1: 151; Limbrey v. Wilson, 1638, HCA 13/54, f. 89; Schedules to Mary Limbrey v. Edward Wilson, 15 June 1638, HCA 24/94.

attention from the Crown, which sought from 1620 to divert as much
revenue from the weed as possible into its notoriously underfilled coffers.

Political culture played a controlling role in these developments: Warwick and other patrons would not have been cognizant of what was going
on in America without the efforts of their clients on the ground. Powell
and his brother Henry, as agents of Sir William Courteen as well as
Warwick, were in the thick of English pursuits in the Caribbean. John
Powell became the first Courteen-appointed Governor of Barbados after
Henry had established Sir William's colony on the island in 1627. The
Courteen venture, however, ran afoul of an alliance formed by the two
other claimants, and the Earl of Carlisle assumed the proprietorship of the
"Caribbee Isles" in the following year. With his new power, Carlisle
granted a syndicate of London merchants headed by Marmaduke Raw-
don 10,000 acres of Barbados land; their own agent, Charles Wolverston,
used that authority to assume the government over the entire island.[32]
Predictably, Powell did not recognize either Wolverston's or Carlisle's
authority. Another of the Carlisle's clients, Henry Hawley, then arrived in
Barbados and arrested Powell. The ensuing feuds that turned early Barbados into a political hothouse constitute an interesting element of colonial history, especially since this scenario was replicated at some level
throughout Anglo-America. Yet the links between the Powell brothers
and other godly participants in seventeenth-century English overseas
trade and colonization have rather greater significance.[33]

Moreover, Warwick's connections transcended the Caribbean, just as
his interests did. For instance, the Powells knew both Henry Winthrop
and Henry's father, John Winthrop, the Governor of Massachusetts Bay.
Prior to his own migration to America, the elder Winthrop, through
Henry and his acquaintance with the Powells (who served as postmen
for the Winthrops), knew all about the importance of tobacco and bound
labor for Anglo-American colonies. He also knew, probably not coincidentally, both that slavery existed as a labor option for Anglo-American
planters and how the American trade in indentured labor functioned.
Henry Winthrop, in relating the wonderful prospects he found in Barbados, asked his father to "send me ouer sum 2 or 3 men yt they be bound to

---

[32] The Earl of Carlisle's Commission granted to Charles Wolverston to be Governor of the
     Merchants Plantations, 3 April 1628, Ms. HM 17, Huntington Library, San Marino,
     California.
[33] The Prologue or Preface, Brief Collection of the Depositions of Witnesses and Pleadings
     of Counsellors at Law in a difference depending in Parliament, 15, 17, 19, 26 March
     1646/7 and 9 April 1647, MS Rawlinson C 94, ff. 1–4 at 2–3, Bodl.

searve me in the West Indyes some 3 yere or 5, wch you doe thincke good
to binde them for, and get them as resonable as you can, promysinge them
not above 10 pd a yere." Although the population of the infant colony
was "but 3 score christyanes and fortye slaues of negeres and Indyenes,"
if his father would supply him with necessities, such as knives, cheese,
wax, thread, and shoes, Henry had no doubt he would send 500 or 1,000
pounds of tobacco to England in six months. John, though, having
already spent £35 on various items and his patience with his "vain,
overreaching" son clearly stretched, was less confident about this prospect, finding the tobacco he had already received to be "ill-conditioned,
foul, and full of stalks, and evil colored," probably due to improper
preparation and shipping. Moreover, Henry's uncle had reported that
none of the grocers with whom he spoke about it would pay five shillings
a pound for it.[34]

The collective goal for the Warwick network – in addition to profit –
seems to have been to carry the fight against the Catholic foe via privateering and colonization, which would also increase English territorial
claims and the flow of revenue to both the Crown's coffers and the estates
of the colonizers. Thus, Warwick and his associates, often styled as
"Puritans," proposed the creation of an English West India Company
following the example of the Dutch West India Company that had been
founded in 1621 in anticipation of the renewal of hostilities between the
Dutch Republic and Spain. While the Earl continued his private war
against the Spanish, however, this particular idea of a company never
came off due to the disputes over the mismanagement of the larger
conflict, including the failure to capture Cadiz and the horribly dismal
attempt to relieve the siege of Huguenot La Rochelle, by Buckingham.
The ensuing demands for investigations into the Duke's activities and a
reluctance to throw good money after bad tied to questions over the
Crown's religious policies and the exercise of the royal prerogative that
Warwick, Saye, and others raised in the parliaments of the first years of
the reign of Charles I. The furor over the Crown's religious policies and its
methods of raising revenue to fight the war for which Warwick and his
associates had clamored culminated in the assassination of the favorite in
August 1628, the submission of a Petition of Right that demanded redress
of grievances, the King's dissolution of the Parliament of 1629, a

---

[34] Henry Winthrop to John Winthrop, 15 October 1627, and John Winthrop to Henry
Winthrop, 30 January 1627/8, in Davis, *The Cavaliers and Roundheads of Barbados*,
33–6.

determination to rule without parliaments until further notice, and the end of the war for which the Crown could not pay. While the proposed English West India Company became lost in these political fights, its spirit remained alive in the form of the Providence Island Company, which Warwick, Holland, Saye, and a remarkably large and important group of partners founded in order to continue harassment of the Spanish as well as pursue other Caribbean prospects.[35]

Thus, the socioeconomic platform for the development of Anglo-America had formed. The demands of colonizers necessitated the development of colonies that produced and consumed commodities that benefited those backers. The running of the plantation trade required agents on the ground; colonizers recruited them with offers including land and the means to transform it into an estate. Those who accepted these invitations also provided leadership for the colony by virtue of their new economic position and their connections. Successful settlements, by definition, require inhabitants and, therefore, the creation of societies. Yet for those involved in the colonial trade the recruitment of labor to cultivate staples held far more importance than the formation of American societies in of themselves did.

---

[35] Appleby, "An Association for the West Indies." For the political and religious differences of the first years of the reign of Charles I, see Cust, *Charles I*, 44–103. A note on the use of "Puritan": this was an epithet for contemporaries and none of the people referenced here would have accepted it as a description of themselves, who instead termed themselves "godly." John Winthrop, though, has become the quintessential American "Puritan," through the influential work of Miller, *The New England Mind*, and Morgan, *The Puritan Dilemma*. With that in mind, Winthrop, Warwick, and many of their partners were staunch Calvinists, who, in 1627, believed in a literal Scripture and in a further reformation of the Church of England to be achieved by protesting the practice of ceremonies they regarded as useless or, worse, "popish," although the list of offending practices could vary from one believer to the next. The literature on "puritanism" is so vast and contentious as to defy ready cataloging in a footnote, but the reader could do much worse than begin with Collinson, *The Religion of Protestants*; Collinson, *Godly People*; and Tyacke, *Anti-Calvinists*.

The Expansion of English Interests

America

The 1637 voyage of the *Abraham* illustrates how metropolitan interests initiated, maintained, and even integrated the spread of seventeenth-century English involvement in the Western Hemisphere following the establishment of tobacco cultivation in Virginia and Bermuda in the 1610s. A regular commerce with Barbados had quickly developed in the first decade after the founding of the colony and the godly London merchant Matthew Cradock and his partners sent this vessel loaded with servants for the island along with such commodities as stockings, candles, sugar, butter, flour, beaver hats, oatmeal, breeches, oil, vinegar, and spirits. Cradock's agents traded these goods with the Barbados planters, acquiring their tobacco crop, which they sold in Middleburg in Zeeland after the vessel recrossed the Atlantic Ocean.[1]

The evidence of this voyage also illustrates that the pursuit of Anglo-American colonization arose from pursuit of profits from the plantation trade. Planters certainly acquired colonial estates that provided the basis for their status within colonial society. They also relied on the tobacco, sugar, and other commodities that their estates produced to acquire the labor and other necessaries that they could obtain only from abroad. For metropolitan merchants, such as Cradock, as well as their planter customers, the return from these export crops constituted the readiest means of securing a return on their investment

---

[1] Ledger for Goods sould in ye Barbadoes by Tho Anthony & James Hooke, sent by ye shipp Abraham @ 1636 & what goodes was returned by the sayd shipp delivered at Middle[burg], 1636, Thos. Anthony's Account, 1637, and Ledger of Ship *Abraham*, HCA 30/636. The vessel left London at the end of 1636 (old style).

in overseas trade. Thus, the promotion of the cultivation of staples constituted their primary rationale for supporting overseas settlement.

The organization of this trade meant, as various colonials observed, that those who controlled it at both ends could act to the detriment of planters, who occupied a lower plane in the political economy of seventeenth-century England. Of course, those who objected to this state of affairs resisted it by resorting to their own political connections, by engaging in smuggling, and by pursuing intercolonial trade. The latter course of action, although this commerce also involved imperial merchants, became a profitable expedient practically from the onset of more extensive Anglo-American settlement and vital for provisioning the Caribbean colonies.[2]

This perspective on the seventeenth-century Anglo-American economy transcends American-oriented analyses that focus on the export of colonial products to Europe and on the exodus of servants and slaves westward. Yet while the vehicle of indentures made it easier to supply servants, the system did not entail the increasing commodification of labor as an integral part of an emerging capitalism as some have claimed: if by emerging capitalism we mean a set of socioeconomic circumstances in which commerce constitutes a prominent – if not necessarily commanding – element it is difficult to say when such a system did not exist in the first instance. Moreover, labor services have always been bought and sold whether in a wage environment or via some variation of servitude.[3]

Rather, as discussed in Chapter 1, the employment of the indenture device filled the preindustrial requirement for bound labor and retained the reciprocity that constituted the social cement – even if only in the

---

[2] E.g., The State of ye Difference as it is pressed between ye Merchants and ye Planters in relation to Free Trade at ye Charibee Islands and ye means of reconciliation and general satisfaction proposed, [1655], Add. Ms. 11411, ff. 3v–5r, BL. For early intercolonial trade, see, e.g., John Winthrop Jr. to John Winthrop, 30 April 1631, WP 3: 31–3.

[3] Souden, "'Rogues, Whores and Vagabonds'." These realities cloud the customary view of the settlement of Anglo-America that regards this phenomenon in terms of "early American history." Even with recent scholarly attention devoted increasingly to slavery and the slave trade and to Atlantic History, the movement of Europeans and the societies these migrants formed out of unfamiliar environments remains the intuitive focus of study as formulated most famously by Turner, "The Significance of the Frontier in American History." Prominent studies that focus on the settlers include Bailyn, *The Peopling of British North America*; Fischer, *Albion's Seed*; Gaskill, *Between Two Worlds*; Lipman, *The Saltwater Frontier*; Norton, *Founding Mothers and Fathers*; Richter, *Before the Revolution*; and Taylor, *The American Colonies*.

abstract – of master–servant relations. The recruitment of servants also entailed an initial voluntarism (again if only in the abstract) on the part of the prospective migrants. Once agreed, the terms of their service were memorialized in a written contract that could be bought and sold by people who had no acquaintance with the qualities of the servant concerned. On the other hand, the servant having engaged herself or himself initially was contractually obligated to render her or his service to whomever acquired the indenture subsequently. The administration of the indenture trade by agents on the ground, such as Thomas Stagg, who oversaw Maurice Thompson's Virginia operations in the 1630s, constituted an important aspect of seventeenth-century colonial servitude.[4]

In addition to servants, though, men of sufficient stature had to be recruited to assume leadership positions both formal and informal. These people might rise from within colonial society, although this could take some time. Generally, though, they tended to come from England with sufficient wherewithal, often provided as an encouragement to take up life across the Atlantic, to translate readily to the upper echelons of their new world. Others had to be content with operating on lower sociopolitical strata whether in the metropolis or overseas; Anglo-Americans such as William Claiborne, George Lamberton, Edward Winslow, and John Winthrop, Jr., sought to extend their personal estates as they promoted the expansion of English territorial and commercial interests just as their metropolitan counterparts did. These colonial-imperialists built on the foundation laid by the likes of John Rolfe and partnered with those who maintained both an expansive territorial and commercial vision and the substance to support that vision from the second quarter of the seventeenth century, such as Sir William Courteen, Cradock, and Thompson. The ambitions of all of these individuals, in turn, provided the basis for the formation of a halting yet palpably coherent set of overseas interests.

Cradock had obviously assumed a mastery of this situation by 1637, just ten years after the founding of the Barbados colony, if the *Abraham*'s case provides any indication. The value of the goods shipped on this voyage amounted to £142 17s 10d. The ship also brought fifty-six

---

[4] Deposition of Thomas Silver, 4 October 1639, HCA 13/55, f. 268; for promotional literature, see, e.g., Wilson, *An Account of the Province of Carolina in America*. These pamphlets were obviously targeted primarily at a literate – and therefore "weighty" – audience, but this did not preclude the circulation of their contents more widely. Wilson's contribution, for instance, claimed that "many persons who went to Carolina Servants, being Industrious" after the expiration of their terms, had prospered "and their Estates still encreasing" (7–8).

servants, whose indentures were sold for 500 pounds of tobacco apiece, which at 6d per pound (the going price for Barbados tobacco in 1637), amounted to £12 10s per indenture. This figure included £6 to pay for the servant's transport, and so the profit for the voyage's investors amounted to £364 in total from the servant trade. In exchange, the ship received 63,364 pounds of tobacco worth £1,583 2s at Middleburg, of which Cradock and his partners had 38,492 pounds worth £962 6s, which cleared a profit of £339 1s 6d.[5]

These sums, while tidy, are not massive in themselves. We can, however, certainly imagine – and the question must be left there due to the lack of a record – that the aggregate volume of the provision trade from the genesis of Anglo-America made involvement in it worthwhile for the likes of Cradock (whether colonies thrived or not). Thus, the apparent ordinariness of this voyage also reflects how the plantation trade in this period manifested the nature of the English Empire in the 1630s. Most important, the agendas of merchants such as Cradock set the territorial, political, social, and economic tone of English overseas interests. Naturally, profit constituted the main aspect of these agendas. Hence, it was determined that the Barbados tobacco should go to the Dutch Republic rather than England (or, for that matter, Hamburg, which was the second market option for the voyage). The continuing profitability of the Dutch tobacco market at a time when the price of the weed had plummeted elsewhere made Middleburg a good prospect for the ledgers of Cradock and his partners. This Anglo-Dutch commerce, however, did nothing either for the colonial planters whose trade was conducted on the basis of English rates for their tobacco or for the government of Charles I, which was deprived of the customs duty that would have paid on it had it been shipped to London (the third and last market option considered).[6]

The most successful merchants controlled both the markets on colonial commodities and the colonial markets for metropolitan goods and labor. Thompson, who controlled the provision trade with Virginia and

---

[5] Journal appertaining to me James Hooke of my dealings in merchandise from the 28 January 1636[/37] in A Journall taken ye of January by me J:H: [James Hooke] of all my dealings in Merchandize at Barbadoes for Shipp Abraham kept by James Hooke or Thomas Anthony, HCA 30/636, f. 2r. For the profit due to Cradock and his partners, see The weight of tobacco as hath been landed of the Abraham in the town of Middleburg in August 1637, and Account of some of the Abraham's tobacco sent from the Barbados to Middleburg and discharged in August 1637 in Receipt Book of James Hooke, HCA 30/636, ff. 5, 6.

[6] Thomas Anthony's Account, HCA 30/636.

Providence Island from the 1630s, realized this and acted accordingly. In 1632, Governor Sir John Harvey of Virginia reported to the Commission for Virginia headed by the longtime backer of the colony, the Earl of Dorset, that his colonists required "shoes and other necessaries." Thompson's partner, William Tucker, however, had left instructions to sell them "at his most excessive rates" and would pay only one penny per pound for tobacco, which did not even cover the cost of the staple, while "our intrudinge neighbours, the Dutch" offered the planters eighteen pence per pound. Harvey, another Virginia veteran, noted sarcastically that Thompson's concern should continue to enjoy its exclusive contract for providing imports, as it had made the "Colony greatlie indebted to them" while they "declare the great good will" that they bear "to his Majestie's service and this Plantation." He pleaded with the commissioners to permit "free trade" for the colony and for encouragement in the effort to find alternative "staple commodities."[7]

The voyage of the *Abraham*, though, scarcely does justice to the scale of the activities of Cradock who was a Committee (Director) of the East India Company and the first governor of the Massachusetts Bay Company. Along with Thompson, he was a member of a "godly" element that participated in an array of seventeenth-century English overseas ventures. The backers of the Massachusetts venture, though, appear to have been exclusively godly in their makeup. In addition to Cradock, the recipients of the company's charter included another omnipresent participant in overseas ventures, Samuel Vassall, as well as Vassall's brother William, Theophilus Eaton, later Governor of the New Haven Colony, Sir Richard Saltonstall, and John Venn, Maurice Thompson's friend and colleague in the Artillery Company of London, all of whom subscribed to fervent Protestant beliefs.[8]

In 1630, this group famously decided to remove their company's operations to America. Cradock, with his vast business interests, resigned the governorship, and John Winthrop, a Suffolk attorney recently discharged from his post in the Court of Wards, agreed to succeed him. This was one Anglo-American colonizing venture that did not require a

---

[7] John Harvey to the Lords Commissioners, 27 May 1632, in "Virginia in 1632–33–34," 149–50. For yet another example of the variety of commodities supplied, see Invoice of Goods Shipped on the *Lion* [for John Winthrop Jr.], 15 July and 2 August 1631, *WP* 3: 41–3.

[8] The Charter of Massachusetts Bay, 1629, http://avalon.law.yale.edu/17th_century/mass03.asp (accessed 29 August 2016).

promotional campaign or the clearing of jails and streets to attract
migrants. Winthrop took the charter and a substantial group to New
England where they would build on the platform already laid (in part to
defeat the claims of others) by a party led by company member John
Endecott. On their arrival, the new governor, perhaps even more famously, exhorted his group when they were within sight of their new home,
to bear in mind that they would be creating "a model of Christian
charity," "a city upon a hill" on which England, if not the rest of
humanity, would gaze.[9]

Putting that prediction aside, the perfecting of its charter by the
Massachusetts Bay Company brought "over fifteen thousand people"
to New England over the ensuing decade, although godly migration to
the Netherlands and the West Indies continued as well: by 1650, the
region had "over forty towns" and a population of European descent
that approached 23,000; by 1689, this figure approximated 90,000.
Moreover, while migration to the other seventeenth-century overseas
outposts of the English-speaking world consisted mostly of men, the
movement to New England had a relative gender balance. Also, notwithstanding the difficult winters in a time of global cooling, the climate
of their new environment enabled its inhabitants to follow the biblical
injunction "to be fruitful and multiply."[10]

This movement of people, unparalleled in terms of its scale in the
annals of seventeenth-century English colonization, has inevitably and
consistently attracted attention, often leavened with hagiography, even
as it was occurring. Why did these godly people – or, indeed, anyone –
cross the ocean to live in a faraway place in the seventeenth century? An
estimated 353,000 "British" people migrated to America between
1580 and 1700 (303,000 of them between 1640 and 1700), and this
figure does not include other Europeans who removed to Anglo-
America.[11]

---

[9] John Winthrop, "A Modell of Christian Charity," *CMHS*, 3rd ser., 7 (1838): 31–48.
[10] Genesis 1:28. The estimates of the number of migrants and of their composition come
from Breen and Foster, "Moving to the New World," 222; Canny, "The Origins of
Empire: An Introduction," 30; Anderson, "New England in the Seventeenth Century,"
200. For evidence of New England and the servant trade, see, e.g., Philip Nye to John
Winthrop, Jr., 21 September [1635], *WP* 3: 211; Lord Brooke to John Winthrop, Jr.,
[c. 1636], *WP* 3: 218–19.
[11] Horn and Morgan, *Settlers and Slaves*, 20–7. The emotions felt by the estimated 375,000
Africans with respect to their being taken to new situations in Anglo-America during this
120-year period must be left to the imagination.

Unfortunately, most people did not record their thoughts; indeed, the extent to which they exercised any choice – while also considering the alternatives that may have been available – in the matter of migration seems generally to have been an open question. For others, such evidence as we have of their motives for making such a seemingly momentous decision is always mixed.[12] Also, the same circumstances that might have motivated some to remove may have motivated others to remain. Thus, while the Huguenot *réfugée* Judith Giton recounted her escape from Louis XIV's *dragonnades* that led to her to remove to South Carolina in the 1680s, the reflections of the godly London turner Nehemiah Wallington on how to respond to his uncertain times led him to remain in England in the 1630s. Still others, including the Huntingdonshire gentleman farmer, Oliver Cromwell, and, for that matter, Maurice Thompson, gave observers the strong impression that they would remove to America, but they ultimately did not leave England.[13]

Trying to bear these issues in mind, we can say that these people departed from an England that they regarded as ecclesiastically and economically (seventeenth-century English people did not draw such distinctions) inhospitable. They also tended, in accordance with the nature of their religious practice, to move with their ministers as gathered churches – the sort of relationship that had alarmed ecclesiastical authorities for decades, if not centuries, and would continue to do so even in New England and other parts of Anglo-America.[14]

Regardless of motive, the scale of this influx of people produced one of the first and foremost episodes of colonial-imperialism in English history as the New Englanders rapidly investigated settlement prospects from Maine to the Delaware River in the 1630s and then spread to the Chesapeake, the West Indies, and Carolina over the next thirty years. This further migration, ironically, derived a considerable amount of its fuel from the differences in approach to religious practice among the godly that their removal to America aggravated. For all of the intentions of the likes of Winthrop and other Massachusetts leaders to devise an orthodox

---

[12] Horn, "'To Parts beyond the Seas'"; Horn, "Moving on in the New World."

[13] For Giton, see Judith (Giton) Manigault's Letter, 1684, Baird, *History of the Huguenot Emigration to America*, 2: 396–7; Van Ruymbeke, "Judith Giton." For Wallington, see Seaver, *Wallington's World*, 95–100; for Cromwell, Morrill, "Rewriting Cromwell." The Massachusetts Bay colony built Thompson a house in 1639 in anticipation of his relocation to the colony; Francis Kirby to John Winthrop, Jr., 26 December 1631, WP 3: 55–6; Hosmer, *Winthrop's Journal*, 1: 310.

[14] E.g., Henry Jacie to John Winthrop, Jr., 9 January 1631/2, WP 3: 57–61.

"New England Way" of church practice and belief, "Puritanism in the early seventeenth century carried within it the seeds of divergent ecclesiologies in a kind of balance that allowed the movement as a whole to retain its unity" only until the godly – in New England as well as in the metropolis – actually had the chance to put their beliefs into effect.[15]

The expansion of the English into the interior of New England began once the colony at Plymouth, founded in 1620 and itself an offshoot of Jamestown, had stabilized. The seemingly familiar "Pilgrim Fathers" came to occupy a mythological place in the United States in the nineteenth century, but their seventeenth-century situation was quite strange in contemporary terms with respect to their belief in the separation of church and state. Thus, the would-be migrants contacted the Virginia Company about the possibility of moving to their province as a group. Instead, they wound up quite far from Virginia and so assumed a right of self-government, although they had no license to be where they were.[16]

Yet the situation of the Pilgrims was also mundane in the sense that, as other Anglo-Americans did, they incurred debts in transporting themselves and their households, which required repayment, and they also needed to maintain themselves after relocating across the Atlantic. As it happens, these colonists had established themselves in a place that was reasonably proximate to areas with quantities of animal skins, especially beaver, whose pelts served as the material for hats that were a fashion craze in early seventeenth-century Europe – recalling that the *Adventure* brought beaver hats to Barbados. There was a catch, however: Europeans had not worked out how to catch the animals themselves, so they had to trade with natives in order to acquire peltries. By 1623, Plymouth Colony traders had developed a commercial relationship with Indians at Buzzards Bay on Cape Cod and over the ensuing decade extended their trading orbit as far west as the Connecticut River, as far north as Maine, and as far south as Narragansett Bay. This expansion, perhaps unavoidably, brought them into conflict with Dutch, French, and Massachusetts interests.[17]

English traders who sought trade with American Indians, like their counterparts in Guinea, had to work out a commercial relationship. In particular, they had to negotiate a situation in which they had to deal with the disadvantages of territorial and cultural unfamiliarity as well as

[15] Bremer, "The English Context of New England's Seventeenth-Century History," 325.
[16] Bradford, *Bradford's History*, 36–50.
[17] Henneton, "The House of Hope in the Valley of Discord."

the preeminence of indigenous economic and diplomatic power, notwithstanding the devastating effects that epidemics of smallpox and other Eastern Hemisphere diseases wrought upon the indigenous inhabitants of the Western Hemisphere. Moreover, in Africa, the availability of gold, the universally recognized medium of exchange, provided a ready basis for trade so long as the English provided commodities that their local partners were willing to acquire in exchange for it. In North America, however, where there was no gold, the Native American traders neither shared the value assigned to gold by other societies nor did they base their economies on the European comprehension of trade. Thus, when the English traded goods, especially metal tools and weapons with which Native American societies lacked familiarity but quickly came to desire, the Indians retained their presumption that the exchange itself provided the value of the interaction; as gift-giving it bound those involved into what the Indians regarded as a diplomatic arrangement rather than an economic one in European terms.[18]

The Indians, though, proved quick studies. They adapted their comprehension of economics to include a European perspective by demanding goods of equal or better value by European definition to the skins they produced. They also tried to maneuver Europeans to their advantage, as also happened in the East Indies and on the Gold Coast. Thus in 1631, for instance, the inhabitants of the Connecticut River Valley invited the Plymouth Colony authorities to establish a trading factory that would help protect them from their enemies, the Pequots. Of course, these diplomatic machinations did not always bring the desired results: sometimes, as in the case of the calamitous Dutch involvement in the Mahican–Iroquois War of 1624 or the English effort to support the inhabitants of Pulau Run in the East Indies in 1616, the European intervention proved of no help to indigenous allies; sometimes, as in the case of the Connecticut River, the establishment of a trading factory provided entrée for the English to entrench themselves with multiple settlements.[19]

The 1636 siting of Hartford, where the noted minister Thomas Hooker located his church, furthered the European identification of the Connecticut as a prime location for the fur trade; their partnership with the Indians enabled the Anglo-Americans to see off the Dutch presence there. In a similar way and in the same year, the Massachusetts Bay Company

[18] Otto, "Henry Hudson, the Munsees, and the Wampum Revolution."
[19] Parmenter, "Separate Vessels," 110–14; Starna and Brandão, "From the Mohawk-Mahican War to the Beaver Wars"; Trigger, "The Mohawk-Mahican War."

member William Pynchon established a factory upriver at Agawam (Springfield), which now constituted the deepest interior location of seventeenth-century Anglo-American settlement and became an immediate competitor of the Dutch post at Fort Orange (Albany). It is possible that Pynchon's religious views, which became increasingly at odds with the state-mandated orthodoxy practiced by the Bay Colony, contributed to his western move.[20]

The establishment of Agawam and Connecticut follows the pattern of seventeenth-century Anglo-American expansion in which colonial-imperialists customarily took territorial and commercial initiatives. From their colonial bases, these individuals invariably acted without involving the metropolitan government and worked either in conjunction with their local governments or without regard for government. The godly inhabitants of New England, many of whom, like Pynchon, held beliefs that did not jibe with those that came to be enforced by the Bay authorities, constituted a central element of this history. Whether as exiles from Massachusetts or moving to seek a less poisonous atmosphere, these migrants founded new settlements at Rhode Island, New Haven, and on Long Island. Not only did this further migration occur without the knowledge of, let alone at the direction of, the government of Charles I, it often happened against the wishes of colonial authorities as well. Rhode Island, also founded in 1636, was settled after its leader, Roger Williams, fell out with his fellow clerics in Massachusetts on the vexing issue of the relationship between church and state. Williams and his fellow settlers were joined by others who made themselves obnoxious to the Bay Colony authorities over the ensuing decade, including, most notoriously, Anne Hutchinson and Samuel Gorton. The leader of the colony was no political naïf: faced with repeated threats to this colony from both the Bay and Plymouth, he drew on the patronage of Warwick to secure a charter for Rhode Island from Parliament in 1644.[21]

The founders of New Haven, established in 1638, envisioned a godly commonwealth that was more Mosaic than that established in other jurisdictions. Unlike Rhode Island, this colony was not conceived out of the tumults that beset Massachusetts; indeed, it joined the Bay, Plymouth, and Connecticut in 1643 as "United Colonies" in order to address issues raised by the unexpected spread of the godly settlement, especially the

---

[20] Gura, "'The Contagion of Corrupt Opinions' in Puritan Massachusetts."
[21] Patent for Providence Plantations, 14 March 1643/4, http://avalon.law.yale.edu/17th_century/rio3.asp (accessed 29 August 2016).

proximity of "people of several nations and strange languages" as well as of Indians "who have formerly committed sundry Insolence and outrages upon several Plantations of the English."[22] But the prospect of living in a particularly rigorous environment of the sort planned by the Reverend John Davenport attracted settlers who founded additional towns on both sides of Long Island Sound.[23]

The New Haven leadership proved to be an especially active group of colonial-imperialists. The extent of their settlements compelled the Dutch to negotiate an agreement in 1650 that divided Long Island into Dutch and English zones.[24] Yet as the articles of this treaty set out, the New Haveners, especially Lamberton, had their eyes on the Delaware River Valley as well. Lamberton's expedition to the Delaware, however, ran afoul of the Swedish colony that had been established there also in 1638. The Governor of New Sweden, Johan Printz, arrested the New Haveners, and it required the intercession of Massachusetts Governor Winthrop to secure their release. Yet even Lamberton's death in the disastrous loss of the colony's ship in January 1646 did not deter New Haven's westerly ambitions. After the colony was absorbed by Connecticut in 1662, migrants from the former New Haven town of Branford finally established a presence between the Delaware and Hudson Rivers, founding Newark in the new colony of New Jersey in 1676.[25]

This demographic and geographical expansion of New England, however, soured Anglo-Indian relations. The Pilgrims had formed peaceable relations with their Wampanoag neighbors, no doubt assisted

---

[22] The Articles of Confederation between the Plantations under the Government of Massachusetts, the Plantations under the Government of New Plymouth, the Plantations under the Government of Connecticut, and the Government of New Haven with the Plantations in Combination therewith, 29 August 1643, http://avalon.law.yale.edu/17th_century/art1613.asp (accessed 29 August 2016). The extensive metropolitan ties and broader perspective on territorial expansion employed by these colonial leaders means their behavior transcended the modern scholarly concept of "settler colonialism"; LeFevre, "Settler Colonialism."

[23] Bremer, *Building a New Jerusalem*; Siminoff, *Crossing the Sound.*

[24] Articles of agreement between the delegates of the Commissioners of the United Colonies of New England and the delegates of the Director-General of New Netherland, 19 September 1650, Davenport, *European Treaties Bearing on the History of the United States and Its Dependencies*, 2: 1–6.

[25] Hosmer, *Winthrop's Journal*, 2: 286–7; Calder, *The New Haven Colony*, 210–15; Weslager, *The English on the Delaware*, 93–100, 107–32, 260–2, 264–5. For the New Haveners founding of Newark, see At a meeting Touching the Intended design of many of the inhabitants of Branford, 30 October 1666, *Records of the Town of Newark, New Jersey*, 2–3.

by the horrible effects of a smallpox outbreak that preceded the founding of Plymouth, and New England traders with the Indians such as Pynchon relied, as their counterparts throughout Anglo-America did, on the cooperation of the locals to provide peltries. Yet the seemingly inexorable movement of the English and their livestock across the landscape correspondingly reduced Indian hunting grounds and circumscribed the mobility of indigenous communities that they required to sustain themselves.[26]

For several decades, notwithstanding these circumstances, Indian polities generally preferred to employ diplomacy and accommodation in their dealings with New Englanders prior to King Philip's War (1675–6).[27] This philosophy, however, meshed with the Anglo-American pursuit of expansion to produce the marked breach of this relatively peaceful period of intercultural relations: the Pequot War (1636–7), perhaps the bloodiest overseas conflict involving English forces prior to 1650 and certainly one of the nastiest in the entirety of English imperial history. Using the alleged murder of an otherwise unlamented drunken mariner as a pretext for curbing the expansion of the Pequots in what is today southeastern Connecticut, for "overawing" other New England Indians for keeping the Dutch out of Long Island Sound, and for opening the Pequot Country to Anglo-American settlement, the colonial governments of New England, except for Rhode Island, allied with that nation's indigenous enemies, the Mohegans, Narragansetts, and Wampanoags, in a deliberate campaign of extermination.[28]

Almost all of the Pequots were killed, dispersed, or enslaved after their defeat. Most of the last group of unfortunates were sent to Bermuda and the West Indies, although some, especially women, remained in New

[26] John Winthrop and other contemporaries claimed the Indians did not "improve" their land – that is, practice husbandry – and did not stay in one place (ironically, given Winthrop's circumstances). Thus, they had no claim to a permanent title to it in the face of competition from "superior" cultivators. This view was, at best, mistaken as Indians who lived south of the Upper Great Lakes all practiced agriculture, and while indigenous communities did migrate every six or seven years, they did so in order in to maintain soil fertility; Cronon, *Changes in the Land*, 82–107.

[27] A note on nomenclature here: contemporary native social, economic, and political formulations did not jibe with European ones, but just as contemporary English observers employed inadequate terminology such as "king" or "nation" when describing indigenous cultures and societies, I shall do the same as an expedient; the difference being, hopefully, that the shortcomings of language are recognized. For the devastating effects of King Philip's War, see, e.g., Cray, "Weltering in Their Own Blood."

[28] Cave, *The Pequot War*, remains the best general account, but see also Lipman, "Murder on the Saltwater Frontier," and Meuwese, "The Dutch Connection."

England as slaves.[29] As it happens, the near-annihilation of the Pequots occurred at a time when African slaves became increasingly available to Anglo-American purchasers who bought into (literally as well as figuratively) this newly available labor source with alacrity to pursue their cultivation of tobacco, cotton, and, ultimately, sugar. A number of English traders in Guinea from the late 1630s, such as Maurice Thompson, were aware of the opportunities presented by furthering links between New England and the West Indies through their associations with New England's leaders.[30] Although the enslavement of Indians always came a distant third to the trade in enslaved Africans and the transportation of servants in terms of volume, it remained an essential component of the Anglo-American socioeconomic schema and, consequently, to territorial expansion. Can the emergence of English involvement in these slave trades have been a coincidence?[31]

Virginia also provided a base for the extension of Anglo-American interests into the interior of North America. As early as 1613, a foray commanded by Samuel Argall had explored the coast as far north as Acadia (Nova Scotia) and Maine and destroyed the French settlements they found there, the first English attack on another European presence in North America.[32] As we have seen, the subsequent "tobacco boom," while creating great hardship, stabilized the colony's population. Then, in the aftermath of the Powhatan attack of 1622, Sir Francis Wyatt, the new governor, pursued a "scorched earth" policy against the Indians seeking revenge for the "massacre" but also to clear the surrounding area of its indigenous presence, thereby enabling the expansion of settlement; the resulting Second Anglo-Powhatan War continued until 1632.

---

[29] Fickes, "'They Could Not Endure That Yoke.'"

[30] Francis Kirby to John Winthrop, Jr., 22 June 1632, *CMHS*, 4th ser., 7 (1863): 13; The Company of Providence Island to Capt. Nat. Butler, Governor, [7 June 1639], *CSPC AWI* 1: 295; Articles of Agreement between the Company of Providence Island and Maurice Thompson, 25 February 1639/40, *CSPC AWI* 1: 309. Thompson contracted with the company to transport one hundred men to their island on 9 March 1640/1; Coldham, *The Complete Book of Emigrants*, 217.

[31] Both the enslavement of Indians by the English (and other Europeans) and the practice of slavery and the slave trade in New England have received a battery of recent scholarly attention; Warren, *New England Bound*; Newell, *Brethren by Nature*; Gallay, *The Indian Slave Trade*; Gallay, *Indian Slavery in Colonial America*. For the enslavement of Indians in Barbados, see Handler, "The Amerindian Slave Population of Barbados in the Seventeenth and Early Eighteenth Centuries."

[32] George Folsom (ed.), "Expedition of Captain Samuel Argall, afterwards Governor of Virginia, Knight, &c., to the French Settlements in Acadia, and Manhattan Island, A.D. 1613," *CNYHS*, 2nd ser., 1, pt. 9 (1841): 335–42.

Meanwhile, Virginia's population grew from approximately 750 inhabitants in 1625 to some 7,600 in 1640. A third war with the Indians ensued (1644–6), which removed the "Powhatan threat" (the now-nonagenarian Opechancanough was captured and murdered) and "opened" further, accordingly, the area south and west of Chesapeake Bay to English settlement as the colony's population increased to an estimated 12,000 inhabitants by 1650. This conflict also brought the demarcation of the Indian-English boundary that also, perhaps paradoxically, established the set location for conducting trade with Indians who lived beyond the line of fortifications that the Virginians built on their self-designated south-western frontier at the falls of the Appomattox and James Rivers.[33]

Those English people who traded in Guinea and the Indian Ocean did not have to worry about the prospect of colonization annoying their local commercial partners thanks to the huge demographic imbalance and the tropical climates in those areas in the Eastern Hemisphere where the English operated. In Anglo-America, though, the expansion of colonization, by generating intercultural conflicts, required striking a balance between the territorial demands of settlement and the need for peace in order to conduct profitable trade with the Indians. These pursuits constituted the driving elements in the history of North America throughout the seventeenth century and afterward. Just as William Pynchon conducted his lucrative trade with natives at Agawam in New England, in Virginia, Abraham Wood, one of the commanders at the fort built at the falls of the James, was prominent in pursuing trade in deerskins with Indians who lived as far south as the Roanoke River in modern North Carolina.[34]

This commerce continued well into the next century, usually in competition with other English traders, especially after the founding of South Carolina in 1670, and with French *voyageurs* after the explorations of the Mississippi River Valley by the Sieur de la Salle and the founding of New Orleans in 1701. The full-fledged and illegal slave trading ring that the South Carolina traders conducted with Indian partners complicated these relations, devastating indigenous communities from the Florida Keys to the Mississippi River and provoking bloody wars in the first decades of the eighteenth century, and also kept that colony's politics on a continuous full boil with the slave traders and

---

[33] Fausz, "Merging and Emerging Worlds," 47–98; Craven, "Indian Policy in Early Virginia," 73–82. Population figures for Virginia come from McCusker and Menard, *Economy of British North America*, 135–6.

[34] Bland et al., *The Discovery of New Brittaine*.

their opponents, who correctly argued that this commerce dangerously destabilized South Carolina's relations with its neighbors.[35]

The uneasy relationship between trade and settlement also manifested itself in the northern part of Virginia, which stretched 200 miles north of Point Comfort pursuant to the terms of the third charter of the Virginia Company (1611) according to expansion-minded Virginians.[36] The leading Virginia Indian trader was William Claiborne. In 1630, pursuant to a patent apparently obtained through the offices of Sir William Alexander, a leading promoter of Scottish colonization during the reign of Charles I, Claiborne formed a partnership with, among others, the Guinea trader William Cloberry and, for a time, Maurice Thompson. Their plans included the "transportation of passengers to Virginia" but concentrated on pursuing trade with the Susquehannock nation that inhabited what is today southern Pennsylvania, central Maryland, and the Northern Neck of Virginia to obtain beaver and other peltries as well as corn and other provisions for Alexander's new colony in Nova Scotia. Thus, Claiborne established a post at Kent Island in the northern part of Chesapeake Bay where his agents conducted a profitable trade, although Alexander's colony ran into the sand, into 1637.[37]

---

[35] Vidal, "French Louisiana in the Age of the Companies." For the Indian slave trade managed from Charles Town, see Wright, *The Only Land They Knew*; Ethridge and Shuck-Hall, *Mapping the Mississippian Shatter Zone*. Most of those seized in these raids were taken to feed the ever-demanding labor needs of the West Indies, like their counterparts from the Pequot War, but some remained in South Carolina: a 1708 census reported 1,400 Indian slaves (and 4,100 enslaved Africans) out of a total population of 9,580; Sir Nathaniel Johnson to Board of Trade, CO 5/1264, ff. 52–7.

[36] The patent set the colony's southern boundary 200 miles south of Point Comfort; The Third Charter of Virginia, 12 March 1611/12, http://avalon.law.yale.edu/17th_century/va03.asp (accessed 6 September 2016).

[37] "Agreement of Claiborne with Cloberry and Others for Trading to Virginia." For Cloberry and his coincidental involvement in Guinea, see Chapter 3. For Claiborne's long career, see Roper, "Charles I, Virginia, and the Idea of Atlantic History," 41. Thompson became involved in the fur trade after an English force captured Québec in July 1629 (a second American imperial success for the English, although one of the few they achieved in their 1627–9 war with France); since a peace had already been agreed when the town fell, it was returned to France in 1632; Petition of the adventurers to Canada to the Privy Council, [September] 1632, *CSPC AWI* 1: 155. The connection with Alexander is not quite firmly established; Brenner, *Merchants and Revolution*, 122–3. For Sir William Alexander's career, see D. C. Harvey, "Alexander, William, Earl of Stirling," in *Dictionary of Canadian Biography*, vol. 1 (Toronto/Montreal: University of Toronto/ Université Laval, 2003–) (accessed 5 September 2016), www.biographi.ca/en/bio/alexander_william_1577_1640_1E.html.

Unfortunately for Claiborne, this promising enterprise to conduct "a very profitable and beneficiall trade" between Chesapeake Bay and Delaware Bay, the Hudson River, and north to Nova Scotia fell victim to particular circumstances that derived from colonizing efforts in this region as well as from the general circumstances in which seventeenth-century English overseas trade and colonization took place. First, while he and Cloberry had been able to call upon a Scottish vehicle for securing a charter, this patent was always subject to being overridden by English claims. Such an English charter came into existence when Charles I granted colonization rights without thought – or perhaps even an awareness – that the territory in question was already occupied by his subjects.

In this case, Kent Island came under the patent granted in 1632 to George Calvert, Lord Baltimore, who had publicly returned to the Roman Catholic faith of his youth and retired from his long service to the Crown as English law barred "papists" from public life. Baltimore had been an early investor in the East India and Virginia Companies but entered the overseas colonization lists in his own right in 1621 when he had received a first patent, substantially enlarged and revamped as a proprietorship in 1623, for "Avalon" in Newfoundland. Other English Catholics had been involved in overseas matters, and, like these other adventurers, Baltimore hoped to use his venture as a practical demonstration as to how Catholics could be integrated into the English political nation. At the same time, a Catholic-led colony could provide a haven for Baltimore's co-religionists where they could practice their religion without fear of incurring the draconian penalties prescribed by the recusancy laws whenever the authorities chose to enforce them strictly.[38]

For Lord Baltimore, Newfoundland was a promising location for such a colony. First, as with the Plymouth establishment of the Separatists, it was far from Virginia and other potential sources of political-religious interference. It also, at least at first glance, presented economic opportunities, especially with its access to the rich fishing grounds off the Canadian coast. Baltimore may have acquired some idea of the place from acquaintances of his who had been involved in the Newfoundland Company (chartered in 1610), which had sought to bring some management to the fishing stations that the English and other Europeans had operated in the area since the fifteenth century. The results, though, proved disappointing to that company's investors, who allowed it to wither, although

[38] Questier, "Catholic Loyalism in Early Stuart England."

Baltimore's new proprietorship inherited several communities that survived. The new Lord of Avalon funded the construction of a new port called Ferryland that became the chief town; he invested as much as £30,000 in his venture, arriving in person in 1627 to oversee progress.[39]

Once again, however, the promise of a successful colony presented by the appearance of green shoots failed to materialize. Avalon endured the usual problems of conflict between colonizers and their agents on the ground over the pace of the colony's progress. It also suffered conflict, in a foreshadowing of the problems the Calverts would endure in the Chesapeake, with claims made to rights that allegedly preceded the proprietary grant by the West Country fishermen who comprised most of the population. But Avalon also had particular issues: the Protestant inhabitants objected to the open practice of "popery"; nasty weather, especially in 1628-9, took its toll; and the French enemy sacked the English settlements in 1629. This combination of blows convinced Baltimore to shift his attentions elsewhere, and he transferred his Newfoundland interests to Sir David Kirke and the Earl of Pembroke and Montgomery in 1637. The Kirke family then became the leading English operators in Canada, as they established firm commercial links between Newfoundland with the wine trade in Spain and its Atlantic islands, and John Kirke was an original patentee of the company that received a trading monopoly in Hudson's Bay in 1670.[40]

Charles I then issued Baltimore a new patent to "Maryland" in 1632 that extended north from the Potomac River to 40 degrees north latitude at Delaware Bay to Baltimore. The former proprietor of Avalon died, though, before he could perfect this grant, and his son, Cecilius, succeeded to the Baltimore title and to the Maryland proprietorship. The arrival of the Calvert colonists in November 1633 triggered a forty-five-year struggle with William Claiborne that finally ended with the Virginian's death in 1677.[41]

Claiborne tried all sorts of maneuvers to have the Calvert grant annulled as he resisted the attempts of Baltimore's government to bring Kent Island under its authority, although his partnership with Cloberry degenerated into acrimony. Having sufficient colonial prominence to

---

[39] Cell, "The Newfoundland Company"; Pope, *Fish into Wine*, 124-32.

[40] See note 39; Miller et al., "'Over Shoes over Boots'"; Pope, *Fish into Wine*, 79-122, 132-44. Sir David Kirke led the force that captured Québec in 1629.

[41] The Charter of Maryland, 20 June 1632, http://avalon.law.yale.edu/17th_century/ma01.asp.

have cultivated powerful patrons to whom he readily exercised recourse, Claiborne submitted a battery of petitions to metropolitan authorities seeking relief from Calvert "tyranny." He also worked with the Earl of Dorset and his commission to "thrust out" Sir John Harvey, who had supported Baltimore's colony in accordance with his orders from the King. The collapse of royal government in England in 1642 presented Claiborne with the opportunity to foment rebellion against Baltimore's supporters – "Ingle's Rebellion" of 1644–6 – followed by another period of outright warfare that culminated in the "Battle of the Severn" (25 March 1655). But all to no avail: the Calvert proprietorship remained in place until 1689 when another rebellion, again infused with confessional overtones, overthrew it in the wake of the Glorious Revolution, a result confirmed by the incoming government of William and Mary.[42]

Amid these tumults, Maryland planters pursued the tobacco-based variation on the customary sociopolitical model that their neighbors had developed. The prospects for extending the colony's settlements received a fillip by the enforced departure of the Susquehannocks and their trading partner Claiborne from the scene after 1676. As happened in the cases of the Pequots and the Wampanoags, the Susquehannocks fell victim to an Anglo-Indian alliance, so the importance of the Indian trade to the colony and the political influence of the province's traders declined precipitously as western land was "opened" for planting by both small-scale farmers and planters with more extensive holdings after 1675.[43]

In his suit against Cloberry, Claiborne alleged he had lost thousands of pounds in the Kent Island venture as early as 1638, and Thompson seems to have lost whatever sums he had invested in this scheme as well. Indeed, the records we have of the careers of overseas merchants and colonizers demonstrate that they routinely incurred substantial losses, in time and effort as well as money, even allowing for exaggerated allegations. Yet despite these occupational hazards, seventeenth-century investors in the expansion of English interests outside Europe generally possessed a

---

[42] "Claiborne vs. Clobery et al. in the High Court of Admiralty." For Claiborne's efforts against Maryland, see Roper, *English Empire in America*, 121–6. The Calverts retained their right to the soil after 1689.

[43] Maryland's estimated population rose from 600 in 1640 to 11,400 in 1670 to 26,200 in 1690; McCusker and Menard, *Economy of British North America*, 136. For estates in seventeenth-century Maryland, see Walsh, *Motives of Honor, Pleasure, and Profit*, 371–3.

remarkable resilience that enabled them to weather such setbacks as befell them and move on to pursue other opportunities.

Thus, we find, for instance, that Thompson and Claiborne enlisted with Warwick and his partnership of aristocrats, gentlemen, merchants, and mariners in the plan to colonize three islands off the coast of modern Colombia in 1630.[44] As we saw at the end of Chapter 1, the purposes of these colonizers reflected their political orientation and relatively extensive overseas experience. They began by looking for bases in the western Caribbean from where to carry on piratical attacks on Spanish trade and shipping, in accordance with their anti-Spanish views, and those of Queen Henrietta Maria and her pro-French allies, after the war with Spain ended. They also included the investigation of further prospects for mines (rumors of the existence of which habitually flowed), the pursuit of (illicit) trade with Spanish colonies and with Indians on the mainland, and the conducting of colonial imperialism by locating additional sites suitable for settlement. Thus, Warwick's piratical client, Daniel Elfrith, searched for mines in the Bay of Darién, while Claiborne received a patent as proprietor of Ruatán Island off the cost of Honduras and Warwick sponsored the settlement of Tobago in 1639, having purchased colonizing rights to the island from the Earl of Pembroke. The Spanish, though, crushed the Darién and Ruatán initiatives, while the Kalinago Indians drove off the Tobago settlers and repeated the exercise in 1642 and 1646 for good measure. The colonization of Providence Island itself spawned such fervent differences between colonists and colonizers over the economic direction of the venture that Warwick contemplated offloading the enterprise to the Dutch West India Company in 1639.[45]

Of course, the backers of Providence Island did not foresee these difficulties when they undertook this venture. They expected that their

---

[44] Kupperman, *Providence Island*, lists the members of the company at 357–60.

[45] For Claiborne's proprietorship, see Kupperman, *Providence Island*, 82. For Darién, see Minutes of a Court for Providence Island, 8 and 25 May 1639, *CSPC AWI* 1: 293, 294. For Tobago, see Boomert, *The Indigenous People of Trinidad and Tobago from the First Settlers until Today*, 118; Description of a rich plantation called "the Tapoywasooze, and the Towyse-yarrowes Countries," lying upon the coast of Guiana, [1640?], *CSPC AWI* 1: 316. Warwick's acquisition of the Pembroke grant provided a pretext for him to pursue a proprietorship over Barbados and the other English islands, and he tried to purchase the Earl of Carlisle's rights, thereby stoking the political fires, although Warwick abandoned his plans; Puckrein, *Little England*, 44–7. For Providence Island and the circle of Henrietta Maria, see Smuts, "The Puritan Followers of Henrietta Maria in the 1630s." For the proposed sale to the West India Company, see Robert Earl of Warwick to Mr. Webster, 9 December 1639, *CSPC AWI* 1: 304.

planters would follow what had already become the colonization norm for Anglo-America and as anticipated by Robert Harcourt: they would exchange the tobacco and other merchantable staples, such as indigo or cotton, that they cultivated for the shoes, clothing, liquor, and labor they demanded in accordance with the operations described at the beginning of this chapter. The Providence Island colonists, though, would have the same reformed religious stripe as those in New England.[46]

Despite its difficulties and ultimate destruction by the Spanish in May 1641, Providence Island constitutes a sort of workshop of English overseas endeavor as this colony involved a significant array of what might be termed seventeenth-century English imperialists who went on to participate in a range of trading and colonization ventures. This colonial episode also exhibited all of the elements, including the ambiguity yielded by the mixture of these elements, which were inherent in the development and management of these activities. The venture's leadership secured the charter from the Crown from which the company derived its powers to establish a government, devise laws, remove people from England, and build forts. They also recruited the officials to manage the colony on the ground, established the lines of communicating the attractions of the place to prospective planters, and provided the investment and made the arrangements for provisions, fortifications, and other necessaries. Mercantile and maritime clients provided advice to these patrons and also acquired the commodities required to sustain the venture. They also provided and skippered the ships that brought those goods across the Atlantic and returned with the colonial products that sustained the estates of planters. Thompson, who assumed a similar role in Virginia at this time, quickly established himself as the manager of the provisioning of Providence Island. Undoubtedly, his extensive involvement in shipping people and commodities to these colonies at this relatively early date provided him with the wherewithal to support his even more extensive involvement in overseas matters after 1640.[47]

---

[46] For indigo cultivation, see, e.g., Minutes of a Court for Providence Island, 9 March 1640/1, *CSPC AWI* 1: 318.

[47] E.g., Petition of Maurice and Edward Thompson and Geo. Snelling to the Privy Council, [1634?], *CSPC AWI* 1: 195; The Company of Providence Island to Capt. Nat. Butler, [7 June 1639], *CSPC AWI* 1: 295–6; Articles of Agreement between the Company of Providence Island and Maurice Thompson, 25 February 1639/40, *CSPC AWI* 1: 309; Minutes of a Court for Providence Island, 4 January 1640/1, *CSPC AWI* 1: 316; Minutes of a Court for Providence Island, 13 February 1640/1, *CSPC AWI* 1: 317; Minutes of a

No one should be surprised to find that the process of planting Providence immediately entailed slavery given the prominence of Warwick,
whose Bermuda plantations employed slave labor from an early date. The
colonization of the island also involved the Earl's clients Elfrith, whose
piracy helped to introduce slavery into Anglo-America, and Thompson,
the organizer of the first English slaving voyage to an English colony, who
had become directly involved in the Guinea trade by 1638: by the end of
the 1630s the island had become the first Anglo-American colony to have
a majority of its population consist of enslaved Africans. Equally unsurprisingly, then, Providence provided the location for the first slave rebellion in Anglo-America even as the directors warned their government
about the presence of "too great a number" of slaves in the colony,
including "Cannibal negroes brought from New England," and tried to
restrict slave ownership.[48]

The rapid prevalence of slaves in Providence reflected circumstances
that made the colony an important part of the conduit, along with its
close contemporary, Barbados, by which slavery came to pervade
Anglo-America after 1630. First, relatively few European migrants
elected to take up residence so close to the Spaniards, while those who
were conveyed to the colony were not particularly keen to render the
service required to defend the island. Then, the development of the
colony coincided with the increased availability of slaves to Anglo-
American planters through the offices of Dutch and English traders in
Guinea after 1635. As their counterparts elsewhere in the Caribbean
did, the Providence planters readily adopted this labor alternative irre-
spective of the potential consequences; it was the availability of Africans
that determined the spread of slavery, not the alleged labor choices of
Anglo-Americans. As for English aspirations in the western Caribbean,
they had to wait until the late 1650s.

Thus, there was nothing particularly, not to mention inherently, distinctive about the short-lived Providence Island colony if we consider its
history in conjunction with the history of seventeenth-century English

Court for Providence Island, 25 February 1640/1, *CSPC AWI* 1: 317; Minutes of a Court
for Providence Island, 29 March 1641, *CSPC AWI* 1: 319.
[48] The Company of Providence Island to Governor and Council, 3 July 1638, *CSPC AWI* 1:
277–8. For Thompson and Guinea, see Warrant to the Marshal of the Admiralty to stay
the *Star* of London and other ships set forth by Maurice Thompson, Oliver Clobery,
Oliver Read, George Lewine, and others, for trade to Guinea and Binney, contrary to the
patent granted to the [Guinea] Company, 5 May 1638, *CSPC AWI* 1: 273. For slavery in
the colony, see Kupperman, *Providence Island*, 165–80.

overseas trade and colonization. All of the colonies that the English founded faced the fundamental problem of recruiting inhabitants. All of them also endured repeated political convulsions, as well as the reluctance people often have to being ordered to perform arduous labor at the behest of a master.[49]

While the Crown played a minimal role in these godly colonization efforts, its interest in the colonial trade commenced practically as soon as the colonists established the cultivation of "sweet-smelling" tobacco in Bermuda and Virginia. Lionel Cranfield, charged by James I with the thankless task of cleaning up the royal finances, implemented a farm for collecting the customs from tobacco as early as 1619, and Sir Thomas Roe, a longtime proponent of expanding overseas interests, and the merchant Abraham Jacob paid the Crown £8,000 for the right to collect sixpence per pound and an additional sixpence per pound as an imposition on imported tobacco. Yet this practice quickly came into dispute. Advocates of "free trade" claimed that removing the monopoly and lowering the duty would result in increased trade that would make up the loss to the government of the set rate by volume, a debate that would continue to rage as English overseas trade continued to expand.[50]

The Crown continued the farm, but Charles I tried several measures to bring more coherence to the collection of tobacco revenue. The earliest and grandest of these involved the appointment under the Great Seal of the diplomat Sir William Boswell and a Huguenot gentleman, the Sieur de Licques, as "receivers-general" of the customs produced by the trade of Virginia and the West Indies. De Licques apparently devised this plan, the original of which has been lost, which promised the King £50,000 along with a new ship for the Royal Navy per annum, while the grantees would receive one-fifth of the income from a plantation set aside for them. This plan, though, never materialized, in another illustration of the cross-purposes by which the Caroline government sometimes seemed to operate: Charles went to Scotland for his coronation there shortly afterward (with Boswell, secretary to the Earl of Carlisle, in his train), then Boswell

[49] Cf. Games, "'The Sanctuarye of our Rebell Negroes,'" 3–4.
[50] E.g., Swingen, *Competing Visions of Empire*, which tracks some of these views, although it is in error with respect to the context and chronology of events. The creation of monopolies provided a lightning rod of grievance throughout the seventeenth century; e.g., Journal of the House of Commons, 20 April 1614, in Jansson, *Proceedings in Parliament*, 109–15 at 110–14.

was appointed ambassador to the Dutch Republic where he remained until his death in 1650; de Licques disappeared from the record.[51]

Another scheme, mooted in 1638, followed a tactic Charles had employed in Ireland to obtain local approval of his plans. This involved securing legislation from the Virginia House of Burgesses that would have approved the reformation of the tobacco trade by collecting exports in set locations, limiting production, maintaining quality control, agreeing in advance how much tobacco the colony would export, providing relief from creditors such as Thompson, and setting a monopolistic contract under which the colony's tobacco would be bought that would hamper Dutch smugglers who continued to operate in the Chesapeake with impunity. Unfortunately for the King, the House of Burgesses was not as malleable as its Irish counterpart nor was Sir John Harvey as capable a parliamentary manager as Thomas Wentworth, Earl of Strafford, the Lord Deputy of Ireland: instead of applying a rubber stamp to the plan, the members denounced it and the motives of those who proposed it. A furious Harvey ended the session and the plan remained stillborn.[52]

Thus, the Crown devised a third idea, possibly at the instigation of its recipient, for regulating the "vast and excessive quantityes" of tobacco that Anglo-Americans cultivated. Since the colonial governors, "by reason [of] their distance one from another," had been unable to resolve tobacco issues, Charles I commissioned Henry Hawley, "Lieutenant general and Governor" of Barbados, to visit the plantations and meet with their governors "and soe many of the Inhabitants as shall be necessary" in order to curb overproduction, set an agreeable "certen price" for the commodity, and transact "such other businesse as by instruccons wee have authorized him."[53]

The imperial intention of this commission is apparent but was reinforced by the appointment of Hawley's brother, Jerome, as the Treasurer of Virginia with the brief to sort out the revenue situation at the same time. Richard Kemp, Secretary of Virginia, had advised the Secretary of

---

[51] For these plans, see Roper, *English Empire in America*, 105–7.

[52] Roper, "Charles I, Virginia, and the Idea of Atlantic History," 41–4. Seventeenth-century English governments were equally unsuccessful in their repeated efforts to assist colonial tobacco production, whether via royal proclamation or Act of Parliament, by halting cultivation of the weed in England; Jonson, "Natural History and Improvement," 122–5. If the metropolitan authorities could not impose their will in Gloucestershire, should we surprised that they were unable to do so in Gloucester County, Virginia?

[53] Copy of Capt. Hawley's Commission to treat for cesation of Plantinge of Tobacco, 27 March 1639 [copy dated 12 December 1639], Mss. Bankes 41/2, f. 125, Bodl.

State Sir Francis Windebank that twenty-one ships had sailed for London from Virginia in 1636 with tobacco the customs from which had been valued at £3,334. Moreover, the merchants had devised such "ready ways for the conveyance of their goods" to escape duties so that the recovery of even one-third of the lost revenue might amount to £20,000 per annum.[54]

Unfortunately for Charles I, though, this idea only constituted another illustration of both the limits of his power to manage matters and the political circumstances under which the seventeenth-century English Empire functioned. The untimely but hardly unforeseeable death of Jerome Hawley only a few months after he assumed his office did not help. Then, the Crown erred – or was perhaps led to error – in styling Henry Hawley in the manner that it did in its petition. Hawley had taken advantage of the endemic factional politics of Barbados and the recent death of the Earl of Carlisle, its proprietor, to claim the governorship of the island, having created a colonial assembly that ratified this maneuver. The commission armed Henry with royal authority, but he proved unable to establish his authority over the island let alone assume the dignity required to carry out his brief.[55]

Then, 1639 proved to be the climax of Charles I's Personal Rule as events came to preoccupy his government until its collapse at the beginning of 1642: in March as Henry Hawley returned to Barbados, the King left for York to deal with rebellion in Scotland. Charles had economized and, as we have seen in the colonial sense, scoured his dominions seeking ways to augment his revenue. He had done so, perhaps in a backhanded approach, in order to deprive those who questioned his government of a legitimate forum – Parliament – in which to air their concerns, as had happened in the late 1620s. Perhaps not coincidentally, many of the most prominent people who had concerns with the Crown's religious and constitutional policies were involved in the Providence Island Company, although to style Warwick, Saye, John Pym, Oliver St John, and the other investors who led the encroachment on royal power after 1641 as an "opposition" group in the 1630s is an overstatement that evokes anachronism. The opportunity to challenge the King presented itself only after Charles sought to impose his religious authority more forcefully on his Scottish subjects through the introduction of a new Prayer Book for

---

[54] Richard Kemp to Secretary Windebank, 11 April 1636, "Virginia in 1637," 170–1.
[55] The political tribulations, which continued until 1652, did not help the socioeconomic development of the place; Puckrein, *Little England*, 40–55.

the Kirk, based on the English version, in 1637. Instead of more dutiful obedience, however, this move provoked rebellion in all three of the Stuart kingdoms.[56]

Meanwhile, matters proceeded on other fronts. While the efforts of Charles to formalize his authority ran into all sorts of obstacles, the scope of English overseas interests intensified even in the face of continuing domestic political animosities and hostility from indigenous and European rivals.

[56] Kupperman, *Providence Island*, 6–14.

3

The Expansion of English Interests

Guinea

In February 1649, the merchant Samuel Wilson dispatched the *Seville Society* from London "direct" for "Guinea." Wilson's ship traded along the Atlantic coast of Africa, probably between Sierra Leone and the Volta River, until the following November when it headed for the West Indies. Arriving in the Caribbean in January or February of 1650 and carrying "about two and hundred and fifty Negers and about three thousand pounds of elephants teeth & several English manufactures and stuff," the vessel called at Barbados and Nevis. The crew, though, seems not to have traded at the English islands but sailed on to Venezuela and Curacao before arriving at Aruba on 7 April 1650. They remained at this island for two months "to refresh ye Negers which the said ship had brought from Guinea" before returning to the South American mainland where they "put their Negers ashore." The English then traded with the Spanish colonists over the next 3 or 4 months, acquiring "a great cargazon," including 300 to 400 cloth pouches of tobacco, 40 tons of salt, 8 to 10 tons of wood, and approximately 3,000 hides that joined the ivory in the hold. Unfortunately for Wilson and his agents, the mouthwatering prospects for this voyage evaporated when five French men-of-war surprised their ship near Caracas and hauled it to France.[1]

What does this episode tell us about seventeenth-century English overseas trade and colonization? First, it reflects the substantial extension of the scope of these activities by the middle of the century, both

---

[1] Deposition of Thomas Hewitt, 22 April 1652, and deposition of William Eales of Limehouse, 22 April 1652, CLA/024/06/004, Depositions (unfoliated), Mayor's Court, City of London, 1652–3, LMA.

geographically and in terms of the number of individuals involved. Second, it illustrates the lack of involvement in overseas trade and colonization of the seventeenth-century English state sometimes to the point of irrelevance, especially in this period in the immediate aftermath of the trial and execution of Charles I on 30 January 1649. Wilson apparently was an "interloper": someone who conducted his activities without having secured a charter or any sort of governmental license to trade overseas and who acted in violation of the particular patent granted to the Guinea Company in 1631.[2] But was he really? Samuel Wilson had close contact with his namesake and possible relative, Rowland Wilson, and other members of the Guinea Company; how vehemently did they object to Samuel's African enterprise?[3]

This incident also underscores how quickly the "Guinea trade" became central to seventeenth-century English overseas affairs. By the time of this voyage – less than a quarter century after Maurice Thompson's three ships delivered sixty slaves to St. Christopher's – Samuel Wilson and his operatives seem to have acquired a comfortable level of knowledge of how to conduct the commerce that connected West Africa with the Americas, Asia, and Europe. Such knowledge, which could be accrued only by someone sailing to Guinea and observing the cultures and governments of its inhabitants, was vital in any event and with African commerce especially. To procure the commodities they sought, Guinea traders needed to be aware of the nature, quantity, and quality of goods that African merchants, such as the Akrosan brothers, John Ahenakwa and John Claessen (a.k.a. John Cloyce) of the Kingdom of Fetu (or Afetu) in modern Ghana, demanded in return. They also had to be aware of and be able to absorb the hazards of conducting affairs in a remote and hostile climate (for Europeans).[4]

---

[2] Order of the Council of State. Samuel Vassall, Peter Andrews, and Company, Mr. Frith, linen-draper, Cornhill, and Company, and Samuel Wilson, of Aldermanbury, and Company, all trading to Guinea, to be summoned to attend the Council on 17th inst, 12 April 1650, *CSPC AWI*, 1: 338.

[3] Rowland Wilson appointed his "loving friend" Samuel as an "overseer" of his will in order to assist Rowland's grandson; Waters, *Genealogical Gleanings in England*, 1: 834–5.

[4] We do not have the sort of reports from the Gold Coast from English factors in the 1640s that we have for the Dutch West India Company perhaps because of the Great Fire of London (1666) or perhaps because the English did not have a base in Guinea to rival the Dutch citadels of El Mina and São Tomé. The Dutch observations, though, can be taken as applicable to the English situation. Certainly, the prospect of the sort of disaster inherent in the sudden consumption by fire (accelerated by the presence of a quantity of liquor in

We should be clear, accordingly, that the Africans with whom Thomas Hewitt, the master of the *Seville Society*, and his counterparts dealt were manifestly not unsophisticated, naïve dupes in either political or economic terms: they knew what they wanted from Europeans, they knew what Europeans wanted, they were well aware of the competition between Europeans over African commodities, and, thus, they knew how to manage their encounters with Europeans to their advantage. Thomas Crispe, chief factor of the Guinea Company, recalled that the King of Fetu had promised him "the country should be mine and that no other white man whatsoever should come ashore or have any trade there at Cape Coast" and that he would have a new factory built for the English. He and the King concluded an agreement to those ends that conveyed the "castle" in exchange for gifts worth ten bendas (twenty ounces) of gold valued at £64 sterling by the Englishman on 20 April 1650 "whereupon ye people gave severall greate shouts, throwing ye dust up in the aire and proclaimed that this was Crisps land." Four days later, though, a Swedish ship arrived on the scene. Its captain quickly ingratiated himself with the locals, gained possession of the new English factory, built his own fort, and commenced undercutting the English trade by underselling goods, overpaying for gold, and drawing away the merchants who had amassed considerable debts to the Guinea Company to its "great prejudice" to such an extent that "it is to be feared will be the ruin of the whole trade upon that Coast."[5]

Needless to say, this sort of turn of events bemused those, such as Crispe, who saw their hopes and expectations dashed. Yet instead of acknowledging that the King of Fetu and his "chief men" had worked out a better deal with the Swedes, the Guinea Company factor found it easier, if not instinctive, to regard this behavior as capricious and,

---

the hold) of the *Nieuw Groningen* "with a good coast cargo," including the loss of eight men of the relief garrison, would have been dreaded at all the European trading forts; Isaac Coemans to Director General van der Wel at St. Thomé, 5 March 1647 (n.s.), FP, The Gold Coast (N 4) (1646–1647), 157–60.

[5] Deposition of Thomas Crispe, London merchant, "having been diverse voyages upon the Coast of Guinea for" Sir Nicholas Crispe and Company, 15 March 1664/5, T 70/169, ff. 35–6. For the power and influence of the Akrosan brothers, see Daaku, *Trade and Politics on the Gold Coast*, 107–11; e.g., "The Title of the English to Cape Coast & the Fort there, is in fact & right this," FP, The Gold Coast (N 5) (1648–1652), 56–7. The Akrosans consistently favored Swedish traders in their dealings with Europeans; for Swedish activity, see Nováky, "Small Company Trade and the Gold Coast." Kea, *Settlements, Trade, and Politics*, 190–2, discusses the currencies and exchange rates in effect on the seventeenth-century Gold Coast.

moreover, a manifestation of the sort of general trait – not racial, in the nineteenth-century sense but nevertheless inherent – among "the Blacks."[6]

Another revealing aspect of the *Seville Society* voyage is the nature of the vessel's cargo, which reminds us that, while modern students naturally tend to dwell on slavery, for contemporary participants, slaves appear to have constituted one of several "desirable commodities" that were obtainable in the Guinea trade. In the English, as well as the Dutch, case, gold, ivory, and dyestuffs seem to have provided the initial attraction to Africa. Yet, well before 1649, the English not only regarded slaves as a "desirable commodity"; they knew the location of markets, beyond the obvious English ones, for slaves and they had ships with the capacity to transport upwards of 250 Africans across the Atlantic along with ivory and other goods.

As we know, the volume of the slave trade undergirded much of the economic character of the Americas between the early fifteenth and late nineteenth centuries and spawned the peculiar version of slavery that existed in the Western Hemisphere with consequences that still reverberate throughout the Americas. This execrable commerce expanded substantially during the seventeenth century, and, following the expiration of the Twelve Years Truce in the Dutch war against the Habsburgs in 1621, the Dutch and the English became rivals with the Portuguese for the leadership of the dubious league of European slave traders.[7]

---

[6] Contemporaries with similar views can be found in, e.g., Hendrick Caarlof, fiscaal, to the XIX, Casteel del Myna, 26 September 1647 (n.s.), FP, The Gold Coast (N 5) (1648–1652), 179–85 at 182.

[7] According to the best estimate, the approximate number of enslaved Africans transported to the Americas rose to 152,373 between 1576 and 1600 and to 352,844 between 1601 and 1625, declined to 315,050 between 1626 and 1650 but rose to 488,065 between 1651 and 1675 and 719,675 between 1676 and 1700. Ships from "Great Britain" (customarily, England in this period) shipped no African slaves, according to the surviving evidence, in the first quarter of the seventeenth century, but the number of slaves shipped by the English rose to 33,695, 122,367, and 272,200 at the ensuing quarter-century markers. The latter figure left the Dutch, fierce rivals of the English, well in arrears: 31,729 African slaves shipped between 1626 and 1650, 100,526 between 1651 and 1675, and 85,847 in 1676–1700. Meanwhile, the number of slaves shipped to America in Portuguese vessels declined from 174,886 between 1600 and 1640 to 116,025 between 1640 and 1700, a period during which Portugal fought a twenty-eight-year war of independence from Spain and lost its trading factories on the Gold Coast (as well as those in Angola and Saõ Tomé temporarily) to the Dutch; *Voyages: The Trans-Atlantic Slave Trade Database*, www.slavevoyages.org/assessment/estimates.html?yearFrom=1501& yearTo=1866&flag=2 (accessed 11 January 2016).

The perpetuation of this reality, especially in a nation that came to postulate that "all men are created equal," has naturally produced considerable indignation among modern historians, who have spilled a considerable amount of ink trying to come to terms with the emergence and development of a labor system that had no apparent precedent and no actual counterpart in the metropolis yet became integral to Anglo-American colonial development. How to account for the wretched state of affairs created by the trans-Atlantic slave trade?

One seam of scholarship, following the lead of Eric Williams, has tied the history of slavery to the history of capitalism whereby, according to Seymour Drescher, the "opening of the Atlantic invited the creation of a virtually unconstrained form of capitalism, whose beneficiaries created and dealt in human chattels as their labor force." In a related vein, John Donoghue has recently fingered "merchant-revolutionaries" and the "revolutionary state," which combined to devise a system whereby "unfree labor" in a variety of forms was supplied to the ever-widening maw of planter demand for field workers. In America, the arrivals – Royalist prisoners of war, Irish Catholics, convicts, the impoverished, as well as enslaved Africans – were subjected to the dehumanizing conditions of plantation life that they naturally resisted. Simon Newman shares these sentiments: "given the opportunity the mid-seventeenth-century Englishmen who became Barbadian planters did not hesitate to use bound white laborers in brutal fashion" with the survivors usually condemned to a life of penury.[8]

As Newman, for one, suggests, Barbados, the most populous and wealthiest (in terms of planter income) part of seventeenth-century Anglo-America, has provided the model both for the colonial pursuit of wealth and for historiographical comprehension of colonial British America. We have now been cautioned about thinking in terms of a sugar revolution as having taken place in the colony around 1640, which gave rise to this situation. Nevertheless, it remains a commonplace in the comprehension of the history of the English "Atlantic World" that all of the "slave societies" that extended southward from Chesapeake Bay transitioned from indentured servitude to slavery as their primary labor system during the later seventeenth century.[9]

---

[8] Donoghue, *Fire under the Ashes*, 214; Newman, *A New World of Labor*, 2; Drescher, "White Atlantic," 33. The classic statement of the proposition that slavery generated capitalism remains Williams, *Capitalism and Slavery*.

[9] Beckles and Downes, "The Economics of Transition to the Black Labor System in Barbados"; Menard, "Making a 'Popular Slave Society.'"

In England, the need of landowners for a successful harvest to maintain their estates – and therefore sociopolitical status as well as wealth – was combined with the need of laborers for year-round security in the form of room, board, and perhaps a wage into the institution of servitude. The creation of Anglo-American versions of this system entailed a substantially lower level of personal relationship between master and servant in the classic scenario to begin with, given that colonization incorporated long-distance migration by definition. It also incorporated a correspondingly greater element of market-oriented behavior. Thus, in addition to formalizing the traditional arrangement, the use of indentures also eroded it: the buying and selling of the contracts replaced the annual selection of servants in colonial scenarios. With respect to enslaved Africans, who arrived in Anglo-America as commodities already, this traditional sociocultural arrangement was never applied intuitively. Thus, commerce, as opposed to capitalism, seems to have begat American-style slavery rather than the other way around. Remarkably, though, American-centered analyses have never considered the reality that, regardless of whenever planters may have come to prefer slave labor, the satisfaction of whatever labor demands they may have had remained dependent on supply and the English did not have ready access to the African slave trade until the 1630s.

Confusion over the status of Africans in Anglo-America, as well as over the level of involvement of the English in the slave trade prior to circa 1660, has arisen due to a lack of an evidentiary "smoking gun" that confirms that Anglo-Americans promptly and generally relegated Africans who arrived in their plantations to enslavement. Other circumstances enable the claim that "the slave trade was as yet of small concern to English traders" prior to the latter part of the seventeenth century. These include the ambiguity presented by evidence that a community of free Africans lived on the Eastern Shore of Chesapeake Bay from the 1620s, the time lag between the first recorded arrivals in various colonies and the creation of colonial "slave codes" that stipulated a link between Africans and enslavement, the seeming objections to buying and selling humans expressed by certain contemporaries, and the language of the patent issued to the Royal Company of Adventurers Trading into Africa in 1660, which makes no express reference to the slave trade (although this was amended in the next version issued in 1663).[10]

---

[10] Rawley and Behrendt, *The Transatlantic Slave Trade*, 77.

On the other hand, recent attempts to answer the eternally vexing questions of the origins of slavery in the "English Atlantic" and, by extension, the United States and the chronological priority of race and slavery have argued – correctly in my view – that African people and slavery were central to the development of seventeenth-century Anglo-America. Yet we need not consult the works of the Jacobean poet-playwright Michael Drayton, not to mention those of the dyspeptic twelfth-century Welsh chronicler Geoffrey of Monmouth or the eighth-century commentator the Venerable Bede, to have a good sense of the attitudes of seventeenth-century English people toward Africans. Those English people who were actually involved in Guinea regarded the slave trade as part of the regular commerce they had with Africans, and they styled the "Blacks," to use the most frequent descriptive in the record, with whom they interacted as "villains" or as possessing "quality" depending on their attitude toward the English.[11]

Clarity on these issues can come only if we apply the concept of *res ipsa loquitur* – "the thing speaks for itself": whatever may have been written and read – and by whom – about slavery and what we call "race" today, various English merchants, mariners, factors, and planters trafficked in enslaved Africans (and American Indians), and none of these people seems to have expressed any apprehensions about what they were doing. This is not to say that English participation in the slave trade amounted to an unthinking decision; rather, it was an uncaring one. In the end, the circumstances of Anglo-American slavery arose from the mundane, but nonetheless appalling, reality that European traders brought shopping lists to Guinea that were given to them by the likes of Maurice Thompson and Samuel Vassall; human beings, which the record of this commerce prior to the 1680s customarily characterized as "Negroes" rather than as "slaves," constituted a high-demand item for these voyages. The agents then resold their purchases, presuming they survived their trip across the Atlantic, to

---

[11] E.g., Roger Chappell, William Hulinge, Wm. Haddoe, Richard Maxwell, William Spencer, Jeremy Sapston to Right Worshipful Company of Merchants Trading for Guinea and East India, London, Corma[ntine] Castle, 10 June 1661, IOR E/3/27, ff. 40–1; cf. Guasco, *Slaves and Englishmen*, 22–5; Coombs, "Beyond the 'Origins Debate'." An economic study of the costs of the trans-Atlantic slave trade has noted that the "supply side" of this commerce "has received much less attention than the demand side"; Eltis et al., "Accounting for the Traffic in Africans," 940–1.

colonial buyers at a generally healthy profit, thereby creating the framework for interactions between people of African and European descent in Anglo-America (and elsewhere).[12]

We can locate English involvement in the "Guinea trade" and, accordingly, an awareness of the practice of transporting enslaved Africans to the Americas to perhaps as early as the second reign of Edward IV (1471–83) but certainly prior to the end of the fifteenth century. A knot of English merchants traded at Seville, the mercantile capital of Castile at this time. That port, by virtue of the commerce that had developed between the Iberian Peninsula, the Atlantic Islands, and the African coast before 1480, contained a noticeable population of free and enslaved Africans. These traders used their relationship with the Duke of Medina Sidonia, who was active in African commerce, and their Genoese counterparts to carve their own niche in Seville's overseas trade, which included slaves to Hispaniola and sugar produced in São Tomé. Their situations make it quite conceivable that they circulated their knowledge of Iberian slavery, including the particular issues that may have related to the use of slaves on American plantations, to contacts in England.[13]

English opportunities for involvement in Spanish enterprises and English access to markets in Habsburg territories became strictly limited after the accession of Elizabeth I in late 1558, as John Hawkins and Francis Drake found to their cost when they attempted to sell African slaves in Mexico in the 1560s. In this same period, Spain assumed full-blown bogey status for certain English Protestants, while Portuguese merchants, by rights under the Treaty of Tordesillas (1494), shipped increasing numbers of slaves to both the Spanish colonies in America and to Brazil, and Philip II (reigned 1556–98) incorporated Portugal into his composite monarchy in 1580. After the forays of Drake and Hawkins into the slave trade ended in their ejection from New Spain in 1568, we have a scattered record of English appearances on the West African coast

---

[12] See, e.g., Deposition of Walter Smith, 8 February 1648/9, HCA 13/61, ff. 268r–269r; The East India Company's Answers to the Assada Adventurers propositions, 19 November 1649, HCA 13/71, ff. 70-1; Examination of Samuel Meade, 14 September 1653, HCA 13/67, f. 496r; Voyage to the Bite [Bight of Benin] by the *Blackamore*, November 1662, T 70/309, f. 5v; Minute Book of the Court of Assistants of the Royal African Company, 29 March 1673 to 28 April 1676, T 70/76, ff. 8v–9r; Instructions to Captain Thomas Woodfine, 10 December 1685, T 70/61, f. 3; cf. Goetz, "Rethinking the 'Unthinking Decision'." The nomenclature suggests that the slave traders had scant regard for the social status of the people they bought, sold, exchanged, and used as currency.

[13] Dalton, "'Into speyne to selle for slavys'"; Ungerer, *The Mediterranean Apprenticeship of British Slavery.*

for the next fifty years. The undertaking of those voyages that were recorded stemmed largely from the attractions of the gold fields in the vicinity: "infestations" of English traders along the Upper Guinea coast were reported to the Portuguese authorities, and William Keeling's narrative of the Third East India Company voyage to Asia included an account of a layover at Sierra Leone in 1607.[14]

The English presence in West Africa became more sustained after the first English Guinea Company received its charter from James I in the same year as the Virginia Company created indentured servitude. This African entity, founded under the auspices of the merchant John Davies, who seems to have developed relatively substantial African experience as early as 1609, seems to have arisen primarily from Davies's interest in redwood (used in dying cloth), which could be obtained in Sierra Leone. Most of the original members of the company, including the Earl of Warwick, who initially headed it, quickly fell by the wayside, and a clutch of merchants, including Nicholas Crispe, John Wood, William Cloberry, Humphrey Slaney, and John Slaney, assumed control of the company after Davies died in 1626. On 25 June 1631, Charles I granted the new leadership a new charter and they quickly took steps to extend their interests to the gold and ivory trades as well as that in redwood, which "Wood, his partners, factors and agents have had the sole trade and traffic from this kingdom in the Sherbro [River of Sierra Leone]" by 1633.[15]

During this period, the circumstances in which the Guinea trade was conducted changed dramatically as the resumption of war between the Dutch Republic and the Spanish monarchy placed the long Portuguese dominance of the trade between Africans and Europeans in jeopardy. In

---

[14] "The Voyage of Captain William Keeling, in 1607, to Bantam and Banda," in Green, *A New and General Collection of Voyages and Travels*, 1: 312–32 at 313–15.

[15] Deposition of John Downe, 29 June 1648, HCA 13/61, ff. 105v–107v at 106r; Deposition of George Frank, shipwright of Southwark, 28 June 1648, HCA 13/61, f. 103. For the Guinea Company, see The humble petition of Humphrey Slaney and Nicholas Crispe to the Privy Council, [1635], Add. Ms. 36488, f. 20, BL; Blake, "The English Guinea Company"; Blake, "Farm of the Guinea Trade." Slaney and Crispe, like a number of other overseas merchants, partnered in other areas; their involvement in the Canary Islands and Brazil included transporting sugar, so they might have been an(other) instigator of sugar cultivation in Barbados; case of Humphrey Slaney and Nicholas Crispe against George Henley, their agent and master of the *Valentine* in 1633–6 sailing to the Canary Islands and then to Brazil and back, 22 June 1638, HCA 24/94. Cloberry sent a ship to Guinea in 1633, but it is unclear whether this was a company vessel or not; Deposition of Henry St. John, 7 June 1638, HCA 13/54, f. 144v.

1621, the Dutch chartered a West India Company (WIC) to combat the Iberian presence in the Americas and West Africa, as they had created an East India Company (VOC) in 1602 to trade and fight in Asia. The WIC's initial attempt in 1625 to corner the Gold Coast trade by capturing the Portuguese stronghold of São Jorge da Mina failed due to a lack of African cooperation. Three years later, however, a WIC fleet captured the Spanish treasure *flota* in the Bay of Matanzas in Cuba, and the company used this windfall to underwrite a series of campaigns it conducted against the Portuguese over the next fifteen years. These ventures included the temporary, as they proved, captures of Pernambuco in Brazil, Luanda in Angola, and São Tomé, but WIC forces also finally secured the vital African assistance and captured El Mina at the second attempt in 1637 before clearing their enemies from the Gold Coast by 1642. These successes brought the Dutch into preeminence in the trans-Atlantic slave trade and opened the Gold Coast and the Bight of Benin more widely to other Europeans.[16]

Can it have been a coincidence that the English participation in the Guinea trade accelerated along with the establishment of new English colonies in America and the corresponding increase in demand for labor in these plantations? Several circumstances strongly suggest that certain English people had developed an interest in the slave trade before 1635. Even as the renewed Dutch-Iberian conflict progressed in the 1620s, Maurice Thompson had dispatched that first English slaving voyage to an English colony. It is also conceivable that his own experience in Virginia caused Thompson to recognize at this early date the profit potential in the slave trade. Profits from the servant trade remained essentially dependent on success in recruiting prospects, while the convict and prisoner trades depended on the vagaries of judicial temper and on the fortunes of war. If, though, African mercantile connections could be maintained, the Guinea trade could yield a steady revenue stream for traders and a steady supply of laborers for plantations without the need to advertise the prospects of a colony. And, of course, slaves, unlike servants, need never be freed and might be obtained at similar rates: the contract of an indenture in 1637 cost £6 plus the purchaser incurred another £6 for transporting the servant, as we have seen. While the different means of exchange that were involved, including but not limited to cowrie shells, iron bars, and fabrics, as well as other variables, notably

---

[16] Klooster, *The Dutch Moment*, 33–73.

the gender of the slaves, make it difficult to translate the costs of African transactions into European terms, the going rate for purchasing slaves in Guinea seems to have fluctuated at around an equivalent level to that of purchasing indentures, while the transportation cost per slave was lower than that per servant. Only two overriding concerns remained: how might slaves readily be obtained in Africa and what would be the status of Africans imported into seventeenth-century Anglo-America?[17]

A reinvigorated Guinea Company seems to have taken a lead with respect to answering the first of these issues. It had suffered a torrid time during its initial incarnation in the 1620s, sustaining calamitous losses in the attempts of its agents to explore the Gambia River. It also faced default on £945 worth of debts amassed by its Deputy Governor, Sir Kenelm Digby, and other members, as well as parliamentary grievances against both its monopoly and its alleged failure to pursue its trade with proper vigor, thereby threatening English interests in Africa.[18]

As early as 1625, though, Crispe and Wood, two of seventeenth-century England's leading authorities on Africa, and their partners had unofficially taken control of the Guinea trade; they steered the company from these mishaps and placed it on a secure footing. In doing so, they established the precedent by which English operations in West Africa were conducted. Traders seem to have been routinely unconcerned about the privileges granted by charters, whether they had, as Crispe and his partners did, official license or not. Of course, if they acted without license, they risked intervention by the authorities if the legal entity complained and so had to conduct their activities with relative discretion. Yet again and again the inexact boundary between "monopolists" and "interlopers" was further blurred.[19]

"Nicholas Crispe and Company," as the 1631 incarnation of the Guinea Company was informally known, primarily sought gold, at least

---

[17] We lack the account books for this period. A 1683 Royal African Company voyage paid £1,235 worth of goods for 320 slaves, which has been worked out to £3 16s per slave, approximately, and the slaves who survived the voyage were sold at an average approximate price of £16 10s for males and £14 16s for females; Eltis et al., "Accounting for the Traffic in Africans," 942–4. This calculation of the purchase price of slaves in Guinea, though, seems low; see Chapter 9 for further discussion.

[18] Porter, "The Crispe Family and the African Trade in the Seventeenth Century," 58–61.

[19] Account of losses sustained by the Company of Adventurers in voyages of discovery to Guinea, Binney, and the River Gambia, in 1618, 1619, and 1620, December 1621 [?], *CSPC AWI* 1: 27; Petition of Humphrey Slaney and Wm. Clobery to the Council and Petition of Humphrey Slaney, Nicholas Crisp, and [William Clobery?] to the Council, both [1629?], *CSPD* Charles I 4 (1629–31): 136, 145.

initially, and Wood returned to Sierra Leone where he established his control over the redwood trade. To further its aims, the company engaged a new factor, Arendt de Groot, a former Dutch West India Company agent, to use his experience against his former employer and other European competitors. We do not know the full particulars of what happened, but we can say that, following the return of Wood and De Groot to Guinea and by the mid-1640s, at least four phenomena occurred: the volume of English trade there increased substantially, and more English traders, such as Samuel Wilson, pursued the opportunities offered there; conflict between the English and Dutch on the Gold Coast correspondingly increased; the number of Africans conveyed to the Americas by English traders also increased substantially; and English traders developed the capacity to convey increasingly large numbers of enslaved Africans to American buyers, whether English or otherwise.[20]

Over twenty years ago, John Appleby noted the long-held "accepted view that the English slave trade was 'of small proportions' before 1660," while acknowledging that the nature of the evidence made it difficult to confirm this proposition. Appleby himself published an analysis of an early 1650s London slave trading voyage that shed some light on pre-1660 slaving. We also have records from the High Court of Admiralty and other courts that contain evidence of earlier English trafficking in Africa that reduces even further the darkness that shrouds the early English involvement in Guinea. These records, although painstaking to use, make it clear that in actuality the slave trade had actually become an attractive proposition for English merchants, notwithstanding its hazards, by the mid-1630s.

The members of the Guinea Company and other traders obviously thought so. In 1636, for instance, George Lamberton of the New Haven Colony sent a ship to Africa seeking gold and ivory. The fate of Lamberton's voyage reminds us of the difficulties with which Guinea adventurers had to deal in their quest for profits. Having found a crew willing to serve on an African voyage, which Appleby reminds us was by no means a given, as London mariners were well aware of the threats to their health posed by the African climate, shipwreck, and pirates, Lamberton's ship

---

[20] For the African experience of Wood, De Groot and Crispe, see, in addition to above, Note of things desired from Guinea, July 1625 [?], *CSPC AWI* 1: 75; Petition of Humphrey Slaney, Nicholas Crispe, and William Clobery, merchants, to the Privy Council, April [?] 1630, *CSPC AWI* 1: 114; Deposition of Michael Woodcock, 1 July 1648, HCA 13/61, ff. 122r–123v; Deposition of John Wood, 7 September 1639, HCA 13/55, f. 235v; Deposition of Arent de Groote, 5 September 1639, HCA 13/55, f. 236v.

set sail. After twenty days at sea and the weather turning hot, his crew required watering but had difficulty acquiring a sufficient quantity at the Cape Verde Islands where the inhabitants "were in great want of water for their cattle there, & threatened to cut their throats if they took in any more water there." Lamberton and his men had better luck securing water from the Guinea Company's factory at "Sea Lion" (Sierra Leone), but the company's agents allegedly cheated him.[21]

Despite such difficulties, the record indicates that a sort of "slave rush" manifested itself by 1640. The year following Lamberton's misadventure, the Guinea Company successfully sought government intervention to prevent John Crispe (probably the son of Nicholas) "and others" who intended "to trade upon the coasts of Guinea, to take 'nigers' and carry them to foreign parts." In addition to these newcomers, though, the company also had to deal with the ever-ambitious Maurice Thompson as a serious rival.[22]

Frustratingly, if Thompson ever set down some sort of business plan or reflected in any way on the course of his career, it has not survived. Indeed, we have little direct evidence that this ubiquitous participant in English overseas activity between 1625 and 1665 was even involved in the Guinea trade except that provided by legal proceedings. These depositions and interrogatories, though, provide enough evidence on which to assert confidently that Thompson, in addition to holding the dubious title of the first Englishman to send slaves to an English colony, was among the primary movers of the commerce, especially the slave trade, which bound Africa and Anglo-America by 1640.

Most particularly, the name of one of Thompson's ships, the *Star*, recurs in the record of both the Guinea and plantation trades, a record that is also suggestive of the fluid relationship between chartered interests and alleged interlopers. In 1638, the Guinea traders, having successfully blocked John Crispe's intended voyage, again approached the Privy Council seeking to stay the departure of the *Star* along with the detention of the vessel's owners, including Thompson and Oliver Cloberry (William Cloberry's brother), in order to prevent them from trading in violation of the company's patent. The nature of this voyage, however, remains

---

[21] *Cloberry v. Lamberton*, 4 May 1636, Deposition of Thomas Brooks, HCA 13/52, ff. 381v–384r. Brooks's evidence clearly indicates that he had made previous voyages to Guinea, at 381v. For the tricky logistics of preparing a Guinea voyage, especially one that involved slaves, see Appleby, "'A Business of Much Difficulty,'" 4–7.

[22] Privy Council to Sir John Pennington, 11 November 1637, *CSPC AWI* 1: 259.

unclear. Three years later, though, the *Star*, whose owners now included the Guinea Company leaders Nicholas Crispe and John Wood, "sold a cargo of slaves in Barbados." The vessel's fitness for slave trading purposes is confirmed by another slaving voyage it made to the English Caribbean the following year.[23]

It has remained a historiographical constant that it was the incessant labor needs of planters that arose from their cultivation of staple crops that English supplies could not meet, which generated a planter preference for slaves and, in turn, the inexorable rise of slavery in Anglo-America. Thus, "the sudden appearance of slaves in the Barbados deeds" in 1641 reflected a "shifting in the early 1640s to the very labour-intensive production of sugar," as the colony's planters experimented with alternative crops to tobacco (notably cotton) that required "gang" labor to produce.[24]

Given the timing here, though, is it not possible to argue rather that the pursuit of slaves in Guinea from circa 1635 or even 1630 secured the future of Anglo-American colonization? Could then the increasing involvement of the English in the Guinea trade, which translated into greater availability of slaves, have accelerated the Anglo-American quest to find new crops to cultivate in order to replace tobacco, the price of which, as Thompson for one well knew, had sunk like the proverbial stone by this time? Certainly, the greater competition in the Guinea trade after 1635 seems to have created a greater supply of slaves from this time, so can we properly conclude that "planter

---

[23] Warrant to the Marshal of the Admiralty to stay the *Star* of London and Order of the Privy Council, 5–6 May 1638, *CSPC AWI* 1: 273. In the latter case, the council soon ordered the release of the ship of Thompson and his associates; Warrant to the Marshal of the Admiralty for discharge of the *Star* of London with all the men and goods belonging to her that she may proceed in her intended voyage [to Guinea and Binney], 14 May 1638, *CSPC AWI* 1: 273. For the 1641 voyage of the *Star*, identified now as a Guinea Company vessel, see Gragg, "'To Procure Negroes'," 72; for the *Star*'s 1642 voyage, see Heywood and Thornton, *Central Africans, Atlantic Creoles, and the Foundation of the Americas*, 45–7 at 46, but this mistakenly characterizes the vessel as a Barbadian one. The Trans-Atlantic Slave Trade Database includes only one voyage of the *Star* from 1641; www.slavevoyages.org/voyages/a6OlvmyM (accessed 22 December 2016).

[24] Menard, "Plantation Empire," esp. 310–13; Debe and Menard, "The Transition to African Slavery in Maryland"; Coombs, "Beyond the 'Origins Debate'," which correctly places the introduction of slavery to the Chesapeake rather earlier than others have and rightly notes the controlling importance of events outside North America to historical developments there, but errs (at 348) in its assessment of the timing of the acceleration of the trans-Atlantic slave trade.

demand" served as the controlling factor in the increasingly African demographic of Anglo-America after 1640?[25]

For that matter, a number of "planters," including, for instance, Thompson and one of his regular partners, William Pennoyer, took the lead in the slave trade at the time; among other endeavors, the duo owned a plantation in Barbados to which they sought leave to transport horses for their sugar works in 1647 (and so the construction of their sugar plantation would have been completed earlier). Moreover, while planters certainly regarded the price of exports as a vital aspect of their lives, that price held equal importance for merchants, such as Thompson and Pennoyer, who supplied planters with shoes, shirts, liquor, and other commodities in exchange for plantation staples as discussed in Chapter 2. Now that it is clear that the Dutch did not have primary responsibility for introducing a "sugar revolution" in Barbados, is it more likely that colonists on the ground led the turn to sugar that began in 1641–2 or that they were led to do so by those whose geographic, political, and economic perspectives made them best placed to direct the colony's future and to their own advantage?[26]

Meanwhile, De Groot, according to his own account, which naturally refuted the Dutch characterization of his behavior, began his English service by arriving on the Gold Coast in 1632 where he established the first English trading fort at Cormontine. There, to the fury of his former employers, who claimed their own prior exclusive agreement, he made an agreement with the local ruler, the Brasso of Fante, which secured the Guinea Company's right to conduct trade. The WIC also claimed that De

---

[25] Samuel Vassall was buying slaves on the Gold Coast by 1632–3. The logistics of arranging the voyage necessitated advance planning, so someone involved with it would have acquired some familiarity with the region at least a year beforehand; The humble answer of the Guinea Company unto the Remonstrance of Mr. Samuel Vassall, 25 May 1650, CO 1/11, f. 29.

[26] Thompson testified in the High Court of Admiralty (on behalf of his late partner's widow) in *Limbrey v. Wilson* that St. Christopher's tobacco sold at 6d per pound in London in 1637; Deposition of Maurice Thompson, London merchant, [May–June 1638], HCA 13/54, ff. 137r–137v at 137v. Thompson was part of a group that had substantial control of the Virginia tobacco trade from the 1630s; e.g., Governor Harvey to the Virginia Commissioners, 27 May 1632, *CSPC AWI* 1: 151; Sir Henry Marten to the Lords of the Admiralty, 7 January 1636/7, noting that Thompson and his associates had 155,500 pounds of Virginia tobacco seized by "Dunkirkers" valued at £15,500 sterling (£100 per thousand weight); *CSPD* Charles I 10 (1636–7): 350. For the Barbados plantations of Thompson and Pennoyer, see Thompson & al. Leave to carry Oxen from Virginia to Barbadoes, for their Sugar Works, 23 October 1647, *LJ* 9: 4–5; Order of the Council of State, 22 May 1649, *CSPC AWI* 1: 329.

Groot plotted "to incite the Blacks" to "massacre" Dutch traders and to take away a flag of the Prince of Orange. Wood renewed this agreement in 1636 when he succeeded De Groot as chief factor. Although the burning of the Cormontine factory in contentious circumstances in September 1640 undoubtedly set back the company's progress, the English were now on the Gold Coast to stay, a reality reinforced by their establishment – "at the desire of the Futu [Fetu] King and his subjects" – of another Gold Coast post, Cabo Corso (Cape Coast) in 1647.[27]

The vexing issue of who was to have charge of that presence and derive corresponding benefits from it, however, remained. During the 1620s, the original Guinea Company, plagued by the debts and other distractions of its members, had not been in a position to enforce its monopoly rigorously. Two decades later, it had seen off the encroachments of the likes of the Scottish Guinea Company, but an ever-increasing number of well-backed rival traffickers and, especially, the outbreak of the Civil Wars in 1642 put paid to its ability to keep out those whom its membership regarded as threats to their interests. Regardless of their official station, though, by 1648, Guinea traders had developed a capacity to conduct extensive operations that enabled the transportation of 250 or more slaves to America as Samuel Wilson's voyage did.[28]

---

[27] Protest of Arendt Jacobsz van Amersfoort against the English, 19 June 1640 (n.s.), FP, The Gold Coast (N 3) (1639–1645), 46–50 at 47–9; Protest of Arent de Groot, for the English, FP, The Gold Coast (N 3) (1639–1645), 51–60 at 51–5 (Protest van Arent de Groot voor d'Engesen, 26 August 1640 (n.s.), inv. 013 I, ff. 22–43 at 23–4, 32, Nationaal Archief, The Hague; my thanks to Jaap Jacobs for a copy of this original document). For the establishment of Cabo Corso in response to which the Dutch constructed a "Lodge" at Aja, one-half mile away, "at the entreaties for long years of the Brasso of Fantyn," see Letter from Hendrick Caarlof, fiscaal, to the XIX, 26 September 1647, FP (N 4) (Gold Coast, 1646–1647), 179–85 at 179. The reports of West India Company factors on the Gold Coast include almost continual observations on their English competitors from 1645; Ratelband, *Vijf dagregisters van het kasteel São Jorge da Mina (Elmina) aan de Goudkost.*

[28] We do not have the sort of figures for the Guinea trade from this period that provide a relatively clear picture of the profitability of the slave trade in the late eighteenth century, and these transactions did not involve cash, which further clouds the picture. In 1662, though, Isaac Bowles and John Gregory admitted owing £3,982 18s 7d for 195 "Negros living of 217 taken in Guinea and disposed of as by their account" in the West Indies, which works out to £20 per slave; T 70/309, f. 8r. That same year, the *James* brought a cargo valued at £242 3s 3d (887 iron bars worth £202 8s 3d (approximately four shillings and six pence per bar) and 120 guns worth 7s each to trade, or £42 altogether). If the entire cargo was exchanged for, say, 100 slaves who survived the trans-Atlantic voyage (not counting those who would have been part of the compensation of the ship's officers) and were sold for £20, the profit from this voyage would have been approximately £1,757 (less other costs such as "provisions for Negroes"), or approximately £17 10s

Meanwhile, Nicholas Crispe had provided much of the financial and political support for the Guinea Company but found himself sidelined as a supporter of Charles I as the King's crisis with Parliament passed the breaking point in August 1642. Crispe raised a regiment in support of his sovereign, but his Royalism cost him his place in the House of Commons and his company shares. It also cost the Guinea Company its patent, which Parliament recalled as a monopoly while the parliamentary navy blockaded the Guinea coast inorder to prevent gold from reaching the King. In 1647, at the end of the first Civil War, this pioneering Guinea trader entered exile in France and then endured a spell in prison for debt.[29]

Crispe's enforced departure from the company left Wood to pick up the pieces; he managed to secure new partners who were well set both economically and politically. In 1646, Rowland Wilson assisted Wood in a complaint against the New Englanders Robert Shapton, Miles Cawson, and James Smith, who, they claimed, had unlawfully seized and enslaved Africans during a voyage the previous year. There can be no question that this New England trio had a record of this sort of behavior and they probably were not the only English arrivals who seized or murdered unfortunate Africans or who resorted to extortion in order to secure "merchandise" when conventional trading opportunities failed to present themselves.

Here, though, they claimed to have acted in accord in the employment of the noted slave trader, supporter of overseas trade and colonization, and friend of the godly, the Earl of Warwick. Their irregular and very risky ventures triggered legal attention across the Atlantic as well as in London: the arrival of Captain Smith and his mate Thomas Keyser in Boston with two slaves drew the censure of Sir Richard Saltonstall

per slave (although this figure would probably have varied for men, women, and children); T 70/309, f. 5r. For "Negroes" as compensation, see, e.g., Agreement of the Adventurers of Assada with Walter Clinch, surgeon, 22 March 1648/9, IOR E/3/22, ff. 15r–15v; Orders of Council and Petitions and other Business at Court relating to the Royal African Company of England, 3 March 1681/2 to 22 September 1696, T 70/169, f. 6. For other "interloping" voyages, see, e.g., Deposition of Philip Jordan, 1 January 1647/8, HCA 13/16, f. 11; Deposition of Raphe Langley, 13 May 1648, HCA 13/61, f. 57v, Deposition of William Zanes, May 1648, HCA 13/61, ff. 63v–65r; Deposition of John Downe, 29 June 1648, HCA 13/61, ff. 105v–107v; Deposition of Henry Izod, HCA 13/61, ff. 223v–224v; Deposition of Walter Smith, 8 February 1648/9, HCA 13/16, f. 268r–269r.

[29] For Crispe's Civil War career, see Porter, "The Crispe Family and the African Trade," 67–8; Eveline Cruickshank, "Crisp, Sir Nicholas (c. 1598–1666) of Hammersmith, Mdx." In *History of Parliament Online*, www.historyofparliamentonline.org/volume/1660–1690/member/crisp-sir-nicholas-1598–1666 (accessed 4 July 2016).

in Massachusetts Bay, part-time resident of that colony and another full-time godly supporter of colonial expansion. Sir Richard claimed the two slaves had been seized after Smith and Keyser, who had offended godly sensibilities already by brawling, had overseen the killing of almost 100 other Africans, allegedly in revenge for an attack on other English traders. Since it deemed this attack to have defiled the Sabbath, the colony's General Court ordered the two survivors, including an all-important interpreter, released; the fate of their English enslavers, though, remains unclear.[30]

This sort of behavior, veteran Guinea hands warned, threatened the reputation of the English with African nations and, thus, put the entire Guinea trade at risk. African goodwill was essential to the successful conduct of this commerce as Wood, for one, well knew: loss of it not only entailed denial of access to African commodities, but those Europeans whom African governments and merchants regarded as threats could easily find themselves in danger of the loss of their stock and their lives. It did not take much persuasion for hostility to develop with Dutch factors ever ready to work any fissures in Anglo-African disputes to their greater advantage.[31]

Meanwhile, Maurice Thompson became further involved in the African trade; by 1647, he seems to have joined the Guinea Company, at least unofficially. In the event, his name appears with those of Wood and Samuel Wilson as owners of the *Star* who traded for gold, according to Robert Brenner, in Guinea at that time; since this vessel was employed

---

[30] Blakemore, "West Africa in the British Atlantic," 303–8. Blakemore references an earlier voyage from 1643 in his discussion. It is unclear to what degree, if any, this result is indicative of the existence of contemporary English – particularly "Puritan" – qualms about enslaving Africans; equating complaints about the behavior of slavers with reservations about slavery may be, at best, anachronistic; Warren, *New England Bound*, 39–47. The court's confusion lay with the issue of jurisdiction over the "slaughter" committed in Africa and the allegation of "revenge" there rather than any problem with enslavement in the abstract: it did not review the legal justifications for slavery, "just wars," and "lawful commerce"; Hosmer, *Winthrop's Journal*, 2: 252–3. On the other hand, John Winthrop's nephew, George Downing, and his son, John Winthrop, Jr., had become well aware of the sensibility, which had become established before 1645, that the provision of slaves had become vital to the success of – and to success in – Anglo-America; Sir George Downing to John Winthrop, Jr., 26 August 1645, *CMHS*, 4th ser., 6 (1863): 536–40 at 537–9.

[31] E.g., Continuation of the daily Journal sent to the Hon. Gentlemen at the Assembly of the XIX by the ship *Haarlem* of Amsterdam, & now begins on 1st June 1646, FP (N 4) (The Gold Coast, 1646–1647: The Dutch Director over the North Coast of Africa and the Island of St Thome), entries for 5 July and 28 July 1646 (n.s.), 69–113 at 77, 80.

in the slave trade, as we have seen, as early as 1641, though, it is possible that slaves were involved in this voyage as well.[32] Also, by this time, the most successful of the unlicensed merchants, Samuel Vassall, who partnered with both Wilson and Thompson over the course of his long career in overseas trade and colonization, had reentered the African scene. In 1647–8, three ships of a Vassall-led group brought slaves from Guinea to the Spanish colonies as Wilson's voyage did the following year and, like Wilson's voyage, brought no joy to its backer as it returned losses of between £20,000 and £40,000: the Spaniards captured two of the vessels after they had conveyed 400 slaves to Santo Domingo, while the third escaped after embarking 174 slaves out of its original consignment of 251 individuals.[33]

Undaunted, Vassall contested the Guinea Company's patent before the Council of State, alleging that the company had fulfilled no public purpose since it had found no gold, although this mission had been the purported rationale behind its quest for a charter back in 1618. Instead, his remonstrance charged, the company members "yearly make their private benefit by wood, elephants' teeth and hides and such small quantities of gold as the Blackmoores bring in trading to their ships at Cormontine or their pinnaces near the seaside." If the Council would dissolve the company and issue a "commission" to five "fit and experienced men" who would "manage the said trade for the sole benefit of the State," they would eliminate the Dutch and Portuguese from the gold trade in the Gambia by establishing a fort (with the permission of "the King of Setico") that would provide access to Timbuktu and to gold production exceeding £300,000 per annum.[34]

The Guinea Company's response to these claims naturally emphasized its contributions to the good of the commonwealth and the expenses it had incurred in maintaining the English position in Africa. These included the £10,000 in gold it had paid to Charles I in 1631 to obtain its charter

---

[32] Brenner, *Merchants and Revolution*, 192.

[33] Voyages #21879, 26255, and 26256, Voyages Database, 2009, *Voyages: The Trans-Atlantic Slave Trade Database*, www.slavevoyages.org (accessed 20 March 2013); Appleby, "English Settlement during War and Peace, 1603–1660," 98–9. In 1650, Vassall and his Guinea trading partners, including Samuel Wilson, were ordered to appear before the Council of State, Order of the Council of State, 12 April 1650, *CSPC AWI* 1: 338.

[34] [Samuel Vassall], A Remonstrance humbly presented to the Hon. Council of State for their honour and profit and for the general good of the land by the Trade of Africa for gold and other very good commodities, [about December 1649], CO 1/11, ff. 25r–25v.

as well as the charges it had incurred in fortifying and manning as many as sixteen trading posts at one time (although presently none "due to interruptions"). It denied that it had "engrossed" the entire Guinea coast and hampered other English merchants "to the prejudice of the Commonwealth."

Three of Vassall's allegations required further responses. To the first, that a jointstock company was not the best vehicle for pursuing the Guinea, the company replied that its corporate form enabled it to employ seventeen ships that carried "large" cargoes on a scale beyond the capacity of individual traders. Vassall also claimed that the company traded English-made goods in "buying & transporting of Negroes." The respondents denied this, claiming in their turn that they only exchanged "foreign commodities for the buying of Negroes," although they admitted that they did use English commodities "for the supplying the plantations with them" when necessary. They also insisted that they had only done "what those plantations shall require" and lamented that in their pursuit of profit, some "interlopers" had "taken Negroes away by force," thereby "setting the Negroes against our factors that they have been murdered." Finally, the company refuted Vassall's contention that his agents were the first Englishmen to settle at "Wyamba" (Winneba, Ghana) in 1632–3, claiming that they "bought some Negroes" but did not establish themselves until much later when they began attacking the company's men and property, including burning the Company's trading house. In the end, the response claimed, if the Dutch were to be kept "from planting at Wyamba," the Guinea Company offered the best means of keeping them out.[35]

In the end, the company's view prevailed and the Council of State issued it a new charter on 9 April 1651 to run for fourteen years but that restricted the area of its monopoly to an area twenty leagues (just over sixty-nine miles) east of Cormontine and twenty leagues east of Sherbro.[36] It is conceivable that this result, which followed his 1647 debacle, may have contributed to Vassall's abandoning his maverick course to follow the poacher-turned-gamekeeper precedent set by Thompson and Nicholas Crispe. In the event, Thompson and Vassall joined Rowland Wilson and

---

[35] The humble answer of the Guinea Company unto the Remonstrance of Mr. Samuel Vassall, 25 May 1650, CO 1/11, f. 29.

[36] Order of the Council of State. Approving report of the Council of Trade concerning the trade to Guinea, and recommending to Parliament a grant being passed as is therein expressed, 9 April 1651, *CSPC AWI*, 1: 355.

Wood in this new version of the Guinea Company. This corporate reincarnation undoubtedly suffered spectacular losses, but its history also demonstrates the success these merchants had achieved as well as their determination to continue their African-oriented pursuits. Moreover, just as the English were now a permanent presence in Guinea, that presence facilitated their pursuits elsewhere.

This was by no means a straightforward process, however, to be sure. The new company devised a grand plan for perfecting its position that was ready by mid-August 1651. On 22 August, its ship, *Friendship*, and two pinnaces, the *John* and *Supply*, were loaded with iron bars, along with oznabrigs, calicoes, gingham, and other cloths and various liquors and crystal for trade, as well as provisions for the Gambia. The following month, Wood, Thompson, and Rowland Wilson commissioned James Pope to organize this project "to our most advantage, for hides, wax, and teeth, gold, Ambergreez, or any other merchantable Comodity you shall meete withal" by acquiring as much of these goods as possible even by underselling in exchange, to "prohibite all private Trade," especially of hides, and to "buy for us 15 or 20 lusty young Negers of about 15" years of age to be brought to London.[37]

Three months later, the Guinea Company instructed Bartholomew Haward to take his ship to the Gambia where he was "to lade aboard her as many Negors as she can carry, and in default thereof to fill her up with Cattle" before making for Barbados. Haward was to take precautions "to put aboard your Pinck *Supply* 30 paire of shackles and boults for such of your negers as are rebellious and we pray you be veary carefull to keape them under and let them have their food in due season that they ryse not against you, as they have done in other ships," while noting that they planned to buy 200 slaves in the Gambia the following year so long as the prospects for their availability were favorable. To further that end, the company instructed Pope and Haward to assess the potential demand for "East India Cristall beads" at the company's factories.

Then, anticipating that the fleet commanded by Sir George Ayscue then making its way to America would succeed in reducing Barbados and Virginia to the authority of the new Commonwealth of England, the ship

---

[37] Deposition of Thomas Wall on behalf of the Guinea Company against the Portugals, 17 August 1653, HCA 13/67, f. 423r; Deposition of Richard Webster, merchant of London, 21 August 1653, HCA 13/67, ff. 423v–424r; The Guinea Company to James Pope, 17 September 1651, in *DIHSTA*, 1: 126–8.

was to head to that island, where, the company's leaders had agreed, the slaves would be kept at John Wood's plantation on the island until they were sold. Meanwhile, Francis Soane, the company's Barbados factor, "may make use of their Labour in Lieu of their dyet" while awaiting suitable purchasers, thereby avoiding the accumulation of debt; if "any of the said negers should be sick," the cost of their food could be charged to the company's account.[38]

This scheme, though, ran afoul of the vagaries of the Guinea trade. First, an unhappy accident with gunpowder killed one of the company's Gambia factors and destroyed part of its trading house along with a substantial quantity of its goods, including "teeth," that had been stored there. Then, sickness carried off another factor; since the ship's arrival, twenty-three men had died and none of the company had escaped illness: the captain observed, "I never see men dye so soudainely in my Life." Even so, and despite the presence of "Flemish" and Danish competitors, the survivors managed to acquire some 600 hides. On 2 March 1652, however, the ship was surprised by the Royalist fleet of Prince Rupert – allegedly guided by a Portuguese pilot whose services, necessary for navigating the "very dangerous" Gambia, had been provided by the Governor of Santiago in the Cape Verde Islands. Rupert's force seized their cargo, valued, according to the company, at £10,580, and allegedly rewarded the Portuguese governor with a share of it.[39]

Rupert thus also come to realize the importance of the Guinea– Caribbean commerce as he carried on the quixotic cause of his nephew, the would-be Charles II. He turned up in the Caribbean at least twice in 1652 after his Gambia raid. In the first instance, "he surprised some 4 or 5 vessels," including a London ship "trading for Negroes & taken in his loading of sugar." His second swoop netted the cargo, including sugar, of the *Hopewell* at Antigua that "damnified" its owners of

---

[38] The Guinea Company to Bartholomew Haward, 9 December 1651, in *DIHSTA*, 1: 129–30; The Guinea Company to James Pope, in *DIHSTA*, 1: 130–2; The Guinea Company to Francis Soane, 9 December 1651, in *DIHSTA*, 1: 132–3. Wood's Barbados plantation produced sugar, and also indigo, by this time; The Guinea Company to Bartholomew Haward, 11 December 1651, in *DIHSTA*, 1: 133.

[39] Petition of the Guinea Company to the Council of State, 21 June 1652, CO 1/11, f. 152; Captain John Blake to the Guinea Company, 15 February 1651/2, in *DIHSTA*, 1: 134–6; Deposition of William Coxon of Ratcliffe, Middlesex, HCA 13/67, f. 425r–425v; Deposition of Thomas Bonner, Lime-house, HCA 13/67, ff. 426r–426v; Appleby, "A London Slaving Venture, 1651–1654."

approximately £3,500. This vessel had brought 250 slaves to Barbados from Guinea before sailing to the smaller island.[40]

Rupert's depredations did not constitute the only hazard to the English trade in Guinea at the midpoint of the seventeenth century. The continuing efforts of the Dutch to hamper their English rivals – and vice versa, of course, although the Guinea Company chose not to emphasize its anti-Dutch activities in its public entreaties – intensified as the English presence in Africa became more substantial from the late 1630s. While continuing to monitor and disrupt English operations on the ground, the "Hollanders" began harassing their rivals at sea.[41]

Both sides were well aware of what was at stake here. Twenty years after he had relayed his views on the state of Barbados to his cousin in New England (see note 30), Sir George Downing, now a knight and ambassador of Charles II to the Dutch Republic, observed to the Secretary of State that the States General, as the English government, was well aware "that if ye English should at this time clear ye coast of Africa of the Dutch & get ye gold trade & Negro trade to themselves that it would be of greater import than the East Indies trade."[42] Meanwhile, in September 1652, the Guinea Company's members had reminded the government that they had invested "about £70,000 with severall ships and pinnaces for discoverie and trade, and have yearly vented many manufactures, and returned gold, hides, wax elephants teeth redwood guinea grain &c to a considerable value" to the Commonwealth of England, although they left unmentioned the further value of the now-lucrative slave and plantation trades that their pursuits made possible. Absent strong and swift measures, they warned the Council of State, Dutch predations threatened the future of these vital economic conduits.[43]

---

[40] Governor Daniel Searle [of Barbados] to Council of State, 30 June 1652, CO 1/11, f. 159; Examination of John Swift, 14 September 1653, HCA 13/67, ff. 491r–491v; Examination of Arthur Perkins, HCA 13/67, f. 492v–493r; Examination of Samuel Meade, HCA 13/67, ff. 496r–497v; Examination of William Jackson, HCA 13/67, ff. 506r–507v; Examination of John Farrington, 22 September 1653, HCA 13/67, ff. 536r–538v.

[41] Dutch complaints about the English on the Gold Coast include a recollection in 1663 that sixteen years previously "your nation presumed" to bribe Africans and "vassals of our state," as well as "suborned" the Swedes and Danes against Dutch interests; John Valckenburgh, Director-General of the North coast of Africa and the island of St. Thomas to Francis Selwyn, Agent of the Royal English company trading to the coast of Africa, 11 June 1663, CO 1/17, ff. 82–6 at 83r–83v.

[42] Sir George Downing to Sir Henry Bennett, 4 August 1664, SP 84/171, ff. 106–10 at 108r, TNA.

[43] To the Right Honorable Council of State The humble petition of the Guinea Company, 25 September 1652, CO 1/11, f. 187.

In terms of the second question posed above – the status of Africans purchased and then transported across the Atlantic by Europeans for resale in the New World – the ready answer was another variation on the servitude practiced in England as sketched in Chapter 1. Unlike migrants who traveled to Anglo-America under an indenture, though, Africans did so as commodities, without contracts, against their will, and lacking the rights under contract and social custom held by servants. Masters/purchasers thus had complete legal sway to treat their purchases as they saw fit. Having made the decision to spend upward of £15 per head and taken possession of another human being, owners had little pause in making it the practice to consign these newcomers to English ways to perpetual and hereditary servitude. Although it took time for the various colonies to devise "slave codes" that officially consigned Africans to slavery, the law always responds to developing social norms.[44]

In the meantime, since the slave trade rendered the persons of perpetual servants as commodities, rather than the labor of that person only, the architects of Anglo-American societies could and did adapt the social framework that governed master–servant relations to the social institution of slavery as it suited them, both individually and collectively: limitations on this power existed only if and when masters had some sort of sensibility of the humanity of their property. Moreover, prospective European servants, with the exception of convicts and prisoners of war, retained the option of declining whatever opportunities were advertised in Anglo-America, and word about the abuse of servants could get around. The options for slaves seeking to avoid a trans-Atlantic voyage were limited to suicide and escape regardless of the level of their awareness of circumstances in America. Then, across the Atlantic, of course, servants – and even convicts – had the prospect of legal freedom after their terms ended; slaves could entertain no such hope, although the state of the record includes next to nothing in terms of direct evidence of the perspectives of the Africans who were transported during this formative period of Anglo-American history – a historiographical insult added to the deep injury of their enslavement. Thus, this system worked all too naturally for the traders who developed it as well as for those Anglo-Americans able and willing to buy slaves. "What is truly surprising about British abolitionism," then, as Christopher Leslie Brown has observed, "is that such a campaign ever should have developed at all."[45]

---

[44] Roper, "The 1701 'Act for the Better Ordering of Slaves.'"
[45] Brown, *Moral Capital*, 462.

4

The Expansion of English Interests

Asia

English indignation over Dutch behavior in Asia actually preceded the complaints in Africa by almost three decades. But concerns with the Dutch also reflect the integrative nature of seventeenth-century English overseas trade and colonization. In addition to providing pepper and other spices for European markets from the Middle Ages, commodities from "the Indies," notably cloths, constituted important means of exchange in other parts of the world: the New Havener George Lamberton brought "East Indies stuff" to trade for gold and ivory in Guinea in 1636.[1]

We should bear in mind that English people interested in overseas ventures always regarded Asia as the brass ring. Asian endeavors hold chronological pride of place, excepting John Cabot's inconclusive voyages to America of 1497 and 1499, in the history of English overseas trade and colonization, and while these pioneering feelers ran into predictable difficulties, they did demonstrate that Asian commodities, especially pepper, were worth the trouble for contemporaries. The issue with grasping the ring, of course, arose from the hazardous, lengthy journey, whether by land or water, to the East.

Agents of the Muscovy Company, founded in the mid-sixteenth century, tried to approach Asia both through a Northeast Passage through the Barents and White Seas as well as overland from Russia via Persia (Iran). Their Levant Company counterparts, based in Aleppo (then located in the Ottoman Empire), established contact with the Indian

---

[1] *Cloberry v. Lamberton*, 4 May 1636, Deposition of Thomas Brooks of Wapping, Middlesex, boatswain's mate on the *Patience*, for George Lamberton, HCA 13/52, ff. 381v–384r.

subcontinent via a Central Asian route in the 1580s. The jointstock vehicle by which these chartered ventures allocated risk and conducted their business was naturally adopted by the backers of a far grander venture for pursuing Asian interests, the East India Company (EIC), which received its charter from Elizabeth I on 31 December 1600. The group of merchants who thus acquired control of English interests in South and East Asia differed from their predecessors, though, by sending voyages directly from London to the Indian Ocean via the Cape of Good Hope; this route, which bypassed the uncertainties of Mediterranean and Near Eastern circumstances, quickly became the preferred one for conducting Asian operations.[2]

English pursuit of opportunities in Asia endured a familiarly torrid beginning, which was aggravated by the farther distance and challenging environmental factors involved, notably the monsoons. These realities were compounded by the lack of interest on the part of Asian people, unlike American Indians, in acquiring European commodities, which were either redundant (as in the case of woolens) or inferior in manufacture. In order to entertain any hopes of prospering, then, the EIC, as Professor Chaudhuri has observed, had to purchase "East India stuffs" for the home market with bullion, the export of which it obtained by special license pursuant to its charter, and it would have to set up some control of the Indian Ocean carrying trade. The success of this approach, as well as the acquisition of the requisite knowledge and experience of the trade and the circumstances in which it took place, required the establishment of trading factories at strategic points especially in the subcontinent and in the East Indies.[3]

Unfortunately, the Dutch had arrived there first. The ensuing long and fierce Anglo-Dutch competition for Asian trading partners and goods constituted England's first imperial crisis. Indeed, the Anglo-Dutch rivalry might well have greater significance, certainly from a global or imperial perspective, than either its Anglo-Spanish or Anglo-French counterparts for all of the attention that has been lavished on these latter imperial relationships.

In the case of Spain, the English registered only very limited success in the long and long-winded campaign against the Spanish notwithstanding

---

[2] For early English interaction with Russia, see Willan, *The Muscovy Merchants of 1555*; Willan, *The Early History of the Russia Company*. For the Levant Company, see Wood, *A History of the Levant Company*.

[3] Chaudhuri, *The English East India Company*, 14–19.

the enduring fame of Sir Francis Drake's circumnavigation of the globe (1577–80), the other exploits of the "seadogs" memorialized by admirers of derring-do, the defeat of the Spanish Armada (1588), and the steady dissemination of anti-Spanish rhetoric from Elizabethan printing presses and pulpits. In actuality, the East India Company achieved most of the few substantial English contributions to the reduction of Iberian global influence prior to 1660: one of its fleets overcame Portuguese military and diplomatic opposition to secure a presidency at Surat on the Arabian Sea in 1613 and another allied with Shah Abbas I in his 1622 capture of Portuguese Ormuz in the Persian Gulf. This latter enterprise, though, also illustrates the checkered early history of the EIC: while a grateful Shah granted it a moiety of the customs revenue at his new port of Gombroon (Bandar-e Abbas), since it had acted without government approval and exceeded its charter powers, the Duke of Buckingham could claim a fine of £10,000 from it; when James I heard of this, he demanded £10,000 from the company as well.[4]

In terms of France, hostility and fear certainly had important global aspects, but Europe remained the focus, while, notwithstanding the greater fighting in North America and the Caribbean, Anglo-French conflict in Asia and Africa never matched the scale of its Anglo-Dutch counterpart, with the possible exception of the Indian theater in the Seven Years War. In the event, Anglo-Dutch animosity first became apparent at a time when the governments of Elizabeth I and James I and the apostate Huguenot Henri IV (1589–1610) were friendly, while French overseas trade and colonization did not become competitive until after Louis XIV reached his majority in 1661. Thus, the English seventeenth-century rivalry with the Dutch also constituted the first case in English – not to mention European – history in which international disputes originated from places outside of European environs. Moreover, those faraway conflicts remained the core of dispute as Anglo-Dutch competition spread from Asia to Africa and America.

The very birth of the EIC constituted a response by its backers to the news of a successful Dutch trading expedition that had returned from the East Indies in 1599. In the view of these merchants, this voyage foreshadowed the Dutch cornering of the spice trade. This prospect required forceful countering although perhaps not with the same virulent justification as accompanied demands for anti-Spanish measures; after all, the

---

[4] Chaudhuri, *The English East India Company*, 29–30.

Dutch were co-religionists to whom the English had lent substantial support in their war of independence. Now, at the dawn of the seventeenth century, certain English merchants, in planning an East India Company, committed to trading with Asia via a water route. Their approach also served notice that they were willing to compete with the Dutch for Asian commodities, eliminate Dutch middlemen by transporting Asian goods to English markets directly, and furthering the carrying trade around the Indian Ocean.[5]

Initial EIC efforts signaled plenty of promise notwithstanding concerns about the Dutch: the company's first two voyages in 1601 and 1606, even operating without established factories, brought in so much pepper from the Spice Indies that the price of this commodity sank, thereby encouraging the company to send a third fleet to the Red Sea and then to the west coast of India in search of alternative locations and commodities. While its efforts along the Arabian Peninsula came to naught, as did probes to Basra in the Persian Gulf, Siam (Thailand), and Japan, the EIC did manage to establish factories at Bantam at the western end of Java, at Jambi in Sumatra, and at Macassar (Makassar) in the East Indies, as well as the aforementioned Surat base and another at Madras in India, during the first four decades of its existence.

Such progress as the company achieved, though, came in the teeth of immediate, consistent, and often fierce Dutch opposition especially in the Spice Islands. From 1603, agents of the East India Company and its Dutch counterpart, the VOC, maneuvered and countermaneuvered around the Indonesian chessboard while the states of the archipelago sought to make the best of the arrival of these newcomers. Initially, the EIC, in addition to its posts at Bantam, Jambi, and Macassar, founded a factory at Jacatra (Jakarta) in west-central Java and pursued relations with the societies inhabiting the Banda Islands, the world's sole producer of nutmeg and mace at this time, which are located at the eastern end of the Moluccas. The EIC, though, perhaps relying on their common anti-Iberian sensibilities, may not have being fully cognizant of the determination of their VOC rivals to control the spice trade.

The Dutch company cared nothing for the history of Anglo-Dutch relations. In addition to sending more and better-equipped fleets to the Indian Ocean, as Martine van Ittersum has observed, the VOC devised a much more streamlined and centralized framework, headed by a

---

[5] Chaudhuri, *The English East India Company*, 10–13.

governor-general, for managing its affairs than its English counterpart did. Instead, prior to 1613, the EIC constituted each of its voyages as a separate entity; after that date it created presidencies at Bantam, Surat, and Madras. This decentralized approach followed customary imperial practice: the English never created overseas offices with expansive powers in any of their seventeenth-century establishments with the possible exception of the Dominion of New England at the very end of the period of study, while English interests in Asia were not placed under the authority of a governor-general until 1774. This practice may have saved the company the not insubstantial costs of constructing forts and warehouses on the ground, as well as paying officials, factors, and soldiers to maintain these facilities, but it also deprived it of an overarching administration with a clear chain of command and a permanent base; the Dutch took full advantage.[6]

At the same time, VOC operatives stressed to local rulers that their presence brought the prospect of relief from the aggression that the Portuguese at Malacca (Melaka) brought to bear against native polities. Of course, the bestowal of such protection came in return for a guarantee that those protected would sell all of the spices they harvested to the VOC at a rate set by the protectors. This method proved particularly effective for Dutch domination of the smaller islands, such as the Moluccas, whose dimensions, demographics, and lack of military resources made them especially vulnerable to intimidation and threats, as opposed to their larger neighbors in Java and Sumatra. Meanwhile, the English cultivated relations with the island states in a rather more diplomatic manner.

Dutch behavior often slid into high-handedness from Indonesian and English perspectives; pressure to secure the nutmeg of Pulau Run in the Bandas provoked the islanders to ambush and kill forty-six Dutchmen in 1609. To stave off the inevitable retribution of the VOC, the Bandanese leaders (*orangkayas*) made several overtures to East India Company officials seeking their protection, initially without success. In 1615, the *orangkayas* went so far as to send a delegation to the EIC's Bantam factory. On this occasion, an agreement was purportedly reached that, the English claimed, placed the little chain of islands and their inhabitants under English sovereignty, a claim echoed by the strikingly similar appeal made just before this by the Chickahominy people to the government of Virginia. The *orangkayas* and EIC representatives allegedly ratified

---

[6] Van Ittersum, "Debating Natural Law in the Banda Islands," 468.

further treaties in March and December 1616 that confirmed their new relationship, although the Dutch disputed both the form and substance of these negotiations from the first.[7]

Meanwhile, the differences that had developed between the two companies prompted what might be termed the first European diplomatic conference for resolving grievances that arose "beyond the seas" that began in 1613. These negotiations culminated in a treaty in 1619 that proclaimed an Anglo-Dutch union against the Iberians in Asia and divided the whole of the East Indian pepper trade in half and the Moluccas spice trade into respective spheres with the VOC having two-thirds and the EIC one-third. Moreover, each company was to contribute ships and arms to a common force and to participate in a Council of Defense that would arbitrate future differences between them. Instead of settling matters, however, this agreement, since the English favored its terms and sought to apply them while the Dutch did not, only exacerbated ill feeling. It also sparked a long debate over the respective Asian claims of the Dutch and the English that provided an important element in a general dispute over the nature of sovereignty in terms of access to trading and fishing rights, in which such intellectual heavyweights as Hugo Grotius and John Selden were employed.[8]

Whatever the English may have thought and whatever the Bandanese and other native inhabitants of the East Indies may have hoped would result from these negotiations, the VOC operatives, especially those in Indonesia, were not going to permit the diversion of the valuable produce of these islands to their rivals. Yet neither the Bandanese nor the English were prepared for the vigor exercised by Jan Pietersz Coen, VOC Director-General from 1614 and Governor-General from 1617. Certainly, no seventeenth-century figure on the ground pursued English overseas interests with the firmness and directness that this Dutchman did on behalf of his employers. Coen recognized firsthand the grave threat posed to the VOC by both English alliances with Indonesian societies and Anglo-Dutch agreements that permitted English access to the spice trade. His view received ready confirmation when forces of the Sultan of Bantam combined with an EIC fleet commanded by Sir Thomas Dale to depose

---

[7] Anon., *A courante of newes from the East India*; *The Hollanders declaration of the affaires of the East Indies*; Clulow, "The Art of Claiming," 29–36; Loth, "Pioneers and Perkeniers," 16–21.

[8] Clark and van Eysinga, *The Colonial Conferences between England and the Netherlands in 1613 and 1615*; Van Ittersum, "The Long Goodbye."

the Sultan of Jacatra (friend of the Dutch) at the end of 1618. Coen had to withdraw but returned in May with his own fleet that reversed the situation in Java dramatically: now "exceedingly strong in these parts, but exceedingly hated and abhorred of the inhabitants," the Dutch seized and destroyed Jacatra and then blockaded Bantam. Coen then rebuilt the Javanese town as a fortified port and seat of VOC operations, which was renamed Batavia.

This place proved a splendid location for continuing the assault against the Anglo-Bandanese alliance that brought the Banda Islands firmly under Dutch control. From 1617 to 1621, VOC ships intercepted and sank English vessels, tracked down and killed English agents, and blockaded, cajoled, threatened, manipulated, and, ultimately conquered the Bandanese. They pursued these courses in accordance with, they claimed, principles of "just" wars undertaken both against the "illegal" attempts by local rulers to interfere in the spice markets, viz., deprive the VOC of pepper, mace, nutmeg, and others, and to protect those same rulers from the encroachments of the Iberians.[9]

The results of this campaign were dismal for everyone concerned except the VOC. As for the English, the East India Company was expelled from Batavia and from the Bandas, although the Dutch retention of Pulau Run remained a fierce bone of contention for the next half-century. In 1639, for instance, the EIC claimed that, in addition to losses of £74,638 15s at the hands of the Dutch "previously detailed," the VOC had caused it £50,000 in damages (estimated as the value of crops produced on the island) by refusing to restore Pulau Run in defiance of treaty, £20,158 for commodities supplied to the Dutch, £77,200 (converted from 102,959 rials) for EIC property seized by Indian officials retaliation for which the Dutch had prevented, £20,000 in customs due on Dutch goods traded in Persia, £50,000 from the burning of the English factory at Jacatra, and £600,000 in trade lost through the VOC's six-year blockade of Bantam. Additionally, Charles I claimed losses for the deaths of "150 of his native subjects of Pulo Run, and the enslaving of 800 more" along with "plunder" taken from that island that the English valued at £125,000.[10]

---

[9] Van Ittersum, "Debating Natural Law in the Banda Islands"; Loth, "Armed Incidents and Unpaid Bills."

[10] This figure did not include claims for losses caused by "the massacre of their factors at Amboyna," Statement, 15 March 1639, of the Losses Sustained by the Proceedings of the Dutch since the Accord of 1623, *CCMEIC* 1: 303.

The English might have claimed a billion pounds in damages for all the Dutch cared about their complaints. While the EIC and the government resorted to the conference table and the printing press to air their litany of complaints, the VOC blithely added to that list. Most particularly (and infamously from the English perspective), it completed the erasure of the English presence east of the Celebes with the execution by VOC agents of thirteen Englishmen and twelve Japanese servants of the EIC on charges of conspiring against Dutch authority in the Moluccan island of Ambon in 1623. The English invariably cited this "Amboyna Massacre" as a preeminent example of Dutch treachery and cruelty over the next sixty years.[11]

Matters were even worse, however, for the indigenous inhabitants of the Bandas whom the Dutch killed, removed, or enslaved. The exiled population was replaced by slaves who toiled under the *perkenier* system of nutmeg plantations that the VOC established to secure the production of the spice, Coen's vision of a society peopled by free Dutch inhabitants having fallen victim to the general preference of his contemporaries to avoid his example of pursuing lives and careers in the East Indies.[12]

English interests in India fared rather better. Happily for the EIC – although perhaps this is counterintuitive in terms of considering the history of European overseas expansion – the Mughal Empire in 1613 was in an infinitely better military and diplomatic position to arrange matters to its own satisfaction than its counterparts in the Spice Islands. Thus, Indian rulers and officials could ignore Dutch and Portuguese blandishments and threats and indeed make good their own threats when it suited them. Accordingly, the Emperor Jahangir could grant a license (*firman*) to the EIC to conduct trade at Surat, and the English would have no concerns about possible interference from other Europeans so long as they retained Jahangir's favor. The EIC's factors, fully aware of the importance of imperial support for their position, continued their efforts to negate Portuguese influence at the

---

[11] For denunciations of Dutch "cruelty" and "treachery," see, e.g., Hall, *The History of the Barbarous Cruelties and Massacres, Committed by the Dutch in the East-Indies*; Settle, *Insignia Batavia*; Anon., *The English and Dutch Affairs Displayed to the Life by a true Lover and Asserter of his Countries Honour*; Anon., *A True Relation of the Unjust, Cruel, and Barbarous Proceedings against the English at Amboyna in the East-Indies by the Netherlandish Governour and Council there*; Anon., *The Second Part of the Tragedy of Amboyna*; Browne, *Vox Veritas*; Chancey, "The Amboyna Massacre in English Politics"; De Britaine, *The Dutch Usurpation*.

[12] Winn, "Slavery and Cultural Creativity in the Banda Islands."

Mughal court and succeeded in establishing additional factories at Agra, Ahmedabad, and Burhanpur.[13]

Once ensconced, the traders suggested that the company send a person of appropriate substance to serve as resident ambassador to the Emperor. The EIC Governor, Sir Thomas Smythe, recommended Sir Thomas Roe, Virginia Company backer and extensive voyager who had just returned to England from his exploration of Guiana, for this position. The nature of the Mughal political world enabled – indeed obliged – the EIC to enlist Crown support for sending a duly constituted royal ambassador to Agra; Jahangir would not receive the representative of a mere company of merchants, however many powers and privileges their monarch may have granted to it. As an emissary of James I, though, Roe had the brief to negotiate a clarification, ideally including further privileges, of the EIC's position in India, while William Keeling was appointed Factor-General with the brief to oversee the company's trade. Pointedly, Sir Thomas seems not to have exercised power equivalent to that of the VOC's Directors-General at Batavia. After some discussion, the company's membership and King James agreed on his appointment, and on 2 February 1615, Roe took ship for India.[14]

Roe departed the subcontinent in 1619 having overcome, with the assistance of additional naval successes, fervent Portuguese opposition and latent hostility at the Mughal court to cement the position of the EIC. This included crucial permission "that the English be allowed to live 'according to their owne religion and lawes' without interference" in their trading factories.[15] We should certainly not discount this result especially given what was going on in the East Indies at this time. Yet Roe's Indian career provides another example of the fitful character of the administration of English overseas trade and colonization. For the ambassador remained frustrated in his efforts to secure imperial licenses for the further extension of the EIC presence into Sindh and Bengal. Then, as we have seen with his counterparts in the East Indies, he also had to deal with

---

[13] Chaudhuri, *The English East India Company*, 45–55.

[14] Foster, *The Embassy of Sir Thomas Roe to the Court of the Great Mogul*, 1: i–ix. The EIC apparently envisioned the creation of four presidencies, at Surat, Bantam, the Coromandel Coast, and Patna in Bihar, from which its operations would be conducted. In the event, only the first two came into being and were joined later by Madras; Chaudhuri, *The English East India Company*, 46.

[15] Sir Thomas Roe's Negotiations with Prince Khurram, August 1618, Foster, *The English Factories in India*, 38–40 at 39–40; Watson, "The Establishment of English Commerce in North-Western India in the Early Seventeenth Century."

Dutch encroachments to which his range of responses, notably in terms of the use of force, was limited by the desire for peace in the metropolis. Finally, he had to deal with a lack of clarity, which fed resentment of his presence, with respect to the scope of his authority and a breakdown in cooperation. As a royal ambassador, Roe claimed authority over the company traders at Surat, which the EIC merchants denied. The factors objected further to the ambassador's efforts to pursue commercial prospects in Persia and Arabia that they regarded as costly drains on their own interests. In the end, Roe was never replaced nor was anyone else ever appointed to fill a similar position in the seventeenth-century history of English overseas interests.[16]

A case could be made that prioritizing the "voyage" vehicle for acquiring pepper and other Asian commodities served the EIC well at least in the immediate term. Yet Roe, for all of his concerns about the VOC, recommended that the English adopt the Dutch approach in Asia, observing that its rivals, "who seeke Plantation heere by the Sword ... turne a wonderfull stocke, they proule in all Places, they Posses some of the best; yet ther dead Payes consume all the gayne."[17]

The examination of the returns of the early voyages sent out by the East India Company that Chaudhuri has made provides support for Roe's view. "Pepper was a profitable commodity during this period," reaching

---

[16] Roe regarded himself as the Crown's minister to the Mughal Emperor; e.g., Sir Thomas Roe to King James I, 15 February 1617/18, Foster, *The Embassy of Sir Thomas Roe to the Court of the Great Mogul*, 2: 495–7; he carried instructions from the king, 29 December 1614, ibid., 2: 551–3. The terms of his appointment with the company, however, expressly placed the management of the EIC factories outside the scope of his appointment; The Company's Agreement with Roe, 16 November 1614, ibid., 2: 547–51 at 548. None of this prevented Roe from trying to order around the traders threatening royal wrath if they did not cooperate; e.g., Sir Thomas Roe to the Factors at Surat, 8 October 1617, ibid., 2: 428–30. The problem of two masters revealed itself when a Dutch fleet turned up at Surat to the consternation of the English traders there. The merchants feared competition, especially if the newcomers were to build a factory "where they would both out-present, out-bribe and out-buy us in all things," and hoped that an English fleet would arrive to disperse the unwanted visitors. Roe, for his part, had instructions from England to avoid hostility toward the Dutch, but did everything he could to encourage their rapid departure; ibid., 1: 228–9. The ambassador was well aware of the "insufferable insolencies" of the Dutch in Asia, which, he warned, required correcting; Sir Thomas Roe to the East India Company, 14 February 1617/18, ibid., 2: 466–85 at 481; Sir Thomas Roe to the Expected General who shall arrive this year, 30 August 1617, ibid., 2: 407–11 at 407; Sir Thomas Roe to the King's Majesty, 29 January 1615/16, ibid., 1: 120–1. For difficulties between Roe and the Surat merchants, see ibid., 1: xlviii–li.

[17] Sir Thomas Roe to the East India Company, 24 November 1616, Foster, *The Embassy of Sir Thomas Roe to the Court of the Great Mogul*, 2: 342–52 at 344.

its height in 1617; when company ships brought home some two million pounds of the spice, the EIC set the price of Jambi pepper at 26d per pound and of Bantam pepper at 25d per pound. The conflict with the Dutch in the East Indies, though, meant no pepper was transported in 1619, and from the following year, the price began to edge downward, although not as dramatically as that of American tobacco did during the ensuing decade. Now the Dutch strategy began to pay dividends: since the VOC had closed the English out of the Spice Island trade except for smuggling cloves at Macassar, it was difficult for the EIC to find adequate sources of new commodities while its costs for pepper rose and the price it could set continued to fall. Aggravated by ravaging famine in Gujarat in 1630–1, the death of Shah Abbas and the cool attitude of his successor to the English, as well as the mismanagement and concentration on their private trade by its factors, the company had to adopt the recourse of selling all of its pepper in bulk to the customs farmer and financier Philip Burlamachi in order to obtain the best price. Burlamachi, acting on behalf of four other prominent merchants of the day, Sir John Wolstoneholme, Sir Paul Pindar, Abraham Jacob, and Charles Cockayne, bought some £10,000 worth of the commodity, paying 18d per pound for Jambi pepper and 19d per pound for Priamon pepper. By 1630, though, the price of pepper had dropped to 15d per pound and did not begin to rebound until 1636.[18]

Indigo constituted another important import of the EIC in the second decade of the seventeenth century, but its price plummeted in 1619 and fluctuated wildly thereafter while supplies fell and costs rose. Saltpeter and sugar constituted alternative commodities but did not generate significant traffic. By 1635, the company's situation was grim: it had amassed a capital fund of £420,700 four years previously in its Third Joint Stock but had not paid a dividend and had announced that no return could be expected for the next one or two years while massive debts swamped its factors in Asia. Perhaps even more ominously, this set

---

[18] Chaudhuri, *The English East India Company*, 140–67. These merchants and others, including Courteen, were among the select group on whose ready willingness to "lend" money to the fiscally challenged governments of James I and Charles I relied, a reality they used to ingratiate themselves with the Crown; Ashton, "Revenue Farming under the Early Stuarts." Burlamachi, an associate of Sir William (both were among those fined for exporting bullion illegally in 1619) who operated on the fringe of overseas activities, had the wherewithal to purchase the EIC's entire pepper cargo as well as to front the dowry of Elizabeth of Bohemia, but his political and economic clout still could not prevent his bankruptcy in 1633; Judges, "Philip Burlamachi," 285–6, 289, 291.

of circumstances brought dissent and demands for accounting within the EIC as well as seriously dampened the enthusiasm of investors for its future.[19]

At least one knowledgeable albeit anonymous observer warned that, absent Crown intervention on the company's behalf, "a dissolution was inevitable."[20] Unfortunately for the membership, royal involvement seemed highly unlikely in 1636–7: the same writer sensed that Charles I held an "ill opinion of their persons and endeavours" of the EIC, which is why it was in such a poor state. This concern was aggravated by royal support for a plan that created an alternative entity to promote English interests in the East that was initiated by two former employees of the East India Company, John Weddell and Nathaniel Mountney, and under-written by Endymion Porter, a groom of the royal bedchamber, and Sir William Courteen. This Courteen Association envisioned the restoration of English fortunes in the East and beyond albeit without necessarily diminishing the company's position; indeed, it is unclear whether Cour-teen even regarded himself as a rival of the EIC.[21]

Regardless, Sir William pursued a plan that would have superseded the EIC and its alleged waste of its powers with a new venture that was intended to further English interests throughout the Indian Ocean but also beyond it to China and Japan and even across the Pacific Ocean. This breadth of vision attracted the uniquely direct involvement of Charles I, who announced that he would make a £10,000 personal investment in the joint stock to which Courteen and his partners had already contributed £120,000.[22]

In addition to making this contribution, the King tendered a commis-sion that authorized Weddell and Mountney, who had previously con-cluded a truce with the Viceroy at Goa permitting free trade in Portuguese-controlled areas of Asia, to conduct a voyage of trade and "discovery." This would promote "the venting of English goods and

---

[19] *CCMEIC* 1: v–xxxvi at vii.

[20] Memorandum of the East India Trade, [May 1637?], *CCMEIC* 1: 273–4.

[21] *CCMEIC* 1: v–xxxvi at xiv–xvi. We have evidence of friendly relations between Sir William Courteen and the company in 1634, when he recommended one Robert Freeman for reemployment, although it "rejected" Freeman; Court minutes of the East India Company, 7 March 1633/4, *CSPC EI* 8: 529–30; see also Court minutes of the East India Company, 25 June 1625, *CSPC EI* 6: 78.

[22] The King's Undertaking to join in the Adventure to the Indies, 6 December 1635, *CCMEIC* 1: 123–4; Reasons to move the King to confirm under the Great Seal Captain Weddell's Commission, [May 1637], *CCMEIC* 1: 274–5.

manufactures" in the East Indies since the East India Company had "neglected" its business, thereby threatening public employment, trade, and customs revenue. Accordingly, the Crown granted the Courteen voyage the authority to call at Madagascar, Mozambique, the Arabian and Indian coasts, the Spice Islands, Macau, Japan, and California "on the backside of America" – wherever the EIC did not maintain factories – in search of "such Commodities and Merchandizes as you in your Judgements and discretions shall think may bee of best value and advantage to the Merchants and Adventurers in this voyage," as well as to seek the Northwest and Northeast Passages. In addition, Charles I authorized the voyagers to investigate further prospects for trade, allegedly left moribund by the company's febrile efforts; engage in diplomacy with the governments they would encounter, notably the Emperor of Japan and claim territory for future colonization; and to take prizes. In the event they found new lands, "the discoverers" would receive half of the customs revenue that these places brought by way of "trade, plantation, or otherwise." This authorization did not, however, grant the Courteen group such rights as the power to build forts, remove people from England, or commence plantations and establish governments for them as royal charters did: this was to be an exploratory and trading endeavor, not a colonizing venture. On 14 April 1636, six ships duly set sail from the Downs to carry out this commission.[23]

The history of the Courteen Association began with a series of fiascos, but ultimately brought transforming results for the history of seventeenth-century English overseas trade and colonization. Thus, we should be clear about the stakes involved for those concerned. The pain of this imperial episode arose from the behavior of competing groups, both of which regarded themselves as also acting in the public interest, who solicited the government to back them. The nature and relatively large scale of government involvement in the Courteen venture does constitute a major distinction from other such cases, but still

---

[23] Royal Commission to Captain John Weddell and his associates, 12 December 1635, Instructions for our Trusty and Wellbeloved Captain John Weddell and Nathaniel Mountney imployed by especiall Commission from us under our Royal Signature and Signet, 12 December 1635, *CCMEIC* 1: 128–9; Instructions given by the King to Captain John Weddell and Nathaniel Mountney, 12 December 1635, *CCMEIC* 1: 130–1; Royal Commission to use Martial Law, 12 December 1635, Royal Commission for Taking Prizes, 19 December 1635, Charles I to Captain Weddell, on the return of the *Planter*, confirming previous grants, 14 March 1637/8, Temple, *The Travels of Peter Mundy* vol. 3, part 2, 429–55, quotations at 433, 445.

illustrates the reactive role that the state played in terms of initiating and overseeing overseas activities: firm encouragement from Charles I could not prevent the Courteen business from crashing on the shoals of royal obfuscation and EIC and Dutch opposition. Such encouragement as the government did offer still did not come close to an application of a new broom to Asian affairs, and it is curious that the Crown, given the deep dissatisfaction that Charles expressed with the efforts of the East India Company, did not pursue the ultimate sanction – a *quo warranto* judgment that would have annulled the corporate charter – as it sought against another corporate entity, the Massachusetts Bay Company, whose behavior displeased it at this time.[24]

Another important distinction here was the scale of the stakes involved: Sir William's heirs and creditors later claimed that the Courteen venture incurred damages that totaled in excess of £150,000, a vast sum – even allowing for the likely inflation of such claims: by way of comparison, it amounted to almost one-tenth of the estimated annual revenue collected by the Protectorate government between 1655 and 1660, a period of almost unprecedentedly high taxation. Unless it was wildly inaccurate, the assertion of this figure demonstrates the seriousness of the commitment that Courteen and his partners brought to their endeavor. Thus, despite its failure, the consistent neglect or dismissal of the Courteen Association in the historiography of the Anglo-British Empire is curious.[25]

The problems that dogged this scheme began when Sir William took sick and died within three months of the departure of the fleet, which deprived the partnership of its chief proponent and financial backer. The loss of the association's namesake and mercantile chief then compelled Mountney to seek reemployment with the East India Company.[26]

---

[24] Instead, the King promised the EIC that he would call in the Courteen patent and renew its charter, while the EIC agreed to call a new subscription; At the Court at Whytehall, 10 December 1639, PC 2/51, ff. 165–8 at 167. This agreement seems to fallen afoul of the company's terrible state, which deterred investors followed by the distraction of the government after 1640, *CCMEIC* 2: iii–vii.

[25] For the Courteen claims reported at £151,612, see Graves, *A Brief Narrative and Deduction of the several Remarkable Cases of Sir William Courten, and Sir Paul Pyndar*, 5. For the estimates of the total revenue of the government in the mid-seventeenth century, see Aylmer, *The State's Servants*, 321.

[26] For Mountney's request to return to the employment of the EIC, see A Court of Committees, 10 August 1636, *CCMEIC* 1: 189–90. For the continuation of the Association following Sir William's death, see Thomas Knyaston and Samuel Bonnell to Edward Nicholas, 10 August 1636, *CCMEIC* 1: 190–1; Samuel Bonnell to Edward Nicholas, 17 August 1636, *CCMEIC* 1: 191; Draft Articles of Agreement between Endymion

Meanwhile, Barbary pirates seized one of the ships off Land's End. Then the mariners suffered continually from malaria and mortality while their overtures at Madagascar, at Bhatkal (in the Carnatic), and at Macau met with hostility from the inhabitants. Frustrations in China convinced Weddell not to attempt Japan, let alone California.[27] Then, despite the good relations that supposedly existed between Weddell and the Portuguese at Goa and the captain carrying a passport from Charles I to the VOC at Batavia, Asian-based Europeans harassed the English fleet on both its outbound and return voyages: two of the remaining five ships, including the flagship, *Dragon*, never returned to England; "had they come home," claimed one veteran of the expedition, "they had made a Ritch voyage for them selves as well as the Imployers," upwards of "probably more than" £150,000.[28] Back in England, pressure from Sir William's creditors from the voyage, uncertain about the future of their investments, drove his son, also named William, abroad to escape them. This plight brought more kingly sympathy for the Courteen venture: Charles directed the customs farmers to provide a loan to relieve William until Weddell's fleet returned. Some of the farmers agreed, but others expressed a preference that the East India Company assume control of "the adventure."[29]

The creation of the Courteen Association, though, seems to have breathed some new life into the East India Company, which responded with alacrity to the perceived encroachment on its chartered rights and the perceived treachery of its former employees. The company had two of the

Porter, William Courten, Executor to Sir William Courten and Assignee of Samuel Bonnell, and Thomas Knyaston, [August 1636], *CCMEIC* 1: 191–3.

[27] Mundy's Notes to Relations XXI–XXX, Temple, *Travels of Peter Mundy*, vol. 3, part 2, 424–8 at 424 (Barbary pirates), 425 (problems in China and the death of Sir William Courteen), 427 (loss of Weddell and the *Dragon* and the *Catherine*). For the China leg of the voyage, see Relation XXVI: From the tyme of our departure from Tayfoo untill our arrival att Macao againe in China, Temple, *Travels of Peter Mundy*, vol. 3, part 1, 235–316 at 300–1. The Canton mandarins ordered the Portuguese to remove the English to Macau and then send them away; Copy of the contract which the City [of Macao] made with the Mandarins of Canton, respecting the English who were in the said port, [October 1637], Temple, *Travels of Peter Mundy*, vol. 3, part 1, 250.

[28] D[arell], *Strange News from the Indies*, 34; Letter from His Majesty of Great Britain, Charles I, to the representatives of the Dutch East India Company in India, 20 February 1635/6, Temple, *Travels of Peter Mundy*, vol. 3, part 2, 427 (loss of Weddell and the *Dragon* and the *Catherine*), 443–4.

[29] The King expressed concern that Courteen would suffer "through the perverseness of some" and insisted that the farmers set out whether they would help him or not and if they would not why they would not in writing, [Secretary Windebank] to the Farmers of the Great Customs, 10 June 1636, *CCMEIC* 1: 180–1.

Associates arrested for causing it to incur an alleged £120,000 in damages by the sending out of Weddell's expedition, and it ordered its agents everywhere to deny the Courteen fleet any sort of assistance. At the same time, it lobbied the Crown to renew and clarify its rights. Then, the EIC complained to the Privy Council that Weddell and his men had seized two of its junks at the mouth of the Red Sea and conspired with the Governor of Surat to imprison the company's president and council in violation of express royal orders that they should "not act to the prejudice" of the East India Company.[30]

The responses of Charles I to this petition, however, demonstrated both how the situation of the EIC remained parlous and how the future of English involvement in Asia had become particularly dependent on royal favor. First, having been reluctant to characterize the alleged seizure of the junks either as piracy or as having been perpetrated by Englishmen, the King determined that the offending vessels had not been part of the Courteen fleet. Moreover, he ordered that Courteen "should not be questioned or vexed by the East India Company." Then, he renewed the Association's commission.[31]

The Crown not only had to arbitrate here, since a duly chartered company was one of the parties concerned, but the case of the East India Company constitutes one of the two instances in the history of English trade and colonization prior to the Restoration where the monarch intervened – in both cases at the instigation of a rival – to assess the performance of a company that it had duly chartered – the other being that of the Massachusetts Bay Company. Since the issues over religious policy that attracted governmental attention in the Massachusetts case did not appear in the Indian one even though the East India Company Committees included such godly stalwarts as Matthew Cradock, Thomas Spurstowe, and Rowland Wilson, we can only attribute this extraordinary scenario to the importance that the prospects for the Asian trade held at this time.[32]

---

[30] George Lowe to the Earl of Middlesex, 6 February 1635/6, *HMC Fourth Report, Part One* (London: H.M.S.O., 1874), 292.

[31] Order of the King in Council, 6 January 1636/7, *CSPD* Charles I 10: 342; Petition of William Courteen, 7 February 1636/7, *CCMEIC* 1: 226; A Court of Committees, 27 February 1636/7, *CCMEIC* 1: 232–3; His Majesty to Captain Weddell, 14 March 1636/7, *CCMEIC* 1: 241. For the Crown's contemporaneous investigation of the Massachusetts Bay Company, led by Archbishop William Laud, chair of the Committee for Foreign Plantations, see Bremer, *John Winthrop*, 229–40.

[32] A General Court of Election, 3 July 1640, *CCMEIC* 2: 60–1.

The EIC certainly held few illusions about its own future given the royal support bestowed on its rival. Thus, on 31 January 1638, the company's "generality" expressed the view that to send another ship to the Indies amounted to throwing good money after bad and so "were almost unanimously in favour of dissolving the trade." The members observed further that the Crown had already shorn their privileges by granting new patents and cited a rumor that more restrictions were to come. The Governor and Committees defused this sentiment only by invoking the prospect of royal disapproval – Charles having assured them of his continued favor – if the company was to cease trading. On a more positive note, they reported, the Crown had appointed Wolstoneholme and Pindar to resolve the differences with the Courteen Association and they had recommended that Courteen sell out to the company. If they could arrange "suitable terms," the Governor and Committees advised the members, they would buy out the Associates; they awaited Courteen's offer. If not, it had been reported that another group had approached the King with a plan to pursue the East Indian trade "with equal advantages to His Majestie and the profitt of the State." If these men were in earnest, the company "is ready to surrender its charter, but also to transfer its servants, ships, wharfs, &c. on moderate terms."[33]

Ascertaining, not to mention maneuvering around, the royal will could be difficult at any point in time, but reading the signs was notoriously so when the sovereign in question was Charles I. Contemporaries and generations of historians have contributed their views on the character of this ill-fated monarch, especially in terms of his capacity for sincerity, his vacillating, or, alternatively, his desire to reach compromise. We are not particularly concerned here about the status of Charles as historiographical victim but we would like to be able to have a sense of what the East India Company and the Courteen Association made of the King's behavior. Because, on the one hand, it could have reflected an aim for compromise: to modify the EIC patent to allow the Courteen group to manage a substantial share of the Asian trade in areas where the company had no presence. On the other hand, it could have been indicative of royal irresolution.[34]

[33] Narrative of what has been done since the King's last answer to the East India Company, February 1637/8, *CCCMEIC* 1: 292–3. For government encouragement of an EIC buyout of Courteen, see Order of His Majesty in Council, Whitehall, 25 May 1638, *CCMEIC* 1: 295–6; Summary of Proposals for a new East India Company, June 1638, *CCMEIC* 1: 296–7.

[34] Cust, *Charles I*, provides a balanced treatment of this ill-starred, controversial monarch.

In the event, just six weeks after the EIC officers sought to placate their irate members with assurances of royal support, Charles reconfirmed his appreciation of Weddell's services and of the "good beginning" he had made. As a mark of his "continued esteem" for the captain and his partners, the King confirmed his previous commission to them. In hopes of avoiding further confusion Charles ordered the EIC not to trade on the Malabar Coast and that the Courteen Association should "not prejudice the trade of our East India Company."[35]

Royal hopes for an accommodation between the rivals, however, failed to materialize. Unfortunately, the King's alternative plan of treating them as separate but equal entities with authority over their respective baili-wicks did not curb their animosity. The EIC consistently referred to the chronological priority of its patent, claiming that any subsequent license granted to conduct trade in the Indian Ocean infringed on its rights. The company's view was undoubtedly bolstered by the King's intent to renew the EIC charter "with such fitting enlargement as may be for their better encouragement and the better government of that trade" in September 1638.[36]

By this time, however, rebellion had broken out in Scotland over the Crown's religious policy in that kingdom and would soon be followed by the "Bishops' Wars" (1639–40). Preoccupation with Scottish affairs nat-urally diminished the government's ability to act on its concerns over the Asian trade even as it sought to resolve the EIC–Courteen differences. The success of the Scottish rebels thus removed the pressure for a merger between the two ventures as well as the prospect of dissolution for the East India Company. More significantly, Scottish progress rendered the issue of royal favor, on which the Courteen Association still depended in order to make good its claims for equal status with the company, increas-ingly irrelevant – and even dangerous to pursue – after 1640.

The EIC slowly made its advantages tell after what proved to be a final attempt to reach an agreement with Courteen failed. On 4 March 1642,

---

[35] Petition of the Governor, Deputy, and Committees of the East India Company to the King, 30 September 1638, *CCMEIC* 1: 298–9. For Charles I's approval of Weddell's conduct on his voyage, see The King to Captain John Weddell, Commander of the Fleet whereof the *Dragon* is Admiral, 14 March 1637/8, *CCMEIC* 1: 294. The Courteen Association claimed the EIC had never traded on the Malabar Coast south of Surat and that the "Kings of Batacola and Cannanore [Kannur] offer land and assistance in building forts," Mr. Courteen's Factory at Batacola [Bhatkal], [March 1637/8], *CCMEIC* 1: 294–5.

[36] Order of His Majesty in Council, Oatlands, 2 September 1638, *CCMEIC* 1: 298.

the company submitted a petition to Parliament (the King having left London two months previously) complaining of the injuries done by the Dutch and English rivals to their trade. In reply, it received an order to sort out their differences with William Courteen. Thus, two weeks later, the company offered to buy all of Courteen's goods and his shipping for cash and invited him to invest in the next EIC voyage "and not to send out any more" himself. Courteen, though, was preparing five ships for a new voyage and wanted the company to pay for the goods contained in three of them (two were to go to India unladen) and to have the company collect his factors and goods from Asia. The EIC, however, rejected these proposals, claiming to Parliament it had done their best to preserve the trade while reminding Courteen of the injuries his activities had cost it.[37]

At the time of this final impasse, the East India Company had recovered to the extent that it was able to launch its Fourth Joint Stock, with a capital fund of £105,000, to support a voyage of four vessels. This reserve was sufficient to sustain a loss of some £30,000 due to the sinking of one of these ships in a storm on its return home as well as to ride out the uncertainties created by the outbreak of civil war in 1642. Meanwhile, EIC factors acted to preserve previously precarious outposts, such as Balasore in Bengal, and secured a new *firman* from the new Emperor, Shah Jahan, in 1643. They also undertook a new program of expansion, which withstood the continued attempts of the Dutch to make inroads at the Mughal court and in Persia. While much of this came to naught, such as the feelers sent to Manila and Macao, and some ran afoul of Dutch aggression as at Ceylon (Sri Lanka), it did result in the founding of the Madras presidency in 1639.

This new establishment on the Coromandel Coast at last met the EIC's desire for a presence there. Yet while the fort that the English built and the city – Madras – that grew up around it from the preexisting Indian town of Madraspatnam bore some resemblance to the model of Batavia, essential differences between the two places existed: first, the company acquired its territory from the local ruler, who also granted it permission to set up a government of the town and to construct Fort St. George (completed in 1644), whereas the VOC had destroyed the Javanese town,

---

[37] Such details of these negotiations and their sticking points as we have are memorialized: A Meeting of the Special Committee to Consider the Petition presented to Parliament, 4 March 1641/2, *CCMEIC* 2: 234; A Court of Committees, 19 March 1641/2, *CCMEIC* 2: 239; A Court of Committees, 21 March 1641/2, *CCMEIC* 2: 239–40; A Court of Committees, 22 March 1641/2, *CCMEIC* 2: 241–2.

expelled the local ruler, and erected their own fortified port. Then, while Batavia constituted the administrative center of Dutch Asia, Madras was one of three equal EIC presidencies.

These distinctions were reflected in the reality that Madras could not provide the hoped-for springboard for dominating trade in the Bay of Bengal in the way that Batavia had done in the East Indies. Not only did the English town have generally larger and stronger neighboring polities than the VOC's headquarters did, but "the Bay" included more open ocean than the waters surrounding Java did and incorporated no straits where naval force could be strategically applied to control trade. Even so, Fort St. George did provide security for conducting trade for Coromandel cloths against the Dutch factory at Pulicat, as well as a platform both for supplying the company's surviving operations in the East Indies and for moving into Bengal. By 1646, the returns from Bengali commerce had shown marked improvement, and by 1664, the first available year for which such data exist, Coromandel cloths constituted 48 percent of textiles imported by the EIC into Europe, with Gujarati cloths accounting for 35 percent and Bengal 17 percent. By 1684, the company's cloth trade had reached 1.76 million pieces with a value of £670,000, or 83 percent of the import value of its entire trade.[38]

The Courteen Association, though, had not been idle and was working to take advantage of the presence left by Weddell's voyage, which, in addition to Carwar (Karwar) and Bhatkal on the Malabar Coast, included factories at Aceh in Sumatra and Rajpur in Gujarat.[39] By 1641, Courteen had addressed his debts, which one writer later calculated at £140,000 and another at £100,000, by assigning all of his Asian interests to his brother-in-law Sir Edward Littleton. William and Littleton then bolstered their finances by recruiting Pindar to invest £36,000 (or £24,800 depending on the writer) in a new undertaking that sent five ships to the Indian Ocean.[40]

---

[38] Foster, *The English Factories in India, 1642–1645*, v–xxxvii; Foster, *The Founding of Fort St. George, Madras*. For the value of the EIC textile trade, see Prakash, "The Dutch and English East India Company's Trade in Indian Textiles in the Seventeenth and the Eighteenth Century," 188–9.

[39] E.g., Relation XXII: Our departure from Goa and arrival at Battacala in East India, where was settled a factory, Temple, *Travels of Peter Mundy*, vol. 3, part 2, 69–107 at 94.

[40] For estimates of Courteen's debt and his attempt to dispose of it, Graves, *A Brief Narrative and Deduction of the several Remarkable Cases of Sir William Courten, and Sir Paul Pyndar, Knights*, 3; E.W., *Severall Remarkable Passages concerning the Hollanders*, 57–8; D[arell], *The East-India trade further discovered*, 7.

Unfortunately for its backers, this voyage, like its predecessor, ended poorly and the Courteen Association collapsed into debt and, thus, acrimony. More important, though, in terms of the future of English overseas trade and colonization, the conception of this voyage included trading in Guinea for gold to employ in trade in Asia and investigating the prospects for planting a settlement in Madagascar (also known as St. Lawrence to the English at this time). It thus marked the first practical English attempt to integrate operations in Africa and Asia.

Initially, matters went well: Courteen ships brought home "3600 hundred weight of rough Salt-petre or thereabouts" in January 1644, which William contracted with Parliament to refine for a payment of £10,000, while the *Lioness* exchanged £2,500 worth of commodities on the African coast for "about £6000" worth of gold before it headed for the Indian Ocean.[41] Then, however, *Lioness*, carrying the Guinea gold along with two brass cannon intended as gifts for Asian trading partners, was seized at Madagascar either by EIC agents, as Courteen alleged in his ensuing complaint to Parliament, or by Courteen's creditors seeking to attach its cargo toward their debts, according to the company.[42] Even more devastatingly, the Dutch seized two of the other vessels, the *Bona Esperanza* and the *Henry Bonadventure*, in the Straits of Malacca as they made their way from Goa to China on the grounds that they carried Portuguese goods; "thereupon inevitably followed not only the immediate ruin of the said forts and factories but also the loss of the China trade to the great prejudice of this kingdom & the damage of near two hundred thousand pounds," according to the complaint made by Courteen's son twenty years later.[43]

The management of the business might have been better, according to other observers. The Surat President of the EIC found three Courteen ships at Rajpur "in a deplorable and desperate condition expecting lading for England where appeared neither goods nor moneys to purchase."

[41] Ordinance concerning Salt-petre and Courteen's Agreement; with the Committee of Safety for Salt-petre, January 1643[/4], *LJ* 6: 403–4; Contract for Salt-petre, *CJ* 3: 365; Andrew Trumbull and Thomas Chambers in Jaitāpur Road to the Company, 11 February 1645/6, Foster, *The English Factories in India, 1618–1669*, 26–7. For Courteen's intention to colonize Madagascar in the spring of 1644, see Boothby, *A breife description of the most famous island of Madagascar*, 66; Smith, "Canaanising Madagascar".
[42] Reparation of Courteen's Damages to be demanded of the States, 19 March 1646/7, *LJ* 8: 220; Courteen and the E.I. Co., 12 March 1646/7, *LJ* 9: 58; Courteen and the East India Company, 6 April 1647, *LJ* 9: 125–6.
[43] Petition of William Courteen III to the King, 25 June 1663, Sloane Ms. 3515, f. 4, BL; E.W., *Severall Remarkable Passages Concerning the Hollanders*, 58.

Only one was able to obtain any commodities in India and was "very poorly served" in what it could obtain even so. A second wound up carrying ballast as it could not locate any goods at all. The third (*Lioness*) supposedly carried the gold brought from Guinea, but its officers, "daring to trust the agent therewith" given their inability to locate commodities, found themselves at a loss about how to proceed. Voyages to Mokha and Basra fared no better, which increased the indebtedness of the Association to Indian merchants – another grievance of the EIC since locals were quick to cast general aspersions of misbehavior by English merchants no matter who they represented.[44]

The plan to investigate Madagascar went no better. By 1644, when the Courteen Association sent its settlers to this sizable island located at the western end of the Indian Ocean, a number of English people had already considered the possibilities of this place. Inevitably, the character of imperialism as it was constituted during the reign of Charles I came into play. In 1636 or 1637, the King received favorable reports about colonizing Madagascar, probably from Thomas Howard, Earl of Arundel, the main supporter of pursuing ventures to the island. These made particular reference to its purportedly favorable location and climate for "refreshing and succouring" English traders to the East Indies. Charles also noted "that the King and others of that country have invited the English to plant there" and announced, to the decided bemusement of his sister, Elizabeth of Bohemia, that her son, Prince Rupert, should have the charge of settling a plantation there. Elizabeth soon put a stop her to her son's involvement but Arundel still "worked exceedingly hard at it," despite its "impracticability," reported a dubious Venetian Ambassador.[45]

The opportunity for Arundel to take charge of his Indian Ocean dream did not present itself until the failure of the army under his command to defeat the Scottish rebels in the First Bishops' War cast him into disfavor with the King. Apparently agreeing that their relationship might improve

---

[44] President Breton and Thomas Merry at Swally Marine to the Company, 31 March 1647, Foster, *The English Factories in India, 1618–1669*, 113–15 at 115; Francis Breton et al. from Swally to EIC, 30 March 1646 (received 30 August 1647), IOR E/3/20, ff. 2–8 at 6v–7r.

[45] King Charles to [Prince Rupert] [unfinished draft by Secretary of the Admiralty Edward Nicholas], [March 1637?], *CCMEIC* 1: 244; Anzolo Correr, Venetian Ambassador in England, to the Doge and Senate, 10 April 1637, no. 194, and same to same, 17 April 1637, no. 199, "Venice: April 1637," *Calendar of State Papers Relating to English Affairs in the Archives of Venice, Volume 24, 1636–1639*, ed. Allen B. Hinds (London, 1923), 175–93, *British History Online* www.british-history.ac.uk/cal-state-papers/venice/vol24/pp175-193 (accessed 15 July 2016).

if substantial distance was put between them, Charles granted the Earl
leave to depart from court and lent him one of his top ships, newly
refitted, for six months. Arundel then started a publicity campaign to
recruit investors and migrants, with an enthusiasm manifested in the
portrait painted of his wife and himself considering their soon-to-be
new home on a globe, in the autumn of 1639.[46]

That, however, was as far as Arundel went with his Madagascar plans,
for which he never seems to have received a charter in any event.
According to Richard Boothby, whose Asian career began with the EIC
but who became a Courteen partisan, the plans for the summoning of a
parliament that commenced in December 1639 brought the Earl's project
to a halt. Alison Games, who has provided the most recent historiographical treatment of seventeenth-century English designs on the island, in
addition to the forthcoming parliament, cites "Lady [*sic*] Arundel's reluctance to move her household to Madagascar," "insufficient financial
support," as well as "Arundel's poor health" as the reasons for the
"collapse" of the Earl's "vision." After the dissolution of the Short
Parliament in May 1640, Arundel accompanied Princess Mary on her
journey to the Netherlands to marry the *stadhouder* William II in
1642 and never returned to England, dying in Italy in 1646.[47]

Courteen and Captain John Bond both tried to keep the Madagascar
flame lit. The advocates of colonizing the place regarded it, as
Charles I had been advised, as an essential waystation on the route to
the East Indies, but given its size and the supposedly benign climate for
humans and livestock, along with the tractable nature of its inhabitants
(suppositions quickly proven wrong by bitter experience), the colony
would, along with the opening of the Asian trade to all comers, contribute
to English wealth and stature in its own right and provide a helpful
anchor for combating Dutch pretensions in Asia. If ignored, the VOC
would grab the island just as it had seized Mauritius in its westward
spread across the Indian Ocean from Batavia.[48]

---

[46] "The Madagascar Scheme," 6 September 1639, Hervey, *The Life, Correspondence and
Collections of Thomas Howard, Earl of Arundel*, 506–8; Thomas Smith to Robert Reade,
8 October 1639, *CSPD* Charles I 16 (1639–40): 19.

[47] Boothby, *A breife description of the most famous island of Madagascar*, 70; Games, *Web
of Empire*, 190.

[48] E.g., Hamond, *A Paradox Prooving, that the Inhabitants of the Isle called Madagascar*;
Boothby, *A breife description of the most famous island of Madagascar*, 24–31; D[arell],
Strange News from the Indies, Bond's Patent, 13 February 1642/3, *CJ* 2: 963.

In actuality, the East India Company, which consistently opposed all colonization plans for Asia, was responsible for the demise of Arundel's plan as well as the one pursued by Thomas Wriothesley, Earl of Southampton, for Mauritius. In yet another manifestation of both the conduct of seventeenth-century English imperial initiatives and of the approach of Charles I to government – vacillation or compromise – the monarch, at the company's behest, stopped Arundel and Southampton's ventures.[49] While one EIC Governor Sir Maurice Abbott and some Committees had allegedly opposed the planting of the island as "unhealthful,"[50] the company also opposed Asian colonization since it feared that a colony would provide a base for conducting piracy in the Red Sea (water route for the *hajj*). It acknowledged that company ships would be able to refit on the island "at a cheap rate, but whether this will be so when Englishmen are seen fortifying on the island is to be questioned." But the real fear was that the planting of any colony within the territorial limits of the EIC patent would draw off trade from the company's factories to its "prejudice" and, by extension, damage English interests in Asia generally. This argument, as the EIC warned Bond, would serve to stop his endeavor in its tracks just as it had curbed the Indian Ocean ventures of Arundel and Southampton, and it was correct: Parliament revoked its earlier order allowing Bond to proceed in March 1643, and evidence of his venture disappears from the record.[51]

The EIC did not limit its anti-colonization strategy to petitioning and counseling the government about the alleged evils of pursuing Asian plantations; it also accepted the Courteen challenge to a pamphlet war and presented its case to the court of public opinion. Just as the Association employed ex-EIC men to present its case for the damages caused it by the Dutch and the East India Company while offering Madagascar as a prospective new home for willing migrants, the EIC backed a countering view of the island's features penned by another former Courteen factor who had returned to the company fold. Unfortunately for the Courteen

---

[49] At a Court at Whytehall, 10 December 1639, PC 2/51, ff. 165–8 at 167; A Court of Committees, 19 December 1642, *CCMEIC* 2: 295–6. For Southampton and Mauritius, Boothby, *A breife description of the most famous island of Madagascar*, 22; D[arell], *Strange News from the Indies*, 11. The King ordered the EIC to "fully reimburse" Southampton and his partners; Orders of His Majesty in Council, 26 January 1639/40, *CCMEIC* 2: 8.

[50] Boothby, *A breife description of the most famous island of Madagascar*, 10.

[51] A Court of Committees, 19 December 1642, *CCMEIC* 2: 295–6 at 296; Order revoked, 18 March 1642/3, *CJ* 3: 9.

Association, the reality of the destruction of their colony made Powle Waldegrave's contemptuous firsthand account of the 1644 attempt to settle Madagascar – "whereof not Twelve" of the 140 colonists survived – and of the descriptions of the island offered by pro-colonization authors Boothby and Walter Hamond, rather more compelling.[52]

The Courteen venture proved such a spectacular failure that the vast sums involved prolonged the disputes over Sir William's estate and the alleged injuries and damages it had incurred in the East (as well as the West) Indies until the 1680s. By this time, William Courteen III, Sir William's grandson, had charge of the crumbs of his family's fortune and the case had come to involve an array of aristocrats and merchants as well the English and Dutch governments in a battle over the thousands of pounds alleged to be at stake and who had done what to whom. In the shorter term, meanwhile, the East India Company had seen off the challenges to its monopoly.[53]

Meanwhile, however, the Courteen imperial concept and the vestiges of the apparatus created to implement it came under the control of a group of men led by the ubiquitous Maurice Thompson. By 1642, "M.T." had joined the Courteen Association. Within four years, Thompson had obtained Courteen's commission to trade in Asia and had taken direction of the surviving Courteen interests. In December 1649, Thompson acquired Courteen's papers either from Lady Katherine Courteen, Sir William's daughter-in-law, or from John Darrell, another Courteen partisan who had served as the group's trader at its chief Indian factory at Carwar.[54]

As the Civil Wars drew to a close in the late 1640s, Thompson and his own associates began to build on what they had acquired and, in doing so, carried on the fight with the East India Company over the best means of encouraging English interests in the East Indies as well as, of course, pursuing personal profits. In the course of this battle, Thompson and his partners formulated their own plan, based on the Courteen vision, for the better ordering of English affairs in the Indian Ocean that similarly linked their activities in Asia, Africa, and America. In sum, these "new

---

[52] Waldegrave, *An Answer to Mr. Boothbies Book*, 4.   [53] Carew, *Lex Talionis*.

[54] Alderman Thomas Andrewes, Robert Heynes, John Lewis, and Thomas Best at Gombroon to the President and Council at Surat, 4 March 1646/7, Foster, *The English Factories in India, 1618–1669*, 109–11 at 110; Edward Thompson [aboard the *Ruth*, Maurice Thompson's ship] at Goa, to the President and Council at Surat, 26 August 1647, ibid., 148–50 at 149. The Thompsons also appear to have been involved with the EIC by 1644; Waldegrave, *An Answer to Mr. Boothbies Book*, 22.

modelers," as Darrell styled them, planned "to settle Factories and plant Collonies after the Dutch manner," although the level of their esteem in which they held the Dutch example was more than matched by the depths of the suspicion they held for those who had devised it. Moreover, in pursuing their plan, they proved rather more capable, formidable and perhaps more fortunate opponents of both the East India Company and the Dutch than their predecessors in interest had been.[55]

[55] D[arell], *Strange News from the Indies*, 11 (for Madagascar and Mauritius), 24 (for the 1642 involvement of "Mr. M.T." in the Courteen project), 29 (for "M.T." acquiring the papers related to the Courteen enterprise and reference to "new modelers"); Graves, *A Brief Narrative and Deduction of the several Remarkable Cases of Sir William Courten, and Sir Paul Pyndar*, 4, asserted that Thompson acquired these East India papers from Lady Katherine. For the Courteen attempt to colonize Madagascar, see complaint of Thomas Andrewes, Francis Allen, Steven Eastwick, George Thompson, Samuel Moyer, and Maurice Thompson, merchants against the East India Company, 1651, C6/114/6, f. 6, TNA.

5

Civil War and English Overseas Interests

The implementation of their scheme required that these "new modelers" exercise an authority that they did not enjoy in 1641. A decade later, though, they had certainly achieved a position that enabled them to initiate and direct matters as they desired. How had they achieved this? How revolutionary was the overseas program envisioned by these "new modelers" – an obvious reference to the New Model Army whose victory in the English Civil Wars brought expectations of the application of a new broom to many aspects of society? Did the coming to power of "M.T." and his cohort reflect the social and political changes effected by their military counterpart during the 1640s and 1650s? What connected the development of the English state and that of overseas trade and colonization after Charles I abandoned his increasingly rebellious capital in January 1642?

These questions have, of course, received plenty of scholarly attention, and Robert Brenner's conception has provided the most influential analysis. Grounded in impressive archival research, Brenner argued that "new merchants," including notably Maurice Thompson, in pursuing commercial opportunities beyond the traditional northwestern European venues after 1550, overthrew the established leadership of the City of London. Then, as they transformed the scope of English commerce over the course of a century, the last generation of these "interlopers" took control of the city's government and used their accumulated wealth and power to transform the English sociopolitical landscape by 1653. Brenner's analysis has provided an attractive platform for those who believe that what took place in England during the mid-seventeenth century constituted a revolution and one brought about by economic forces.[1]

This comprehension, though, presumes that the likes of Thompson acted as interlopers against the positions of politically established merchants. Given the nature of the relationship of the English state to overseas trade and colonization, however, the lines Brenner drew between the interests of the historical actors appear to be too firm: people like Thompson, not to mention his patron, Warwick, had little difficulty working with the government when it suited them as, for instance, in Providence Island; when it did not, they did not bother with it as, for instance, in Guinea. Every other overseas trader and colonizer engaged in similar competition and behaved in similar ways: if they could secure the approval of the state, so much the better; if they could not, then did it really matter given the inability of the government of Charles I to achieve much of an imperial reach? Correspondingly, does a characterization of these people as engineers of social, political, and economic overhaul jibe with our understanding of the history of seventeenth-century English politics, economics, and society? Did a revolution take place in mid-seventeenth-century England? Where did overseas trade and colonization fit into what was happening in the metropolis in the 1640s and 1650s during this period? How did metropolitan circumstances affect English colonies and English long-range endeavors, and vice versa?

Reaching helpful answers to these questions necessitates clarification with respect to what it is we are talking about. First, a case might be well made for a "revolutionary England," if the historian ends the enquiry in 1653 as Brenner did. Such a study would thus include the English Civil Wars (1642–8) that resulted in parliamentary victory; the execution of Charles I; the abolition of monarchy, episcopacy, and House of Lords; and the uncovering of previously unimagined (and unimaginable) social and political views, such as those articulated by the Levellers and the Diggers. Ending the analysis in 1653 also enables the historian to ignore what came after April of that year: the dissolution of the Rump Parliament, which marked the end of the short-lived English Republic

---

[1] Brenner, *Merchants and Revolution*, references Thompson in particular over 100 times (732). Recent work that relies on Brenner as the platform for their own characterizations of the history of mid-seventeenth-century England and its Empire includes Donoghue, *Fire under the Ashes*, 334, 337, and Pestana, *The English Atlantic in an Age of Revolution*, 19.

(1649–53) and the founding of the Cromwellian Protectorate (1653–9), followed by the restoration of monarchy, episcopacy, and House of Lords in 1660. This was accompanied by the return underground of those radical socioeconomic views that confused and horrified so many contemporaries.[2]

While this turn of events constituted a revolution in the seventeenth-century terms, which tended to define these things in a planetary sense, the return in the 1660s – even superficially – to the orthodox forms of the 1630s requires a clearer explanation if one wishes to apply a revolutionary label to the post-republic period of English history. The same problem of assessing the pace, nature, and scope of change also arises if the chronological frame starts too far before the breakdown of the government that occurred at the start in 1642. Brenner, for instance, begins his account in 1550 in accordance with the view of the English Revolution as a long-term concept with myriad preconditions held by his mentor, Lawrence Stone.[3] Yet while our understanding of seventeenth-century England and its Civil Wars has moved on since 1972, certain American historians of seventeenth-century English overseas trade and colonization seem to have been slow in accepting that it has done so. Indeed, in a recent analysis, which focuses on a "transatlantic network" that incorporated London's Coleman Street ward and New England, "no space" is "wasted discussing whether these events (ca. 1640–60) amounted to a revolution" as it "is self-evident that such profound changes were fundamental, systematic, and therefore revolutionary in nature."

This a priori approach to the study of the past enables the hauling of the Marxist view of the unfolding of the past out of mothballs albeit in an "Atlantic" winch. It also provides the opportunity to bemoan a good revolution turned sour: the "revolutionary" changes that occurred in England also "helped give birth to the frontier and the plantation as colonial institutions that became integral to the formation of seventeenth-century racial hierarchies, steeped as they were in the blood and violence of mass enslavement, settler annihilation of Indian peoples, and catastrophic wars fought for the glory and power of empire" outside the metropolis. Moreover, the attendant and "needless killing and enslavement of hundreds and thousands of people from around the

---

[2] Lake and Como, "'Orthodoxy' and Its Discontents"; Como, "Secret Printing, the Crisis of 1640, and the Origins of Civil War Radicalism."
[3] Stone, *The Causes of the English Revolution.*

English Atlantic for the sake of profit, Protestantism, and English imperial glory," not to mention "the violence of imperial expansion" and "its corollary, the proliferation of global capitalism," were "orchestrated in large part" by the "elite" denizens of Coleman Street over the "radical" opposition of their "class-conscious" neighbors. The parish's "most militant republicans" objected to the "massive scale of corruption, slavery, and carnage" that merchants, aristocrats, and their clerical supporters perpetrated in the course of their activities. These radicals, who "hailed from classes and occupations that ranged from printers and merchant clothiers to sailors and cobblers," also "challenged the Revolutionary state and its imperial ambitions" – support for which was "orchestrated in large part by their elite peers on Coleman Street" – "as gross betrayals of the Revolution" by "championing religious toleration and democratic republicanism."[4]

This English Revolution also spawned an enduring paradox in imperial terms, according to Michael Braddick: "The foundation of the navigation system [created in 1651 with the first Navigation Act] was the foundation too of the first English (later British) empire, and it contained the central contradiction of later imperial life – the forcible imposition of English liberties, and their costs." Who was responsible for this? Braddick nominates the "circle" of the energetic intellectual emigré from the Continent, Samuel Hartlib, draughtsman of the Navigation Act, imperial thinker, scientist, and pursuer of knowledge, and another group "with which his interests eventually intersected": citing Brenner, Braddick argues, "Bound together by their hostility to the great merchants of the monopolistic Chartered Companies, men like Maurice Thompson, William Barkley, and Owen Rowe can be seen at the cutting edge of the radicalization of the parliamentary cause throughout the 1640s. Their time was to come in 1651, when their influence can be seen at work in the transformation of state regulation of overseas trade."[5]

The revolutionary qualities of the events of the mid-seventeenth century may be "self-evident" to some modern observers but they were rather less so to contemporaries, which has been one of the sticking points in the eternal debates over seventeenth-century English history. One can certainly be appalled at the behavior entailed in seventeenth-

---

[4] Donoghue, *Fire under the Ashes*, 3–8; Pestana, *The English Atlantic in an Age of Revolution*, 2, 4.
[5] Braddick, *God's Fury, England's Fire*, 458, 588.

century overseas trade and colonization, but does the pronouncement of moral condemnation 375 or so years after the fact actually shed helpful historiographical light on the subjects at hand? And what was the intent of contemporaries here? To what degree – and why – did their agendas change over time? To what extent did the economic interests of opponents of the Caroline regime contribute to – let alone create – the distrust of Charles I that, in some cases, translated into a demand for regicide and an end to monarchical government? And to what degree did these political and governmental changes translate into economic and social ones?

"No one" after all, as Blair Worden has noted, "expected the extent of the Puritan Revolution. Unrevolutionary purposes bore revolutionary results": what had begun as revolt against Charles I ultimately did bring sweeping, if temporary, changes in both institutions and society. The parliamentary army that fought and won the battles against the Royalists had the chief responsibility for this: it backed the Protectorate against both Royalists and republicans; it had (reluctantly and briefly) governed the country; and General George Monck and his troops, a number of whom came from New England, engineered the return of kingly government in 1660.[6]

Many people, including Maurice Thompson and his sometime partners Thomas Andrews, Samuel Moyer, and William Pennoyer, supported the campaign against the Crown in each of what might be termed its phases. As noted above, the initial question of how to frame one's subject has constituted a central issue in coming to terms with mid-seventeenth-century English history since time immemorial. When did resistance become rebellion? When did rebellion become revolution? Yet the historiographical analyses of the sort cited above give the impression that these merchants took the lead in directing, both philosophically and fiscally, a revolutionary English state to take an imperial turn. First, though, this state had to come into existence and it did so only after those who came to control it had assumed power within the shell of the old regime. This enabled them to further overseas ambitions that they had already been pursuing, for years in some cases. Furthermore, this entity was not some sort of autonomous abstraction: those pursuing overseas commercial and colonization aims used their positions, as well as the personal and political affinities they had with other participants in the

---

[6] Worden, *God's Instruments*, 1.

Interregnum regimes, to control the levers of state power after March 1642. They did so to the advantages – indistinguishable as they saw them – of themselves and the nation. There is no evidence to support the view that the involvement of the Thompson group in overseas trade and colonization had any necessary bearing on their support for Parliament. Indeed, a number of their counterparts and partners, such as Nicholas Crispe, became Royalists when the lines between supporters and opponents of the King became more clearly drawn after 1641.[7]

While bearing in mind the concerns about anachronism and teleology that the study of the Civil Wars often raises, it is neither anachronistic nor teleological to recognize that serious concerns with Crown religious policies, which entailed economic, political, and constitutional elements, manifested themselves from the onset of Charles I's reign. For instance, it had been the practice of a parliament called at the accession of a new monarch to grant that new sovereign the right to collect tonnage and poundage customs for life; that is, until the Parliament of 1625 gave Charles I a desultory grant of these revenues for one year only. Regarding this maneuver as an encroachment on his prerogative as well as an insult to royal honor that compounded the injury of his barren treasury, the King continued to collect these duties after the parliamentary grant expired. This practice aggravated the concerns that he was exceeding that prerogative at the expense of the liberties of his subjects.

This dispute was incorporated into the rancorous exchanges over the government's disastrous conduct of the wars of the 1620s against Spain and France, over the ham-fisted attempts it employed to pay for these campaigns, and over the expanding influence of Arminianism and its adherents in the Church of England. This heated atmosphere became further aggravated by the assassination of the detested Duke of Buckingham in August 1628, the ratification of the Petition of Right that demanded the King address the concerns raised in Parliament, and the resulting decision by the monarch to govern without the necessity of parliaments, economizing and resorting to fiscal creativity as necessary to keep the Crown's finances afloat, after 1629.[8]

---

[7] E.g., An Act for the Advancing and Regulating of the Trade of this Commonwealth, [1 August 1650], *AOI*, 403–6, includes Thompson among the names of the commissioners charged with regulating trade.

[8] For this history, see Russell, *Parliaments and English Politics*; Thompson, *Parliamentary History in the 1620s*; Cogswell, "A Low Road to Extinction"; Cust, *The Forced Loan and English Politics*. Orthodox Calvinists such as Warwick, Saye, Matthew Cradock, Maurice

Charles might have sustained this course and continued to deprive those of his subjects who objected to his policies of the constitutional platform of a parliament in which to air their grievances. His attempt to introduce a new Prayer Book into the Scottish liturgy, however, resulted in the rejection of royal religious policy and the adoption of a National Covenant in the King's northern realm in 1638; the ill-prepared, ill-equipped, and ill-led army sent to recover the situation predictably failed to achieve victory over the resolute, well-trained Covenanters. The catastrophe, in addition to the military fiasco, for Charles in his conflict with this Scottish subjects was the financial drain it placed on an exchequer already stretched to the breaking point: this meant that he had to entertain summoning an unwanted parliament. Moreover, the control of Scotland by the rebels invited the prospect of an alliance with those who had become disaffected by the philosophy of the Caroline government in England.

What did this defining series of events in seventeenth-century English history have to do with overseas trade and colonization especially? A review of the chronology reminds us how the collapse of the Caroline regime in 1640–2 created the opportunity for those who worked against that regime, including certain promoters of overseas trade and colonization, to take control of an alternative state. A number of promoters of overseas initiatives made the airing of their concerns with the character of the Church of England and other Crown policies a consistent irritation for the monarch. Among those unhappy with the state of England in the late 1630s who held longstanding interests and involvement in overseas trade and colonization included the Earls of Warwick and Pembroke, Viscount Saye and Sele, and Lords Robartes, Wharton, and Brooke. This knot of aristocrats had worked hand-in-glove with their extensive clientage in pursuing an anti-Spanish agenda overseas and protecting godly ministers from the attentions of the ecclesiastical authorities carrying out Archbishop William Laud's views on religious practice, which stressed prayer, contemplation, and ceremony at the expense of the sermons and disputation of Scripture by the laity

Thompson, and John Winthrop regarded the Arminian view that human behavior could influence the divine judgment on an individual's salvation as the thin wedge of "popery" and undoubtedly regarded its ascendancy at court as an indication that Charles I tended toward the contemporary religious and constitutional views of the French monarchy and the Holy Roman Empire where efforts to roll back Protestant liberties were in full throttle; Wilson, *The Thirty Years War* 197–266, 347–61, 375–9.

preferred by the godly.[9] Warwick and Saye also organized resistance to the collection of the Forced Loan that Charles sought in 1627 to pay for the war against France and Spain after Parliament failed to vote him subsidies. They did the same when the King sought to extend the ship money writs – levies the monarch could order collected for the preservation of the realm's coasts and ports – from the coastal shires to the entire kingdom – without recourse to a parliament.[10]

The mercantile clients of these aristocrats, including Maurice Thompson, worked with Warwick, most particularly. They gained influence over the City Artillery Company, which boasted a membership of some five hundred men, had a substantial quantity of arms, and conducted regular drills. At the same time, they continued work on Providence Island and seeking out new prospects for colonization, such as Tobago, as well as privateering. Warwick, who acquired the Caribbean interests of Pembroke in 1638, increased his involvement in America as the 1630s wore on.[11]

This is not to say, however, that such networks functioned as the tools of their aristocratic leaders. The clients here certainly gravitated to those who could offer them substantial advantages such as land, capital, office, and connections as per norm, while patrons sought clients who could render valuable service and do the hard work. But the affinity here went deeper as the people who formed these associations had strong common religious, as well as economic, ties. As Calvinists and as orthodox members, as they saw it, of the Church of England, they sought, if not expected, a further reformation of that Church in strict accordance with Scripture (the precise strictness could be a bone of contention). Yet even those adherents of predestination who did not identify with a hotter religious sensibility could regard the continuing promotion of the free-will doctrines of the sort ascribed to the Dutch theologian Arminius as dangerous. Accompanied by the

---

[9] Atherton, "Cathedrals, Laudianism, and the British Churches."

[10] For the refusal of Warwick and Saye to pay the Forced Loan, see Gardiner, *History of England*, 6: 150; to pay ship money, 8: 93, 203. Warwick worked with his client, the sometime Massachusetts Bay colonist Sir Richard Saltonstall, against the levying of ship money from 1635 until the Long Parliament put an end to the collection; Holmes, *The Eastern Association in the English Civil War*, 20–1.

[11] Adamson, *The Noble Revolt*, 65–82, which notes that the Artillery Company was not necessarily as "puritan" as the presence of the Warwick associates might suggest: Sir Paul Pindar and Nicholas Crispe, whom Adamson identifies as Thompson's "arch-enemy" for some reason, were also members (70).

attempts of ecclesiastical authorities to root out godly ministers from the Church – rather than promote them as the likes of Warwick believed was the proper function of bishops – constituted an alarming turn. Thus, the concerted episcopal assault on the godly from 1628, when Laud was translated to the see of London, provided a mass of carefully assembled evidence that, so far from subsiding into extinction, a refreshed "popery" was again threatening "liberty" – a concept that was inextricably intertwined with religion for seventeenth-century English people.[12]

Those who objected to Arminianism, to the questionable financial recourses employed by the Crown, and to those "evil counsels" who advocated these policies seized with both the hands the opportunity presented by the King's Scottish misadventures. When the Short Parliament convened in April 1640 the members refused to grant the Crown any subsidies until their grievances were redressed. Charles, though, refused to be cowed and dissolved the assemblage after just three weeks. This, however, did nothing to address the problems of the English army, and – almost certainly with the approbation if not at the instigation of Warwick and his associates – the Scots duly invaded England. When Philip IV of Spain suddenly diverted funds in order to suppress a revolt in Catalonia that had been earmarked to help Charles pay for his army, the English monarch was left with an empty exchequer with little prospect for filling it while the morale of his troops was at a similarly low ebb. The attempt to repel the Scots resulted in the embarrassing loss of Newcastle, the port from which London received its fuel, along with the entire northeast of the country by the end of August. A truce was reached but the Covenanter army remained in the field collecting a substantial annuity.[13]

On the heels of this disaster, a group of peers, led by Warwick and Saye, petitioned Charles to summon another parliament. These lords had command of the situation thanks to the control of London exercised by their clients. Following the dissolution of the Short Parliament, apprentices, artisans, and mariners rioted in Lambeth against Laud in May 1640, although the motivations for the attack on the

---

[12] Tyacke, "The Puritan Paradigm of English Politics, 1558–1642"; Bremer, *Building a New Jerusalem*, 83–99; Hunt, *The Puritan Moment*, 163–72.

[13] By 21 January 1640/1, the cost of the Scottish invasion to the Crown was given at an astronomical £514,000, or, Adamson observes, about one-half of its annual revenue prior to the invasion; *The Noble Revolt*, 171.

Archbishop's palace remain unclear. Then, in September, Thompson and his fellow overseas merchant and Artillery Company member, John Venn, took the lead in circulating a "City Petition" to the King, signed by a reported 10,000 inhabitants, which demanded a new parliament and end to the war with the Scots; Thompson himself led the delegation that brought this petition to Charles at York, where he had taken personal charge of the renewed campaign against the rebels, on 16 September.[14]

Bereft of funds, the debt to the Scots increasing daily and disaffection with the lack of a result achieved by the Short Parliament continuing to manifest itself in the capital, the King, in the end, had to accede to the clamor for another parliament. He became convinced, however, that he might turn the situation to his advantage, issuing the writs for the new assembly to convene on 3 November.[15]

Unfortunately for Charles, his opponents were more than ready for this gathering and their mood had not improved since the abrupt dissolution of their last assembly. They immediately moved for a redress of their grievances but also targeted those royal advisors they regarded as particular threats to the realm, to parliaments, and to themselves. At the top of this list was Thomas Wentworth, Earl of Strafford, who had been a leading proponent of the Petition of Right along with many of his enemies before becoming one of the King's chief advisors during the Personal Rule. In addition to improving the royal administration of Ireland as Lord Deputy, Strafford had evidence of treasonable correspondence between his enemies and the Scots. Unfortunately for him, though, his enemies struck first, bringing charges of high treason against him based on a letter in which Strafford invited the King to use an Irish army to put an end to his English troubles. The Earl was imprisoned in the Tower and the Lords eventually attainted him. Popular demonstrations against the Earl compelled Charles to sign the death warrant of his devoted servant, to whom he had pledged his honor and support, and Strafford went to the block on 12 May 1641. The spectacular demise of this once-powerful Crown official provided a clear indication of the impotence of the King and the ascendancy of Strafford's enemies: Warwick and Saye were

---

[14] Adamson, *The Noble Revolt*, 79–80.
[15] The widening of the crisis put paid to any lingering Madagascar dreams that Arundel might have entertained as the Earl Marshal found himself on 1 September 1640 in charge of arranging defensive preparations in London against an expected insurrection in the capital; Adamson, *The Noble Revolt*, 54–5.

among the official witnesses of the Earl's execution. The character of their animosity toward Charles I himself, though, remains unclear: while many of those sitting in parliament (and elsewhere in the realm) entertained the notion of placing restrictions on this monarch, especially his selection of his advisors, there was no agitation for his removal and certainly no one conceived of overthrowing the monarchy in 1642.

With Strafford removed, though, rebellion broke out in Ireland at the end of October while Charles was in Edinburgh failing to reconcile with his Scottish subjects. The assaults – real and imaginary – perpetrated on Protestants put the Parliament on high alert. Their fear of "bloodthirsty papists" combining with "evil counsels" to the monarch to destroy religion and liberty, however, along with the convenient absence from England of the King, provided the parliamentary leadership with the opportunity – or the pretext – to take effective control of the government. Having had the first reports of the revolt, they were able to take the lead in raising the money and organizing the force required to subdue the Irish rebels. They also launched a(nother) simultaneous campaign to crack down on Catholics in England. The maneuver, as John Adamson has noted, "effectively removed the business of government from the king's hands. An entire political system, in which royal favour had been an essential prerequisite of political power was subverted, if not wholly eradicated."[16]

Eradication, though, did come in fairly short order and in the teeth of fervent opposition from a furious Charles as well as within the Parliament. First came a rehearsal of "the multiplicity, sharpness and malignity of those evils under which we have now many years suffered" accompanied by a series of "humble desires of your people in a parliamentary way, for preserving the peace and safety of the kingdom from the malicious designs of the Popish party" in the Grand Remonstrance. Although couched in language of dutifulness and obedience, this document unequivocally declared the allegiance of a narrow majority of MPs to "the state" above their obedience to the monarch.[17]

---

[16] Adamson, *The Noble Revolt*, 428.
[17] The Remonstrance passed the Commons by a vote of 159 to 148. Imperial thinking, in accord with the views of the Providence Island group (whose colony had been overrun by the Spaniards at the end of the previous May) appears in the third grievance among those grouped as evidence of the "greatest sway" of the "Jesuited counsels" to support Spain "whereby to make way for the change of religion which they intended at home." It laments further the "diverting of His Majesty's course of wars from the West Indies, which was the most facile and hopeful way for this kingdom to prevail against the

The remonstrance, having been presented to Charles on 1 December and then published, received a predictable if moderate rejection on 23 December. A week later, Parliament debated a Militia Bill to raise and support an army for Ireland that provided for parliamentary appointment of state officers and included language that these officers held their positions by virtue of parliamentary – rather than royal – authority. This maneuver furthered the move to deprive an untrustworthy monarch, ostensibly in the clutches of "evil counselors," of access to any revenue or to any force not controlled by Parliament.

The King, incensed by the restrictions on his prerogative that he had already been compelled to accept, absolutely refused to accept this further and highly public encroachment on his powers and renewed his efforts to regain control of the situation. His reaction justified the enduring suspicions the parliamentary leaders had of the level of sincerity entailed in his promises to work with them. Unfortunately for Charles, then, his attempt to seize five MPs on 5 January 1642 failed spectacularly: they not only escaped arrest but the King's blatant violation of parliamentary privilege poured a huge quantity of fuel onto the belief that he was untrustworthy and tyrannical. The resulting furor led Charles to decide that London was no longer safe; he and his family departed the capital on 10 January. He did not return until his execution seven years later.

The King's withdrawal created an extraordinary, not to say unprecedented, scenario. Previous coups d'état had either brought the accession of a new monarch, such as Edward III in 1327, or war between competitors for kingly power, as with the fifteenth-century Wars of the Roses. In 1642, though, no rival claimant to the throne around whom opponents of Charles could assemble existed. Instead, Parliament provided the vehicle both for fighting the King and for claiming the authority to rule in the name of the sovereign. Thus, the English state as it had been understood since the creation of Parliament in the thirteenth century was fractured: Parliament retained its authority to pass bills and to form committees in accordance with its preexisting functions, but the monarch would not sign the bills he was sent nor would he subject his official appointments to parliamentary vetting, while his opponents, for their

Spaniard, to an expenseful and successless attempt upon Cadiz, which was so ordered as if it had rather been intended to make us weary of war than to prosper in it"; The Grand Remonstrance, with the Petition accompanying it, presented to the King, 1 December 1641, Gardiner, *Constitutional Documents of the Puritan Revolution*, 202–32 at 203, 204, 207–8.

part, would not recognize those appointments he made without their approval. This situation quickly approached a paralyzing crisis when Charles again refused to consider the Militia Bill leaving open the response to the Irish rebellion, control of the armed forces, the power of official appointment, and, indeed, the entire conduct of state power.[18]

While some MPs and others resolved this vexing problem by joining Charles, the parliamentary leaders took the view that the King's departure left the government in limbo; he had not abdicated but remained under the sway of evil counsels. In their minds, only Parliament, which had already secured legislation against its dissolution without its agreement as well as a statute that guaranteed the summoning of a parliament every three years, possessed the requisite constitutional status to fill the governmental vacuum: a monarchy in which subjects ruled on behalf of the monarch. Thus, Parliament would continue its functions of proposing, debating, and approving bills, including those related to the levying and assessment of taxation, without regard for the royal assent, but it would now also establish new councils and appoint military and other officers required for running the state. It began by converting the Militia Bill into a Militia Ordinance that gave its control over the kingdom's armed forces in March 1642 and appointed lords-lieutenant for the various shires, including Warwick for Essex, Holland for Berkshire, and Robartes in Cornwall. This act also gave the crucial oversight of London to a group that included the overseas merchants and radicals Owen Rowe, Stephen Estwick, and John Fowke.[19]

It is no accident that C.H. Firth and R.S. Rait began their edition of *Acts and Ordinances of the Interregnum* with this statute: simply put, its approval signaled the completion of the displacement of monarchical authority for the first time in English history. After enacting it, the Parliament appointed Warwick Lord High Admiral and the Earl of Essex as Captain General of the army. Meanwhile, the King, having been refused entry into Hull, where he intended to secure "his" magazine but had been barred by the governor, and having failed to secure control of the Navy, made his way to York where he issued a commission of array. In August, his army engaged its parliamentary counterpart at Edgehill: civil war had begun.

---

[18] This bill passed the Commons by 158 votes to 125.

[19] An Ordinance of the Lords and Commons in Parliament, for the Safety and Defence of the Kingdom of England, and Dominion of Wales, [5 March 1641/2], *AOI*, 1–5.

Those who frame the English Revolution in modern terms miss the point of what happened. First, the coup against Strafford was initiated and directed by aristocratic leaders, such as Warwick, although this movement necessarily entailed the full participation of their clients just as their pursuit of overseas commercial and colonizing ventures did. Thus, without in any way minimizing the significance of the shifts caused by the assumption of state authority by the Parliamentarians, these networks continued to operate in accordance with the customary sociopolitical formula through 1645. Three years before, the sight of the King trudging away after his humiliating rejection at the gates of Hull must have led the Warwick group to think the struggle for power at court was over. Against expectations, though, Charles succeeded in rallying his party and forming an army that nearly carried the day at the first civil war battle at Edgehill in August as well as at Turnham Green near London the following year.[20]

This Royalist persistence, which flickered until the Battle of Preston (17–19 August 1648), obliged Parliament to ramp up a war effort to an extent that obliged the clarity of goals and motives beyond hedging the power of an untrustworthy monarch. Thus, it shifted the command structure of its army from the local, militia-based framework to a national, regimental one. This move also facilitated *esprit de corps* among the New Model Army that blended with the essentially egalitarian nature of Calvinist belief – but only with respect to other members of the elect – and the crushing of the Royalist army at Naseby on 14 June 1645 to promote a sense of the Army's special role in furthering the providential course of history against the royal Antichrist. It also stimulated the emergence of new sorts of religious, social, and political views that based an individual's worth on their godliness rather than on their estate or lineage, although the degree of popularity that these views were held by contemporaries remains the subject of considerable debate. While the Levellers and the other radical groups of the late 1640s subsided almost as quickly as they emerged, less enthusiastic but no less committed reformers, notably Oliver Cromwell, who not coincidentally came to prominence at this time, could come to the view that the removal of the monarch and then of monarchy was required.[21]

The connections between this history and overseas matters came, first and perhaps foremost, in the eternally vexing case of Ireland, whence

---

[20] Hutton, "The Structure of the Royalist Party."
[21] Worden, "Providence and Politics in Cromwellian England"; Gentles, "The Politics of Fairfax' Army, 1645–9."

rebellion had added a match to the overheated atmosphere of 1641. For English governments, the neighboring island's proximity had long encouraged a sort of dual sensibility of Ireland as both a dangerous haven for enemies abetted by "ungovernable" elements in that kingdom and a treasure room from which to extract rewards for loyal followers. The rebellion that had kicked over the traces of Strafford's government brought the former of these concerns to the forefront of English consciences.

For godly people the collapse of the Caroline regime provided the opportunity for truly reformed Christian beliefs and their practitioners to flourish. Indeed, events had presented them with the opportunity to mesh economic and imperial agendas with their deeply Calvinistic world-view, including the self-regard of the believer as a chosen member of the elect and an enduring fear and loathing of popery when the Irish revolt broke out at the end of October 1641, even before the departure of the King from London and relations between Parliamentarian and Royalist became increasingly ossified. To godly minds, if they did not seize this opportunity, the consequences of that negligence would not bear contemplating.[22]

Thus, we should note that a number of overseas merchants responded immediately to the Irish emergency without regard, of course, to their attitudes toward subsequent developments. This intervention, however, further illustrates the problem with conceiving of the Civil Wars and the advance of overseas trade and colonization in grand terms such as "revolution." As early as February 1642, "a group of London merchants approached the house of commons with a plan for the suppression of the Irish rebellion," and in March this plan was secured with two and one-half million acres of rebel land and the subscription collected an impressive £306,718. In June, Parliament approved an Irish Adventure, whose backers included Maurice Thompson, John Wood, Thomas Andrews, Moyer, and Pennoyer.[23]

---

[22] Morrill, *The Nature of the English Revolution*, 58–65.
[23] The Ordinance for the Sea Adventure to Ireland, 17 June 1642, *LJ* 5: 145. The list of Adventurers who drew Irish land in the lotteries of 1653 and 1659 after the "settlement" of the island includes Thomas Andrews (790 acres), Nicholas Crispe (901), Richard Crispe (600), Stephen Estwick (1,550), John Fowke (600), Richard Hutchinson (760), William Jessop, secretary to the Providence Island Company (310), Martin Noell (1,040), William Pennoyer (900), and Maurice Thompson (3,243); Bottigheimer, *English Money and Irish Land*, appendix B: 198–213.

The "Adventurers" quickly involved themselves more deeply in the parliamentary government, especially those aspects that dealt with religion, finance, and, of course, overseas matters. Thompson was appointed to a four-man commission sent by Parliament to the Netherlands in July 1643 to acquire property and raise funds via subscriptions that would be repaid as loans (Thompson's Courteen ties came into play here again as Sir William's nephew, Bouden, a merchant in Middleburg, was appointed as one of the receivers for this venture) "for the relief of Ireland."[24] Having subscribed £1,075 in return for 16,218 acres in Counties Armagh and Antrim, he also received a commission for another £1,670 8d in 1645; in 1648 Andrews and Thompson led another Irish subscription of £83,129 13s 4d, for which they also served as treasurers. Moyer and Thompson's brothers, William and George, also made regular contributions to the Irish war effort.[25]

Many of Thompson's partners, including Warwick, Pembroke, Wharton, Saye, and Samuel Vassall, served on the commission that oversaw the levying and collection of the excise on various commodities such as liquor to support the Parliamentarian effort.[26] In January 1643, Andrews, Thompson, Fowke, Richard Chambers, William Barkley, Francis Allyn, and Estwick became Commissioners of the Customs, having advanced Parliament £20,000 for the right to collect that sum

[24] Ordinance appointing Commissioners to receive Subscriptions in Holland for Ireland, [29 July 1643], *AOI*, 220–1.

[25] *CJ* 2: 671–3; *CJ* 4: 303–5; Contract for supplying the Forces in Ireland with Provisions and Cloaths, 21 March 1647/8, *LJ* 10: 157–61. This private force, although the statute included Lord High Admiral Warwick as one of its commanders, thus operated without any check, aside from a £2,000 bond to cover cases of pillage of "the King's Subjects, Friends, or Allies," on its behavior outside that of the subscribers; Lindley, "Irish Adventurers and Godly Militants in the 1640s." Several analyses, noting the participation of these colonizers in suppressing it, stress the importance of the Irish rebellion to English imperial history. These argue that the contempt and fear with which the English held the rebels translated into, first, an unprecedented state commitment to directing overseas action that provided a precedent for future cases and, then, into the creation of a new state-appointed bureaucracy to oversee imperial policy while captured rebels were added to the coerced labor mix of Anglo-America; e.g., Games, *Web of Empire*, 255–87; Pestana, *English Atlantic in an Age of Revolution*, 181–93. Ireland, though, must be regarded as a distinctive case from other areas of English overseas activity: it was officially a kingdom, whose administration was appointed directly by the Crown, rather than a colony. Then, while colonization certainly took place there, this was enabled by the defeat of rebels rather than by "discovery." Then, as sketched in above, these private interests, rather than the state, led the response to the 1641 rebellion as well as provided the impetus for Cromwell's expedition of 1649.

[26] Ordinance for regulating the Excise, [6 June 1645], *AOI*, 691–2.

out of the monies they received, plus 8 percent interest. Thus, the collection of customs operated, albeit with Parliament rather than the King appointing the farmers, as it had prior to 1642.[27]

Then, after Parliament removed the bishops, it appointed a committee to oversee religious matters to assume the erstwhile episcopal function of overseeing orthodox practice. The membership of this new entity included Warwick, Wharton, Saye, Robartes, Vassall, George Fenwick, and Venn.[28] At the end of December 1647, when war threatened to resume, Parliament appointed Moyer, Thompson, and Pennoyer to the Militia Committee for Tower Hamlets, the mandate of which included rating, assessing, and collecting money to support the Army and punishing delinquents.[29]

In terms of the institutions of the English state and the wider world, with which of course they had particular concern, Warwick and his associates assumed oversight of the plantations on 2 November 1643. This parliamentary commission constitutes the third governmental institution to have been dedicated to colonial affairs in English history. Its immediate predecessor, the Commission for Foreign Plantations, created in April 1634 (recommissioned in 1636) and chaired by Laud until the Archbishop's impeachment in early 1641, had claimed extensive powers of oversight and coordination, including first, and perhaps foremost, "to impose penalties and imprisonment for offenses in ecclesiastical matters," as well as to review and replace governors, establish courts and appoint magistrates, to receive and resolve "all manner of complaints from the colonies," to regulate charters and patents, and to revoke those surreptitiously or unduly obtained.[30]

---

[27] For which see Chapter 4, note 18. This authority was renewed for another year on 25 March 1643, Ordinance for the Commissioners of the Customs to repay themselves 20000l. advanced for the Navy and to remain in Office a Year, 25 March 1643, *LJ* 5: 670–2.

[28] An Ordinance to exclude improper persons from the Sacrament, [5 June 1646], *AOI*, 852–85.

[29] An Ordinance for Constituting a Committee of Militia within the Hamblets of the Tower of London, 8 January 1647/8, *AOI*, 1057–8.

[30] Ordinance for the Government of the Plantations in the West Indies, 2 November 1643, *AOI*, 331–3. The commission was renewed and several members, including the Anglo-American Fenwick, added in 1646, Ordinance to continue and amend the One concerning Foreign Plantations, 21 March 1645/6, *AOI*, 840. For its predecessor, see Commission to William Laud, Archbishop of Canterbury, Thomas Lord Coventry, Lord Keeper, Richard Neyle, Archbishop of York, Richard Earl of Portland, Lord High Treasurer, Henry Earl of Manchester, and seven other officers of state, 28 April

A comparison of the makeup of Warwick's commission with that of its predecessor illustrates the comprehensiveness of the triumph that the Earl and his allies had achieved. The Earl of Manchester was the only holdover on this committee from 1634 to 1643, while the detested Archbishop was now incarcerated in the Tower. Since Warwick now had the tiller of overseas matters he also now had possession of the governmental rubber stamp of approval of his longstanding personal anti-Spanish foreign policy, whereas in the 1630s he and other militant opponents of Spain had been obliged to conduct their activities with discretion.[31]

On closer examination, however, the ascendancy of Warwick and his allies to their government brought little practical change to English overseas trade and colonization in terms of what we might call imperial oversight or even in terms of the relationship between the colonies and the metropolis. The patterns of commerce, territorial expansion, and imperial administration that had been established prior to 1641 remained essentially in place; indeed, they intensified. Thus, the Guinea traders carried on their business; slaves were taken before, during, and after the Civil Wars and the scale of this trade had even accelerated prior to 1642. Then, while the Guinea Company was denounced as a monopoly it continued to conduct its business with Wood, Vassall, and Thompson maintaining the preeminence they had already achieved in African commerce. A similar scenario remained in place in Asia. Again, 1642 was the benchmark year, as Thompson, Pennoyer, and Moyer stepped into the Courteen Association's shoes thereby revitalizing its competition with the East India Company.[32]

With respect to Anglo-America where, unlike Africa and Asia, the English had established plantations, colonial-imperialists continued their explorations through the 1630s. In the decade after 1642, partly in response to the political turmoil of the period, those

---

1634, *CSPC AWI* 1: 177; renewed 10 April 1636, *CSPC AWI* 1: 232; Andrews, *British Committees, Commissions, and Councils of Trade and Plantations*, 16–17.

[31] Craven, "The Earl of Warwick, a Speculator in Piracy." As further evidence of the intimate connections between the parliamentary state and overseas traders, Simon Groenveld has noted that about half of the "Parliamentary Navy" at the beginning of the Civil Wars consisted of ships hired from godly merchants. These owners also leant their expertise and experience to the parliamentary naval administration; "The English Civil Wars as a Cause of the First Anglo-Dutch War," 548.

[32] Deposition of Thomas Crispe, London merchant, "having been diverse voyages upon the Coast of Guinea for" Sir Nicholas Crispe and Company, 15 March 1664/5, T 70/169, ff. 35–6.

colonial-imperialists continued these efforts. In addition to the continuing probes of New Englanders, Virginians spread south and west, while settlements in the Bahamas and Surinam were founded by migrants from Bermuda and Barbados.[33]

Accordingly, trans-Atlantic links strengthened since the war encouraged a substantial number of Anglo-Americans to return to England either permanently or for an extended period. Colonists had operated politically and economically on both sides of the Atlantic since the establishment of Jamestown, but after 1642 the political and commercial connections between colony and metropolis became increasingly integrated. The outbreak of civil war enabled a group of New England colonial-imperialists to contribute their talents, first, to the parliamentary cause and, then, to the creation of the Interregnum regimes, in addition to fomenting territorial expansion in North America: Richard Hutchinson, who became Deputy Treasurer and then Treasurer of the Navy under Cromwell, George Downing and Downing's cousins Stephen Winthrop and Fitz-John Winthrop, who joined the parliamentary army, as well as the "Pilgrim Father" Edward Winslow, were among those who combined what we would call today a lobbying practice on behalf of their colonies as well as themselves with the rendering of service to the state. In addition, various New England families, such as the Hutchinsons and Hulls, conducted operations in Newfoundland (fish), the Canary Islands (wine), and the West Indies (provisions). While the rest of seventeenth-century Anglo-America continued to rely on the Matthew Cradocks and Maurice Thompsons of this world, as discussed in Chapter 2, for supply, these American-based merchants provided both an alternative route for servicing New England with the manufactures its colonists desired as well as another route for carrying on the political and commercial interactions that typified seventeenth-century English overseas relations.[34]

---

[33] For the expansion of Virginia, see, e.g., "Francis Yeardley's Narrative of Excursions into Carolina, 1650," in Salley, *Narratives of Early Carolina*, 22–9. For the attempt to colonize the Bahamas, which emanated from Bermuda, see Miller, "The Colonization of the Bahamas."

[34] The classic analysis of these traders, Bailyn's *The New England Merchants in the Seventeenth Century*, observes that they "from the start conducted their trade mainly within the confines of the British [*sic*] commercial system" (91). But how could it be otherwise since these colonial-based merchants occupied a secondary status in the wider Anglophone world of the seventeenth century? For discussions of this reverse migration, see Moore, *Pilgrims*, and Cressy, *Coming Over*.

The metropolitan government – whether royal or parliamentary – played practically no role in these developments. This did not mean, however, that it played no role in overseas affairs whatsoever. In addition to trying to extract revenue from tobacco, the state continued to serve as the final court of appeal for entertaining the intercolonial issues of colonists and anyone else with an interest in colonies after 1642. Civil war actually aggravated this scenario since more colonial cases came before both the High Court of Admiralty and Warwick's committee as more people, especially from the ever-growing colonies, became involved in overseas trade and colonization.

Warwick's commission, like its predecessor, entertained these petitions. Among the most prominent of these was the application of Roger Williams for a charter for the colony of Rhode Island and Providence Plantations he had established after his exile from Massachusetts Bay in 1636. In addition to his heterodox views on the relationship between church and state that had brought his expulsion from "the Bay" in the first place, Massachusetts, along with its southern neighbor, Plymouth Colony, had designs on the territory that Williams claimed for Rhode Island. In December 1643, the Warwick Commission awarded Massachusetts all of Narragansett Bay south of Plymouth. Williams, though, went to London to dispute the Massachusetts claim and was successful in securing the commission's reversal of its decision and "a free and absolute charter" for his own colony in the Narragansett territory. New Haven, founded in 1638, also planned to use the newly favorable attitude to godly interests in the government to secure a charter from the Warwick Commission, but the ship carrying the petitioner, the colony's leading merchant – and Guinea trader – George Lamberton, along with approximately seventy other people and a cargo valued at £5,000, sank in a storm; that colony arguably never recovered from this "sad affliction."[35]

Although certainly religiously sympathetic to the leaders of New England, Warwick's primary American concern remained the

---

[35] Grant by Robert Earl of Warwick, Governor-in-Chief and Lord High Admiral of all the Plantations in America, and others joined in commission with him, to the Governor, Assistants, and Freemen of Massachusetts Bay, 10 December 1643, *CSPC AWI* 1: 325 (grant to Massachusetts); Grant by Robert Earl of Warwick, Governor-in-Chief of the Plantations in America, and other joined in commission with him, to the inhabitants of the towns of Providence, Portsmouth, and Newport, 14 March 1643/4, *CSPC AWI* 1: 325–6. For Lamberton's ill-fated voyage, see Hosmer, *Winthrop's Journal*, 2: 286–7.

Caribbean. His appointment as Lord High Admiral, in conjunction with his leadership of the plantations committee, would have given the Earl considerable discretion to pursue his American interests except that the parliamentary fleet had to support the invasion of Ireland and measures against Royalists in England and on the high seas.[36]

In order to resume his anti-Spanish campaign in America, Warwick turned again to privateering. Thus, he granted letters of marque to various New Englanders to conduct raids, but he also recruited one of his old skippers, Captain William Jackson, to lead a more substantive voyage against the old enemy in 1642. Warwick and Jackson's partners in this venture included a number of Providence Island veterans, including the settlers and officials Samuel Axe and William Rous, who served on the expedition, and Maurice Thompson, who inevitably provisioned the venture. Jackson, no doubt deliberately recalling the careers of Sir Francis Drake and the Elizabethan predators of three-quarters of a century before, spent three years raiding Spanish ships and towns, collecting loot (and slaves), spreading pandemonium and diplomatic consternation, and receiving the acclaim of godly people as he brought substantial numbers of African and Indian slaves and other "plunder" to Bermuda and New England. He also captured Spanish Town in Jamaica and collected a ransom before returning it to Spanish control. Yet, as with the depredations of Drake, Jackson's attacks had only epiphenomenal effects on the American situation: the Spaniards rebuilt and the English retreated.[37]

Meanwhile, the continuing tumult of the 1640s, which a small but growing number of people attributed to the duplicity and obstructionism of "that man of blood" Charles Stuart, led to the trial of the King followed by his execution on 30 January 1649: the actual revolutionary moment in all of this. It was accompanied by the

---

[36] Kerrigan, "Ireland in Naval Strategy, 1641–1691."

[37] Harlow, *The Voyages of Captain William Jackson*; Kupperman, *Providence Island*, 315–16; Hanna, *Pirate Nests and the Rise of the British Empire*, 89–93. Mariner Edward Hatfield, who made three voyages across the Atlantic between 1643 and 1647, testified in the High Court of Admiralty that "it was commonly accounted and reported that there was open war and hostility and open war between the subjects of the respective kings [England and Spain] in these seas and coasts"; Deposition of Edward Hatfield, Wapping, 24 May 1648, HCA 13/16, ff. 63r–70r at 63r. William Zanes, who made two voyages to America from Guinea between 1645 and 1648, likewise testified; Deposition of William Zanes, May 1648, HCA 13/61, ff. 63v–65r.

termination of the House of Lords, which brought the withdrawal of Warwick, Saye, and their counterparts from public life. Thus, the regicide and the ensuing replacement of the monarchy by a republic brought even greater involvement in public affairs and the opportunity to direct governmental policy for those who supported these events. Even so, the level of revolutionary commitment held by those concerned with these events can be tricky to discern: some of them, notably Andrews and Rowland Wilson, who were named to the special court created to try Charles, obviously supported the regicide. Yet while Thompson and Pennoyer apparently wholeheartedly participated in and benefited from the various Interregnum regimes, they suffered no punishment at the Restoration.[38]

In the event, the receding prospects of the would-be Charles II coincided with the increasingly bright prospects of Thompson and his cohort whether they were firmly committed republicans or not. Now, having expanded their various interests during the 1640s while simultaneously devoting their persons and purses to secure the final triumph over the reprobate forces of Charles I, this corps of godly merchants was ready to seize the opportunity provided by the regicide to pursue their enterprises with redoubled vigor.[39]

Although this group held sway domestically, foreign obstacles to their plans remained, especially the Dutch. As it happened, 1648, the year in which the English Civil Wars wound down, constituted a crucial year in the imperial history of these arch-foes of seventeenth-century English overseas interests. On the one hand, it marked the Peace of Westphalia, which brought the Thirty Years War to a close. The end of this exhausting conflict ended inter alia the longer war between the Dutch Republic and Spain and finally guaranteed Dutch independence; indeed, these formerly bitter enemies quickly became friends. This turn of events, with which the English had had little to

---

[38] An Act of the Commons of England Assembled in Parliament, for Erecting a High Court of Justice, for the Trying and Judging of Charles Stuart, King of England, 6 January 1648/9, *AOI*, 1253–5, lists the king's judges. Moyer was imprisoned in the Tower with Sir James Harrington, Praise-God Barebon, and others as part "of a great clapping up of some old statesmen" after the Restoration (Pepys, *Diary and Correspondence of Samuel Pepys, F.R.S.*, 238 (entry of 1 December 1661)), but was released in 1667 without going to trial; Greaves, *Deliver Us from Evil*, 78–80.

[39] Thus, Thompson could prepare "propositions for the reduction of Barbadoes," then resisting the Rump's authority, for government consideration in 1650, Orders of Committee of the Admiralty, 10 September 1650, *CSPC AWI* 1: 342.

do, now meant, first, that any Elizabethan-style harassment of Spain would come without Dutch assistance.[40]

On the other hand, 1648 saw the collapse, in practical terms, of Dutch dreams of empire in the Western Hemisphere. The revolt of Portuguese planters against the West India Company (WIC) that had broken out in 1645 had reduced the Dutch presence in Brazil to the city of Recife and a handful of other outposts, and this effort had provided the platform for the successful Portuguese attacks against São Tomé and Luanda. Even more importantly, the WIC had incurred huge losses in its fruitless attempts to maintain its Brazilian enterprise. These costs drove the company to the wall. In order to pick up the pieces of the Brazilian catastrophe, resist English pretensions to their remaining American operations, and maintain their relatively dominant position in Asia (unaffected by the Portuguese war), the Dutch would have to continue their practice of responding to English complaints over their behavior with delay, obfuscation, and the feigning of ignorance along with the new friendship between the Republic and Spain.[41]

From an English perspective, however, Dutch smugglers, traders, officials, and diplomats had gone about their business in areas that the English regarded as theirs with relative impunity due to the fiscal and bureaucratic impotence of the Caroline government and, in Anglo-America, the cooperation of locals who were generally unperturbed by the prospects of getting caught. If English overseas trade and colonization were to progress now that England had joined the Dutch in throwing off kingly government, the festering resentment that had increasingly permeated Anglo-Dutch relations over the previous thirty-five years needed to be resolved, whether by diplomacy or by force. As it happened, the Civil Wars had yielded another important, if paradoxical, result along with the end of the monarchy and the House of Lords: the victorious new Commonwealth of England was endowed with a new strength and a sense of purpose, and its leaders were prepared to bring this power to bear. Thus, the opponents of the Dutch could call on their ready access

---

[40] Solana, "A Network-Based Merchant Empire." The shift in the relative naval power of the Dutch Republic and Spain (along with the impotence of England at that time) was manifested in the comprehensive victory of the Battle of the Downs (21 October 1639) in which Admiral Tromp's fleet destroyed Admiral Oquendo's much larger one while an English squadron watched.

[41] Recife finally surrendered in 1654 and the Dutch-Portuguese war ended officially in 1661; Klooster, *The Dutch Moment*, 77–96.

to the resources of this excise-fueled and confident state they had helped
to create in order to expand English overseas trade and colonization on a
much greater scale. In the minds of this freshly triumphant cohort, those
who stood in their way could expect to receive swift and powerful
punishments.[42]

[42] Although Professor Aylmer could not provide concrete figures, he estimated roughly that
the parliamentary state might have claimed an annual taxation revenue approaching two
million pounds between 1643 and 1652, or approximately twice that of the Caroline
government prior to 1640. Of course, its expenditures were substantially higher but it
also had a significantly larger army and navy; Aylmer, *The State's Servants*, 319. The size
of the English Army stood at between 11,000 and 47,000 men in 1647–60. More
important, in terms of dealing with the Dutch, between 1643 and 1645, the state had
164 ships and pinnaces (up from 42 ships totaling 23,000 tons in 1642) with their crews
totaling 16,723 men; 216 ships (about half of which were prizes and half newly built)
were added to the navy between 1649 and 1660, making it the strongest in Europe;
Braddick, "Review."

6

New Modelers

For all of the contemporary expectation of – and modern attempts to characterize – the "new modelers" as revolutionaries, their understanding of religion, society, and politics remained the same as it had been prior to the regicide notwithstanding the deep surgery they had performed on pre-1642 hierarchical sensibilities. What had changed was the direct access to the corridors of power at Whitehall and the validation of the righteousness of their cause that their victory had brought them; these developments fueled their greater sense of purpose. In terms of overseas affairs, Maurice Thompson and his associates brought their new situation to bear against their Dutch competitors, although the question of how to deal with these rivals was not the only one they had to address in their pursuit of a further reformation of society and, by extension, their wider interests.

Following the purge of MPs conducted by Colonel Pride and his troopers on 6 December 1648, the Rump Parliament declared itself "the supreme power in this nation" on 4 January 1649. This action facilitated the execution of Charles I on 30 January and the subsequent abolition of the monarchy; England became a "commonwealth and free state" governed by the "representatives of the people" in May. The immediate concerns of these "representatives" – that is, the Rump and its hand-picked Council of State – were to stamp out the smoldering embers of Royalism and to secure the recognition of the new republic from other European nations, a number of which had regarded the beheading of a duly anointed monarch askance.[1]

---

[1] An Act Declaring and Constituting the People of England to be a Commonwealth and Free State, [19 May 1649], *AOI* 2: 122.

The Rump's goals shared important aspects with the longer imperial game to preserve and extend their control of overseas matters that the new modelers played. These included the crushing of resistance to parliamentary authority in the American colonies and curbing smuggling in Anglo-America, especially of tobacco. Thus, Parliamentarians who were not involved in overseas affairs worked hand-in-glove with Maurice Thompson and his cohort to bring state power to bear on such issues as the opening of Spanish America to English trade, the coordination and expansion of the Asian trade, and the recovery of compensation from the Dutch for their past affronts. For addressing those issues that had less immediate concern for other Commonwealthsmen, Thompson and other politically connected merchants took the lead; they were free to pursue their integrative imperial vision that placed West Africa, the source of both the gold essential for successful trading in Asia and of the slaves essential for generating wealth in America, at its core.

Overseas initiatives also now incorporated colonists to a greater extent than hitherto. The geographic, social, and political growth of English settlements over the previous twenty or thirty years meant that Anglo-Americans, following the examples of Thompson and James Drax, could draw on existing patronage and also form new relationships in order to elevate themselves politically and socially. This greater enmeshing of Anglo-Americans into the increasingly expansive political associations that developed after 1642 embedded these connections more firmly in overseas settings, better enabled the more intelligent and ambitious pursuit of overseas ambitions by their constituents, and further strengthened the social, political, and economic ties that bound Anglo-America and the metropolis.

Yet while further imperial integration in terms of both philosophy and personnel became increasingly marked after 1642, the English state continued to lag behind events even as it assumed new forms. To add further confusion over the mid-seventeenth-century reconstitution of that state, ideological fissures, which proved irreparable and therefore fatal to the Commonwealth, occurred among those who had obtained power in 1649. One significant crack developed between those who believed Providence had ordained the final triumph of a republican government and those more willing to engage in political and ideological compromise in order to achieve pragmatic results in the shorter term. In a related sense, the republicans came to regard the army that had brought them their triumph over the King as an instrument of tyranny. On the other hand, the Army came to regard the Parliamentarians as do-nothings whose excessive dithering threatened the nation's future, especially with respect to paying the soldiery. Having tossed out monarchy, bishops, and House of Lords, how many of the remnants of the ancient constitution could be – or should be – retained in the future? This was the question to which leaders of the Interregnum found it impossible to agree on an answer.[2]

This failure to reach a settlement on what was to be the nature of a post-monarchical and post-episcopal English society, however, was certainly neither unavoidable nor even unexpected until the prospects for a restored monarchy suddenly appeared on the cards around the beginning of March 1660. Yet those who were involved in overseas trade and colonization between 1649 and 1660 had to work within this often vitriolic situation as well as negotiate with those who had conflicting views with respect to foreign policy, trade, and, ultimately, the purpose of the Commonwealth in order to achieve their aims. In the end, such success as these architects of Interregnum imperial policy achieved came despite indifference and sometimes opposition to important aspects of their endeavors; the impetus for sending a fleet to subdue Barbados and Virginia, for instance, arose from the aforementioned meshed motives. In the immediate aftermath of the regicide, the new political and economic leaders of England had to agree if only tacitly that some sort of governmental imperial policy had to be devised formally for the first time. Thus, English territorial and commercial advancements (outside Ireland) made during the Interregnum were manifestly not "occasioned by the Revolutionary state's decision to launch an ambitious project of empire-building around the Atlantic world."[3]

Before considering this situation further, however, some words of caution are in order. While it might seem clever to style 1676 as the year

---

[2] Hirst, "The Failure of Godly Rule in the English Republic." The sort of disputes that developed among metropolitan "Puritans" in the 1640s and 1650s appeared in other English-speaking places where the godly had political ascendency. Instead of generating religious unity, these secular triumphs invariably resulted in vehement differences over theology and religious practice, schism, and the departure of significant numbers of inhabitants for new pastures as in Rhode Island in the 1630s and the Bahamas in 1649. The prolix Presbyterian attorney, William Prynne, pointed to the altercations in Bermuda that gave rise to the latter colonization attempt as the inevitable "horrid" result of Independents and other radicals gaining power that should serve as a stark warning to England; "A Transcript of a Letter lately written from the Sommer Isles to William Prynne of Lincolns Inn, Esquire" attached to *A fresh discovery of some prodigious new wandring-blasing stars, & firebrands, stiling themselves new-lights.*

[3] Despite the claim to the contrary made by Donoghue, *Fire under the Ashes*, 7.

that marked the "end of American independence,"[4] it is, in the first instance, quite misleading to comprehend the seventeenth-century relationship between England's colonies and the metropolis in terms of American independence. Contemporaries may have resorted to hyperbole in characterizing the political behavior of certain colonies as that of a "free state," but no American colony exercised or pursued independence in our period. Indeed, the contrary was invariably the case: notwithstanding the disputes that certainly existed between metropolitan governments and colonists during the seventeenth century, no Anglo-American ever proclaimed her- or himself, let alone their colony, as free of obedience to an imperial authority. The imperial question between 1649 and 1660 arose from the claim to that authority made by the Rump; colonial rebels proclaimed themselves instead to be loyal subjects of Charles II. In the end, though, these proclamations did not matter as the Council of State sent a fleet, at the encouragement of those who had charge of overseas matters, which ended any pretenses to colonial detachment from the Commonwealth in 1652.[5]

In Virginia, the only Crown Anglo-American colony in 1649, Sir William Berkeley, the vigorous and experienced governor, regarded the regicide as abhorrent and proclaimed "Charles II" on having the news of it. On top of his fiercely anti-republican views, Sir William, who had held his office since 1641, subscribed to the position held by many planters that the colony had long suffered from its addiction to tobacco production. This had resulted in an ongoing depression in the staple's price after its collapse at the onset of the 1630s and the pernicious control over the economy exercised by the cabal of merchants who acted in concert to keep the wholesale price of tobacco down to their advantage and the disadvantage of the grower.[6] Berkeley thus proposed that Virginia wean

[4] Webb, 1676.

[5] For contemporary characterization of Barbados as a "free state," see, e.g., John Bayes to the Council of State, 30 June 1652, CSPC AWI 1: 384.

[6] The wholesale price for Virginia tobacco slumped from two or three shillings per pound during the "tobacco boom" of the 1620s to one penny per pound in the 1670s. Lorena Walsh has observed that production costs plummeted as well, however, so the situation was not as universally bleak as it might seem, notwithstanding the laments of contemporaries; Walsh, *Motives of Honor, Pleasure and Profit*, 181–2. The proverbial shoe appeared on the other foot for Sir William at the end of his long stint as governor when a cohort of colonists, disaffected by the governor's Indian policies and led by the newcomer Nathaniel Bacon, drove him from Jamestown in 1676. Bacon's Rebellion, suppressed with the assistance of troops sent from England, brought the recall of Berkeley in disgrace. As this event involved an early North American assault against the royal governor (but not royal

itself from tobacco and that planters be permitted a free trade, especially with Dutch merchants, who offered a better price for the weed. Perhaps accordingly, the governor had maintained good relations with his neighbors in New Netherland, long viewed as a smuggling hotbed by the tobacco interests in the metropolis. Of course, from the Commonwealth's perspective, Dutch smuggling diverted the tobacco trade from English merchants and its customs from the state; indeed, it had clouded relations between the colony and the Crown since the 1620s. Moreover, Sir William, a skillful politician, had secured the approval of his House of Burgesses for his support of the pretensions of Charles Stuart.[7]

Rejecting the Rump's claim to imperial authority also provided a ready pretext for rejecting the efforts of the Rump's partners, such as Thompson, to control the colonial economy by controlling the price that would be paid to planters for their tobacco. The "Man in the Moon," a Royalist gazetteer, emphasized the ties between tobacco, empire, and the sensitivity of Interregnum politics by citing the allegedly pernicious effects that the state of the tobacco trade had on Virginia. This author scoffed at the "fine new Liberty" presented by the excise, including a two-shillings-per-pound impost on tobacco ("though the Commodity be not worth six pence the pound"), which the king-killing "twined Snakes" had enacted; he wondered "how the Forraign Plantations, and Merchants will thrive by this?"[8]

The rejection of parliamentary authority in Barbados, arguably the most important Anglo-American colony geographically and economically in 1650, arose from distinctive circumstances. As Virginia's political situation had stabilized under the leadership of Berkeley, so seemingly had that of the island colony during the contemporaneous tenure of the former Providence Island Governor Philip Bell. The Civil Wars, however, fractured this quiet as defeated Royalists made their way to exile in

authority), and came to incorporate a wide range of grievances, it has generated inordinate historiographical attention; Musselwhite, "Bacon's Rebellion." The Bacon rebels, in typical seventeenth-century fashion, insisted that they were fighting to uphold the royal prerogative after the "abuse" it had allegedly suffered at the hands of the governor and his "evil councilors"; Copy of Mr. Bacons Declaracon in ye Name of ye People, 30 July 1676, in *CMHS*, 4th ser., 9 (1871): 184–7.

[7] Commission to Governor Berkeley and Council, 3 June 1650, "Virginia in 1650," 134–41; "Speech of Sir William Berkeley, and Declaration of the Assembly, March 1651."

[8] [John Crouch], *The Man in the Moon*, no. 36, 26 December 1650–2 January 1650/1, 286. Parliament had imposed an excise of four pence per pound on tobacco imported from Anglo-America in 1643; An Ordinance concerning the Excise of Tobacco, [23 September 1643], *AOI* 1: 361–2.

Barbados, as they had in Virginia, where they acquired plantations with the acquiescence of Bell, notwithstanding the potential for the aggravation of political and religious differences. Unlike their Virginia counterparts who lived peaceably, the Barbados Royalists picked up where they had left off in England.

One of them, Humphrey Walrond, arrived in the island in 1645. According to an unsympathetic account of his career, after the regicide the Royalists led by Walrond and his brother began to harass those who had supported the Rump's proceedings. These "new-modell'd Magisters" then took control of the colony's Council and Assembly and refused to entertain the petitions for elections brought by other planters, whom they denounced as "Independents."[9] If this pamphlet is to be credited, this upheaval commenced from the desire of the Royalists to cast off the debts they owed to metropolitan figures. Thus, in order to build up the numbers of his supporters, Walrond recruited "agents and factors" of "London merchants and others" who allegedly turned to the rebels for "preferment" in order to avoid having to provide an accounting to their employers.

On the other hand, the Walrond group identified "that seven-headed Dragon of Westminster" James Drax and his metropolitan associates as the ringleaders of the campaign to enslave the planters, deprive them colony of their liberties, and bring them under the tyranny of the usurpers in the metropolis. Having defeated the attempt to regain the Barbados situation for Parliament, the Royalists proclaimed Charles II on 3 May 1650 and then arrested Drax along with 121 other "Independents" and fined him 80,000 pounds of sugar before banishing him to England. After arriving in the metropolis, Drax and several of his counterparts called on their contacts there to prod the Council of State into taking the case into hand. They also recommended that it appoint the deeply experienced and qualified Edward Winslow, who had returned to England from the Plymouth Colony to serve in the Commonwealth government, as the new governor of the colony.[10]

---

[9] Religious Independents, such as Thompson and John Winthrop, subscribed to a hierarchy-free form of church government in which congregations chose their own ministers, while Presbyterians favored a truncated hierarchy in which the pastorate governed the laity rather than vice versa.

[10] Foster, *A Briefe Relation of the Late Horrid Rebellion Acted in the Island of Barbadas in the West Indies*, 28–9, 36, 50 (Drax's fine); "Humble proposals of several Barbadeans" to the Council of State, 22 November 1650, *CSPC AWI* 1: 346; Pestana, *The English Atlantic in an Age of Revolution*, 93.

Meanwhile, another defeated Royalist, Francis, Lord Willoughby of Parham, arrived in Barbados on 29 April 1650 armed with a commission as governor from the second Earl of Carlisle endorsed by "Charles II" that compelled the Walronds to subside and the bedraggled Governor Bell to withdraw. This document also included an agreement with the Stuart pretender that entitled his governor to one-half of the profits of the island for twenty-one years. Once installed in office, Willoughby took a rather different tack than Berkeley did in securing his authority along with that of the King. Rather than work with the colony's Assembly, the membership of which included many supporters of the Walronds and who may have regarded Willoughby's checkered support of the royal cause with suspicion, the governor unilaterally proclaimed Charles II as king on 7 May 1650. He then committed other acts "dishonourable to the present established Government of this Commonwealth," including excluding from power those, such as the Walronds, who had not rallied to his standard. Thus, Willoughby may have achieved the result sought by his masters, but his commission only papered over political cracks. Moreover, as a newcomer, Willoughby, unlike Berkeley, had developed no support among the colonial leadership to call upon when political issues came to a boil; the situation remained edgy as the Walronds, Parliamentarians, and other opportunists monitored the situation.[11]

The cases of Barbados and Virginia provide helpful illustrations of how patron–client relationships worked with respect to seventeenth-century overseas affairs and how Anglo-Americans benefited from these associations. Sir John Danvers, who had been involved in Virginia for forty years and served on the Council of State and its Committee of Admiralty, and Maurice Thompson, appointed Commissioner of the Excise, were both part of the Rump's government in 1650.[12] Both had long and extensive involvement in Virginia. Both favored an ordering of the tobacco trade, including the identification and punishment of interlopers, and both played a leading role in developing the plan to reduce Virginia.

The stakes involved here were, of course, very high. The Rump's failure to heed the concerns raised by the likes of Drax and bring these colonies under its authority would mean the end of any pretense to an

---

[11] Gragg, *Englishmen Transplanted*, 45–50. For Willoughby's career, see Barber, "Power in the English Caribbean."

[12] For Thompson's appointment, see 18 July 1650, *CJ* 6: 443.

English Empire in America before the concept had gained much ground. Even worse, successful colonial opposition to the Parliament's authority could fan the smoldering resentment against the regicide into a conflagration if Charles Stuart could coordinate strategy with his American supporters. To lend further urgency to the matter, negotiations had begun between the man who would be king and his Scottish subjects, who were having second thoughts about their relationship with the Commonwealth, about bringing Charles to his northern throne. The establishment of a Royalist Anglo-America would have encouraged the King's supporters everywhere at a time when the Rump's army was still in the process of subduing its enemies in Ireland. It would also have provided Royalists with a base from which to harass the Commonwealth and its supporters, as evidenced when Barbados provided a haven to Prince Rupert's fleet when it harassed Caribbean shipping. Moreover, the interruptions to the Anglo-American and Guinea trades of the sort that Rupert perpetrated threatened the commercial interests of the republic's supporters, but hostile colonial governments also obviously threatened the plantation operations of those merchant-planters within their jurisdictions.[13]

Thus, in the autumn of 1649, the Committee of the Admiralty sought advice on Virginia from Thompson, William Pennoyer, Benjamin Worsley, and "such others as Thompson and Worsley shall think fit" in order to determine "what is requisite for reducing Virginia to the interest of the Commonwealth, and to be placed in such hands as the State may confide in, that the trade of that plantation may not be destroyed by its disaffection to the Commonwealth."[14] Duly informed, the Committee recommended the appointment of commissioners to assume the government of the colony with power to appoint a new governor and council. It took until September 1650, though, for the preparation of legislation authorizing the use of force against Barbados, Bermuda, and Virginia – the draft of which "having been read in the presence of divers Barbados men." The committee then entertained

---

[13] The Scots and Charles agreed the Treaty of Breda on 1 May 1650, a week before Willoughby's proclamation. Charles landed in Scotland on 23 June and was crowned on 1 January 1650/1, but the defeats at Dunbar (3 September 1650) and Worcester (3 September 1651) forced him back into the exile. The Commonwealth's fleet finally reduced Rupert's force to one ship by 1653; Woolrych, *Britain in Revolution*, 505.

[14] Order of Committee of the Admiralty, 29 November 1649, *CSPC AWI* 1: 331; Order of the Committee of the Admiralty, 20 December 1649, in "Virginia in 1641–1649," 21.

Thompson's "propositions concerning the reduction of Barbados" before Parliament declared Antigua, Barbados, Bermuda, and Virginia to be in rebellion.[15]

In December, the Council of State appointed Sir George Ayscue commander of a fleet to reduce Barbados but diverted it against the Scilly Isles, a hive of privateering the geographical proximity of which dictated that their subjection be a priority; Ayscue's force did not leave for the Caribbean until August 1651. Meanwhile, the Council of State finally approved a plan for Virginia the following month: Ayscue was still to proceed to Barbados, but if he succeeded there in timely fashion he was to meet another fleet headed for Virginia and assist it against the mainland colony. The Virginia commissioners were Captain Robert Dennis, commander, Edward Custis, and three longtime partners of Thompson, Thomas Stegge, Richard Bennett, and William Claiborne.[16]

These representatives of the Rump and fifteen ships rendezvoused with Ayscue's command at Barbados, which having arrived there on 15 October 1651 had received encouragement from the news of the comprehensive parliamentary victory at Worcester. Willoughby, meanwhile, had prepared the colony's defenses, and a standoff ensued. This situation continued into January when a group of planters led by Thomas Modyford assisted Ayscue in effecting a landing that compelled Willoughby to accept terms on 11 January 1652. In return for accepting parliamentary authority (the Rump having called in Carlisle's patent), the planters received liberty of conscience, the right to tax themselves in their assembly, confirmation of land titles, indemnity for their rebellion, the return of any property lost or seized, free trade "with all nations that do trade with and are in amity with England," the right to depart the island, and the retention of existing government institutions. Willoughby was allowed to remove to his plantation in Surinam or return to England.[17]

The submission of Virginia went rather more smoothly. Although Berkeley made a show of force in accordance with his commission to the extent that his biographer says "for a few days in March it looked as though blood might actually run" until "at the last moment," it seems unlikely that the situation would have ever deteriorated to that extent.

[15] Order of Committee of Admiralty, 9 January 1649/50, "Virginia in 1641–1649," 22–3; Order of Committee of the Admiralty, 10 September 1650, *CSPC AWI* 1: 343; An Act of Parliament Prohibiting Trade, 19 September 1650, "Virginia in 1650," 143–4.
[16] Order of the Council of State, 16 December 1650, *CSPC AWI* 1: 347; Order of the Council of State, 26 September 1651, *CSPC AWI* 1: 360–1.
[17] *Articles of Agreements, Made, and concluded the 11th day of January 1651.*

After all, Sir William achieved some favorable terms when he surrendered on 12 March 1652: the right of Virginians to tax themselves, confirmation of the colony's boundaries, permission to use the Book of Common Prayer for one year (the use of which Berkeley had encouraged in defiance of parliamentary statute), and the confirmation of land titles. Thus, he fulfilled his duty to Charles Stuart with a great show of bluster and secured the persons and property of his colonists. Claiborne and Bennett certainly had no objection to Sir William's goals, but they also negotiated the retirement of the governor to his Green Spring plantation and an end to free trade in the colony (unlike the Barbados agreement). Bennett became governor and secured the surrender of Maryland, the last Royalist outpost in Anglo-America, two weeks later. One suspects that this scenario would have been reversed had the arriving fleet been Rupert's armed with a royal commission.[18]

The Commonwealth's need to eliminate Royalist resistance in the colonies dovetailed with its need to sort out its relations with the Dutch Republic. On the one hand, the Dutch were fellow republicans and staunch Protestants.[19] In the view of Oliver Cromwell, who had rapidly come to preeminence through his military performance and joined the Council of State at the creation of the Commonwealth, close cooperation – ideally a union – with the Dutch was natural as well as desirable in order to promote a common religious and governmental sensibility. The English Republic duly dispatched an emissary, Isaac Dorislaus, to pursue this possibility in April 1649.[20]

Yet matters were not so straightforward. In the first instance, while certainly powerful, Cromwell was not in a position to direct policy prior to April 1653 when he and his supporters staged their coup against the Rump. Moreover, he had been away from England leading the Commonwealth's successful campaign against the Royalists in Ireland in 1649–50. Then, after his return to England, his position and influence could be neutered by the more committed republicans such as Sir Arthur Heselrige, another metropolitan politician with overseas associations.[21]

---

[18] Article seven provides free trade for Virginians "according to the lawes of [England]"; Articles at the Surrender of the Country, 12 March 1651/2, Hening, *Statutes at Large,* 363–8; Billings, *Sir William Berkeley and the Forging of Colonial Virginia,* 108–12.

[19] Propositions to the King, 1 June 1642, *CJ* 2: 599–600; Parliament's Petition and Propositions to the King, 1 June 1642, *LJ* 5: 97–9.

[20] Woolrych, *Britain in Revolution,* 507–9.

[21] Morrill, "Cromwell, Parliament, Ireland and a Commonwealth in Crisis: 1652 Revisited." Sir Arthur was a cousin of Edward Winslow's; Aylmer, *The State's Servants,* 15.

On the Dutch side, the Commonwealth had to deal with the strong Orangist party led by the *stadhouder* Willem II (and son-in-law of Charles I), whose party supported Willem's aspirations to greater power and opposed the execution of Charles I as well as the pretensions of the Rump to legitimacy; when Royalist agents murdered Dorislaus on 2 May 1649, they managed to avoid arrest. The *stadhouder*'s enemies accused Willem of scheming to become king, while his saber-rattling, as the chief military officer in the Republic, conflicted with the strong preference of Holland, especially Amsterdam, for peaceful foreign relations so that trade would remain uninterrupted. Willem's sudden death from smallpox in 1650 prevented him from staging a planned coup and provided the Estates-General the opportunity to eliminate the hereditary character of his office and to reduce the size of the Dutch Army dramatically. Yet Orangist sentiment did not dissipate, and its monarchical overtones as well as its relationship with the Stuart cause, together with the endurance of Royalism in Ireland, Scotland, and Anglo-America, remained a substantial concern.[22]

The grievances of English overseas adventurers over Dutch behavior festered in the midst of these circumstances. As their activities intensified during the 1640s, especially in Africa and Asia, and ran up against their adversaries accordingly, these merchants responded to their rivals both directly and by employing their new relationship with the English state. The extraordinary scope of imperial comprehension for the time that Thompson's group possessed along with the power that its members exercised at the outset of the Interregnum became evident in the negotiations they entered into with the Rump and the East India Company with respect to the direction of English affairs in Asia. These discussions began with the Thompson group's petition to Parliament for the right to plant a colony on the island of Assada (Nosy Be) off the northern coast of Madagascar. The EIC, headed by its governor, William Cockayne, naturally regarded this plan as a threat to its monopoly and moved to oppose the government approval that Thompson and the other Assada Adventurers sought.[23]

---

[22] Groenveld, "The English Civil Wars as a Cause of the First Anglo-Dutch War."

[23] The company seems to have had its first report on the Assada Adventurers, at least some of whom, including Thompson and Samuel Moyer, were also members of the EIC at the end of September 1649; A General Court of all the Freemen and Adventurers, 28 September 1649, *CCMEIC* 3: 358–9.

This Assada initiative, as with most failed colonizing ventures, has not received much scholarly attention. Moreover, such analysis as has been produced has, unfortunately, misapprehended the nature of the enterprise and, accordingly, failed to grasp its significance for the development of English overseas interests. First, Assada constituted a key element – but only one element – in a comprehensive plan to integrate English operations in the Eastern Hemisphere with those in the Western Hemisphere. Then, while those who conceived of the colony almost certainly had the Barbados model in mind – Thompson and his partners had amassed over twenty years of experience supplying Caribbean plantations by 1649 – it was manifestly not the plan of either Robert Hunt, the colony's governor, or of Cromwell (who was in Ireland at the time it was devised). Rather, the Assada Adventurers, whose leader, Thompson, undoubtedly knew the "godly" ex-governor from their mutual involvement in the Providence Island colony and their mutual association with the Warwick, enlisted Hunt to serve in a similar capacity on the other side of the world.[24]

Moreover, notwithstanding the ultimate abandonment of the Assada scheme, the vision that it incorporated remained firmly in the minds of its backers. Being quite familiar with the risks and rewards involved in colonization, they may even have anticipated failure in the form of, as actually happened, attacks by indigenous people on the settlement. Thus, Assada might be likened to Virginia, whose early settlers suffered early reversals and moved to abandon their colony on at least two occasions. For instance, although the North American colony (and Maurice Thompson) survived the Indian attack of 1622, can it have been a coincidence that metropolitan interest in founding Anglo-American plantations turned to places where there were no indigenous populations, such as Barbados, after that date? A similar scenario emerged with respect to Africa and Asia: after the devastation of Assada the Adventurers shifted their planting focus to the uninhabited island of St. Helena.

Nor did the Assada endeavor constitute an attempt by interlopers to divert trade surreptitiously from the East India Company; rather, the

---

[24] Cf. Games, *The Web of Empire*, 208–15; Brenner, *Merchants and Revolution*, 177; Eacott, *Selling Empire*, 46; Pincus, *Protestantism and Patriotism*, 40–57. For Hunt, who succeeded Philip Bell as governor of Providence in 1636, see Hunt, *The Island of Assada Neere Madagascar Impartially Defined*; Newton, *Colonising Activities of the English Puritans*, 252–4. The Adventurers included, in addition to Thompson, his perennial associates William Pennoyer, Nathaniel Andrews, and Jeremy Blackman; A Meeting of Divers Committees and Others of the Assada Adventurers, 27 November 1649, *CCMEIC* 3: 379.

Adventurers, a number of whom were members of the company to begin with, approached the Council of State to secure rights that the company, in their view, did not possess. Furthermore, Thompson and Cockayne, the EIC Governor, had a longstanding professional relationship, the endurance and nature of which must cast doubt on any argument that regards Thompson and his Assada friends as elbowing aside vested interests.[25]

Indeed, there is substantial evidence to support the proposition that Thompson regarded himself as the legatee of Sir William Courteen's vision as well as of the Courteen interests in Asia; he allegedly went so far as to secure Courteen's "Books and Papers of Instructions for [the East Indies] trade" from Sir William's widow personally "soon after" the Dutch committed their "Spoils and depredations" of the Courteen Association.[26] In America, Thompson had abandoned whatever interest he may have ever had in governing plantations but still turned up to testify in support of the opponents of Carlisle's claims in 1647 as befit an associate of William Courteen. Moreover, he and his partners negotiated with their counterparts within the company in order to achieve a mutually satisfactory solution rather than plotted to displace their rival.[27]

The comprehensive plan that the Assada Adventurers presented to Parliament incorporated a newly ambitious scope: they sought a charter that incorporated the plantation of Assada into "a national settlement" of the Indian Ocean trade that, in turn, would link "Asia, Africa, and America." This commerce would exist independently of the East India Company, since "a free well regulated trade might be more advantageous to the nation" as opposed to the moribund jointstock approach of the EIC. Having already raised £80,000 and expecting to issue an additional £200,000 worth of stock to provide the capital for their plans, Thompson and his cohort now asked the Council of State to settle "all former differences with the Dutch in India" and to grant the Adventurers permission to trade in places that the Company had allegedly ignored or abandoned over the years, such as Japan. The first goal here was "to get mace

---

[25] Legg and Symons, 7 October 1644, *LJ* 7: 16–17; Cockayne had also partnered Thompson's early associate Matthew Cradock in the plantation trade prior to Cradock's death in 1641; Deposition of Matthew Cradock, September–March 1637, March–July 1638, HCA 24/94.

[26] Graves, *A Brief Narrative and Deduction of the several Remarkable Cases of Sir William Courteen, and Sir Paul Pindar, Knights*, 4.

[27] Briefe notes upon Examination of wittnesses before a secret committee of Parliament in March & April 1646/1647, MS Rawlinson C 94, f. 4, Bodl.; Davis, "Papers Relating to the Early History of Barbados and St. Kitts," 332.

and nutmeg of our own growing and a free trade in the South [manuscript torn] as formerly and that we should settle the plantations and fortifications and erect a state of trade with English government in those parts." This, of course, meant a resumption of competition with the Dutch for control over the mace and nutmeg trade and renewing the long dispute over Pulau Run.[28]

The plantation of Assada constituted a second phase of this scheme: "free planters that will go to Assada at their own charge" would pay £10 per head for passage and £4 per head for goods and receive the same liberties as the "free burgesses" of Portuguese Goa and Dutch Batavia. They would, though, be unable to trade in "the company's commodities," which would include, in addition to mace and nutmeg, pepper, cinnamon, cloves, indigo, cardamom, and calicoes, although they could acquire "Negroes, clothes, calico and all necessaries" for the colony. Perhaps most significantly, this commerce was to be attached to the Guinea trade in "[elephants'] teeth and gold," with the Council of State to choose fifteen "able merchants" to serve on a "Grand Committee to manage the affairs of Guinea, Assada, & India." The Council was sufficiently impressed with this plan that it ordered the incorporation of the Assada Adventurers into the East India Company in order to effect it.[29]

This Assada business illustrates how imperial policy – "mercantilism" – was conducted customarily in seventeenth-century England. The state became involved in overseas trade and colonization only when the promulgators of those activities solicited its involvement, such as when they required clarification of the legitimacy of their pursuits or when other European interests were concerned, as with the status of Pulau Run. In this case, though, larger issues were at stake: state approval of the plans of the Assada Adventurers gave official imprimatur to their anti-Dutch attitude, as nervous observers across the North Sea noted.[30]

---

[28] Papers of ye Merchants trading to Assada giving reasons why they refuse to join with the East India Company in a 5-year voyage upon the old joint stock, 10 November 1649, CO 77/7, f. 66.

[29] The Agreement between the East India Company and the Assada Adventurers, 21 November 1649, *CCMEIC* 3: 377–8. The Company, striving to preserve as much of its monopoly under the joint stock as possible, responded tepidly to these overtures on 19 November 1649, CO 77/7, ff. 70–1, with agreement between the parties achieved on 21 November 1649, CO 77/7, f. 72, and parliamentary approval given on 31 January 1649/50, CO 77/7, f. 76.

[30] Contenant diverse Instructions et memoires touchants la navigation des Hollandais aux Indes Orientales et l'effet des affaires de ces pays deduit dans les quartorze articles Suivans, CO 77/7, ff. 58–61. Brenner and Games have noted that the Adventurers did

So what to do about the Dutch? They had habitually frustrated English diplomats with delay and claims of ignorance while habitually frustrating their English rivals with blockades and underpricing punctuated by incidents of outright violence. With the Irish campaign winding down by the middle of 1651, the new modelers could now devote more attention to this vexing problem. Since those who sought reparations for the alleged misdemeanors committed by the Dutch as well as the further extension of English overseas interests could find some basis of agreement with those who envisioned an Anglo-Dutch union of Protestant powers – so long as England would be the dominant partner – another diplomatic overture to achieve that end was agreed.

Thus, in March 1652, this special embassy, led by Oliver St John, whose longstanding connections to godly political and mercantile figures included investment in the Providence Island Company, and Sir Walter Strickland arrived in the Dutch Republic with its brief. Unhappily for the prickly ambassadors, but predictably, their efforts were met with the customary lack of cooperation freshly flavored with the vegetables with which Orangist mobs, encouraged by Royalist exiles, pelted them as they traveled on their business. In the event, the Dutch government had no interest in accepting a junior partnership even within a "Protestant Union." The insulted and disappointed emissaries returned to Westminster emptyhanded.[31]

This failure ended English patience. The first target of the more aggressive anti-Dutch program that resulted was smuggling. Dutch "insolence" on this point had directly threatened the Commonwealth by depriving it of revenue and encouraged the rebellious attitude of Virginia and Barbados. Thus, having already dispatched Ayscue's fleet to America, the Rump passed a Navigation Act on 9 October 1651, which was based on the statute of 1650 that banned trade with rebellious colonies and subjected violators to seizure of their goods.

---

follow the Dutch model in Asia by envisioning Assada as a colony from which trade could be conducted, as the Dutch did at Batavia. Their analyses, though, overlook the previous existence of the East India Company's base at Madras (established in 1639) as well as the reality that the Adventurers' plans for Assada constituted only one element of their strategy for dealing with the Dutch; cf. Brenner, *Merchants and Empire*, 168–81; Games, *Web of Empire*, 211.

[31] Aside from an entire lack of interest in subordinating Dutch overseas interests to English ones, the Dutch had significant commercial interests in the Baltic, the Mediterranean, and the Spanish domains; Rommelse, "The Role of Mercantilism in Anglo-Dutch Political Relations," 595–7.

The new legislation banned foreign ships without a government license from the plantation trades and restricted the importation of "foreign goods" to and exports from overseas (with certain exceptions granted for the East Indies trade) to English ships from 1 December. The proponents of the statute were none other than the same Thompson-led group that had planned the Ayscue expedition against Barbados, and the success of this venture reflected the greater degree of coordination between the interests of these men and English overseas policy that their access to state power had enabled: when Ayscue arrived at Barbados he found some two dozen Dutch ships trading in violation of the embargo that the Rump had placed on the island, and he confiscated a reported £100,000 worth of goods. This seizure, not to mention the views that underpinned it, both infuriated and alarmed the Dutch. The Republic sought, on the one hand, to resume diplomacy; on the other, it began preparations for war.[32]

Meanwhile, the merger of the East India Company and the Assada Adventurers provided the opportunity to articulate English protests against the behavior of its global adversary more coherently and forcefully. This began with a demand that the Council of State pursue the recovery of itemized damages totaling £1,681,996 15s for "particular and real losses" it had incurred at the hands of the VOC dating from the Anglo-Dutch treaty of 1622.[33] But the advocates of this militant agenda ratcheted up the pressure on both the Council and their overseas rivals working with their clients from "below." Thus, in the spring of 1652, someone went through the trouble of preparing and collecting thirty-six petitions "of divers sea commanders, mariners, widows, and orphans," all living in the environs of Ratcliffe where Thompson and his partners held sway. These petitioners, some of whom signed their complaints with their marks, sought the issuance of letters of reprisal to privateers to attack VOC shipping in order to recover damages for lost property

---

[32] John Paige to Gowen Paynter and William Clerke, 16 February 1651/2, and same to same, 13 March 1651/2, "Letters: 1652," Steckley, *The Letters of John Paige*, 57–82; An act for increase of Shipping, and Encouragement of the Navigation of this Nation, *AOI* 2: 559–62; Farnell, "The Navigation Act of 1651, the First Dutch War, and the London Merchant Community," esp. 440–3.

[33] An abstract of the particular and real losses which the English Company have sustained in divers parts of the East Indies by the proceedings of the Netherlands Company being come to our knowledge from the Indies since the treaty here in England in Anno 1622, Abstract of some particular damages which we likewise have received from the said Netherlanders Company, CO 77/7, [January 1651/2], ff. 83r–84r.

and wages dating back to between 1616 and 1620, such as Barbara Cowley's request for £1,500, Margery Carter's for £1,200, and Katherine Dove's for £3,000. Cockayne then presented these claims to John Thurloe, Secretary to the Council of State, for action.[34]

The Dutch responded to this pressure by sending out a fleet to protect their shipping. This squadron's encounter with an English counterpart in April 1652 led to an English declaration of war on 8 July. This conflict, which should be regarded as a global one given its geopolitical scope, did not go quite as well as those who had sought it had hoped. Certainly, the English fleet in the "Narrow Seas" dealt serious blows to the enemy, including the death of Admiral Maarten Tromp, but in the wider world the limitations under which the English state still operated were exposed: even in the relatively proximate Mediterranean and Baltic Seas, the Dutch were able to cut off English trade, while privateers hampered English commerce with Asia. The inability of the Commonwealth to achieve a comprehensive victory aggravated the increasing sense that this government could not achieve anything. This irritation, augmented by the increased taxation and other hardships that always accompany war, contributed to the demise of the Rump.[35]

The war also inexoraably renewed the involvement of army and its officers, notably Cromwell, in political life. They drew on public unhappiness to stage a coup in April that expelled the Rump and then established the Cromwellian Protectorate on 16 December 1653. The new Lord Protector still preferred to find a diplomatic solution to Dutch issues in pursuit of his hope for a permanent union of the Protestant republics, as Cromwell regarded the exigencies of combatting "popery" and the Houses of Stuart and Orange as more important even than English commercial interests, despite the belief of the radically millenarian Fifth Monarchists that defeat of the Nicodemian money-grubbers from across the North Sea constituted another step toward the ultimate triumph of the saints. He even proposed dividing the global interests of the nations, as Pope Alexander VI had done in 1494 with Portugal and

---

[34] William Cockayne, Governor, and Council of the East India Company to the Council of State, 29 January 1651/2, CO 77/7, f. 93, with The humble petition of divers sea commanders, mariners, widows, and orphans to the Council of State [May 1652], CO 77/7, ff. 97–181, with Cowley's petition at f. 109, Carter's at f. 136, and Dove's at f. 147.

[35] Woolrych, *Britain in Revolution*, 515. For a brief review of the war, see Israel, "The Emerging Empire," 424–5.

Spain, with the Dutch receiving free rein in the East Indies and the English holding sway in the Western Hemisphere.[36]

Accordingly, the Protector declined to capitalize on Dutch desperation, and the resulting Treaty of Westminster cannot have pleased the backers of English overseas interests any more than it did the Fifth Monarchy Men. The only success achieved by this accord from their perspective was the retention of the Navigation Act, although it did include the promise (Article XXVII) that the States General "shall take care that Justice bee done on those who were Authors or Abettors of the Murther committed upon the English in Amboyna" – if any of them were still alive after thirty years. On the other hand, Article XVI provided that an alleged violation of the treaty in Africa, America, or Asia would not "interrupt" the "amity" between the nations that the pact secured; rather, offender(s) would be punished on a case-by-case basis. Then, Article XXIV proscribed the issuance of letters of marque, a practice to which English merchants had resorted in order to secure direct remedies for Dutch injuries, while Article XXX mandated the appointment of commissioners by both nations to review and settle the global disputes between their people going back to 1611; any case on which they could not reach an agreement was to be submitted for arbitration by the Swiss Cantons. Unfortunately, the Swiss seem to not have been consulted about taking up this role beforehand and they declined to accept it, so a mutually agreeable process for bringing these issues to a final resolution of grievances remained elusive.[37]

In the immediate term, the end of the Dutch war enabled Cromwell to turn his attention to Spain, which he still regarded, in what had become an old-fashioned view, as the chief threat to English domestic security and overseas ambitions. In reality, the long, exhausting reign of Philip IV (1621–65) had blunted the Spanish edge; having waged relentless war for decades with little to show for it and having had to deal with a series of rebellions, this monarch needed to stabilize his position especially with respect to France and the Spanish Netherlands. Thus, Dutch-Spanish relations had continued to warm as the latter regarded their erstwhile

---

[36] Prestwich, "Diplomacy and Trade in the Protectorate"; Woolrych, *Commonwealth to Protectorate*, 279–88.

[37] This 1654 treaty may have been the first diplomatic agreement in English history that sought to resolve issues on a global scale; e.g., Article XIV that applied its terms to places beyond the Cape of Good Hope and in America; Davenport, *European Treaties Bearing on the History of the United States and Its Dependencies*, 2: 17–20.

fierce enemies as their best prospect for an anti-French alliance and perhaps for the recovery of Portugal. So, the Protector's perennial anti-Spanish sensibility retained a spit of common ground with the anti-Dutch views of those English people whose expectations for the recent war had been defeated by the terms of the peace. While those same people may not have cared too much about Spain (and a number of them conducted business in the Canary Islands that an Anglo-Spanish war would inter-rupt), they would have entertained hopes of conducting their trade with Spanish America, as in the case of the slave trader Samuel Wilson cited at the beginning of Chapter 3, legally if Spain could be compelled to open its colonial markets to English traders.[38]

Thus, the undertaking of "Oliver Cromwell's Western Design" in 1654 against the Spanish West Indies – "a single moment in the development of an English imperial vision," as Carla Gardina Pestana has styled it, and a central aspect of the "imperial moment of the English republic," as discerned by David Armitage – was by no means foreordained.[39] After all, Spain was not necessarily the first target of the Protector's Protestant millenarian views: France, another powerful Catholic neighbor of England and whose monarch, the minor Louis XIV (1643–1715), was a cousin of Charles Stuart, also presented an option for confessional ani-mosity. It required the diplomatic skills of Cardinal Mazarin, chief advisor to Louis's mother and regent, Anne of Austria, to keep the Protectorate's hostility trained upon Spain – and the Dutch Republic. The Protectorate, its Council having considered the issues involved in pursuing war against either Spain or France, concluded a defensive treaty with the latter in October 1655 and an offensive one in March 1657.[40]

---

[38] In addition to the Thirty Years War, which confirmed the independence of the Dutch Republic, Philip also lost Portugal (although its independence was not confirmed until 1668) and had to devote substantial attention and resources to revolts in Catalonia (1640–52) and Naples (1647). Studies in English of Philip's reign, during which his dominions never enjoyed a day of peace, include Elliott, *The Count-Duke Olivares*, and Stradling, *Philip IV and the Government of Spain*. For English trading in the Canaries, see, e.g., Steckley, *The Letters of John Paige*, ix–xxxix.

[39] Pestana, "English Character and the Fiasco of the Western Design," 1. According to Armitage, this "imperial moment extends from the peace settlement which concluded the first Anglo-Dutch War in 1654 to the second Protectoral Parliament of 1656," so, oddly, it includes neither the enactment of the Navigation Act nor the Commonwealth's subju-gation of Barbados and Virginia; Armitage, "The Cromwellian Protectorate and the Languages of Empire," 533.

[40] Edward Montagu's notes on the Debates in the Protector's Council concerning the last Indian Expedition, 20 April 1654, Clarke, *The Clarke Papers* 3: 203–6; Smith, "Diplo-macy and the Religious Question: Mazarin, Cromwell and the Treaties of 1655 and

The ensuing Western Design certainly constituted the first instance of an English government sending an armed force outside the British Isles and northwestern Europe. The significance of this reality should not be downplayed, but did this expedition actually constitute a seminal imperial moment in English history? After all, the career of this foray demonstrates yet again the nature of the relationships that propelled the seventeenth-century English imperial reach and how that reach often continued to exceed its grasp.

From Cromwell's perspective, this expedition was a disaster. The grand scheme may have envisioned the ultimate conquest of Spanish America by the self-styled forces of godly righteousness, but the immediate goal was only "to gain an Interest in that part of the West Indies in the possession of the Spaniard." The Protector and his Council thus suggested to General Robert Venables, commander of the mission's army, that after recruiting additional forces in the English Caribbean, he might attack either Santo Domingo or Puerto Rico before attempting to take Havana. Certainly, bringing those islands under English possession would, it was argued, attract settlers and provide bases for future military operations in America. Alternatively, Venables could bypass the islands and make directly for Cartagena, the seizure of which would provide a preexisting town as the basis of an English colony on the South American mainland and enable the control of the English flow of treasure from Peru.[41]

To oversee the logistics of the invasion, the Protectorate appointed a group with deep experience of overseas trade and colonization as commissioners. Maurice Thompson, unsurprisingly, had a place, as did his frequent partners, the chair of the commission Andrew Riccard, John Limbrey, Martin Noell, and William Ryder.[42] These commissioners, in turn, recommended that Edward Winslow, along with Daniel Searle (who had succeeded Willoughby as Governor of Barbados) and Gregory Butler, accompany the fleet to facilitate the recruitment of additional soldiers and to secure necessary provisions from the English islands.[43]

1657"; Battick, "Cromwell's Diplomatic Blunder." The Design also presented a means of removing "knowne idle masterlesse vagabonds and robers, menn and weomen, the only instruments of troble, plots, and projects in the commonwealth" from Scotland; Instructions to the council of Scotland, [November 1655], *TSP* 4: 129–30.

[41] Instructions unto General Robert Venables given by His Highnes by advice of his Councel upon his expedition to the West Indies, in Firth, *The Narrative of General Venables*, 111–15.

[42] Mr. Andrew Riccard, &c. to the Protector, 14 August 1654, *TSP* 2: 542; Commissioners for the southern expedition to the protector, 7 March 1654/5, *TSP* 3: 203–4.

[43] Bangs, *Pilgrim Edward Winslow*, 384–401.

Nothing, though, went according to plan after the force departed for the Caribbean in December 1654: the deity, confounding godly expectations, mysteriously and consistently withheld support from the endeavor, the commanders bickered, the poorly trained and poorly equipped men feuded, and foul weather caused fatal delays. Moreover, the Barbados planters declined to render sufficient assistance (bread had to be brought from New England), while they permitted the Dutch to conduct free trade in accordance with the articles of capitulation agreed with Sir George Ayscue.[44]

The invaders decided to attempt Santo Domingo, but two attacks made by the disease-riddled, ill-led, morale-free force were repulsed by the surprisingly well-led and well-fortified defenders. These setbacks led to a debate over what to do next. Most significantly, the commanders decided not to abandon the endeavor – which would have strangled "the imperial moment" in its infancy. Winslow proposed a third assault on Hispaniola. Disease, however, carried him off, and the surviving officers rejected his view in favor of diverting to a much more modest target: the relatively poorly fortified Jamaica (the designated alternatives of relatively well-defended Puerto Rico, not to mention Cartagena, seem to have received no consideration in the discussions).[45]

This move salvaged the Western Design. Indeed, the decision to attempt Jamaica constituted a singular imperial instance of extricating triumph from the jaws of defeat, as the island became the wealthiest and most important Anglo-American colony in the eighteenth century.[46]

Who was responsible for enabling this? Admiral William Penn and General Venables can claim no credit aside from supporting the idea of attacking Jamaica: after bickering over strategy and landing the troops on the island, the commanders departed the scene at a speed deemed unseemly enough that they were sent to the Tower on their return to England. Meanwhile the miserable men they left behind had to deal with the guerrilla campaigns conducted over the next five years by the Spaniards and the attacks of the slaves the Spaniards had freed when the English landed.[47]

---

[44] Bangs, *Pilgrim Edward Winslow*, 386–92.   [45] Ibid, 396–9.

[46] Burnard, "'Prodigious riches.'"

[47] E.g., A letter from Jamaica, 2 September 1656, *TSP* 5: 374; Edward D'Oyley to Martin Noell, 5 July 1657, Egerton Ms. 2395, f. 128; William Brayne to Thomas Povey, Martin Noell and William Watts, 8 July 1657, Egerton Ms. 2395, ff. 129–30, both BL.

Nor can we assign Oliver Cromwell any meaningful imperial role here beyond his approval of the Design in the abstract. After all, the Protector had no knowledge whatsoever of the change of plan to attack Jamaica. Moreover, the failure to take Santo Domingo, by all accounts, had the further effect of holing the aura of invincibility that had come to surround Cromwell following the occupation of Ireland and Scotland and the defeat administered to the Dutch. After the return of the expedition's commanders, though, this once-steely sense of self-purpose collapsed into self-recrimination and self-doubt. Thus, while the Protectorate's alliance with the French resulted in the capture of the pirate nest of Dunkirk in 1658, it entertained no further overseas ambitions.[48]

So what to do with Jamaica? With the island more or less under English control, those who tracked Anglo-American opportunities did not require further involvement by the state beyond maintaining its defense in order to pursue opportunities there. Situated 119 miles west of Santo Domingo and 957 miles west of Nevis, the closest English colony, and 1,200 miles from Barbados, Jamaica was a bit closer to the English islands and so was easier to defend than Providence Island had been. Yet while it certainly remained vulnerable to Spanish attack, it also provided decent proximity for harassing Spanish shipping, for establishing plantation agriculture, and for pursuing logwood in the Bays of Campeche and Honduras that had been English targets since the days of the Providence Island Company.[49]

Thus, soon after the English established themselves in Jamaica, reports on the prospects for the place began to circulate, and Drax, Thomas Povey, Lord Willoughby, and William Watts "being many waies engaged in the prosperitie of the West Indias and of ye Highness affaires there" created a West India Company "on their own charge." This group petitioned for "encouragement" from the Protector in the form of a £1,300 contribution from the state for an attack on Florida, in conjunction with "the King there," who had indicated his support for the undertaking. This

---

[48] Woolrych, *Britain in Revolution*, 633–4. The crew of the *Marston Moor* sent by Cromwell to confirm the capture of Jamaica mutinied rather than return there; C. S. Knighton, "Myngs, Sir Christopher (bap. 1625, d. 1666)," *Oxford Dictionary of National Biography*, Oxford University Press, 2004; online edn., Jan 2008, www.oxforddnb.com/view/article/19708 (accessed 13 August 2016).

[49] Craig, "Logwood as a Factor in the Settlement of British Honduras"; Information of John Bant concerning the logwood trade, 2 July 1672, CO 1/29, f. 4; An Extract concerning the Logwood Trade out of Sir Thomas Lynch his letter 10 March 1671/2 to the Council of Plantations, CO 1/28, ff. 127–8.

would "interrupt" the Spanish trade in the Gulf of Florida, enable commercial relations with the Indians in the area, "tempt those colonies of the Spaniards who are under his tyranny to a trade and commerce with us," and, at the least, provide a base for conducting trade with New England. All that was required was a two-hundred-ton ship with twenty mariners and their provisions and wages for eight months. The result "will then very much to the honour and the advantage of your Highness and this Commonwealth."[50]

But in what other ways could the newly conquered island be used to further "the honour and advantage" of the nation? What were the best methods for pursuing these plans? The recommended device, of course, was a jointstock company that "we are persuaded . . . may tend much to the service of his Highness and the advancement of his affairs in the West Indies as well as to the private profit of adventurers." This "West India Company," once it had received its charter, would raise £12,000 and use privateering vessels provided by the government to attack the Spanish, including their Pacific holdings, while it undertook the settling of Jamaica. The formation of the company, the petitioners claimed, would "free the State from further charge in the West Indies," although they recognized that the "encouragement and foundation of such an undertaking must be from the State," especially in terms of a fleet and encouraging the migration of servants to increase the small population of the island.[51] These appeals for a chartered company seem to have fallen on deaf ears, although the Protectorate did form a commission "for encouraging the affairs of Jamaica and other your Highness' affairs in the West Indies" on 15 July 1656, the membership of which included an array of imperialist perspectives such as Limbrey (son of Maurice Thompson's late partner), Stephen Winthrop (son of John Winthrop and brother of John Winthrop, Jr.), and the Barbados planter-turned-London merchant Martin Noell.[52]

The pace of progress of matters on the Jamaican front was not helped by difficulties that beset the Protectorate as Cromwell tried to get the

---

[50] Certain queries concerning his Highness interest in the West Indies [1656?] and A proposition for the erecting of a West India Company and the better serving of this Commonwealth, [1656?], Egerton Ms. 2395, ff. 85, 87, and 107–13 at 107–8, BL.

[51] Proposition for the improving the interest of this Commonwealth in America and tending either to the continuing of the war with the Spaniard to more advantage or the necessitating him to seek a peace, Egerton Ms. 2395, ff. 91–2, BL.

[52] Andrews, *British Committees, Commissions, and Councils of Trade and Plantations,* 44–6.

nation to reform itself in accordance with his godly comprehension of progress. In the midst of the creation of the West Indies commission, for instance, Cromwell announced elections for the second Protectorate Parliament. Unfortunately for the Protector, this session, which lasted from September 1656 to June 1657, allowed for the venting of considerable resentment against military government and sectarians that drove his government to distraction. Cromwell then started afresh, dissolving the Parliament and revamping the Protectorate, even considering at some length a petition, ultimately deciding in the negative, that he become King.[53]

Meanwhile, the West Indies commissioners did not remain idle. They warned Cromwell that the maintenance of Jamaica "as your principal fort and settlement in the West Indies" required immediate attention in the form of increased population. This, they noted, "cannot be carried on by the planters yet there nor by the soldiers nor by the merchants here" without state assistance and recommended that "a settled course be taken with the commander in chief and the Council in Scotland" to send Highlanders "and others as may be best spared" to the island as servants to bolster the demographics. If the government lacked readily available ships to transport servant prisoners, it could contract with merchants to send these people over at customary rates (£5 10s per head), which, they added, even at a cost of an additional thirty shillings for clothing and hammocks would not exceed a cost of £7 per head. This migration would then reconfigure Jamaica from its present "garrison" status into something resembling an actual plantation. This revamped image would, in turn, encourage merchants and others to "forthwith send cargos and servants" while "planters of other parts will speedily transplant and repair thither."[54]

The Protectorate, however, remained generally unresponsive to these suggestions. Indeed, although it gave the "care & management of the Affairs of Jamaica and the rest of America" to the renamed "Committee of America" in October 1657, it seems to have been unable or unwilling to pay any heed the flow of warnings about Jamaica's insecurity that the committee produced over the next year. Fortuitously for this far western outpost of the English Caribbean,

---

[53] Woolrych, *Britain in Revolution*, 651–60.
[54] Report Concerning the Affairs of America from Tobias Bridge, Martin Noell, and Stephen Winthrop to the Protector, 2 June [1657], Egerton Ms. 2395, f. 123, BL.

the Spanish government remained preoccupied during the second half of the 1650s with its own troubles and so did not sustain the resistance to English occupation of the island.[55]

Thus, the history of the Western Design also underscores how the enduringly symbiotic relationship between public and private interests constituted the platform for pursuing seventeenth-century English overseas ventures. As the first direct state-sponsored overseas initiative in English history, it constituted a novelty in terms of how such projects were pursued, but did this amount to an alteration in the management of imperial matters as far as contemporaries were concerned? Previously, as we have seen, those who led the pursuit of overseas trade and colonization resorted to the government only when they sought legitimacy for their activities or when they employed state institutions, notably courts, to defend their interests. The scale of military force that the Design required, of course, exceeded the capacity of those who hitherto had charge of English affairs in the Western Hemisphere. The promoters of the Design expected that the vigor of the Protectorate grounded in that government's millenarian-tinged anti-Spanish attitude would bring the desired result. As they learned the hard way, however, the English state still required the resources of individuals and groups in both the metropolis and on the ground if overseas projects were to have any decent prospects.

Instead of demarcating the line between the interests of the state and those of its citizens more clearly, the increasing involvement in the direction of state policy by "new modelers" thus blurred the lines between "private" and "public" even further. The likes of Pennoyer, Thompson, and Noell still did not separate – nor still were they expected to separate – their pursuit of overseas initiatives from their governmental relationships: with respect to overseeing areas in which they had particular expertise, such as Anglo-American colonization or Asian trade, they *became* the state, while, at the same time, they carried on trading and colonizing with increasing vigor. After all, to their minds, the work they performed as they moved seamlessly from merchant to commissioner and back improved their situations along with that of the nation.

---

[55] Report of Thomas Povey, John Mill, Stephen Winthrop, Martin Noell, John Lymbrey, Tobias Bridge, Robert Bowes, and Richard Sydenham to the Privy Council, 29 October 1657, Egerton Ms. 2395, ff. 136r–137v, BL; Committee of America to the Protector [Richard Cromwell], 17 October 1658, Egerton Ms. 2395, ff. 158v–159r, BL; Wright, "The Spanish Resistance to the English Occupation of Jamaica."

7

Interregnum, Restoration, and English Overseas Expansion

The Thompson group drew the English state into greater involvement in the Eastern Hemisphere as they gained control of English interests in Asia just as they had done in the Western Hemisphere; this pattern persisted after the return of kingly government in 1660, although the personal importance of Thompson receded. The Protectorate's grant of a new charter to the East India Company on 19 October 1657 brought an end to the squabbling between the company and its equally well-connected and wealthy competitors that had plagued English interests in the Indian Ocean for two decades. The state's intervention here demonstrated some degree of commitment to Anglo-Asian affairs as it did with respect to Anglo-America. It did not, however, extend its role beyond the customary: the reconstituted East India Company acquired its renewed sense of purpose from the former Assada Adventurers, who now assumed the direction of the company. Consequently, Maurice Thompson and his partners, who had nurtured their expansive view of managing overseas interests for almost two decades, were now in a position to apply the additional resources of the EIC in order to realize that vision, while the vehicle for managing those interests in the Eastern Hemisphere remained corporate.

The situation of the English east of the Cape of Good Hope was dire in the mid-1650s. While the East India Company and the Assada Adventurers had officially merged in 1650 after prodding from the government, their bickering had continued since the members could not agree on the desirability of continuing operations under a joint stock format. Governor William Cockayne and other holdovers from the pre-merger EIC favored the customary way they had done business, in which investors contributed to the stock fund on which the company drew to conduct its voyages and pay dividends, as applicable. On the other hand, it had always been the strong preference of the Assada group to use the corporate entity to oversee common interests, such as the maintenance of factories; members would contribute to the general fund that covered such expenses but would be free to conduct their own trade under the company's license. This debate over method of operation drained the EIC's capital and, perhaps, morale as it left present and prospective investors unsure of the company's strategy and even of its ability to conduct a strategy. Thus, the EIC lacked the means to cope with either unaffiliated traders or the VOC, which, like its WIC counterpart, had used the distractions to its English rivals brought by the Civil Wars to good advantage. It even created two independent stock ventures, the Fourth and the United Joint Stocks.[1]

The condition of foreign affairs made this bad situation worse. Although the war with Spain (1655–60) went reasonably well for the English generally, it hampered overseas trade by enabling enemy fleets and privateers to threaten East India Company shipping, in particular, with impunity. At the same time, the Dutch turned to their familiar tactics of delay and obfuscation when the EIC demanded the return of Pulau Run in accordance with the determination of the arbiters appointed pursuant to the Treaty of Westminster. Then, the government compelled the company to "lend" it the £85,000 awarded to it for injuries it had incurred at the hands of the Dutch. To compound these issues, the two Joint Stocks presented competing claims to these damages as well as to the island.

Only the state could mediate this situation. Curiously, though, instead of withdrawing from the company and working to dissolve it before pursuing their personal interests in an open environment, the former Assada Adventurers joined their rivals in petitioning for intervention from the Protector. With cooperation rather than confrontation now the modus operandi of the EIC, a satisfactory arrangement was reached even though the distractions caused by the government's other matters had resulted, to the company's mind, in an inordinate delay. During this time, private traders, desperate to gain business, severely undercut one another in their dealings with Asian merchants; privateers diverted the fruits of

---

[1] For the arbitration award, see A letter of intelligence from The Hague, 18 September 1654, *TSP* 2: 592. For the company's complaints and disputes, see *CCMEIC* 2: xx–xxiv; *CCMEIC* 3: iii–vii; A General Court of Election of the Adventurers in the United Joint Stock, 14 August 1655, *CCMEIC* 3: 51–2.

such business as was conducted; and the Dutch imposed another blockade of the Bantam factory on their usual pretext that they were at war with the Sultan there.[2]

The issuance of the new charter resolved some of these problems and provided a foundation for resolving others. In the first instance, it confirmed Governor Cockayne's preference for the joint stock method. In every other respect, however, it incorporated the views of the erstwhile Assada Adventurers. To demonstrate the company's new direction, Maurice Thompson, freed from his Western Design responsibilities, was elected governor, while Cockayne returned to the Committees.[3] This reorganization enabled its officers to invigorate the company's finances operations on an unprecedentedly firm footing.[4]

Was it coincidental that the East India Company enjoyed a massive influx of capital after Thompson assumed its leadership? Did investors commit their funds to the company with the general expectation that unity would bring success after years of sputtering? Did the particular plan of Thompson and his partners, held over from their Assada days, contribute to the renewed appeal of the EIC as an investment opportunity? We have no record of the thinking of investors on these issues. Nevertheless, after almost twenty years of work, this successful recapitalization gave the Thompson group a substantial fillip toward the realization of its conception of overseas trade and colonization. Once

---

[2] *CCMEIC* 3: x–xvi.

[3] The 1657 charter has been lost but its terms were directly incorporated into the 1661 version issued by the Crown. The company promptly opened a new joint stock subscription in conjunction with the approval of the charter; Preamble to the subscription to the New Joint Stock, [19 October 1657], *CCMEIC* 3: 173–5. The "new adventurers" leading the EIC included Cockayne, Andrew Riccard, Alderman Thomas Foote, Alderman Nathaniel Temms, Pennoyer, Alderman John Lewis, Thompson, Thomas Andrews, Martin Noell, Samuel Moyer, William Ryder, William Vincent, Nathaniel Wyche, John Banks, Richard Ford, Captain Crowther, William Garway, Thomas Kendall, Edward Peirce, Thomas Winter; Robert Cranmore, Captain Brookhaven, Thomas Breton, and Richard Davidge, A General Assembly of the New Adventurers, 3 November 1657, *CCMEIC* 3: 179–80. *A List of the Names of all the Adventurers in the New General Stock to East-India, who have taken the last Oath agreed on by the generality, December the 8th 1657* was published. When the company had to obtain its new charter after the Restoration, there were ten holdovers: Riccard (the new governor), Lewis, William and Maurice Thompson, Ford, Drax, Vincent, Kendall, Moyer, and Ryder; Letters Patents granted to the Governor and Company of Merchants of London, Trading into the East-Indies, 3 April 1661, in Shaw, *Charters Relating to the East India Company from 1600 to 1761*, 33–4. Five of these received knighthoods: Riccard, William Thompson, Ford, Drax, and Ryder.

[4] The 1657 subscription effected £739,782 10s, an amount greater than the Third, Fourth, and United Joint Stocks altogether; *CCMEIC* 3: xx.

they secured the management of the East India Company, they moved quickly to put their plan into effect: just four days after his election as EIC Governor, Thompson, who now led both companies, "treated with" the Guinea Company to hand over to its East India counterpart the remaining seven and one-half years of its patent along with a lease on its factory at Cormontine and its other property in return for £1,300. The EIC immediately assumed control of these facilities.[5]

After its own reorganization in 1651, the Guinea Company, like its Asian counterpart, also had a reunified management. The deeply experienced recipients of the new patent –Thompson, John Wood, Rowland Wilson, and their associates – had already taken a lead in expanding English involvement on the African coast between the Gambia River and the Bight of Benin and encouraged the coincidental increase in the exportation of slave labor to Anglo-America from the mid-1630s, as discussed in Chapter 3. After settling their dispute with Samuel Vassall, they sent a fleet to the Gambia with hopes of maintaining a large-scale slave trade there. These hopes, however, were dashed in 1652, as we have seen, by Prince Rupert's fleet, and it took at least two years for the company to recover before the war with the Dutch intervened. Over the next six years, its operations continued to be impeded by privateers, by its Dutch adversaries, by the Spanish after the outbreak of the Anglo-Spanish War, by unauthorized English traders, and by traders operating legitimately twenty leagues east of Cormontine. By 1657, the company's position was scarcely better than that of the EIC. According to the standard account of English in West Africa prior to 1700, it "had ceased to function as an effective trading body," although it retained its presence at Sherbro and on the Gold Coast.[6]

Thompson and his partners, however, evidently felt this was a situation that was worth salvaging. Even though the monopolies granted by

---

[5] A Court of Committees for the New General Stock, 18 December 1657, CCMEIC 3: 199; A General Court of Election begun and continued the 10th, 11th, 12th, and 14th December, 1657, at Merchant Taylor's Hall and finished the 17th December at the East India House, CCMEIC 3: 197.

[6] Hair and Law, "The English in Western Africa to 1700," 254. For the generally permeable line between unlicensed and chartered interests, as in the case of Samuel Vassall, see Scott, *The Constitution and Finance of English, Scottish and Irish Joint Stock Companies to 1720*, 1: 247–50; Appleby, "A Guinea Venture, c. 1657." For the Spanish, whose fleet was inconveniently based along the London–Guinea route, see To the Venetian agent, 17 March 1657 (n.s.), TSP 6: 104; for the Dutch, see Extract of the register of the resolutions of the high and mighty lords states-general of the United Netherlands, 8 March 1657 (n.s.), TSP 6: 78.

their respective charters had proven previously unenforceable by the two companies, their union under one government provided sufficient resources to give those who controlled the new entity substantial control over the commodities that fueled the Guinea and Indian Ocean trades and, by extension, trade with America. With their superior connections, access to capital, and trading forts, as well as experienced and trusted factors, they expected to gain a permanent ascendancy over rivals domestic and foreign.

Having made their legal and financial preparations, the EIC leadership sent detailed instructions to their factor at Cormontine, Lancelot Stavely, about the conduct of their new intercontinental trade. Gold, perhaps inevitably, played a key role here as it was the principal medium of exchange: Africans, as the eponymous Gold Coast suggests, had it and Asians wanted it, while Asians had fabrics and cowrie shells, which Africans wanted. Thus, Stavely received the charge to work with factors sent from England to manage the company's voyages between Guinea and Indian, the arrangements for the first of which began within two weeks of the issuance of the new charter to the East India Company.[7] Ivory came second in terms of the value accorded by Asians to Guinea commodities. This trade involved substantial sums: James Conget, who succeeded Stavely, informed his employers that he had loaded approximately £100,000 worth of gold and 1,823 pounds of ivory for Surat and hoped to send another £10,000 worth of gold in six weeks.[8]

The company for its part made clear that it had "appropriated unto themselves the exportacion and importacion of severall Commodities outwards to, and homewards from Guinea and the East Indies."[9] Cormontine, however, was not only an entrepôt: like Bantam and Surat (and Boston and Bridgetown for that matter), it constituted a commercial

---

[7] East India Company in London to Fort Cormontine, 31 December 1657, *TGC*, 1–2; Commission and instructions given to Ralph Johnson by the East India Company in London, 31 December 1657, *TGC*, 3–5. For the use of cowries in African trade from the end of the fifteenth century, see, e.g., Fage, "African Societies and the Atlantic Slave Trade," 105.

[8] James Conget at Fort Cormontine to the East India Company in London, 27 December 1658 with copy letter, 8 October 1658, *TGC*, 27–30 at 27, 29. For ivory expectations, see, e.g., Maurice Thompson, Governor of the East India Company in London, to Lancelot Stavely at Fort Cormontine, 15 July 1658, *TGC*, 14–15. The company also used slave labor at its factories; James Conget at Fort Cormontine to the East India Company in London, 10 July 1658, *TGC*, 13–14.

[9] Extracts from the commission and instructions issued by the East India Company in London to Captain Henry Tyrell of the *Surat*, *TGC*, 17–18.

center from which merchants conducted trade with an extensive area. Stavely requested two pinnaces "for the Benen & Gaboone Trade" and to go "to the Bight [of Benin]" to acquire ivory despite continuing Dutch interference.[10]

The EIC's correspondence from this period makes it clear that Thompson and his associates relied on their agents in a number of places, such as Amsterdam, to secure commodities (especially certain kinds of cloth), to conduct business honestly, and to provide intelligence on the ground for the best way to acquire African goods. Thus, Stavely asked his employers to send "linnen Sheetes large Brass the light Est that can be Gotten, Iron Flemish sayes, Ruggs, Niccanees, Brawles, Guinea Cloth, a few Tapseeles" as well as "Cargoes of Cormandell long Cloth, Booke Callicoes, Booges, Bright Maniloes, 5 or 6 pieces of Red Cloth upon Each, Rangoes the Deepest black Coullers." He also advised them of the presence of "Interlopers" trading for slaves and gold and of the merchandise preferences of Africans, who, for instance, "now desire all old heavy Gunns" not "the new slender Musketts" provided by the company that often broke when fired.[11]

The opportunity to acquire more Asian commodities and more directly provided by the merger also enabled greater access to the third African commodity highly desired by the English in the seventeenth century: slaves. The slave trade to Anglo-America continued to grow during the 1650s, despite the wars with the Dutch and the Spanish, although the normally impressive Trans-Atlantic Slave Trade Database yields little evidence of this, probably since more voyages than usual went unrecorded and others appear to have slipped through the net for some reason, such

[10] Stavely to East India Company, 22 February 1657/8, *TGC*, 8. For Dutch harassment, see, e.g., Cormontine to Right Worshipful Company, 18 February 1661/2, IOR E/3/27, ff. 106–7.

[11] E.g., Maurice Thompson and Thomas Andrew, Governor and Deputy of the East India Company in London, to John Bancks in Amsterdam, 5 March 1657/8, *TGC*, 6–7; same to Jonas Abeeles in Amsterdam, 5 March 1657/8, *TGC*, 7. For Stavely's requests, see Lancelot Stavely at Fort Cormontine to the East India Company in London: undated letter said by Company to be written 1 May 1658 with copy letter 22 February 1657/8, *TGC*, 7–9. Most of these goods were Indian cloths. Africans also sought muskets (the company put 300 of them aboard the *Marigold* on the first voyage to Guinea) and iron (the *Marigold* carried 20 tons of it); Commission and instructions to Robert Johnson, 31 December 1657, *TGC*, 4. This pattern remained in place; see, e.g., List of documents sent on the *Surat* for Fort Cormontine, 15 July 1658, *TGC*, 15, and East India Company in London to the Agent and factors at Fort Cormontine, 16 July 1658, *TGC*, 15–16.

as that of the *Hopewell* seized at Barbados by Rupert after delivering "on or about 250" slaves from Guinea in 1652.[12]

Moreover, the correspondence between the company and its factors on the Gold Coast makes infrequent mention of trading in slaves perhaps since the trade was conducted via Barbados (where many company ships called on their way from Africa), and so there would have been no need to send accounts to Cormontine. In September 1660, the Thompson group even directed their factor "to forbeare the buying and selling of any Negroes, being it hath proved very much to our prejudice formerly and will so continue," and to try to stop others from engaging in the slave trade.[13] Thus, there has been reluctance to identify the company and its successor in interest, the East India Company, as an active slave trader. This view meshes with the belief that the English were not involved in the slave trade to a substantial extent prior to the creation of demand for slaves by the cultivation of sugar on Barbados in the 1640s. Whatever English slave trade that did exist prior to the 1660s was conducted "illegally on the Gold Coast and legally further east," we have been told.[14]

It is difficult to accept these claims. First, the advice from the EIC to their Cormontine factor to eschew the slave trade did not convey any sort of intention to abandon that commerce by men who had been as deeply involved in it as any English person had for thirty-five years and who, notwithstanding this letter, remained deeply involved in it. Also, there is direct evidence that the East India Company did trade in slaves: it proposed during the subsequent negotiations that wound up its involvement

[12] Llewellyn and Company against Henry Powell, late master of the *Hopewell*, Examination of John Farrington, 22 September 1653, HCA 13/67, ff. 536r–538r. The *Hopewell* did not make any slave trading voyages between 1650 and 1659, according to the Trans-Atlantic Slave Trade Database, www.slavevoyages.org/voyages/Cz5LK6qY (accessed 9 August 2016). The database lists twenty-seven voyages made from Africa to the Caribbean (including, for instance, Martinique) and North America in "British" and "Dutch" ships between 1650 and 1657. These vessels disembarked 203 slaves on average (267 having embarked on average originally). Twelve voyages ended at Barbados; this would translate into approximately 2,500 African arrivals there during these eight years; www.slavevoyages.org/voyages/PLobHg4S (accessed 9 August 2016). The population of Barbados has been estimated at approximately 53,300 in 1660, of which some 27,000 were Africans and some 26,000 were Europeans; McCusker and Menard, *The Economy of British North America*, 153.
[13] East India Company in London to Edmond Child at Fort Cormontine, 14 September 1660, TGC, 78.
[14] Hair and Law, "The English in Western Africa to 1700," 254–5; Makepeace, "English Traders on the Gold Coast."

in Guinea that "Their factors shall furnish the factors of the Royal Company [of Adventurers Trading into Africa] with such an assortment of goods as shall be necessary for the advantage of their trade of negroes to the value of £6,000 a year." Therefore, it seems much more likely that the company's caution about the slave trade reflects the concern of its members over the future of their African operations in the aftermath of the Restoration. For Charles II and his friends had taken an immediate interest – unprecedented for English government leadership in the history of English overseas expansion – in the highly lucrative Guinea trade, especially its slave component. As early as 18 December 1660, the Crown had granted a one-thousand-year patent to the African coast from the Gambia River to the Cape of Good Hope "for the sole use of" the Duke of York (the King's brother) "and others," which, of course, conflicted with the East India Company's plans. Given the involvement of so many EIC Committees in the Interregnum governments, it is certainly conceivable that they did not wish to risk offending the King by standing in his way on this point.[15]

Also, it may have suited the East India Company to keep the record of its commerce in gold and ivory separate from its other interests; this would explain the relative dearth of references to slavery in the company's archive. Yet it begs credulity to accept necessarily that Thompson, Vassall, Wood, Martin Noell, James Drax, William Pennoyer, and their associates abandoned the increasingly lucrative slave trade after years of engaging it and after years of pursuing a plan that incorporated the plantation trade into what might be termed a seventeenth-century global enterprise. Moreover, were these experienced and determined businessmen unaware of the continuation of these developments they had initiated that could permit an observer in Surinam in 1663 to identify "Negroes" as "the strength and sinews of this Western world"? After all, Thompson, Vassall, and Wood had looked forward to sending slave trading voyages from 1651 until Rupert's intervention, while Andrew Riccard, Noell, Richard Ford, William Ryder, and John Banks readily involved

[15] The Company's Proposals to the Duke of York touching Fort Kormontine, 3 September 1662, *CCMEIC* 4: 250–1. If this was the case, the effort was largely successful: holdovers Riccard, Richard Ford, William Ryder, Sir George Smith, John Bence, Sir Martin Noell, and Thomas Povey joined the returning Guinea veteran Sir Nicholas Crispe, the Barbadian Sir John Colleton, York, Prince Rupert, and others in the Royal African Company, which received a monopoly to the Guinea trade; Warrant to prepare a bill for the King's signature, containing a grant to the Royal Company of Adventurers Trading into Africa, [10 January 1662/3], *CSPC AWI* 5: 120–2.

themselves in the Guinea Company's successor, the Royal Adventurers Trading into Africa, whose participation in the slave trade is beyond doubt.[16]

The East India Company also bought slaves for its own use whom it intended to deploy at the island of St. Helena, situated some 1,100 miles west of Angola and 1,300 miles south of the Bight of Benin in the South Atlantic, which it had obtained as part of its new patent to serve as a locus for the transshipment of commodities and for the establishment of a plantation.[17] Madagascar and Assada had proven unsuitable locations for an English colony and were located on the "wrong" side of Africa for linking Asian trade with the Gold Coast and America. The EIC, probably at the suggestion of James Drax, decided to undertake the plantation of 158-square-mile St. Helena. The prospects afforded by this place had been apparent to those involved in Asian commerce for years; like the similarly sized Barbados, it offered a useful rendezvous for trading fleets to refit and to escape pirates and other enemies. Indeed, the Dutch had made a couple of abortive attempts to settle the island.[18] By the summer of 1659, the EIC had completed its preparations for colonizing the island "both to the advantage of the Adventurers, and the honor of the English Nation."[19]

While the East India Company Committees plotted the planting of St. Helena, they also recognized that the success of their larger scheme required their ready accessibility to Asian commodities. It is, of course, a commonplace of imperial history that the English planted colonies with

---

[16] Letter from Surinam, 8 November 1663, CO 1/17, ff. 226r–227r at 226v–227r. For the Guinea Company holdovers and Sir Nicholas Crispe, see, e.g., meeting of the Court of Assistants of the Royal Company, 8 March 1663/4, T 70/75, f. 6r; for Banks, see, e.g., Meeting of the Court of Assistants of the Royal African Company, 10 September 1674, T 70/76, f. 18.

[17] James Conget to EIC, 10 July 1658, FP, Correspondence from the Gold Coast (E4) (1658), 12; James Conget at Barbados to the East India Company in London, 4 February 1659/60 with copy letter from Fort Cormontine, 20 June 1659, TGC, 50–3 at 50.

[18] For the importance of St. Helena, see, e.g., The humble petition of diverse merchants trading to the East Indies to Richard Cromwell, 24 September 1658, CO 77/8, f. 115. For the intermittent Dutch presence at the island, see, e.g., Samuel Browne from St. Helena to EIC, 27 April 1650, IOR E 3/22, ff. 2–3; CCMEIC, 3: xxix–xxx. For the involvement of Drax, also a "new adventurer," in the patent, see A Court of Committees for the New General Stock, 5 January 1658/9, CCMEIC 3: 305; Foster, "The Acquisition of St. Helena." The 1661 patent reconfirmed the company's right to erect colonies and plantations at St. Helena (and elsewhere "within the Limits and Bounds of Trade"); Shaw, *Charters Relating to the East India Company from 1600 to 1761*, 45.

[19] Extract from instructions issued by the East India Company in London to Captain George Swanley of the *Truro*, 23 June 1659, TGC, 41.

migrants from Africa and Europe in seventeenth-century America and established trading factories with few European inhabitants in seventeenth-century Africa and Asia. By 1650, it was apparent that the American model would not work in Asia, as the failures to colonize Madagascar and Assada provided painful reminders of the added difficulties of colonization in the Indian Ocean; the English made no further attempts. For the EIC's purposes, though, this did not matter, as the labor required to produce calicoes, chintzes, and other cloths for the Guinea trade as well as for export to Europe had to be skilled. The only means of generating a reliable stream of "Asian stuffs" then was to attract local weavers to places where the company held the government, which gave them the authority to attract migrants, and it directed its factors to recruit these workers on the best terms possible.[20]

Of course, the skills these weavers possessed compelled the EIC to have more consideration of the circumstances of their workers than, for instance, the Caribbean sugar planters did in dealing with theirs, or risk alienating them. Hence, for instance, the outrage of the Committees at the practice at Madras of "engrossing rice," thereby raising the price of this essential foodstuff and thereby angering these vital workers who threatened to take their skills to a more accommodating place; the factors there must "endeavor" to keep the price of "rice and other provisions reasonable and moderate" so "our Weavers may not be disheartened but our manufacture of cloth may be promoted and our Weavers civilly treated and encouraged by you."[21]

Around 1670, though, the company's agents, worked out a system – an Asian version of Anglo-American indentured servitude – that ensured that weavers remained at their looms and sufficient quantities of cloth flowed into the EIC warehouses. Drawing on preexisting Indian legal and economic practices, the company attached their workers to advance contracts whereby the payment of deposits ensured supply while the weavers received the security of advance orders to fill; if though, for instance, famine intervened as it did in the late seventeenth-century, this security become a trap as contracts had to be honored. Even so, during

---

[20] At Carwar, the factors, acting on instruction from Surat, had made a large investment to secure weavers "from all parts": "we had engaged ourselves so far in the business we could not easily go back without great discouragement to ye weavers." "Against all expectations," though, the cloth did not sell; Cesar Chamberlain, Charles Bendish, Thomas Sherlock to Surat, Carwar, 19 November 1670, IOR H/33, ff. 147r–148v at 147r.

[21] East India Company to Fort St. George, 2 February 1661/2, IOR H/33, f. 12.

our period weavers enjoyed a relatively healthy position due to the demand for their services from other European employers as well as from western Asia.[22]

St. Helena actually constituted one of the bookends in the East India Company's larger plan. The other was Pulau Run, which the company remained determined to reoccupy almost forty years after its expulsion from the island by the Dutch. In the autumn of 1657, the EIC Committees heard a report on the Banda Islands from Captain John Dutton, who had served the VOC there despite his English birth. Dutton provided an insight "which fully satisfies" his listeners and included his estimates for the necessary "men, materials and provisions" sufficient to support a plantation in the Moluccas that convinced the company's leaders to take up the colonization of Pulau Run again.[23] The following year, they appointed Dutton as the island's governor but decided, in the interim, to add St. Helena to his brief and to send him to manage the plantation of that island first.[24]

The Dutton mission, then, constituted another seventeenth-century English imperial moment: the successful establishment of colonies at Pulau Run and St. Helena would have set the termini of a safe route for East India Company shipping through the Indian Ocean. The factory in the Banda Islands would also have served as the eastern end of a string of posts ranging from Bantam in Java to Gombroon in the Persian Gulf. It would thus have provided a better platform for conducting operations in East Asia, even though the directors continued the conservative policy of the Cockayne administration on the issue of establishing new factories especially on the Asian mainland east of Bengal. The revitalized company had already revitalized English involvement in the spice trade: eighty-seven ships would sail from Java to London between 1659 and 1681 when the Bantam factory was lost to the Dutch, "the highest level it ever reached in the seventeenth century."[25]

The pursuit of this scheme entailed renewed competition with the company's Dutch adversaries (who had blockaded Bantam from

[22] Chaudhuri, *The Trading World of Asia and the English East India Company*, 256–62.

[23] A Court of Committees for the New General Stock, 22 December 1657, *CCMEIC* 3: 202.

[24] Dutton was appointed Governor of St. Helena on 17 December 1658; A Court of Committees for the New General Stock, 17 December 1658, *CCMEIC* 3: 302, and received his commission on 11 January 1658/9; IOR E/3/85, f. 96. He was appointed Governor of Pulau Run on 11 October 1658; A Court of Committees for the New General Stock, 11 October 1658, *CCMEIC* 3: 288.

[25] Bassett, "The 'Amboyna Massacre' of 1623," 8–9.

1656 to 1659). The EIC's attempt to achieve this employed a carrot as well as a stick, although the carrot proved insufficiently attractive and the stick insufficiently big to encourage or compel the VOC to allow a greater English presence in the East Indies. For instance, the EIC thought "it would be a good thing for both Companies if some regulation were settled concerning the buying of pepper in the Indies and selling it in Europe" and suggested a common purchase price of 2d per pound and a common selling price of 18d per pound with the VOC having two-thirds and the EIC one-third of the trade (as opposed to the even division agreed in 1619), but the VOC rejected this proposal.[26]

Certainly, no progress had been made in terms of perfecting the company's claims to Pulau Run since the end of the war seven years previously and the Dutton expedition manifested a desire to end its frustration on this point.[27] Yet just as the Anglo-American "imperial moment" of the Western Design amounted, at least in the short term, to a damp squib, so did this Eastern design. The East India Company may have imagined that Dutch resistance to its possession of its rightful property would result in another drubbing of the sort that the English had previously administered. This belief, however, would have overlooked the reality that England was now involved in a long war with Spain; after the Western Design, the Protectorate was in neither the fiscal nor mental condition to undertake further aggressive moves overseas.

Even with the prospect of cooperation on the part of the company and the state, however, the success of an anti-Dutch strategy was not assured. In the first instance when the Protectorate's new envoy to the Hague, George Downing, presented the EIC's grievances, supported by masses of depositions and other documentation it had assembled, to the States General, pursuant to the terms of the treaty, the Dutch refusal to respond to this petition substantively "greatly disappointed" the EIC.[28]

Then, in December 1657, having received Dutton's report, the Court of Committees was informed that the VOC had maintained their blockade of Bantam and continued "to obstruct the trade of the English in the

---

[26] Maurice Thompson to Jonas Abeeles [at Amsterdam], 26 February 1658, *CCMEIC* 3: 233–4.
[27] Petition of East India Company to Lords of Trade, 27 November 1660, Add. Ms. 25115, f. 39, BL.
[28] The Company to George Downing at The Hague, 26 March 1658, *CCMEIC* 3: 244–5.

South Seas." The company responded to this news by asking Downing to seek passports for EIC agents from the Dutch that would allow them to conduct their trade without interference. Cromwell himself asked "for a narrative of all affronts and indignities which can be proved to have been put lately upon the English by the Dutch in the East," promising that he would see to the satisfactory redress of them. The EIC duly presented him with its grievances, but once again nothing came of it.[29]

Meanwhile, it took Dutton two years to establish the East India Company plantation at St. Helena, but on 6 May 1661, he finally boarded the *African* to take up his other government at the other end of the Indian Ocean. The company had sent thirty slaves to Pulau Run in anticipation of establishing plantations there. Unfortunately for the English, this episode turned into bitter farce. After calling at the EIC factories at Bantam and Macassar, shadowed by Dutch ships, Dutton arrived at Pulau Run with his commission on 11 March 1662 and announced his arrival to the Dutch Governor Van Dam the following day, who responded two days later "with an impertinent answer." Several days later, Dutton wrote again to Van Dam "concerning the quiet and peaceable delivery of Poularoone into our possession," only to receive a response in which the governor "absolutely denied the surrendering up of that island to us, and very much slighted our gracious sovereign's commission." Dutton protested to no avail, then

---

[29] The Protector, however, insisted that the company refer its grievances with the Dutch to his government rather than approach the Dutch ambassador directly (A Court of Committees for the United Joint Stock, 2 September 1657, *CCMEIC* 3: 161–2) or take action against the Dutch itself; Francesco Giavarina, Venetian Resident in England, to the Doge and Senate, 30 November 1657, *Calendar of State Papers Relating to English Affairs in the Archives of Venice, Volume 31, 1657–1659*, ed. Allen B. Hinds (London, 1931), 123–35, *British History Online*, www.british-history.ac.uk/cal-state-papers/venice/vol31/pp123-135 (accessed 18 July 2016); Collections taken from several persons and letters lately returned from India concerning several abuses and indignities put upon the English nation by the Dutch, presented to His Highness, 9 September 1657, *CCMEIC* 3: 163–5; A Court of Committees for the New General Stock 28 December 1657, *CCMEIC* 3: 204–5. Martin Noell seconded the company's efforts by relating its concerns to Downing personally; A Court of Committees for the New General Stock, 29 December 1657, *CCMEIC* 3: 205; The Lord Protector to George Downing, Resident at The Hague, [February 1657/8], *CCMEIC* 3: 231; The Company to the Honourable George Downing at The Hague, 23 April 1658, *CCMEIC* 3: 255. For Cromwell's intervention, see A Court of Committees for the New General Stock, 4 January 1657/8, *CCMEIC* 3: 207–8; The Remonstrance and Petition of the Company to the Protector, [18 January] 1657/8, *CCMEIC* 3: 215–16; A Brief Relation of Several Abuses received from the Dutch in the East Indian Seas, 18 January 1657/8, *CCMEIC* 3: 216–17; Deposition of Quarles Browne, Presented to His Highness, 18 January 1657/8, *CCMEIC* 3: 217–18.

the Dutch seized a boat from one of the English ships and also took "Mr. Marston his Black Boy" from the *Discovery*.[30]

This stonewalling produced the desired effect: unable to compel the handover of the island, Dutton's little fleet departed Pulau Run "under a constant watch" on 14 April 1662. His humiliation and frustration, however, did not end with the failure to assume his government. On 3 May he arrived at Macassar for a month's stay, during which time "the insolent Hollanders flouted us sufficiently; for in a jeering manner they went up & down pointing at us & saying these are the men that would have the Poula Roone but are returned like fools." Six weeks later, the English called at Jepara in central Java where "one Holland great sloop which came near our junk hailed her and in a jesting manner demanded if we had taken Pulau Run." The only consolation in the middle of these humiliations was news of the exploits of the Ming pretender/"pirate" Coxinga, whose capture of Fort Zeelandia, the VOC post in Taiwan, and attack on the Philippines "did greatly affright the Hollanders." Dutton and his family limped back to the Atlantic.[31]

The conception, execution, and collapse of the St. Helena–Pulau Run project occurred during a tumultuous, defining period in English history between the death of Oliver Cromwell on 3 September 1658 and the Restoration of Charles II in May 1660. The latter event remains a benchmark of English history even as the Interregnum has received much more attention in its own right in recent years. To what extent did the return of kingly government constitute a shift in the history of English overseas interests, including the relationship between the English state and its colonies? To what degree, correspondingly, did those who had assumed responsibility for overseas matters after 1642 surrender that responsibility to those who returned with the King? To what degree did the Restoration government provide the impetus for imperial projects on a greater scale than its predecessors? To what degree – and why – did it exercise greater oversight over imperial affairs? To what degree – and why – did English territorial and commercial overseas interests expand between 1660 and 1689? To what degree, then, does tracking the careers of the

---

[30] The fate of the slaves, shipped from Guinea to the Moluccas in three groups in the fall of 1661, remains unknown; "The Madras Agency, 1661," Foster, *The English Factories in India, 1661–64*, 32–59 at 50–1.

[31] John Dutton, A Brief Relation of a Voyage from St Helena to the Coast of Africa to Bantam in India begun the 6th day of May 1661 and from thence to England With the most Remarkable Observations and Passages which happened during the said Voyage, Lansdowne Ms. 213, ff. 435–41, BL.

managers before, during, and after the Restoration help us gauge the course of mid-seventeenth-century English history?

In the historiography of the English Empire, the Restoration customarily constitutes a turning point in the nature of empire when the English state became increasingly involved in initiating and pursuing, as well as defending, English overseas interests. This view jibes with the reality that the restored monarchy inherited a greater capacity to oversee matters from its predecessors, while the definition of what constituted a state matter had widened. It also, though, derives from the conception of the Restoration as the end of the English Revolution and, in terms of Anglo-America, an American perspective that sees the return of kingly government in the metropolis as enabling increased prospects for state intervention in the lives of colonials, which colonials often resisted.[32]

In metropolitan terms, it can be tempting to regard the dizzying collapse of the Caroline order and the equally dizzying emergence of an array of radical prescriptions for changing society with their references to liberty, social welfare, and "leveling" as the advent of modernity. It can also be tempting to view the return of the old regime forms as a frustration of the aims of the Levellers, Ranters, Diggers, and Fifth Monarchists, among others. In stymying the more radical views of the 1640s and 1650s, the tyrannical attempts to control the people by the Protectorate followed by the later Stuart monarchs left this revolutionary legacy to be picked up by future generations.

First, though, the history of the English Civil Wars and the Interregnum unequivocally demonstrates the general lack of enthusiasm among the English for liberty as the concept was defined by certain contemporaries, not to mention by twenty-first-century students, of these events. Having said that, significant changes unquestionably took place in English society, religion, and government after 1641. Unquestionably also, though, the pace of change slowed after 1652 and reversed, arguably to a significant degree, after 1660. Then, in terms of overseas trade and colonization at least, such changes as did occur amounted to increments rather than transformations; the pattern by which English imperial oversight had been conducted for fifty years continued.

The career of Sir Nicholas Crispe sheds additional light on the background of English backers of seventeenth-century overseas trade and colonization but also points to the dangers inherent in the attempt to

---

[32] Games, *Web of Empire*, 286–7; Richter, *Before the Revolution*, 241–56; Koot, *Empire at the Periphery*, 5–6; Pestana, *The English Atlantic in Age of Revolution*, 181–90.

equate political behavior with socioeconomic status in seventeenth-century England. As a founder of the English Guinea trade, as a supporter of the suppression of the Irish rebellion, and as someone who found his fortune in London, Crispe's life tracked that of Maurice Thompson, William Pennoyer, and the other "revolutionary" merchants featured in Robert Brenner's analysis. Sir Nicholas's ardent support for Charles I, however, enables Brenner to dismiss him as a "courtier-merchant."[33]

Perhaps accordingly, Crispe returned to political and economic prominence at the Restoration, serving again in Parliament and becoming a leader of the East India Company as well. In 1662, he transferred that Guinea Company patent that he had accordingly recovered at the Restoration (and was due to expire in three years anyway) to the Company of Royal Adventurers Trading into Africa, then in the process of putting the East India Company out of the Guinea trade. He then joined that Crown-sponsored venture.[34]

Yet despite the losses he suffered for his Royalism and the corresponding rewards, including a knighthood, which he received when Charles II assumed power, Sir Nicholas headed a family with intimate links with the Parliamentarians, although Brenner seems to have missed this. Indeed, Crispe might easily have remained in his place undisturbed during the Civil Wars and the Interregnum as, for instance, his son Thomas, who established the Guinea Company's factory at Cormontine and its other operations on the Gold Coast in 1649–50, and his brother and fellow company member Samuel did, but his orthodox religious beliefs seem to have prevented him from doing so.[35]

The Crispe family had remarkably radical overtones. Another of Sir Nicholas's brothers was Dr. Tobias Crispe, accused of "antinomianism" before his death in 1643. Tobias and Samuel both married daughters of their brother's pre–Civil Wars partner and Guinea trader Rowland Wilson (d. 1654): Anne Wilson (whose second husband was the regicide and overseas merchant Owen Rowe) wed Tobias, and Mary Wilson wed Samuel. Sir Nicholas must have regarded these unions favorably, since "sister Rowe" received a bequest of £20 in his will "to buy her a Ring," while Mary and Samuel's two daughters both received legacies of £800

---

[33] Brenner, *Merchants and Revolution*, 163–4.
[34] Porter, "The Crispe Family and the African Trade in the Seventeenth Century," 72–5.
[35] For Thomas Crispe, see Deposition of Thomas Crispe, London merchant, "having been diverse voyages upon the Coast of Guinea for" Sir Nicholas Crispe and Company, 15 March 1664/5, T 70/169, ff. 35–6; for Samuel Crispe, see, e.g., A Court of Committees, 11 September 1639, *CCMEIC* 1: 324–5.

and their two sons received £500 each. Nicholas Crispe himself married Anne Goodwin, sister of Reverend Thomas Goodwin, the author of the revised Westminster Confession of 1658, a clear statement of Independent principles, and chaplain to Oliver Cromwell. If the bequests she made in her will to "brother Goodwin" and his fellow Independent divines and co-authors, Dr. John Owen and Reverend Philip Nye, provide any indication, Lady Anne Crispe never abandoned her godly beliefs. Did these relations remain on professional, not to say cordial, terms despite taking opposite sides in the Civil Wars? Regardless, notwithstanding his official withdrawal from the Guinea Company in 1643, did Nicholas Crispe actually sever his associations with the Guinea trade while his brother-in-law gained preeminence in the African trade in 1644–54 through his support of the parliamentary cause? Moreover, given the continuing close social associations of these men, can we regard the behavior of Rowland Wilson and his partners, at least with respect to their overseas interests, as revolutionary?[36]

And what are we to make of the substantial continuity in the composition of the managers of English overseas affairs between 1657 and 1665? When the East India Company received a new royal charter in 1661 to replace the one granted it had received four years earlier from the "usurper" Cromwell, the twenty-four recipients included ten adventurers in its 1657 joint stock issue: Andrew Riccard (the new Governor), Drax, Ford, Thomas Kendall, John Lewis, Samuel Moyer, William Ryder, Maurice Thompson, William Thompson, and William Vincent. Another recipient, Theophilus Biddulph, had served as an EIC Committee during the Interregnum, while other adventurers from 1657, including John Banks, John Joliffe (later Deputy-Governor), Noell, and Pennoyer, had remained active in the company after the Restoration. Eight of these men received knighthoods: Riccard, Banks, Drax, Ford, Lewis, Noell, Ryder, and William Thompson.[37] Then, Riccard, Ford, Ryder, Noell, George Smith, John Bence, and Thomas Povey joined, among others, Crispe, Sir

---

[36] Will of Sir Nicholas Crispe, 25 February 1665/6, Crisp, *Collections Relating to the Family of Crispe*, 32–4; Will of Anne Crispe, 31 May 1669, ibid., 36–7.

[37] A General Assembly of the New Adventurers, 3 November 1657, CCMEIC 3: 179–80; *A List of the Names of all the Adventurers in the New General Stock to East-India* (London, 1657); Shaw, *Charters Relating to the East India Company from 1600 to 1761*, 33–4; A General Court of Election for the Fourth Joint Stock, CCMEIC 5: 153 (for Biddulph); A General Court of Election begun and continued the 10th, 11th, 12th, and 14th December 1657 at Merchant Taylors' Hall and finished the 17th December at the East India House, CCEIC 5: 197–8 (for Biddulph, Joliffe, and Noell); A General Court of the Adventurers in the United Joint Stock, 17 November 1663, CCMEIC 5: 358–9 (Pennoyer); A Court of Committees, 18 November 1663, CCMEIC 5: 359 (Banks).

John Colleton, the Duke of York, and the Guinea Company's foe, Prince Rupert, as members of the new Royal Company of Adventurers Trading into Africa, which took over the EIC's Guinea operations in 1663. In the meantime, though, tensions with the Dutch continued on the ground: "two Blacks of Morea," at the behest of "the flemins," burned the company's Cape Coast factory to the ground, and "the villains of Blacks" stole most of the goods that had survived. The company required the good offices of the great merchant John Claessen Akrosan to get to the bottom of the matter.[38]

Still, there were aftershocks. For one, the sectaries, quite a few of whom were, like Moyer, deeply involved in overseas matters at various levels, suffered in civil and political terms for their now-heterodox beliefs. The fear roused in contemporaries by the proliferation of the extreme views, notably those of the Quakers, which emerged after the collapse of the Established Church in the 1640s, rose to an extent that it is possible to regard it as a contributing factor in the desire to bring back the familiar pre-1642 institutions; this was manifested further by the hysteria that followed the determined attempt of some fifty Fifth Monarchists led by the former New Englander Thomas Venner to overthrow the new monarchy on 1–4 January 1661 that never entirely evaporated over the ensuing decades. Certainly, many members of the Cavalier Parliament were keen to blame "Phanaticks" for the convulsions of the preceding two decades, and Venner's attack fueled fears of a return to those convulsions subscribed to this view even if the new King and some of his ministers were less inclined to hold it.[39]

---

[38] Warrant to prepare a bill for the King's signature, containing a grant to the Royal Company of Adventurers Trading into Africa, [10 January 1662/3], *CSPC AWI* 5: 120–2. For the destruction of the Cape Coast factory, see Roger Chappell, William Hulinge, Wm. Haddoe, Richard Maxwell, William Spencer, Jeremy Sapston to Right Worshiful Company of Merchants Trading for Guinea and East India, 10 June 1661, IOR E/3/27, ff. 40–1.

[39] Although the Fifth Monarchists, among the most radical millenarians, rejected orthodox social, religious, and political views, their own vision of reality was eschatological, grounded in their reading of divine providence. This could certainly incorporate their remedies for reforming society's ills, but they were not egalitarian in the modern sense of that concept (although Venner, a cooper, was not a political leader in the conventional sense of the seventeenth century, either). Thus, they believed their actions furthered the demise of ungodly regimes and the attendant coming of the fifth monarchy of King Jesus as prophesized in the Books of Daniel and Revelation. Venner, who apparently regarded the Restoration as more of the same, had led a similar attack on the Protectorate in 1657. The desperate violence of Venner and his associates deeply shocked most Nonconformists, even moving the Quakers to adopt their pacific principles formally; Capp, "*A Door of Hope* Re-opened."

Thus, a number of vocal supporters of "the Good Old Cause" were exempted from the Act of Free and Generall Pardon for treason and other high crimes committed after 1637, including the Reverend Hugh Peter (another ex-New Englander), Rowe, and Robert Tichborne (who had served as an EIC Committee with the Thompson brothers, Riccard, and the other holdovers in 1657). They were condemned to the gruesome punishment levied on traitors: hanging, quartering, and the display of their body parts on the gates of the Tower. Several others, such as Thomas Andrews, Sir John Danvers, and John Venn, had died before 1660, but their property remained subject to forfeiture for their treason. Moyer, a particularly active republican and godly individual, endured a five-and-a-half-year stint in the Tower on suspicion of sedition (although his son was knighted in 1701).[40]

Yet quite a few of those active in overseas commercial and colonizing matters, as well as in the government, during the 1640s and 1650s, entirely escaped punishment, even though some of these men might have boasted similar revolutionary credentials as their partners. For instance, despite his consistently active hostility to royal policy for forty years, Vassall remained at liberty to pursue another attempt to settle Carolina, where he died in the mid-1660s, as well as to petition Parliament to collect money the state owed him for contributing to the Irish expeditions of the 1640s. Perhaps the most remarkable case, though, was that of Maurice Thompson, who had been among the most active and consistent supporters of the parliamentary cause and ensuing governments from the beginning of the revolt against Charles I as well as having been arguably the most active participant in English overseas ventures over the previous thirty years. Notwithstanding a career that really had no distinctions from those of his partners Rowe, Tichborne, Venn, and Andrews, Thompson entertained no fear of the gibbet, having secured a pardon from Charles II just three days after the King returned to England from his exile. And while the bestowal of a knighthood seems to have been rather too much, Thompson's son, like Moyer's, received a baronetcy.[41]

---

[40] For Moyer's religious and political orientation, see *The Humble Petition of Many Inhabitants in and about the City of London*; for his incarceration, see *Diary of Samuel Pepys*, entries for 1 December 1661 and 16 May 1667, www.pepysdiary.com/diary/1661/12/01/, www.pepysdiary.com/diary/1667/05/16/ (accessed 6 October 2016). For his son's baronetcy, see Burke and Burke, *A Genealogical and Heraldic History*, 378.

[41] For Vassall, see Vassall's Claims, 18 August 1660, *CJ* 8: 127; Vassall's Claims, 29 August 1660, *CJ* 8: 142. For Vassall and Carolina, see *CRNC* 1: 14–16, 42–3, 102–14. For Thompson, see Declarations of Maurice Thompson of Stepney, Middlesex, and others

In the same vein, Povey seems to have assumed responsibility for overseeing imperial affairs following the collapse of the Protectorate until Charles established his government. Then, he and Noell were asked to submit – or submitted on their own initiative – "Overtures touching a Council to be erected for foreign plantations." In their view, the proposed council (proposed by whom remains unclear) should provide the means "to regulate and improve what is already ours," which would "revise and raise our reputation among such as are or like to be our enemies" and "give a new spirit and genius to our countrymen quickening and advancing trade," as prospective overseas adventurers would see the monarchy's care for "those distant affairs." They also recommended a streamlining of colonial administration, so "hereafter they may become as one embody commonwealth whose head and center is here." This reformation would start with requests made to the colonial governors "requiring an exact and particular account of the state of their affairs of the nature and constitution of their laws and government and in what model it moves, what numbers of men, what fortifications and other strengths and defenses are upon the place," both for information and to demonstrate royal concern "for the general good"; such reports should be issued annually. Then, colonial governors should receive new commissions, while those colonies governed by chartered entities should be put under equivalent jurisdictions and incorporated "into a more certain civil and uniform way of government and distribution of public justice." Finally, Jamaica should be promoted both on its own terms and in order to make further attacks on the Spanish as well as to encourage coastal trade with Spanish subjects in order to detach these "oppressed people" from Spanish "tyranny."[42]

Whether or not the impetus for preparing this memorandum came from the state, only some of its suggestions were implemented by the Crown, and this result reflects the haphazard approach that the reconstituted monarchy took to empire; those initiatives as did take place after May 1660 still stemmed from people outside the government. Yet the Crown did take the advice to form a council for trade and plantations. The return of the King also brought the return to power of the surviving

"of their acceptance of the King's pardon and of their loyalty and fidelity," 28 May 1660, *CSPD* Charles II 1 (1660–1): 447. The political career of Thompson's son John, first Baron Haversham, transcended the Glorious Revolution; www.thepeerage.com/p549.htm#i5485.

[42] [Draft] Overtures touching a Council to be erected for Foreign Plantations, [1660], Egerton Ms. 2395, ff. 270r–271r, BL.

aristocracy who had found the regicide or Cromwell intolerable as Charles II fostered an air of reconciliation during the period immediately prior to and after his return to England. The makeup of the Council for Foreign Plantations that was created on 4 July 1660 thus included Viscount Saye and Sele as well as such prominent servants of the Protectorate as the Earl of Manchester, Lord Robartes, and a relative newcomer to the public scene, Sir Anthony Ashley Cooper.[43]

When it formed a new and larger Council of Trade and Plantations at the end of 1660 the Crown again appointed additional aristocrats of different political stripes with a particular interest in overseas matters: the Earl of Marlborough, Lord Wharton, Lord Willoughby, John, Lord Berkeley, and Sir George Carteret. It also followed the Interregnum practice of involving merchants and others who held a direct interest including colonial leaders: the names of Riccard, Povey, Noell, Sir William Berkeley, William Watts, Colleton, Thomas Kendall, Crispe, John Limbrey, Ford, Sir John Wolstoneholme, Downing, Joliffe, Sir William Thompson, and Drax all appear in rolls of the council's membership.[44]

These new bodies, which received official briefs also novel in scope, necessarily had to address the state of affairs left by the failure of the Commonwealth. Most important, the Crown inherited the messy state of imperial relations with the Dutch, including the festering anti-Dutch sentiment fueled by continuing frustration with the republic's lack of effort toward resolving English grievances; this delay itself became a chief grievance as Dutch "insolencies" continued in the course of the fierce competition for commodities, markets, and suppliers. This rivalry also affected English imperial relations, since smuggling, abetted by the distractions of the run-up to the Restoration, affected the tobacco and sugar interests of metropolitan-based merchant-planters and their colonial associates, while Anglo-American planters could obtain the best price for their crops from the foreign interlopers.[45]

---

[43] Order appointing a Committee for Plantation Affairs, 4 July 1660, *DRCHNY*, 3:30.

[44] Patent of Charles II constituting a Council for Trade, 7 November 1660, *DRCHNY* 3: 30–2; His Majesty's Commission for a Council for Foreign Plantations, 1 December 1660, *DRCHNY* 3: 32–4.

[45] E.g., Petition of the Earl of Bath and Sir Henry Bennet to the King, [August 1662], *CCMEIC* 4: 241–2; Adams, *A Brief Relation of the Surprizing several English merchants Goods, by Dutch Men of Warre*; Anon., *The Dutch drawn to Life*, esp. 143–56; W.W., *The English and Dutch Affairs Displayed to the Life*; Woofe, *The Tyranny of the Dutch against the English*.

Those who had been unable to secure satisfaction from the Dutch still had a direct line to the government. If anything, they had even better access since Charles, being unsympathetic to republics and sensitive to the position of his nephew in the Republic, shared their concerns about the Estates-General. The King, accordingly, retained the most prominent anti-Dutch figures of the Interregnum as advisors, including Manchester, Ashley, and, perhaps most crucially, Downing, who made the transition from scourge of Royalist exiles to loyal Crown servant with notorious ease; he remained in post as ambassador to The Hague and kept English demands for redress at the forefront of the foreign policy concerns of Charles II's government until he lost that office in 1671.[46]

Given this atmosphere along with its need for funds, it is unsurprising that the government moved to reenact and extend the Navigation Act in 1660 and again in 1663, especially since its 1651 predecessor, enacted during the "usurpation," had been erased from the statute books. This law, which colonial governors were sworn to uphold, required inter alia that goods transported to England from Africa and Asia as well as sugar, tobacco, dye stuffs, cotton, and ginger cultivated in Anglo-America had to be shipped in English vessels; the owners of vessels engaged in the plantation trade had to supply a bond of £1,000 (if smaller than 100 tons) or £2,000 (if larger than 100 tons) that was forfeit if their voyage violated the act.[47] The 1663 version of the statute further proscribed the shipment of any foreign commodities directly to English plantations except in English vessels. It also increased the penalties for growing tobacco in England and Wales.[48]

---

[46] E.g., Sir George Downing to The Lord Chancellor Clarendon, 21 June/1 July 1661, Downing to Clarendon, 15 July 1661 (n.s.), Clarendon to Downing, 16 August 1661, Downing to Clarendon, 18 September 1663, Lister, *Life and Administration of Edward, Earl of Clarendon*, 3: 144–8, 152–5, 166–9, 249–53; Desires of the East India Company to the Lords Commissioners appointed to treat with the Dutch, [February 1660/1], *CCMEIC* 4: 86–8. The return of Saye, who had expressed concerns about the Dutch presence in North America since the 1630s when he became involved in the Saybrook colony, to public life also signaled the Crown's intent to pursue a more vigorous policy against the Republic; Appendix received from My Lord Say, Read 9th August 1642, *DRCHNY* 1: 128.

[47] Charles II, 1660: An Act for the Encourageing and increasing of Shipping and Navigation, *Statutes of the Realm: Volume 5, 1628–80*, ed. John Raithby (s.l, 1819), 246–50, *British History Online*, www.british-history.ac.uk/statutes-realm/vol5/pp246-250 (accessed 15 July 2016).

[48] Charles II, 1663: An Act for the Encouragement of Trade, *Statutes of the Realm: Volume 5, 1628–80*, ed. John Raithby (s.l, 1819), 449–52, *British History Online*, www.british-history.ac.uk/statutes-realm/vol5/pp449-452 (accessed 13 July 2016).

Concerns with the Dutch also carried great weight in the negotiations over the marriage of Charles II. At the Restoration, Portugal, which had provided relatively constant support for Charles Stuart during his Interregnum wanderings, had been at war with the Dutch Republic and Spain, coincidentally the enemies of the Cromwellian Protectorate. With Spain and its traditional enemy France having concluded the Peace of the Pyrenees (1659), however, the Portuguese needed a new friend of their own.[49]

This necessity translated into a substantial imperial coup – at least on paper – when the House of Avis promised to cede Tangier and Bombay along with free trade to Brazil and the East Indies and 2,000,000 livres as the dowry of Catherine of Braganza pursuant to the marriage treaty agreed on 23 June 1661. The most recent discussion of the English acquisition of Tangier, the Moroccan port on the African shore of the Strait of Gibraltar, includes a salutary reminder of the importance of the Mediterranean to English commerce. It also claims that "Charles II, some of his ministers, and a range of observers envisioned the North African city as a hub within England's trading empire and accordingly sought to transform it into an entrepôt and safe harbour linking the increasingly global threads of English commerce." After obtaining Tangier, the Crown made it a free port. This tactic, however, "departed from the legally defined national and corporate trades that increasingly linked England to its overseas possessions," as manifested in the Navigation Act, for instance.[50]

It does not seem, though, that the inclusion of Tangier and Bombay in his domains caused the King to abandon his usual approach to government. Rather, the idea of the transfer of these ports seems to have originated with the Portuguese, who were trying to get rid of them before they lost them to the Spanish or the Moroccans in the case of Tangier or to the Dutch in the case of Bombay; did Charles even know the location of the latter city in 1661? Presented with this opportunity, however, the King's advisors found the prospect of a base that could command the Mediterranean trade that Tangier seemed to afford too important to pass up – at the least, the Dutch had to be prevented from securing it. It might also provide a location from which to interfere with

---

[49] Belcher, "Spain and the Anglo-Portuguese Alliance of 1661"; Grose, "The Anglo-Portuguese Marriage of 1662."
[50] Stein, "Tangier in the Restoration Empire," 986.

the longstanding practice of enslaving English (and other European) mariners and passengers that was conducted from the neighboring Barbary States.[51]

Unfortunately, the English were unable to improve the desperate situation bequeathed to them by the Portuguese at Tangier. The idea of making the place a free port might seem counterintuitive in terms of creating an increasingly protected empire – at least to some modern historians – but it is not clear that "Restoration imperialists" identified and pursued a mercantilist policy in the modern sense. Moreover, they had the Dutch example of *mare liberum* (albeit applied hypocritically from an English perspective) as a way of managing overseas trade. Then, the administrative alternatives for Tangier, acquired uniquely as part of a royal dowry, included creating a proprietorship (individual, partnership, or corporate) for it along the lines of New York or Carolina or retaining it as a royal colony like Virginia or Jamaica. Those colonies were quite different from Tangier, however: no English person would go to Morocco to plant the equivalent of sugar or tobacco (not in the least since venturing beyond the walls of the place meant taking life in hand). The new acquisition, though, already had a population of merchants of diverse backgrounds who might be encouraged to remain if customs duties were waived and a mole built. Unfortunately for Tangier's advocates, the cost of maintaining the garrison in the teeth of vigorous Moroccan hostility, not to mention constructing the anchorage, vastly outweighed the benefits of governing the city. Charles II, still short of funds in 1684, thus had to abandon the place and suffer the indignation of destroying the mole, thereby ending the seventeenth-century English imperial experiment in North Africa.[52]

Bombay proved to be another dubious acquisition as far as the English government was concerned, although António de Mello de Castro, specially appointed to handle the cession of it by the Portuguese, had recognized its possibilities. Thus, like his Dutch counterpart at Pulau Run, he tried to prevent its handover. Mello de Castro effected a considerable delay, despite the desire of the Indian merchants for the English takeover, but he had to yield at the end of 1665: it was one

[51] Sloane Ms., 3509, ff. 11–12, BL; Edward, Earl of Clarendon, *The Life of Edward Earl of Clarendon*, 1: 494.
[52] Tangier has begun to receive attention in the literature, but the chief published account remains Routh, *Tangier*.

thing to see off three ships commanded by an operative of the East India Company at a small island in the East Indies, but quite another to resist a fleet organized by York, commanded by a peer of the realm (Marlborough), and backed by a marriage treaty between Crowns. Like Tangier, though, by virtue of the nature of its conveyance Bombay was now a royal municipality under direct royal authority – and thus maintained by the threadbare royal purse. Too far away to defend effectively and with its integration into the rest of the English Empire a question to be negotiated while money went to its maintenance, the place looked to be a losing proposition, except that the government finally persuaded the East India Company, whose directors were reluctant to add to their costs by creating new factories, to take it over in March 1667.[53]

The English acquisition of this location, though, proved exceedingly beneficial, as the Assada Adventurers had predicted: Bombay's autonomy and its harbor, coupled with the religiously tolerant attitude practiced by the company's capable officials on the ground – Sir George Oxinden, first EIC governor of Bombay (another Commonwealth holdover) and his successor Gerald Aungier – enabled it to surpass its Portuguese rivals. Indeed, the transfer proved a fortunate one for the English, as the Mughals proved unable to defend Surat, their most important port, successfully; it suffered a devastating and humiliating sack by the forces of Shivaji, the would-be Maratha Emperor, in 1664, followed by his repeated demands for money on pain of further attacks and another raid in 1670. Moreover, the creation of local institutions, especially courts, there established a model for subsequent Anglo-Asian colonization by devolving considerable responsibility for local matters on it while securing the company's control of the town.[54]

While all of this was going on, the Crown also acted quickly to perfect its new interest in the Guinea trade. While its behavior here provides further evidence of the lucrativeness of this commerce, we have no direct evidence as to why the King and his brother, James, Duke of York, had a

---

[53] Ames, "The Role of Religion in the Transfer and Rise of Bombay."

[54] Gerald Aungier et al. to Company, 30 March 1670, IOR E/3/31, ff. 3–6. For the views of the Assada Adventurers, Paper of ye Merchants trading to Assada giving reasons why they refuse to join with the East India Company in a 5-year voyage upon the old joint stock, 10 November 1649, CO 77/7, ff. 66r–66v at 66v; D[arell], *Strange News from the Indies*, 2, suggested Carwar, south of Bombay, as a prime location for trade on the western coast of India; Stern, *The Company-State*, 22–30. For the rapid decline of Surat, see Pearson, "Shivaji and the Decline of the Mughal Empire."

particular awareness of it; perhaps their uncle, Prince Rupert, acquainted them of his raid on the Guinea Company's fleet in the Gambia in 1652. Regardless, the royal brothers, recognizing "how necessary it is to the honour and profit of this our Realme of England that the said trade, and also such others as are hereby granted should be vigourously prosecuted," intervened in African affairs with remarkable rapidity and directness: by the end of 1660 – Charles had been in power only since May – a new Company of *Royal* (emphasis added as this marked the first inclusion of this designation in any English overseas enterprise) Adventurers Trading into Africa had received its charter.[55]

With York at its head, this Crown-sponsored venture pressured the East India Company to hand over its African operations to it. Unable to resist the royal desire for the Guinea trade, the EIC acquiesced, and the arrangements were concluded by 1663, leaving the EIC with St. Helena as a vestige of its interests west of the Cape of Good Hope. Thus, so far from further coordinating and centralizing an English Empire, the government of Charles II severed English commercial and colonizing activities eastward of St. Helena from those in Africa and America in administrative terms. This imperial demarcation also formally quashed the vision of integrated Asian, African, and American interests, as conceived by Sir William Courteen and the Assada Adventurers, just as it was starting to be realized. Instead, York and his partners pursued the perfection of their new patent, sending a first expedition to Guinea commanded by Robert Holmes, one of Rupert's officers in his 1652 voyage, which seized a fort held by agents of the Duke of Courland that occupied territory claimed by the English.[56]

While Asia remained outside their bailiwick, the new "Lords of Trade and Plantation" did assume direct authority over the new royal colony of Jamaica. Thus, they took the lead in the unprecedented governmental involvement in the promotion and administration of an overseas colony, this one acquired by conquest. As early as December 1660, while the possibility remained that Charles II would return the island to Spain, the

---

[55] Copie of ye Royall Companyes Patent, [10 January 1663], CO 1/17, ff. 2–18 at 14r; Petition of the Company of Royal Adventurers in England Trading into Africa, 26 August 1663, SP 44/13, f. 355, TNA.

[56] For the agreement by the East India Company to withdraw from Guinea in favor of the Royal Company of Adventurers, see The Company's Proposals to the Duke of York touching Fort Kormontine, 3 September 1662, *CCMEIC* 4: 250–1; A Court of Committees, 8 October 1662, *CCMEIC* 4: 259–60, and Articles of Agreement between the Royal African Company and the East India Company, 16 October 1662, *CCMEIC* 4: 263–4.

Council of Trade and Plantations received "Considerations about the peopling and settling of Jamaica" from Captain Thomas Lynch, who had served with the army there. Lynch recommended first and foremost that "a person of honor & reputation be commissioned for that government." Sending such a governor would "more fully declare his Majesties estimation of the island and his purpose to settle it and encourage great numbers to transport themselves & their estates" as well as "cause ye [business] & affairs of the island to be more moderately considered at Court." Indeed, "the reputation of his honour and honesty will cause & encourage people of quality & estate to come thither to plant and settle and without such people can no island ever be made rich for poor people are incapable of making any manufacture or of producing the best advantages of the islands," and it is "very probable that if a popular person come in Jamaica, he may in a [short] time effect the peopling of the island." Lynch also recommended paying off the troops still stationed there, permitting customs-free trade for five years, and giving Jamaica some authority over the other Caribbean colonies.[57]

Having decided to keep Jamaica, the Crown began to act on Lynch's suggestions, beginning with the appointment of Thomas, Lord Windsor, as the island's governor on 5 June 1661 and the commencement of a promotional campaign to recruit migrants.[58] As befit this undertaking, the new governor received extensive instructions for igniting the long-delayed and long-awaited establishment of a renewed English presence in the western Caribbean that would be the centerpiece of commercial, if not colonizing, expansion even deeper into the region. Thus, in addition to confirming land titles (while reserving 400,000 acres for the King), confirming a customs exemption for 7 years (with a 5 percent duty thereafter), and seeing to the defense, government, and morals of the island, Windsor was empowered to grant thirty-acre headrights to masters for each servant they brought to Jamaica, to grant official commissions, and to license trade with the Spanish colonies; subsequent instructions authorized him to employ both carrot and stick, as he saw fit, to compel his Spanish neighbors to engage in commerce. He was also charged to improve the island's cocoa walks, to discharge the army occupying the island, except four hundred infantry and fifty cavalry, to make provision for "distributing three hundred negroes that are to be delivered in ten months by the Royal African Company," and "to act for the

---

[57] Considerations about the peopling and settling of Jamaica, CO 1/14, f. 115.
[58] Hickeringill, *Jamaica Viewed.*

advantage and improvement of the island in all things not particularised in these instructions." At the same time, the Privy Council began shipping convicts to the island on a regular basis.[59]

Windsor's brief career as governor provides yet another illustration of the fitful nature of the state administration of English overseas affairs. On the one hand, the colonial government was, for the first time, to pursue commercial relations with foreign neighbors, with aggression if the Spanish attitude warranted it. Yet with the Western Design fleet long gone, Jamaica's governors had no force in place with which either to harass the Spaniards into opening their markets or to defend their exposed colony in the event their neighbors decided to attack them. Windsor and his successors seem to have found an answer to this conundrum by commissioning private vessels with captains and crews of various nationalities to perform naval functions in conjunction, when possible, with the Royal Navy. When the Jamaican government's overtures were rejected at Puerto Rico and Santo Domingo, Windsor ordered a raid on Spanish territory led by Sir Christopher Myngs, who had gained considerable raiding experience and a correspondingly checkered reputation for embezzling prizes as a Cromwellian officer in the Caribbean, "by which meanes possibly other places in the King of Spaine's dominions may be better inclyned to receive the settlement of a trade." Myngs was commissioned to include in his fleet "private men of war taken into your assistance" and to choose commanders for the "volunteer landmen" who have joined the expedition. The designation of Adrian Vandeman Swart, obviously a Dutchman, as deputy commander of the sea forces, reflects the irregular tinge of this force that perpetrated a successful attack on Santiago de Cuba that no doubt confirmed the Spanish view of Myngs as a pirate.[60]

[59] For transportation of convicts, see, e.g., *APC*, 19 June 1661, 310, 24 July 1661, 315. For Windsor's appointment, see At a meeting of the King and Privy Council, 5 June 1661, PC 2/55, ff. 122r–123r at 122v; Instructions to Thomas Lord Windsor, Governor of Jamaica, 21 March 1661/2, *CSPC AWI* 5: 81–2; Additional instruction to Thomas Lord Windsor, Governor of Jamaica [on Spanish trade], 8 August 1662, *CSPC AWI* 5: 85; Additional instructions to Thomas Lord Windsor, Governor of Jamaica, 23 August 1662, *CSPC AWI* 5: 88.

[60] Pestana, "Early English Jamaica without Pirates"; Barbour, "Privateers and Pirates of the West Indies." For the attack on Cuba, see Instructions to Capt. Christopher Mings to force a trade upon the Spanish West Indies, 20 September 1662, Marsden, *Documents Relating to the Law and Custom of the Sea*, 2: 41–5 (similar instructions were issued by subsequent Jamaican governors); [Capt. Chris.] Mings to [Lord Windsor], 19 [October] 1662, *HMC Report on The Manuscripts of J.M. Heathcote, Esq., Conington Castle* (Norwich: H.M.S.O., 1899), 34–5.

Unexpectedly, though, Windsor decided to return to England on 28 October 1662.[61] Following his abbreviated if eventful tenure, the Crown did not repeat the experiment of sending an aristocratic governor directly from England to administer the colony.[62] Instead, it returned to past practices and chose a person with good political instincts and connections on both sides of the Atlantic as well as helpful colonial experience, the Barbados planter and cousin of the powerful General Monck, who had rendered assistance in imperial matters before: Sir Thomas Modyford (also knighted at the Restoration). The selection of the Barbadian as Governor of Jamaica also signaled a shift in imperial strategy. While the Crown would continue to support migration to the island from the British Isles, especially the transportation of felons, "rogues," and other "undesirables," it was now content to delegate responsibility for the government of Jamaica to Modyford and his allies in Barbados and in England. Thus, with the cooperation of Lord Willoughby (now restored to the Barbados government), Modyford published a declaration at Barbados offering terms of settlement of the new colony that had quickly engaged four hundred people to move and convinced him that "3 times that number will follow me" when their affairs were settled.[63]

Although thirty people from the first voyage from Barbados died, Modyford envisioned bright prospects for Jamaica: "a noted Quaker" had ingratiated himself with Willoughby so that "many of that persuasion now go and will come after from hence and he hath sent for his wife and children from England which he tells me will have a great influence; and really Sir it may rake off much of the rudeness of that sect." Meanwhile, he expected three hundred to four hundred passengers to arrive on the

---

[61] Beeston, "A Journal Kept by Col. William Beeston," 277.

[62] Windsor arrived on 11 August 1662 and departed on 20 October; The condition of Jamaica on Lord Windsor's departure, *CSPC AWI* 5: 112–13. Windsor complained about Jamaica's effects on his health that led him to surrender his post; Joseph Williamson to Earl of Peterborough, 14 February 1662/3, CO 279/2, ff. 9–11 at 11.

[63] Modyford to Sir Henry Bennett, 20 March 1663/4, CO 1/18, f. 79. These "further encouragements" were already forthcoming when he wrote, and they included the granting of liberty of conscience, free passage to Barbados (except for food), title to lands, no customs due for twenty-one years, and free trade with all friendly nations "except for Negroes which are to be furnished by ye Royal Company"; Declaration by the King, 2 March 1663/4, CO 1/18, f. 81. Perhaps not coincidentally, Modyford and his partner, Sir Peter Colleton, were agents on Barbados for the Royal Adventurers Trading into Africa; Modyford and Sir Peter Colleton to Governor, Deputy-Governor, Court of Assistants [of Royal Company of England Trading into Africa], 20 March 1663/4 and 31 March 1664, CO 1/18, ff. 84–6. Modyford was appointed formally on 15 February 1663/4, CO 1/18, ff. 35–40.

royal ship *Marmaduke*, and with no land available in Barbados one thousand people would arrive in Jamaica every year; servants, he observed, "must look" to a "very healthy" Jamaica "unless diverted to less considerable places." To prevent this, Modyford offered further suggestions, including the grant of liberal headrights to planters and free passage to Jamaica for servants in Barbados and the Leeward Islands on the expiration of their terms, that "the Royal Company be obliged to furnish so many Negroes yearly as may be taken of," and that the Crown grant denization rights to "Germans now oppressed by the Turke and all other nations" who migrated to the island.[64]

Modyford arrived in Jamaica himself in June 1664 with seven hundred colonists and immediately began working to meet these expectations. Once again, though, the mixed purposes of seventeenth-century Anglo-American colonization manifested themselves. On the one hand, the governor championed the movement of Europeans fleeing persecution or seeking an estate that was beyond their previous circumstances to Jamaica. Yet slavery, the slave trade, and the wealth to be produced by large-scale plantation agriculture, ideally producing sugar – that New World variation on the familiar socioeconomic theme – constituted a greater motivation for the colonizers of the island, as evidenced by Windsor's instructions. Modyford himself accepted his brief of pursuing commercial relations with Spanish colonies, but not only because of his office: he was also the Jamaica agent (an employment he also had in Barbados) of the Royal Company of Adventurers Trading into Africa, which had begun working out a system for shipping regular quantities of "Negroes" to the island and beyond. The English and slavery were in the western Caribbean to stay.[65]

---

[64] Sir Thomas Modyford to Secretary Bennett, 10 May 1664, CO 1/18, ff. 133–6. Modyford's immediate predecessor, Sir Charles Lyttleton, who came to Jamaica with Windsor as deputy, had a rather different view of "this melancholy" and "terrible sick" place "where a great many of died that came with us"; Sir Charles Lyttleton to Christopher Hatton, 13 January 1662/3, Thompson, *Correspondence of the Family of Hatton*, 29–31.

[65] Joseph Martin to Bennett from Port Royal, Jamaica, 26 June 1664, CO 1/18, f. 171, reported on Modyford's arrival. For the Royal Company, including its employment of Sir Thomas Modyford in Jamaica, see Meeting of the Company of Traders into Africa Court, 11 March 1663/4, T 70/75, f. 7.

8

Anglo-Dutch Climax

Did the restored monarchy take charge of overseas matters, and why? Did 1660 actually constitute a turning point in the history of English overseas trade and colonization? Over twenty-five years ago, Robert Bliss suggested that we deemphasize the Restoration as a turning point in the history of the English Empire and that we, instead, center our comprehension of that history in terms of "an understanding of the 'politics of empire,'" rather than focus on the navigation system, "the century's mercantilist consensus," or the employment of military men in colonial situations. Yet despite its deeply contextual approach, Bliss's motion has not provided much impetus for an understanding of imperial development. Instead, the chestnut of mercantilism has received renewed attention, while other comprehensions of the period, all of them concerned with the question of the formation of American identity, still enjoy preeminence.[1]

These preferred historiographical perspectives have substantially clouded the old comfortable understanding of "Colonial America." The resulting blurriness, however, has made it difficult to comprehend readily what was happening in seventeenth-century Anglo-America, especially with respect to the wider world. Furthermore, the quest to find the origins of American society, however defined, in the seventeenth century must be regarded as inapposite. After all, no inhabitant of the seventeenth-century English-speaking world regarded her- or himself as an "American," at least in the sense that modern inhabitants of the United States do.

---

[1] Bliss, *Revolution and Empire*, 3–4.

The increasingly popular idea of "Atlantic History" has offered one prescription for a new synthesis, as noted in the Introduction. The concept of "Anglicization" offers another. This attempt at "a coherent synthesis of the dizzyingly complex world of colonial British America," pioneered by John Murrin, derives from the premise that "the thirteen colonies became more, not less, English over time." Having been devised as "social experiments," especially in New England, the colonies all "ended up failing spectacularly, and nearly simultaneously, to establish their utopian and improved societies" during "a period of acute crisis in almost every Anglophone colony" in the last quarter of the seventeenth century. In the eighteenth century, then, the colonies were ready to participate in the new English "foundation for limited, constitutional monarchy and the fiscal-military state that would propel Britain to first-power status."[2]

Yet the shadow of United States–to-be also hovers over "Anglicization." First, all of the seventeenth-century ideas that were extended to the colonies, including the Calvinist notions of the New England settlers such as John Winthrop, Sr., were just that: extensions and applications of ideas that had developed and continued to develop in England as well as in places where the English came to exercise influence. This reality does not in any way diminish the importance of the application of these views in the colonial environment or that of the societies with whom the English came into contact. It applied in Guinea and the Indian Ocean as well as America; the context in which migration and settlement took place was English.[3]

This reality is further apparent when examining the effects of the Restoration on overseas developments. The rapid strides that were made in colonizing Jamaica went some way toward clearing away the bad taste that the Western Design had left in the English imperial mouth, and by 1660 there was now little question that the continued development of the island – and, indeed, Anglo-America generally – depended on the progress of slavery and the slave trade. The East India Company saw its plans to corner this progress snatched from its grasp, but its successor in interest, the Royal Company of Adventurers Trading into Africa (RCAA), promised to develop even further the trans-Atlantic labor pipeline that the EIC and its predecessors had begun observing: "Plantations depends upon ye welfare of it, for they must be utterly ruined, if they either want supply of

---

[2] Shankman, "A Synthesis Useful and Compelling," 21, 25, 26.
[3] As stressed by, for instance, Cressy, *Coming Over*; Foster, *The Long Argument*; and Moore, *Pilgrims*.

Negro servants for their worke, or be forced to relieve them at expensive rates." If the RCAA delivered on this promise, it would provide planters with a greater availability of permanently bound labor if they were willing and able to pay for it. Sufficient numbers of slaves would enable the production of greater quantities of plantation commodities, thereby enriching both the suppliers and purchasers of slaves and generating additional customs revenue for the Crown. A Jamaican leader certainly subscribed to this belief, reporting that "wee have many hopeful plantations, which will certainly become great (if supplied with Negroes) but our inhabitants are not so numerous as is reported, I doubt 4 or 5000 is the most."[4]

Moreover, with the supply lines now relatively clear, both the company and locals could sell slaves to other colonies from Barbados and Jamaica; the volume of the intercolonial slave trade picked up with the continuing increase of imports from Africa after 1660. Edmund Jennings, acting Governor (1706–10) of Virginia, reported that prior to 1680 the colony had imported its slaves "generally" from Barbados, "for it was very rare to have a Negro ship come to this country directly from Africa."[5]

Prospects for success seemed quite bright at the outset, a recurring theme in the history of seventeenth-century English overseas trade and colonization. The RCAA had inherited a revamped operation in Africa, and in 1664 it claimed it had sent approximately £160,000 worth of cargo to Guinea, "which was more than this company's last predecessors sent out in five years." This had brought its agents "much respect of all the Negro Kings and people in their places that notwithstanding the many private machinations and frequent open interruptions of the Hollanders" had established a string of posts from the Gambia to Benin within one year of the arrival of their first factors. Thus, the company had "furnished all of ye plantations with Negro servants" along with "some 3,500 slaves

---

[4] Royal Adventurers to the Council of Foreign Plantations, [1663], CO 1/17, f. 264; Thomas Lynch, President of the Council of Jamaica, to Secretary of State Sir Henry Bennett, 25 May 1664, CO 1/18, f. 152. For continuing concerns over the prospects of securing sufficient supplies of "sound and merchantable" slaves, see, e.g., Royal African Company to Captain Samuel Richard, 4 December 1688, T 70/61, f. 76; Nathaniel Bradley et al. at Cape Corso Castle, to Royal African Company, 26 April 1680, T 70/1, ff. 54–7; Royal African Company to Captain Thomas Woodfine, 10 December 1685, T 70/61, f. 3; Royal African Company to Captain Thomas James, 18 March 1685/6, T 70/61, f. 6.

[5] Edmund Jennings to Board of Trade, 27 November 1708, *DIHSTA* 4: 88–90, and same to same, 11 January 1709/10, *DIHSTA* 4: 90–1.

supplied per annum from New and Old Calabar in the Bight of Benin
contracted to the Spaniards and worth £86,000 in Spanish silver annually." It expected a yearly return of £100,000 from trading in ivory, wax,
hides, dyestuffs, Guinea grain, and other commodities. These results
generated such expectations that the company reported an increase in
the value of its stock from £17,000 to £120,000 by 1664. It also planned
to obtain a plantation in Surinam and to complete the terms of the
contract it had signed to deliver slaves to Spanish colonies.[6]

The hopes for the Royal Company seem to reflect the generally optimistic atmosphere that surrounded English overseas pursuits prior to the
Second Anglo-Dutch War (1664–7). Predictably, however, this optimism
flagged – another recurring theme in the history of our subject – as
matters did not proceed as the company wished. Most particularly,
planters could purchase the RCAA's slaves if they found the monopoly's
set price acceptable and the company's agents in Africa procured sufficient quantities. If, though, planters found the company's tariff unaccept-
able, they turned to unlicensed traders, who with their lower overhead
could undersell the RCAA (although these shippers also depended on
supply). Then, the flaring of the Anglo-Dutch rivalry on the Gold Coast
presented a large obstacle to the RCAA's plans; even in peacetime, the
WIC agents continued their "insolence." The Royal Company rehearsed
its concerns in a petition for assistance from the Crown "in order to the
exclusion of your petitioners from their just rights." If it did not receive
assistance from the Dutch threat, the RCAA warned, its "care of those
fortifications and jurisdictions on the coast of Africa which do so highly
concern not only the honour of your Majesty's crown in those parts and
the national interest of your subjects in general but the general being of
your Majesty's subjects on the coast of America" would be jeopardized.
This scenario demonstrated the limit inherent in the assumption of imperial obligations by private concerns: if relations with another European
nation became an issue, then the state had to become involved. Even so,
the encouragement of anti-Dutch policy came from those with overseas
interests, although, as noted in Chapter 7, the restored monarchy readily
sympathized with those views and so followed that same policy and

---

[6] A Brief Narrative of the Trade and Present Condition of the Company of Royal Adventurers of England trading into Africa, CO 1/19, [1664], ff. 7r–8r; Meeting of the Court of
Assistants of the Royal Company, 14 April 1664, T 70/75, f. 10 (Surinam); Meeting of the
Court of Assistants of the Royal Company, 20 June 1664, T 70/75, f. 16 (Spanish
contract).

employed the same opponents of Dutch ambitions as its Interregnum predecessors had done to carry out that policy.[7]

Nor did the accession of Charles II alter the character of the "politics of empire" by definition, since it entailed the return of the monarch to the top of the sociopolitical pyramid, and the sovereign again became the focus of social and political activity. The scope of that activity, however, had widened since the withdrawal of Charles I from London eighteen years previously, and the numbers of those with overseas concerns had also increased. In the imperial sense, especially, these people pursued wider and more sophisticated agendas in remarkably sophisticated ways, and they had better political connections. The return of monarchy thus further incorporated colonists into imperial relationships of the sort that had already increased dramatically during the previous two decades before 1660. The Restoration brought many sorts of petitioners from all sorts of places seeking redress, office, favor, and other rewards, and colonials were no exception. In bringing their agendas to court, various subjects of the new King brought proposals to improve the royal interest as well as their own, as their predecessors had done.

John Winthrop, Jr., Governor of Connecticut, who had accured considerable colonial-imperialist experience by 1660, played a central role in the territorial expansion of Anglo-America and illustrates the rapid and substantial degree of importance that colonists assumed in seventeenth-century imperial development. His career began in July 1635, when he accepted the appointment of a colonizing group that included Viscount Saye and George Fenwick to oversee the establishment of Saybrook at the mouth of the Connecticut River. This settlement developed healthy green shoots under Winthrop's oversight before it was absorbed by Connecticut.[8]

Winthrop had all to play for as his colony did not even exist in imperial terms in 1660. Established by migrating settlers from Massachusetts Bay in the 1630s, it had never acquired the requisite charter that would have secured its government and its boundaries and given it the right to enact laws, build forts, negotiate with the Indians, and grant land titles. Since the colony existed in this Hobbesian state of nature as far as the wider world was concerned, the property rights of Connecticut's inhabitants

---

[7] Petition of the Company of Royal Adventurers of England trading into Africa, 3 July 1668, CO 1/23, f. 1; Thomas Pearson to the Royal Adventurers, Cape Coast Castle, 18 February 1667/8, CO 1/23, f. 2.

[8] Agreement of the Saybrook Company with John Winthrop, Jr., 7 July 1635, WP 3: 198–9.

were in jeopardy, as were the colony's territorial claims. The governor, then, had to call on all of his patronage links, powers of persuasion, and knowledge of the Anglo-American scene to achieve a result. At the news of the proclamation of Charles II, Winthrop and the other leaders of the place realized the opportunity the Restoration presented to eliminate Connecticut's legal uncertainty; they made immediate preparations to secure their colony's legitimacy. There was, however, one potential issue: Connecticut was apparently governed by men of the sort who had rebelled against and overthrown the new monarch's father. Would the King entertain sympathy for their applications?[9]

Connecticut's leaders had plans beyond the mere validation of their colony's existence: they sought royal approval to set the boundaries of their colony at Narragansett Bay in the east and the Pacific Ocean in the west. With the assistance of his longtime patrons, including Saye, Lord Robartes, and the Earl of Manchester – all members of the Council of Foreign Plantations – Winthrop nearly pulled it off: in October 1662 a jubilant Connecticut General Court announced that the Crown had granted the colony its charter with the desired limits.[10]

The newly recognized colony thus outmaneuvered and absorbed its neighbor, New Haven, which was in a similar charter-free situation but neglected to take the steps to remove itself from legal limbo. Winthrop, though, was not successful in relieving another neighbor, Rhode Island, of the western shore of Narragansett Bay, as that colony, led by its own experienced and well-connected imperial politician, Roger Williams, also had an agent present in London looking after its interests, Dr. John Clarke. Having received news of the Connecticut charter, Clarke turned to his own connections to secure an annulment of the Crown's grant of the western half of his colony to its aggrandizing neighbor. Winthrop's response to Clarke invoked the customary mixture of public and private interest, as the Connecticut Governor was also a principal in the Atherton Company, which had "planted upon the said Lands Inlarging your Majesties Empire as in duty they are bound." Thus, while the petitioners claimed that they had treated fairly with the Narragansetts, "many turbulent spirited Phanaticks Inhabitants of Road Island" had interfered

---

[9] Preparations for Winthrop's departure for London had begun by October 1660, and the colony's General Court approved his leaving on 7 June 1661; Minutes of General Session, 7 June 1661, and Letter to the Earl of Manchester, [1661], *Ct. Recs.*, 1: 361–2, 369–70, 583–4.

[10] Petition of John Winthrop, 12 February 1661/2, CO 1/16, f. 36.

with the company; consequently, its backers "are discouraged from making further Progress unless they have your Majesties Protection." This spirited defense came to naught: Connecticut received the requested assistance from the Crown against New Netherland but then had to divide the spoils with the Duke of York, and it also had to concede the Narragansett Country to the "Phanaticks."[11]

Winthrop joined a queue of Anglo-Americans that formed in Restoration London to present petitions for the Crown's consideration. His Virginia counterpart, Sir William Berkeley, who had rather better Royalist credentials, brought an agenda that included reopening free trade and, as in Connecticut's case, certifying colonial boundaries. The Virginians had cast their eyes southward, a relatively secluded area the extent of which had been explored in pursuit of trading opportunities with the Indians but also where several colonists whose political and religious views conflicted with Berkeley's had relocated themselves.

In 1663, an expedition was sent to the "Charles River" by backers including Edward and John Winslow, nephews of Plymouth's Edward. New England interest in Carolina coincided with that of expansionists in the West Indies, another area of seventeenth-century Anglo-America where overcrowding had encouraged colonial-imperialism. Captain William Hilton, who made two reports on Cape Fear (in modern North Carolina) to the New Englanders and who also conducted a sounding of the Carolina coastline in August 1663 on behalf of Barbadian interests, may have connected these groups of colonial-imperialists: the younger Edward Winslow married Hilton's daughter.[12]

Another connection came from the longtime investor in overseas ventures and one of the founders of the Massachusetts Bay Company, Samuel Vassall, who had been interested in the area since the early 1630s. As a godly supporter of the rebellion against Charles I he may have been among those who regarded the Restoration as a sign of divine disfavor. In the event, he decided to renew his pursuit under the patent granted by

[11] Petition of John Scott, John Winthrop, Simon Bradstreet, Daniel Denison, Josiah Winslow, Thos. Willet, and Richard Lord to the King, [June 1663?], CO 1/17, f. 145. For the Connecticut–Rhode Island dispute from the Rhode Island perspective, see James, *John Clarke and His Legacies*, 43–82.

[12] Letter from the English Members of the Cape Fear Company to the Lords Proprietors, 6 August 1663, *CRNC* 1: 36–9; Hall, "New Englanders at Sea"; "Depositions of inhabitants of Nansemond County, Virginia concerning the North Carolina/Virginia boundary," 25 March 1708, *CRNC* 1: 676–7; McPherson, "Nathaniel Batts, Landholder on Pasquotank River."

that same monarch thirty years before, claiming that this was still in effect even though his prior colonizing attempt had soured.[13]

Samuel's nephew, John Vassall, joined his uncle in leading the new settlement at Cape Fear that arrived in 1664, although Samuel died shortly after its founding.[14] This venture, while it merged the West Indies–New England interests, necessarily involved imperial politics. The prominent Barbados planter John Colleton also traveled to London to curry the favor of the Restoration government where he received a knighthood and joined the former Barbadian Martin Noell (also newly knighted) on the new Council for Foreign Trade and Plantations. Exercising his consistently keen interest in the slave trade, Sir John became an investor in the RCAA early in 1662, while his son, Peter, accepted employment as a company factor in Barbados.[15]

Colleton also represented a group of Barbadians that included Sir Thomas Modyford and the ex-Royalist Sir John Yeamans, who supported the establishment of new colonies where planters could acquire additional land, which had become a scarce proposition on their island, and increase their estates. Indeed, the ever-increasing population of Barbados, combined with the often combustible politics of the place, had led various Barbadians to pursue colonization with or without the consent of the central government for many years. For instance, the once and future governor of the island, Lord Willoughby, had departed for Surinam after surrendering his government to Sir George Ayscue in 1652, and another colony was attempted at St. Lucia in 1663.[16]

---

[13] State of the case of the Duke of Norfolk's pretensions to Carolina, CO 1/17, f. 106. For Vassall's earlier Carolina endeavor, see Petition of Samuel Vassall to the Lords Commissioners for Foreign Plantations, [February 1635], *CSPC AWI* 1: 197; Kopperman, "Profile of Failure."

[14] Commission to appoint John Vassall as Surveyor General of Clarendon County, 24 November 1664, and Henry Vassall to the Lords Proprietors of Carolina, 15 August 1666, *CRNC* 1: 73, 144–5.

[15] E.g., At a meeting of the Council for Foreign Plantations, 4 March 1660/1, CO 1/14, f. 152v; Debtors to the General Stock of the Royal Company Trading into Africa to the total of £17,400, [1662], T 70/309, f. 1; Meeting of the Court of Assistants of the Royal Company, 20 June 1664, T 70/75, f. 19.

[16] Governor Daniel Searle complained to Thomas Povey about Colleton and Modyford causing him difficulties; Thomas Povey to Daniel Searle, 20 October 1659, Add. Ms. 11411, ff. 90–4 at 91r, BL. It is unclear who took the initiative in the founding of the English colony "Willoughby Land," on the Surinam River in 1650; Barber, "Power in the English Caribbean," 194–7. For St. Lucia, see Lord Willoughby of Parham to Council on Foreign Trade and Plantations, 23 September 1663, CO 1/17, f. 203.

A colony at Carolina suited these expansionist desires as well as those of both Berkeley and Vassall. Settlement of this place also suited influential metropolitan figures, most notably the "architect" of the Restoration, George Monck, Duke of Albemarle, and Anthony Ashley Cooper (now Lord Ashley), absentee Barbados planter and Chancellor of the Exchequer, since it fulfilled such public interests as the expansion of the slave trade and an extension of the English presence in North America that could menace Spanish colonies. This combination of imperial players gained a result when the Crown issued a proprietary grant to the region south of Cape Fear to Albemarle, the Earl of Clarendon, the Earl of Craven, John, Lord Berkeley, Sir George Carteret, Ashley, Sir William Berkeley, and Colleton on 24 March 1663.[17]

The Surinam colony flourished meanwhile. Lord Willoughby, yet another experienced and well-connected Anglo-American political figure, had arrived there in 1652 with about three hundred men together with provisions "at the expense of many thousand pounds."[18] In 1663, a colonist reported, "The country is healthy, pleasant, and fruitfull, the air moderately hot, and of a far more sufferable temper then was rendred to us in England," while its "natives not numerous [were] at peace and amity with the English." The colony already had about 4,000 inhabitants, and nine ships had arrived in two months bringing supplies. With a good climate for sugar production and great prospects, the author was convinced that "were our Nation well informed of the hopes and goodness of this Country, here would quickly [come] thousands of settlers."

All that was lacking to ensure the success of the colony were slaves: if "the Planters supplied with Negroes the strength and sinews of this Western world, they would advance their fortunes and his Majesties customs and make as punctual pay, and in as good commodities as any." Unfortunately, the "sworn enemy of the colony are the Dons of Barbados whose interest is to keep the ordinary planter still resident on that island, without removal to balance the power of their Negroes and therefore they use their utmost means by all instruments how base soever, to disparage the country but their hypocrisies and ends are discovered, and several families are transporting hither." These "eminent Barbadians" allegedly tried to discourage Surinam's prospects by using their connections with the Royal Company to divert "all supplies of Negroes

---

[17] Roper, *Conceiving Carolina*, 15–20.
[18] Reasons offered by the Lord Willoughby why he ought not to be confined to his settlement upon Surinam, [1660], Egerton Ms. 2395, f. 279, BL.

from this place, the which will prove a detriment to his Majesty there being no colony settled by his subjects, more hopeful, thriving, and of greater consequence then this, especially for any design against the Spaniard." If the King would establish a duly constituted government, however, that would correct this situation, according to the writer. In due course, Willoughby arrived to reestablish his authority in "Willoughby Land," which seemed to resolve both the issues with government and access to slaves: in March 1664, the factors of the Royal Company reported that one of the company's ships "hath disposed of all his negroes at good rates & will depart thence laden with his own effects in 6 weeks time."[19]

Thus, the outlook for the English overseas situation in the autumn of 1663 continued to improve: the administration of Jamaica was proceeding; the Portuguese had handed over Tangier with Bombay to follow; and colonists had established footholds in Carolina. The only clouds on the imperial horizon still emanated from across the North Sea. In Asia, the VOC had thwarted the East India Company's attempt to claim its rights at Pulau Run, despite the express agreement to return it under the terms of the 1662 Anglo-Dutch treaty, and it continued to evade its alleged responsibility for older outrages.[20]

Meanwhile, the WIC, even though it had suffered a devastating blow in the loss of its Brazilian colony to the Portuguese, posed an obstacle to the RCAA: in addition to competing for slaves and African commodities in Guinea, it could interfere with English plans for the Spanish market for slaves in America as it continued to smuggle slaves to the English islands and tobacco from Anglo-America, notwithstanding the Navigation Act. Thomas Lynch from Jamaica warned Secretary of State Bennett about the volume of trade the Dutch conducted at Curacao with Spanish America where they had delivered 24,500 slaves over the seven years preceding

---

[19] Letter from Surinam, 8 November 1663, CO 1/17, ff. 226–7; King's bill containing a grant to Francis Lord Willoughby of Parham and Laurence Hyde, of Surinam in Guiana, by the name of Willoughby Land, 6 May 1663, *CSPC AWI* 5: 131–2. For the report of the slave trading voyage, see Sir Thomas Modyford and Sir Peter Colleton to Governor, Deputy-Governor, Court of Assistants [of Royal Company of England Trading into Africa], 20 March 1663/4 and 31 March 1664, CO 1/18, ff. 84–6 at 86v.

[20] The 1662 treaty also expressly recognized the English right to pursue damages for the loss of the *Bona Esperanza* and the *Henry Bonadventure*; Treaty of friendship between Great Britain and the United Netherlands, concluded at Whitehall, 4/14 September 1662, Davenport, *European Treaties Bearing on the History of the United States and Its Dependencies*, 2: 73–85 at 83.

1664; Lynch wondered if "the best way to get the trade & silver of America" might be to expel the Dutch from Guinea.[21] The Crown tried to reinforce its dim view of Dutch encroachments in English plantations by reconfiguring the Navigation Act into the Staple Act of 1663, which removed Ireland as a legitimate trading partner for English colonies, although the efficacy that this legislation achieved remained unclear.

The Dutch also stood in the way of English expansion in North America. New Netherland stretched along the Hudson River from New Amsterdam (Manhattan) to Fort Orange (Albany), while the Dutch had seized the small Swedish colony on the Delaware River in 1655. New Netherland's English neighbors, though, were a rather more formidable opponent than the Swedes and had long had their eye on the Dutch colony. The colonial governments had signed a peace treaty in 1650 that partitioned the region into Dutch and English zones, but the English government had never ratified this, thereby providing Connecticut settlers with the pretext to continue their probing of territory claimed by the Dutch; indeed, the New Englanders had secured government approval to attack New Netherland in 1654, but the end of the First Anglo-Dutch War intervened.[22] Petrus Stuyvesant, the able Director-General of New Netherland, kept the intruders at bay in the first years of the 1660s, but the brief of his counterpart, Winthrop, for his trip to London included the securing of metropolitan assistance in clearing the way for the expansion of Connecticut.

Winthrop's desires, as those of his Carolina counterparts, fit perfectly with other English people with overseas interests at this time, including his cousin, Sir George Downing, who told Johan de Witt, Grand Pension-ary of Holland, when asked about rumors of an English attack on New Netherland, "that I knew of no such country but only in the mapps; that, indeed, if their people were to be believed, all the world were New Netherland; but when that business shall be looked into, it will be found that ye English had the first pattern of first possession of those partes." Downing's subsequent report to the Earl of Clarendon noted that he had raised the issues with De Witt that the English had pressed for years but

[21] Thomas Lynch, President of the Council of Jamaica, to Secretary of State Sir Henry Bennett, 25 May 1664, CO 1/18, ff. 152r–152v.

[22] Jacobs, "The Hartford Treaty." The force that was assembled against the Dutch colony, commanded by the Massachusetts leaders John Leverett and Robert Sedgwick, attacked French Acadia instead; Major Robert Sedgwicke to the Protector, 1 July 1654, and Mr. John Leverett to the Protector, 4 July 1654, *TSP* 2: 419–20, 425–6.

had received no resolution, while there had been "late injuries done in ye East Indies and upon the coast of Africa."[23]

The tone of this letter reflects the expectation that another resort to force of arms would bring the Dutch to the English heel once and for all. Downing and other ministers were aware of the fiscal restraints under which the Crown operated after having paid off much of the army and with Parliament holding the purse strings; the pursuit of war, especially on the global scale that another conflict with the Dutch would entail, would place an alarming drain on the royal coffers. Yet the proponents of war seem to have believed, first, that the Dutch desire for peace and trade was so great that a limited military undertaking might be sufficient to curb their "insolence," a desire aggravated by Dutch concern over the intentions of Louis XIV, especially if the French allied with the English, and depredations of English privateers on Dutch shipping. English militants also believed that a number of Dutch provinces would not support demands "to engage in a warre, and spend their money, to maintaine ye East and West Indie Companies in their robberies and violencies."[24]

In the event, by the time Downing and De Witt had their conversation, those in favor of committing English "violencies" against the Dutch had had their way: a fleet under the leadership of Holmes had sailed for Guinea in December 1663 and captured or destroyed the Dutch facilities on the Gold Coast except for the great citadel of El Mina. The following summer, an expedition of English regulars supported New England colonial troops in an attack on New Netherland that captured New Amsterdam on 27 August 1664 (old style); although there was resistance at the Delaware, the rest of the Dutch colony surrendered peaceably.[25]

These assaults ended the tepid diplomacy between the nations, and the English, having already had "very considerable success," had their imperial wind up undoubtedly also recalling their successes in the 1652–4 conflict. In November 1664, Parliament voted to supply the Crown with an immediate £2,477,500 followed by another £1,250,000, unprecedentedly massive grants. It also approved the use of the Long Parliament's

---

[23] Sir George Downing to the Lord Chancellor Clarendon, 6 May 1664, Lister, *Life and Administration of Clarendon*, 3: 315–21.

[24] Downing to Clarendon, 6 May 1664, Lister, *Life and Administration of Clarendon*, 3: 318.

[25] Sir Robert Nicolls to Lord Chancellor Clarendon, 26 October 1664, and same to same, 21 November 1664, Clarendon Papers, Codex Eng. 2, John Carter Brown Library, Providence, R.I.

detested method of direct assessment of taxpayers rather than the customary but inefficient subsidy method in pursuing the effort against the "continuing insolencies" of the enemy and for "the preservation of Your Majestyes auntient and undoubted Soveraignty and Dominion in the Seas and the Trade of Your Majestyes Subjects."[26] Meanwhile, in mid-February 1665, Anglo-Dutch competition over the slave trade led Governor Modyford in Jamaica to plan an attack on Curacao, the center of Dutch shipping of slaves to the Spanish colonies. This expedition, however, failed in its main objective and only seized the small islands of St. Eustatius and Saba before its men mutinied after the death of its commander.[27]

As was the case with the previous conflict between these nations, then, the clamor for a second Anglo-Dutch War came primarily from the promoters of English overseas trade and colonization. In 1664, the membership of this group had certainly altered from its makeup of a decade before. Much, after all, had happened since 1652: the Protectorate had come and gone, the Commonwealth likewise, and kingly government had been restored with the adherents of the "Good Old Cause" executed, exiled, imprisoned, sidelined, or, perhaps most frequently, cooperating with the regime. Thus, the names of former Royalists, including the Duke of York, Prince Rupert, Sir George Carteret, Sir George Berkeley, John, Lord Berkeley, the Earl of Craven, Sir Nicholas Crispe, and Sir John Colleton, appear among the leaders of the Royal Company of Adventurers Trading into Africa and the East India Company. This reality has enabled Steven Pincus to claim that "war against the Dutch was the manifestation in the realm of foreign policy of the ideological vision of one grouping in the Restoration English polity," urged also by the King, which "understood the workings of European power politics as intimately related to, indeed as a macrocosm of, the English power struggle

---

[26] Charles II, 1664 & 1665: An Act for granting a Royall Ayd unto the Kings Majestie of Twenty fower hundred threescore and seaventeene thousand and five hundred Pounds to be raised leavyed and paid in the space of Three Yeares, *Statutes of the Realm: Volume 5, 1628–80*, ed. John Raithby (s.l, 1819), 525–52. *British History Online*, www.british-history.ac.uk/statutes-realm/vol5/pp525-552 (accessed 14 August 2016); Charles II, 1665: An Act for granting the summe of Twelve hundred and fiftie thousand pounds to the Kings Majestie for His present further Supply [Rot. Parl. 17 C. II. nu. 1], *Statutes of the Realm: Volume 5, 1628–80*, ed. John Raithby (s.l, 1819), 570–4, *British History Online*, www.british-history.ac.uk/statutes-realm/vol5/pp570-574 (accessed 14 August 2016).

[27] Beeston, "A Journal Kept by Col. William Beeston," 285.

between agitators for the Good Old Cause and defenders of the Church by law established and the Stuart monarchy."[28]

Undoubtedly, there were people in the English government in 1664, including the New England apostate Downing, who hated the Dutch for their republican government, their bishop-free church government, and their seemingly incessant pursuit of trade, which was regarded as symptomatic of their problematic national character. Thus, in 1658 "T.P." had sniffed, "Low Dutch that to Religion do pretend, / Your Wits, your Studies and Indeavors bend / To cheat, connive, play Bo-peep and defraud, / Yea, for your profit, you will turn a Bawd." Six years later, the pamphleteer John Crouch, itching for war, demanded, "[W]hy Republicks Priviledg'd are t'usurpe the wide Sea, and the wider Ayre? Is the whole Eastern World your proper due, which Rome ne'er had?" Crouch lamented Dutch "ingratitude" toward their "blest Mid-wife" who had delivered their commonwealth and warned his hypo-thetical Dutch readers, "Where there no satiety is there's little Gaine": "If you with England fight or shall invade / Her Royal Rights or check her Popular Trade; / If you by Spanish Gabells shall annoy / your Fellow Merchants and devest his Boy," the republic would risk the consequences.[29]

But was an anti-Dutch position the sole province of the Francophile York and his circle? Not only had recitations of Dutch "ingratitude" and "grasping" circulated in England for years, but they emanated from various quarters, especially ones inhabited by those pursuing overseas opportunities regardless of their religious stripe.[30] Moreover, while East India Company factors may have had a better grasp of the situation on the ground that led them to express reservations about war, and while the Royal Company's facilities risked destruction at the hands of the Dutch, as Pincus claims,[31] it seems highly likely that the Crown did not intend for the war to last long since it is the rare government that opens hostilities in anticipation of a lengthy encounter. We might regard a plan for a series of quick strikes to reduce the Dutch presence in Guinea, North America, the

---

[28] Pincus, "Popery, Trade and Universal Monarchy," 2.

[29] T.P., *The Low Dutch character'd their Butter-box Opened*; Crouch, *Belgica Caracter-istica*, esp. 7–8.

[30] These continued to mount after the Restoration; e.g. Demands of the English East India Company for Losses Sustained from the Dutch East India Company, [December 1662], *CCMEIC* 4: 286; Demands of the English East India Company for Losses Sustained from the Dutch East India Company, [December 1662], *CCMEIC* 4: 286–7.

[31] Pincus, "Popery, Trade and Universal Monarchy," 4–15.

Caribbean, and the Narrow Seas that would compel the republic to sue for terms while Charles II banked the £2,500,000 granted by Parliament as overly optimistic in retrospect; but was it so in the minds of contemporaries, their vision perhaps clouded by their contempt for their enemies?

Moreover, Royalists did not dominate the entities who maintained grievances against the Dutch. Both of the management lists of the East India and African companies included many veterans of the Interregnum who had a good awareness of Anglo-Dutch history and remained determined to pursue a hostile line as had been done over the previous fifteen years: nothing had changed on the Dutch front, so why should their attitudes have done? In addition to the figures discussed in Chapter 7, this list included John Bence, Noell's partner who had sat in the third Protectorate Parliament and whose wife, Judith Andrews, was the daughter of Peter Andrews, the longtime partner and brother-in-law of Samuel Vassall.[32]

Regardless of all this, the first "European" conflict in which hostilities began outside Europe was declared on 4 March 1665. Unfortunately, though, for its backers, so far from compelling the Dutch to sue for peace quickly, the course of the Second Anglo-Dutch War had turned against the English in Africa even before it had officially begun. As soon as the Dutch government had word of the attack on the WIC posts there, it secretly sent Admiral Michiel de Ruyter with a fleet to recover them and to destroy the English factories – the first English imperial adventure in Africa proved stillborn. Although the coming of peace at least returned the situation in Guinea as it had been in 1662, the WIC's devastating campaign, the RCAA alleged, had "disturbed" an anticipated trade in gold worth £200,000 along with a trade in "servants for the plantations" worth £100,000 and left their "credit extinct and their stock and all that hath been taken at interest being abroad on adventures or owed to American planters."[33]

---

[32] Paula Watson, "Bence, John (1622–1683), of Bevis Marks, London," www.historyofpar liamentonline.org/volume/1660–1690/member/bence-john-1622–88 (accessed 16 August 2016). If Bence was an Interregnum supporter of Charles Stuart, as Pincus, "Popery, Trade and Universal Monarchy," claims (at 14), the family dinners would have been uncomfortable occasions.

[33] The treaty prevented the RCAA from pursuing claims against the Dutch; Davenport, *European Treaties Bearing on the History of the United States and Its Dependencies*, 2: 127–31 at 128. For the company's grievances, see A Brief Narrative of the Trade and Present Condition of the Company of Royal Adventurers of England trading into Africa,

Meanwhile, De Ruyter – whose name English parents of the day might have invoked to render their children obedient – and his squadron sailed across the Atlantic to attack Barbados, the greatest English prize on offer. The Dutch destroyed shipping and fortifications in that colony and then did the same in Newfoundland, although they did not carry out an expected assault on New York.[34]

The English did win the first major engagement after the declaration of war at Lowestoft on 13 June 1665 convincingly, but otherwise the Dutch had much the better of the fighting while their privateers preyed on English shipping with the connivance of both French and Spanish officials. In imperial terms, Tangier was cut off by the Dutch and their Spanish allies by sea and by Moroccans on land, while English trade in the Mediterranean was entirely disrupted, with twenty-three prizes alone at a reported value of £332,500 forfeited at Cadiz in one instance. Also, the English bungled an attempt to capture the VOC fleet from the East Indies at Bergen in Norway: they seized only two vessels, while the violation of Denmark's neutrality kept that country from allying with England. Then, a Zeeland fleet seized Surinam at the end of February 1667, while an embargo on colonial shipping in order to defend the metropolis left the Cape Fear colony to wither.[35]

Meanwhile, France had entered the war on the side of the Dutch in January 1666. This maneuver brought further pressure to bear on the English in Europe and also cost them their colonies in Antigua, Montserrat, and St. Christopher's; Lord Willoughby was lost in a hurricane when leading an expedition to regain the latter island from the French in July 1666. Thus, despite the huge parliamentary grants, the expected victory had not been achieved; the embezzlement, price gouging, and other manifestations of corruption that drained away much of those grants (quite a bit of which seems never to have been collected anyway) added to public frustration at the course of the war. The national mood was not helped by the outbreak in April 1665 of the worst instance of plague in London since the Black Death, which closed the border with Scotland, canceled fairs and other commercial activities, and obliged the court and Parliament to flee the capital. Then came the Great Fire at the

---

[January 1664/5], CO 1/19, ff. 7–8. The company received satisfaction; Warrant to Captain Robert Holmes, commander of the *Jersey* frigate, 7 January 1664/5, *CSPD* Charles II 4 (1664–5): 164.

[34] Klooster, *The Dutch Moment*, 102–3.

[35] Rommelse, *Second Anglo-Dutch War*, 123–74. For the failure of Cape Fear, see John Vassall to John Colleton, 6 October 1667, *CRNC* 1: 159–60.

beginning of September 1666, which consumed most of London but did provide the opportunity for the opening of peace negotiations the following month. The disasters did not end, though: with all of the money from Parliament gone, the Crown had been obliged to mothball the fleet in the Medway; on 3/13 June 1667, the enemy evaded the English defenses with the help of disaffected pilots, captured Sheerness fort, burned thirteen ships, and towed the *Royal Charles*, the Royal Navy flagship, back to the Dutch Republic.

This humiliation accelerated the peace process and the Treaty of Breda was agreed on 13 July 1667. Since this had been a global war, the treaty had quite serious imperial consequences. Under its terms, any territory seized by one side after 20 May 1667 (new style) had to be returned to other. Then, the English finally abandoned their long claims to Pulau Run as well as to other damages that had allegedly arisen from the behavior of the VOC. Moreover, the East India Company lost its factory in South Sulawesi, where smuggling had been a longtime irritant to the Dutch, when the VOC defeated its ally the Kingdom of Macassar in their war of 1666–9 (although the Breda treaty did not include these hostilities).[36]

Then in America, an English force had captured Martinique and Cayenne from the French in July 1667. As this campaign had taken place after the treaty deadline, however, these colonies were returned. The English accordingly retained "New York," as they had renamed the former New Netherland. Meanwhile, Louis XIV and Charles II confirmed their pact of April that inter alia repartitioned St. Christopher's and returned Acadia, previously captured by a New England force, to France.[37]

Thus, the English had been driven from the Moluccas while Surinam remained under Dutch authority, the first territory conceded by the English to a foreign power since the seizure of Calais by the French in 1558. Often, when an enemy's colony was attacked in the seventeenth century – as in the cases of Tobago, Antigua, St. Christopher's, and Montserrat in the 1664–7 war – plantations were destroyed and the inhabitants driven away. Ordinarily, though, those colonies, such as Acadia, were returned at the end of hostilities. The Dutch, having

---

[36] Davenport, *European Treaties Bearing on the History of the United States and Its Dependencies*, 2: 127–31 at 130; Carey, "The Political Economy of Poison."

[37] Treaty of peace and alliance between the United Netherlands and Great Britain, concluded at Breda, 21/31 July 1667, and Treaty of peace between Great Britain and France, concluded at Breda, 21/31 July 1667, Davenport, *European Treaties Bearing on the History of the United States and Its Dependencies*, 2: 119–31, 132–42.

attacked Surinam when the pressure in England for peace had begun to begun to intensify, seem to have had no intention of either destroying its plantations and sugar mills or returning the place at the cessation of hostilities. Instead, perhaps viewing Surinam as a sort of consolation for the loss of Pernambuco to the Portuguese, they took the rare approach of attempting to encourage the conquered population to remain under Dutch authority and maintain their plantations. Even so, the English colonists were permitted to leave and take their property and slaves with them under the articles of capitulation, while the Dutch granted religious toleration and refrained from pressing the stipulated loyalty oath while everyone waited for the war to be resolved. The situation was further complicated when an Anglo-Barbadian fleet recaptured the colony on 7 October 1667 after the signing of the peace but before news of this had reached the Caribbean.[38]

When Abraham Crijnssen's fleet arrived to take possession of Surinam, Henry Willoughby, Lord Willoughby's nephew and the English commander, perhaps drawing on contemporary examples such as the Dutch at Pulau Run and the Portuguese at Bombay, refused to recognize Crijnssen's commission, insisting that he had to have authority to hand over the place either from Charles II or from the Governor of Barbados (Willoughby's father). Unfortunately for Henry, though, he did not receive metropolitan support for this tactic and was obliged to subside: rather than remain under Dutch authority, he and sixty-seven other English planters (with 412 slaves) departed Surinam in February 1668, destroying much of the economic infrastructure of the colony.

A number of English settlers, though, neither wished to leave Surinam nor remain there under Dutch rule, and their attitude received encouragement from Barbados. Their continuing agitation over Dutch "tyranny" and requests that the English government retake Surinam compelled Crijnssen to send the leader of this unhappy group, James Bannister, to Zeeland for trial on charges of sedition in August 1668, where the Provincial States banned him from the colony. Charles II, though, intervened to secure the rebel's release, and Bannister made his way back to Surinam whence he took ninety-eight colonists with him to Jamaica in March 1672. Then, the Third Anglo-Dutch War (1672–4) and Bannister's murder interrupted matters. A further English exodus, directed by Edward

---

[38] Narrative of the taking of the island of Cayenne from the French, and the Fort and Colony of Surinam from the Dutch, by Lt.-Gen. Henry Willoughby and Sir John Harman, July–November 1667, *CSPC AWI* 5: 487–90.

Cranfield, occurred in 1675, and the English did not restore their imperial presence in Guiana until the Napoleonic Era.[39]

Undoubtedly, the failure to retain what had been a promising colony constituted a serious reversal for English overseas interests. Yet recent claims concerning the place of Surinam in the history of the English Empire run afoul of the chronology of events and also misapprehend the nature of seventeenth-century English political culture and imperial history. It might seem feasible to identify the Willoughbys as "Barbadians" whose leadership in Surinam constituted the development of the "most significant" aspect of a "Barbadian diaspora" that is "essential to understanding the development of the early English Empire." It might also seem feasible to blame them for stoking any lingering resentment or apprehension among the English colonists (the desire to recover Lord Willoughby's plantation, valued at a reported £26,000 and bequeathed to Henry Willoughby, may have played a role here) toward the Dutch conquerors, thereby hampering the prospects for co-habitation. And it might also seem feasible to argue that the Crown supported the progress of Jamaica as the center of Anglo-Caribbean operations and gave up on Surinam in order to curb the imperial position of the Willoughbys.[40]

Henry Willoughby, though, died in 1669 and his father followed him in 1673, having spent much of 1668–72 in England. Thus, there was no further Willoughby interest in the Caribbean for the Crown to hobble after 1673. Moreover, the government's plans for Jamaica had already begun to form, as discussed in Chapter 7, in 1661, but the sudden departure of Windsor from the island left matters there in the air and in need of a steady governmental hand. The well-connected and knowledgeable Modyford seems to have been a highly appropriate choice to take charge of this important venture. In the event, he was appointed in January 1664 well before Surinam fell and then was recaptured. Moreover, the Crown ordered the new governor to work with Willoughby and vice versa as Jamaica "became English" over the next two decades.[41]

Even more important, the Willoughbys, but especially Francis, had long involved themselves in overseas affairs, including territorial expansion, just as their counterparts, such as Sir John Colleton, Sir James Drax,

[39] William Willoughby to Arlington from Barbados, 30 July 1668, CO 1/23, f. 51.
[40] Roberts, "Surrendering Surinam," 225; Games, "Cohabitation, Suriname-Style," 208, 209–10, 238–9.
[41] Robertson, "Making Jamaica English: Priorities and Processes"; Schomburgk, *The History of Barbados*, 293–4.

Martin Noell, William Pennoyer, Thomas Povey, and Maurice Thompson, did. Indeed, a number of these Londoners had opposed Willoughby's plans and supported the royalization of Barbados from 1660 only to end up with Crown government but in the person of Willoughby.[42] To what extent then can these men, especially given the geographical scale of their interests, be styled as "Barbadians"? Yes, they pursued an "expansion of Barbados," but did their ambitions and their quests for territorial expansion render them particularly distinctive from anyone else – say, John Winthrop, Jr. – who was involved in English overseas trade and colonization?

Surinam, thus, was another case of seventeenth-century Anglo-American imperial politics as usual but with a stronger foreign flavor thanks to the Dutch. Lord Willoughby had used his control of the Carlisle proprietorship to bring the English West Indies under direct royal authority at the Restoration; most of the planters preferred this after decades of proprietary uncertainty. He had then managed to secure the "4 and ½ percent Act" from the colonial assemblies, which promised, on paper at least, some permanent revenue from the islands' exports to support the government, by taking advantage of the planters' desires to cancel their debts to the proprietor. Why would the Crown have tried to curb the ambitions of such a servant and his family by abandoning Surinam? And in the end, the Treaty of Breda was concluded with no metropolitan knowledge of what had happened in the Caribbean, while a date for ending hostilities had to be set somewhere: would Charles II have risked resuming what had become a humiliating and very costly war just to try to keep the South American colony?[43]

The other "imperial takeover" of the Second Anglo-Dutch War played out in a similar way: New York, after Jamaica, constituted the first territory outside the British Isles with a permanent European population to have been conquered and retained by the English since the Hundred

---

[42] Andrew Riccard, Colleton, William Williams, Noell, and Thomas Kendall were among the "Planters of Barbados inhabiting in and about London" who were allegedly prevented by the Lord Treasurer, the Earl of Southampton, from presenting to the King "some disadvantages that arose in Barbados by the Patent of the Earl of Carlisle." These "disadvantages" included the removal of Governor Searle in favor of Willoughby and the "certain countenance" that "was given to some settlement by Lord Willoughby." The petitioners asked that the Crown make "a resolution of taking the Plantations in America, and particularly Barbadoes into a more immediate dependence on the Crown"; 1 March 1661/2, *CSPC AWI* 5: 14.

[43] Barber, *The Disputatious Caribbean*, 72–5.

Years War (1337–1453). It appears that the Crown intended to keep New York once it had been captured: Charles II had granted it to his brother as part of a proprietorship that extended from Maine to the Delaware River even before the attacking fleet sailed for America. The soon-to-be-former New Netherland had much to commend it from an imperial perspective, such as the location of New Amsterdam, which already attracted a substantial volume of trade according to reports provided by the colonial instigators of the plan, even though James immediately hived off the chunk of this territory west of the Hudson River and granted it to his friends and clients, Sir George Carteret and John, Lord Berkeley.[44]

Also, the English capture of New Netherland was part of the brief of commissioners sent to America to investigate a series of issues, the first incidence of this sort in the history of English overseas affairs. Three of these commissioners, including the commander of the expedition, Sir Richard Nicolls, were officers who had longstanding service with the Duke of York, while the fourth, Samuel Maverick, was a colonist who worked with Winthrop to obtain the necessary metropolitan support for the attack on New Amsterdam. These Crown commissioners met four other Anglo-Americans, including Winthrop, who arrived with their respective forces and signed the articles of capitulation of New Amsterdam. As with the Dutch and Surinam, the English wanted to obtain a settlement as quickly as possible in order to consolidate their position in anticipation of a reprisal of the sort that had happened in Guinea. This was a particularly acute problem given the reality that they now had the government of a substantial population of enemy aliens. The inclusion of provisions for religious toleration and the retention of Dutch local governmental institutions in the surrender terms, though, helped put both conquerors and conquered at ease.[45]

The takeover of New Netherland has long been a centerpiece of the comprehension of "Restoration and Empire" as a manifestation of a centralizing English state's ever-increasing tendency to encroach on liberties, especially of colonists. This particular aspect of the general conception of "Stuart imperialism" carries special weight due to the direct involvement of the Duke of York, often identified as the leading promoter in England of the monarchical philosophy espoused by his cousin Louis

---

[44] Concerning New Netherland, or Manhattan, in *CNYHS*, 1–14.
[45] Jacobs, *The Colony of New Netherland*, 99–103. For English fears of a Dutch attack, see, e.g., Sir George Cartwright to Col. Robert Nicolls, 25 January 1664/5, CO 1/19, f. 43; Earl of Clarendon to Samuel Maverick, 15 March 1664/5, CO 1/19, f. 60.

XIV. To summarize the prevailing view, York refused to grant New York an elected Assembly.[46] Instead, he had a lawyer named Matthias Nicolls draft "Duke's Laws," which Nicolls's namesake, Sir Richard, as New York's governor, presented as the new basis of the government in areas with substantial English populations, while the articles of capitulation applied to the areas where Dutch inhabitants predominated.

Nicolls's statutes, to which many of the English towns objected, eliminated provision for the "democraticall" town meetings by which English towns on Long Island, now under New York's jurisdiction, had governed themselves since their founding. Although the new laws provided for local selection of local governments, they also clearly placed those governments under provincial authority as the governor and his chosen council. These officials also had the power to appoint sheriffs, constables, and other officials, who served as the points of contact between the provincial administration and the localities. The Duke's Laws also, though, secured religious toleration (except for Jews) as a practical matter in a colony that contained, in addition to Reformed congregations, Lutherans, Quakers, and a handful of Roman Catholics among its European population.[47] This squelching of liberties on Long Island reflected, according to this view, the commission's task of bringing New England more firmly under imperial authority as befit the alleged desire of the later Stuarts to pursue "a centralized overseas territorial empire" and "a modern absolutist state."[48]

Once New York had been subdued, the commissioners turned their attention to the rest of York's patent. The Crown did have concerns about the loyalty of Massachusetts, as this colony, armed with its charter, had hesitated to proclaim the accession of Charles II and had received two fleeing regicides, the Cromwellian generals William Goffe and Edward Whalley. The Massachusetts leadership also responded to royal commands with delay, confusion, obfuscation, and protestations of ignorance. Opponents of the "New England Way" thus cultivated the view of "the Bay" as a recalcitrant repository of republicanism whose leaders aspired to establish a "free state"; their anti-Massachusetts stance has led to portrayals of Maverick and the Boston merchant Thomas Breedon as

[46] No such entity had existed in the colony under Dutch rule, while few of the English would have favored the creation of a legislature that would probably have had a Dutch majority – at a time of war against the Dutch Republic.
[47] Ritchie, *The Duke's Province*, 31–42.
[48] The view of the reigns of Charles II and James II proffered by Pincus, *1688*, 6.

"agents" of "Stuart imperialism" who worked to improve the Crown's agenda "of consolidating control over its North American empire."[49]

Instead, as was the case with Willoughby, Berkeley, and so many other Anglo-Americans involved in the "Restoration Empire," Maverick and Breedon came to Whitehall to convince the government to send a commission to investigate New England issues, especially the behavior of Massachusetts, not the other way round. Both of these men had been in trouble with the Massachusetts authorities previously for articulating heterodox religious views, and they allied with a remarkable number of others with grievances, especially territorial ones, against "the Bay" who found themselves in London at the same time. When the Nicolls commissioners arrived in New England, they received a cold shoulder in Boston, to be sure, but they were welcomed everywhere else they went, as for the first time colonists in America had a direct line for airing their concerns to the imperial government. Moreover, the commissioners had no power to adjudicate – let alone compel a result – in the cases they heard; they only collected information and made recommendations that they forwarded to the Council for Foreign Plantations. The Crown then invited Massachusetts, invariably the party complained of, to respond before making any determinations. While the colony's leaders hemmed and hawed, in the end they had to cooperate or risk losing its place in the English Empire and its sacred charter: who knew what would happen in that event?[50]

Meanwhile, Anglo-Dutch hostilities resumed in 1672. Having been burned in the second war, however, the English entered this conflict with considerably less enthusiasm; Parliament would not be granting millions of pounds for the war effort given the previous result, notwithstanding the inability in certain quarters to forget old scores (or, in the case of Surinam, new ones). Rather, this was a war that the Crown wanted and pursued regardless of the consequences: Charles II, for one, wanted revenge for 1667 and still sought to improve the situation of his nephew, William of Orange, in the Dutch Republic. To enable the pursuit of these aims, Charles became a client of Louis XIV. The French King detested the republican form of government and regarded the overseas activities of the Dutch as an obstacle to his own global ambitions. Thus, he agreed to

---

[49] Capt. Thos. Breedon to Council for Foreign Plantations, [11 March 1661/2], *CSPC AWI* 5: 15; Narrative and Deposition of Captain Breedon, 11 March 1661/2 (affirmed 17 October 1678), *DRCHNY* 3: 39–41; Hall, *A Reforming People*, 191–2, 196; Richter, *Before the Revolution*, 254, 261; Bremer, *First Founders*, 221, 223; Bailyn, *The New England Merchants in the Seventeenth Century*, 110–11, 114–26.
[50] Roper, "The Fall of New Netherland," 690–701.

bankroll the Royal Navy under the terms of the secret Treaty of Dover (1670), and the English King canceled his debts by ordering a Stop on the Exchequer the following year in order to provide for the coming war effort.[51]

In a large sense, then, the Third Anglo-Dutch War was not an imperial war as its predecessors had been, but, given that the chief combatants retained interests around the world, it certainly had overseas components: hostilities began with an English attack on the Dutch Smyrna fleet prior to the official declaration of war. Also, in the Caribbean, Sir William Stapleton, who had succeeded the Willoughbys as Governor of the Leeward Islands, directed the seizure of the small islands of St. Eustatius and Saba, whose size belied the annoyance caused by the smuggling conducted from them, while an expedition from Barbados took the opportunity to recapture Tobago. The Dutch, though, recaptured St. Eustatius, the French took Tobago, and Saba was returned at the peace.

Much more important, though, the war made apparent the increasing global prominence of France and the palpable decline of the Dutch Republic in the aftermath of the *Rampjaar* ("Disaster Year," 1672), when French armies occupied the Netherlands as far north as Utrecht. This invasion compelled the Dutch to open their dikes, restore William of Orange to his hereditary military positions, and lynch De Witt, whose attempts to maintain the peace were blamed for the crisis. Perhaps accordingly, English hostility toward France, never far from the surface, became more apparent as the imperial threat from the Sun King continued to increase.[52]

The war and the alliance with France became entangled with another issue that always lay close to the surface in seventeenth-century England: the fear of "popery." Charles II, personally tolerant, had previously issued a Declaration of Indulgence on 15 March 1672. Then, in the middle of the conflict, York announced his conversion to the Church of Rome, his proclivity for which some observers had long suspected. The prospect of a Catholic heir to the throne and James's marriage to the thoroughly Catholic Mary of Modena on 30 September 1673 coupled with the seeming encouragement to popery offered by the royal indulgence alarmed Parliament, which both refused to support the war until the King withdrew his declaration and ratified a Test Act. York was the

---

[51] Boxer, "Some Second Thoughts on the Third Anglo-Dutch War."
[52] Klooster, *The Dutch Moment*, 106–12.

chief target of this statute, which barred Roman Catholics and Nonconformists from military and public office.[53]

Given the attention devoted to thwarting "popish conspiracy" and the
attendant lack of will to fight fellow Protestants, English participation in
this Third Anglo-Dutch War was desultory. Thus, even after the crisis of
the French invasion, a joint Amsterdam–Zeeland fleet was able to demonstrate the continuing frailty of the English imperial grasp. In the
summer of 1673, this force, in addition to recapturing St. Eustatius,
destroyed the Virginia tobacco fleet, thereby pushing that colony's fiscal
situation to the wall. It also retook New York in an almost farcical
fashion and burned the fishing facilities, town, and fort at Ferryland,
Newfoundland; neither the colonies nor the metropolis were able to do
anything about these attacks.[54]

The Governor of New York, Francis Lovelace, had been in Hartford
when the Dutch arrived on 7 August 1673 (new style). By the time he
returned to New York City the town had surrendered without firing a
shot (Lovelace's deputy, Captain John Manning, was cashiered for cow-
ardice), and the rest of the colony surrendered in the ensuing few days.
The Dutch commander, Anthony Colve, assumed leadership of the
colony, which was renamed New Orange in honor of the newly ascendant
stadhouder, and quickly reinstated Dutch governmental institutions. The
seizure of New York, though, gave Connecticut the chance to renew its
quest to annex Long Island, while other colonials appealed directly to the
Crown to retake New York: "the very center and key of his Majesties
Dominions in America," as important to England as Tangier or the
Downs.[55]

---

[53] Boxer, "Some Second Thoughts on the Third Anglo-Dutch War."

[54] Jacobs, *The Colony of New Netherland*, 103–5. For the capture of New York, see, e.g.,
William Dervell to Mr. R. Woolly, 20 September 1673, *DRCHNY* 3: 206. For the
Virginia attack, see Thomas Ludwell, Secretary of Virginia, to Lord Arlington, 2 August
1673, *DRCHNY* 3: 204. For the Newfoundland attack, see Captain Dudley Lovelace, An
Account of the Dutch Fleet upon the Coast of Newfoundland in the Year 1673, 29 March
1675, CO 1/34, f. 85, transcribed by P.E. Pope, www.heritage.nf.ca/articles/exploration/
lovelace-dutch-fleet-1673.php (accessed 19 August 2016).

[55] E.g., The General Court's Letter to the Commander of the Dutch Fleet, 7 August 1673,
Ct. Recs. 2: 561; Letter from the General Court of Connecticut to the General Court of
Massachusetts, 17 October 1673; Part of a Letter from Major John Winthrop in com-
mand of the Connecticut forces at Southold, 25 February 1674, *Ct. Recs.* 2: 563, 567;
Several Propositions Concerning the Consequence of New York being in the hands of the
Dutch, 24 September 1673, CO 1/30, ff. 171–3; Project of Mr. Dyer for reducing New
York, 27 October 1673, CO 1/30, f. 195.

Nothing came of any of this, in the end. In imperial terms, the Dutch were so eager for peace with England they readily agreed to return New York and maintain the status quo ante bellum in the treaty that ended the war.[56] In Anglo-American terms, the settlement of New York's situation with respect to the Dutch meant the return of York's government, but the disgraced Lovelace was replaced by Sir Edmund Andros. Over the next three years, this vigorous and capable officer saw off the pretensions of Connecticut to Long Island by threatening to annex the neighboring colony's territory as far east as the Connecticut River if it did not abandon its claims, and he confirmed the Covenant Chain with his colony's Iroquois neighbors. This latter achievement, in the immediate term, also confirmed the defeat of the Wampanoags, mutual enemy of the signatories, in King Philip's War, and of the Susquehannocks, another ancient foe of the Iroquois, who were regarded as an obstacle to the expansion of Virginia, which had resulted in war in the Potomac River Valley. In the longer term, the Covenant Chain created a perception that the Iroquois and the English were firm friends, while facilitating Iroquois territorial expansion. Andros also began encouraging additional European settlement in the Hudson River Valley.[57]

While the advantage in the Anglo-Dutch rivalry tilted toward the Dutch, its Anglo-Spanish counterpart reached its first official resolution – in itself an English accomplishment – in 1670 with the Treaty of Madrid. Maria Anna of Austria, Queen-Regent of Spain, sought English support against designs of Louis XIV on the Spanish Netherlands, while the English sought to compel Spain to open its markets to English traders with the right to supply Spanish America with slaves constituting the main prize. Meanwhile, Modyford, while trying to negate the Dutch at Curacao, had continued Windsor's policy of encouraging raids on Spanish shipping and providing his island as a shelter for privateers, going so far as to proclaim war against Spain in February 1665.[58] This

---

[56] The Treaty of Westminster confirmed the Treaty of Breda; Treaty of peace between Great Britain and the United Netherlands, concluded at Westminster, 9/19 February 1673/4, Davenport, *European Treaties Bearing on the History of the United States and Its Dependencies*, 2: 229–40 at 239.

[57] Parmenter, "After the Mourning Wars."

[58] Additional factors of the Royal Company arrived at Jamaica in February 1664/5; Beeston, "A Journal Kept by Col. William Beeston," 285–6. Modyford assumed wide discretion in his post, canceling a contract that the company had made in Spain to supply slaves that he found disadvantageous after three Spanish ships acquired "about" 800 slaves in Jamaica; ibid. For the continuation of Modyford's anti-Spanish policy, see, e.g., Modyford to Earl of Arlington, 1 October 1668, CO 1/23, f. 115.

anti-Spanish policy culminated in the sack of Porto Bello in modern Panama, the terminus for silver shipments from Peru, in July 1668 by the privateer Henry Morgan, which netted a reported £75,000 in plunder and earning its mariners in excess of £60 apiece.[59] An ensuing attempt to take Cartagena miscarried, but Maracaibo and Grenada were sacked, bringing the attackers a reported £30,000. Morgan then carried out another attack that destroyed Panama in 1671.[60]

These exploits, needless to say, expanded the popularity of privateering/piracy in Jamaica: £60 was a lot of money in 1668, far more than a small planter, not to mention a servant, could earn even over several years. This reality thus abetted the notoriously lawless situation in Jamaica where the prevalence of the corsairs helped to deter European migration to the island. Yet despite the seeming rise of the buccaneers, the expedient employed by Modyford and Morgan helped to produce the desired imperial result, as the Treaty of Madrid allowed the granting of licenses to aliens to trade in the Spanish Empire for the first time.[61] Unfortunately for those who had envisioned this expansion of English trade and colonization further westward in the Caribbean, however, the RCAA was in no fit state to pursue that vision after the Dutch had devastated its operations, even as it resolved in the middle of the war that "the Negro trade be carried on to the utmost possibility of the stock."[62]

In the end, the best security these Guinea adventurers could find was to reincorporate into a new chartered venture, the Royal African Company, to pick up the pieces. The new incarnation of the RCAA received its patent on 27 September 1672 and the Duke of York continued to lead it. The list of patentees included some unsurprisingly familiar names, including Lord Ashley (now Earl of Shaftesbury), Sir John Banks, John Bence, the Earl of Craven, Sir Richard Ford, Thomas Povey, Dame Priscilla Ryder, widow of Sir William, and Samuel Moyer, now released from the Tower and back at work. It also included Sir Josiah Child, who emerged as one of the leading English promoters of overseas trade and

---

[59] Hanna, *Pirate Nests and the Rise of the British Empire*, 112–13.

[60] Beeston, A Journal Kept by Col. William Beeston, 287.

[61] Davenport, *European Treaties Bearing on the History of the United States and Its Dependencies*, 2: 187–96 at 195; cf. Hanna, *Pirate Nests and the Rise of the British Empire*, 110.

[62] Meeting of the Company of Adventurers Trading into Africa, 26 May 1665, T 70/75, f. 39; Report of Henry Brouncker, deputy governor, 23 January 1665/6, T 70/75, f. 47.

colonization after 1675 and who served as Governor of the East India Company at the end of the period under study.[63]

It took seven years for the chartered company to recover from the Second Anglo-Dutch War. In the meantime, those traders to Guinea not bothered with the niceties of securing a charter continued as they had done since the 1630s. These "interlopers" also seem to have gained an advantage, as the Royal African Company entered what proved to be its last incarnation, in terms of providing slaves to the Spanish. They then used the profits from this trade, as Nuala Zahedieh has shown, to establish a platform of sugar production and slave labor that made Jamaica's planters so wealthy in the eighteenth century.[64]

Thus, the efforts of seventeenth-century Anglo-American colonizers began to be realized by the mid-1670s. Whether they operated under a charter or not, they had devised a system that could deliver bound labor to plantations relatively reliably and without excessive concern about the social aspects of the master–servant relationship as it existed in England. In turn, the colonies provided ready markets for the plantation trade, an extension of the mercantile system that had been established and encouraged for decades, as we have seen. One observer in 1673, Ferdinando Gorges, the descendant of generations of promoters of English colonization, could go so far as to denigrate those "Plantations as are settled upon the continent of America or large islands which do swallow up great numbers of people." These places, according to Gorges, "by reason [of their] vast tracts of land are able to produce both food and raiment for their livelihood and require neither from their Mother Nation are doubtless rather injurious than profitable to this kingdom." In Barbados, on the other hand, the inhabitants "are supplied with a great part of their provisions & all their clothing household stuff horses & necessaries from England to the value of about £340,000 p[er] annum." The purveyors of this provision trade who supported the "few English and their Negroes employ two hundred sail" annually, he claimed, while six thousand mariners "proportionally bring home a native commodity to England" worth £160,000 per annum, "which is no small help to the balance of trade of this nation." Since the Guinea trade also "chiefly depends" on the

---

[63] Charter of Incorporation of the New Royal African Company, 27 September 1672, *CSPC AWI* 7: 409–12. The company retained its monopoly until 1698 and was wound up in 1721.

[64] Zahedieh, "Trade, Plunder, and Economic Development in Early English Jamaica"; Zahedieh, "The Merchants of Port Royal, Jamaica, and the Spanish Contraband Trade."

sugar plantations, "it appears that it is the interest of England to encourage these small sugar plantations & if possible to anticipate other nations their competitors in this great trade & commodity of sugar."[65]

With Jamaica now ready to join and, given its relative size, probably surpass Barbados as a sugar producer, the future had to be bright. All that remained now with the end of the latest Dutch war was to negotiate the price and quantity of the labor to be supplied more particularly. The Royal African Company was ready to take the lead here; its rivals, of course, carried on their business unencumbered by either obligations to pay lip service to the needs of the nation or the costs of maintaining forts.[66]

Planning to these ends could commence in earnest with the quieting of Anglo-Dutch relations after the Treaty of Westminster. Thus, a committee of the RAC considering "what quantities of Negroes it is fit to supply the plantations with" planned to send 5,600 Africans to Anglo-America in 1674: 2,150 to Barbados, 2,000 to Jamaica, 1,000 to Nevis, and 600 to Virginia, whose planters were now fully apprised of the "advantages" of African slave labor. Moreover, the company was now in a position to cast a wider net in its quest for slaves. Its planners thought that it could send a "like quantity" to the plantations in 1675, since it the company had already agreed to send another six ships before Christmas 1674, "which may carry 2000 Negroes from the Gold Coast at convenient times," while the remainder could be acquired "from the Bite [of Benin] & Ardra & Angola."[67]

---

[65] Mr. Gorges concerning the plantations read in Council, 17 March 1672/3, Egerton Ms. 2395, f. 490, BL.

[66] The company promised "to accommodate planters in all things they possibly can but are resolved not to grant licenses"; Meeting of the Court of Assistants, 5 May 1674, T 70/76, f. 7v. Its members heard a report that it had done well in meeting its pledges to provide "Negroes" from 28 February 1672/3 to 28 February 1673/4: Barbados (2,000 pledged), 2,150; Jamaica (2,000), 2,000; Nevis/Leeward Islands (1,000), 1000; Virginia (600), 560; Meeting of the Court of Assistants, 12 May 1674, T 70/76, ff. 8–9.

[67] Report given at a meeting of the Court of Assistants of the Royal African Company that the plantations be supplied as follows from 28 February 1673 to 28 February 1674, 12 May 1674, T 70/76, ff. 8r–8v.

9

A New Empire?

The period from 1675, of course, saw the further ascent of English overseas trade and colonization. It also, not coincidentally, saw the further ascent – or, rather, descent – of English involvement in the trans-Atlantic slave trade as the Royal African Company and its competitors took full and ready advantage of the dependency on slave labor in Anglo-America, which their predecessors had cultivated over the previous four decades. Over twice as many slaves departed Africa in ships flying the flag of "Great Britain" between 1676 and 1700 as had done between 1651 and 1675. Moreover, in the final quarter of the seventeenth century, of the estimated total of 719,675 slaves taken from Africa, 272,200 were taken in "British" ships, a figure that comes a fairly close second in this dubious competition to the 297,272 Africans conveyed by the Portuguese, the perennial leaders.[1]

Thus, there can be no question that the slave trade constituted the linchpin of English overseas activity after the English traders secured a foothold in Guinea from 1635, even though the slave trade constituted just one component of seventeenth-century Anglo-African commerce.[2] This trade also continued to attract participants whose behavior, as invariably happened with seventeenth-century English overseas endeavors, could not readily be regulated: whoever could bring the

[1] The Trans-Atlantic Slave Trade Database records 122,367 slaves taken in "British" ships between 1651 and 1675. All of these figures appear in www.slavevoyages.org/assessment/estimates (accessed 20 August 2016).

[2] Eltis, "The Relative Importance of Slaves and Commodities in the Atlantic Trade of Seventeenth-Century Africa," table 1 at 245, provides data for Royal African Company imports to and exports from Africa at a base year of 1697.

greatest number of healthy slaves at the fairest price for buyers would always prosper, despite the problems for suppliers that were inherent in the trade, including the routinely dreadful mortality among European personnel at African posts and, not to be forgotten, the constant prospect of the enslaved people acting on their resentment at their situation.[3]

Yet the historiography of English involvement in Africa invariably focuses on the Royal African Company and its failure both as a concept – a chartered company – and in practice – as it was unable to defeat its rivals either commercially or politically. The most recent history of the RAC focuses on the debates over the company's monopoly that resulted in the opening of the Guinea trade to all comers in 1712. In addition to facilitating the company's ultimate demise forty years later, this open access "played a critical part in entrenching African slavery as the preferred solution to the American problem of labor supply."[4]

A focus on the Royal African Company, however, misdirects our comprehension of the history of the slave trade and English participation in it, especially during the seventeenth century. First of all, slavery had already become "entrenched" as the "preferred solution to the American problem of labor supply" long before the RAC received its charter in 1672; indeed, the success of the slave trade was arguably the chief reason for investors involving themselves in this venture in the first place. At the same time, since rivalry between traders, chartered or otherwise, had always been a central aspect of English activity in Africa, the extent to which the various creations of chartered monopolies from the 1630s affected the conduct of the Guinea trade remains unclear at best. While unlicensed traders, smelling blood in the water, took pains to submit, in time-honored fashion, rationales for canceling the company's privileges to higher authority, it does not follow that the opening of a trade that had never been closed sparked the further expansion of the slave trade. Rather, the slave trade continued from strength to strength as new colonies, including Jamaica, Carolina, and Pennsylvania, came into existence in the third quarter of the seventeenth century. While these provinces, along with their predecessors, increased in significance after 1690, other markets opened for English slave traders; increasing numbers of Africans

---

[3] For mortality among Royal African Company employees in Guinea, see, e.g., Letter from Agent Nathaniel Bradley, Mr. Henry Spurway, Mr. John Rysing, Mr. John Mildmay, Cape Corso Castle, 26 April 1680, T 70/1, ff. 54–7 at 57. For "unruly" slaves, see, e.g., Edwyn Stede and Stephen Gascoigne to Royal African Company, 28 July 1680, T 70/1, ff. 62–3 at 62.

[4] Pettigrew, *Freedom's Debt*, 15.

were shipped to meet the incessant American demand for labor. The inexorable progress of the trans-Atlantic slave trade also strengthened the commercial as well as the sociopolitical affinities of English interests in Asia and those in the Western Hemisphere and fueled cultural changes in the metropolis (that rippled to the colonies), which provided the foundation for new conceptions of modernity and greater state participation in empire.

Thus, the Governor of Barbados, Jonathan Atkins, reported in 1677 that Spaniards had arrived with cash seeking "to trade with this place for Negroes," having been "resolved to come again by the persuasions of the [Royal African] Company, they being a new society of merchants who have contracted with the Crown of Spain to furnish them with Negroes," pursuant to the Treaty of Madrid. By this arrangement, the company would "be furnished with money that they pay their debts the better and rid themselves at good rates of their refractory, dangerous, and bad Negroes." Barbados, Atkins advised, constituted a splendid location for an intercolonial slave market, as it was close enough – "being within ten or twelve days sail" from Havana – that the traders could maintain "a stock ready upon the island for the Spaniard which will invite him to come to buy because of that certainty," which "will much lessen the charge which a longer voyage puts them to." Consequently, the Royal African Company "will be much advanced in their slaves as well in the number as the prices of their Negroes," while Barbados "by this money trade will increase in wealth and if [the trade] come to be settled it may grow to be so considerable that a duty of some advantage may accrue to his Majesty."[5]

Rivals did make seemingly constant inroads on the RAC's patent. In April 1680, for instance, Edwyn Stede, the Barbados Lieutenant Governor, reported the arrival of an "Interloper" carrying 180 or 190 "good Gold Coast Negroes," whom they delivered to the lee side of the island "without interruption." The company's position was not helped by reports in Barbados that its own agents in Guinea "keep the best of the Negroes to sell to the Interlopers."[6]

Whether they were working against their employers' interests or not, the company's agents in Africa reported on unauthorized traders who "give such extravagant rates for slaves (and there is so few upon the Coast) that

[5] Governor Jonathan Atkins of Barbados to Lord Treasurer Clifford, 13/23 May 1677, Add. Ms. 38714, f. 20, BL.

[6] Letter from Edwyn Stede and Stephen Gascoigne, Barbados, 20 April 1680, T 70/1, f. 48; Stede and Gascoigne from Barbados, 26 October 1680 (sent 31 January 1680/81), T 70/1, f. 67.

without they go for and as &c not one in 6 will gett halfe their comple-
ment." The posting of bonds for good behavior and the threat of fines
seems to have had little effect, if the case of Charles Plummer, who arrived
in the Gambia "to buy Negroes" in 1679, is any indication. Since Plummer
knew the territory and had good contacts among the local merchants, the
company's factor "could not buy a slave of these merchants in 12 or 14
days." To add insult to injury, Plummer reaped sufficient profits to cover
the forfeiture of the bond of £2,000 he had posted not to trade in the
Gambia or along the Guinea coast for one year.[7]

Plummer seems to have been only one of a "great number of interlopers" who operated in Guinea at the end of 1679 and who drove the
RAC to the ends of its collective wits.[8] Royal proclamations having had
no apparent effect, the company asked the Crown to send a round of
letters to governors in the West Indies. If the government did not address
this situation, it was warned, the company would not "be able to support
the great charge they are at in maintaining their forts in Africa."[9] The
Privy Council duly issued the requested instructions but the company's
complaints continued, not all of which were within the power of colonial
governors to address. In August 1682, the RAC noted that "interlopers"
were now building forts at Whydah and Allada, an area east of the
company's traditional theater of operations but one that it envisioned as
an increasingly important area of ever-expanding slave trade.[10]

Meanwhile, the situation of the Royal African Company in Jamaica, its
most promising new market, threatened to become undone. First, the
Lords of Foreign Plantation had entertained a petition from the colony's
planters that the company "did not supply that island with a sufficient
number of Negroes, and that those which were furnished by were at such
price that the planters were greatly discouraged." The Lords ordered the
RAC to "supply the said island with a sufficient number of merchantable
Negroes at the rate of £18 per head to be paid in six months." When the

---

[7] Letter from Agent Nathaniel Bradley, Mr. Henry Spurway, Mr. John Rysing, Mr. John
  Mildmay, Cape Corso Castle, 26 April 1680, T 70/1, ff. 54–7.
[8] Letter from Agent Bradley, Mr Maccabeus Hollis, Mr Arthur Harben, & Mr Henry
  Spurway at Cape Corso Castle, 8 December 1679, T 70/1, f. 50.
[9] Orders of Council and Petitions and other Business at Court relating to the Royal African
  Company of England, 3 March 1681/2 to 22 September 1696, 3 March 1681/2,
  T 70/169, ff. 4r–4v.
[10] Meeting of the Royal African Company, 12 May 1674, T 70/76, ff. 8v–9r; Law, "The
  Slave Trade in Seventeenth-Century Allada." The company also acquired slaves from
  Angola; e.g., Instructions to Captain Thomas James, 18 March 1685/6, T 70/1, f. 6.

company agreed, the Jamaica Assembly promptly passed a statute that set "the price of Negroes positively to the aforesaid rate, upon great penalties," as well as "making themselves the only judges of what are merchantable or not, to your petitioner's great prejudice." Then, the prevalent use of Spanish money in Jamaica had artificially elevated the price of sugar (the island's currency) there, thereby devaluing slaves when the RAC sought to resell that sugar in Europe where the price had plunged. At the same time, the company's competitors had driven up the price of slaves in Guinea. Since the RAC's commanders and masters received part of their pay in slaves, the resulting devaluation of their compensation had made them "terrified and discouraged," so that "many of them absolutely refuse to go to Jamaica." Moreover, the Supreme Court of Jamaica had awarded the company's rivals £1,627 damages for the unlawful seizure of their property by the RAC agent in the colony, holding that it was unclear if prior patentees had surrendered their rights. The RAC reported similar obstruction in Nevis.[11]

Reports from the Gold Coast indicate that the price paid for slaves there between 1660 and 1690 "ranged from 480 dambas in gold [£5] for a boy to 768 dambas [£8] for both adults and children," many of whom had been transported there by traders from the Slave Coast along the Bight of Benin, although the Royal African Company budgeted a cost of £3 per "sound and merchantable slave" at Whydah in 1688. African buyers as well as Europeans paid the same tariff as the company's agents did on the Gold Coast, but other Europeans did not incur the costs of maintaining forts and garrisons that the RAC did, as the company constantly reminded the Crown. Thus, while all slave traders stood to make £10 to £13 per Gold Coast slave under the price established by the Jamaicans, the costs of furthering English interests in Guinea, as the RAC petitions to the Crown always put it, always eroded the company's profit margin. Since the RAC had to pay its suppliers in gold yet remained dependent on the price of sugar in securing its return in the West Indies, its margin came under further pressure.[12]

In response to planter complaints about its pricing policy, the Royal African Company blamed the circumstances of the trade: "for Negroes are not only very perishable and chargeable in our hands but it is wholly

---

[11] Orders of Council and Petitions and other Business at Court relating to the Royal African Company of England, 3 March 1681/2 to 22 September 1696, 6 January 1682/3, T 70/169, ff. 5, 6r, 7r.

[12] Kea, *Settlements, Trade, and Politics in the Seventeenth Century Gold Coast*, 200; Instructions to Captain Samuel Richard, 4 December 1688, T 70/61, f. 66.

unpracticable to keep any quantities many days unsold but we must take for them what we can get." Then, as for concerns that the RAC kept supplies artificially low due to the constant high demand for slaves, it insisted that an examination of its practices would show that it was not "guilty of this fault, but that we have advanced the trade to that degree and supplied all plantations so fully that our factors some of them wish us to desist."[13]

Claiming that "there is now owing to us much above £130,000," the Royal African Company again asked for governmental cooperation. Against those who argued that a free trade would bring a greater supply of slaves to the plantations and so serve as "a general advantage to the Nation," the company claimed that the "manner" of their African trading partners required the maintenance of fortified trading factories in Guinea. It declared further that, if it abandoned its factories, "the potent joint stocks of other nations, but particularly the Dutch" would take them over "and keep the trade to themselves (as they have done in the Spice Islands in the East Indies)." Only by following the Dutch model of having a jointstock corporation conduct long-range trade, the RAC insisted, could the English presence in Guinea flourish. Thus, while the success enjoyed by interlopers might seem to support the free trade argument, without corporate oversight to manage the provision of a regular supply, "plantations would want Negroes wholly to their utter ruin or pay other nations for them twice the price they have paid to us." The company claimed the same liberty to sell their commodities on the same terms as everyone else in Jamaica and other plantations, since, in accordance with its own interests, it would supply that island with enough slaves "to enable them not only to supply their sugar works but also to sell again to the Spaniards to their great advantage, which we have refused (despite several please from the Spanish to do so) or to manage their slaves as they see fit."[14]

This pattern was repeated. The RAC received reports on its rivals, such as its former employee Petley Wyborne, and of the contrivances employed by colonial purchasers of slaves to secure the best arrangements. It then petitioned the Council for Foreign Plantations for governmental action,

---

[13] Orders of Council and Petitions and other Business at Court relating to the Royal African Company of England, 3 March 1681/2 to 22 September 1696, 24 October 1683, T 70/169, ff. 13r–14r.

[14] Jamaica, St. Christopher's, and Antigua also passed laws that obliged creditors, such as the RAC, to accept the valuation of debtors' estates as set by the neighbors of the debtors; Orders of Council and Petitions and other Business at Court relating to the Royal African Company of England, 3 March 1681/2 to 22 September 1696, T 70/169, ff. 12r–12v, 30r.

including the preparation of legislation that would impose a fine of £10 per slave on those found guilty of encroaching on the company's privileges. In lodging its complaints, the RAC reminded the government that, in addition to the trouble and expense it had taken in furthering the public interest, it derived its authority from the prerogative. Thus, violations of its patent constituted an abuse of the royal power that had bestowed that patent. On hearing the RAC's petition, the Crown intervened, but whatever immediate effects soon dissipated; the cycle began again. The Navy sent a frigate to scour the coast from the Gambia to Whydah to hunt for pirates and interlopers and to liaise with the company's factors. Any found were be taken to Cabo Carso for judgment by the Admiralty Court there. The particular RAC–government cooperative effort of 1684, however, seems to have been less than fully effective; one of its chief targets, Wyborne, remained at large.[15]

Two, after all, could play this imperial game: purchasers of slaves in the West Indies not only cooperated with the RAC's rivals and used their own patronage connections to frustrate the company. They also made their own complaints to the Privy Council about the company's pricing policy and the purportedly inadequate supplies of slaves it provided to the colonies. Thus, the RAC found itself pleading the state of its debts in response to the government's commands "that they should supply His Majesty's Plantations in America with such quantities of Negro Slaves as the said plantations could well pay for." The company claimed continuing losses from slave sales in Antigua, Montserrat, Nevis, and St. Christopher's: it had been the longstanding practice in the West Indies to acquire slaves for sugar, but the price of the staple had plummeted in 1687 from 12s 6d per hundredweight to 6s 5d per hundredweight, resulting in an increase in its operating deficit in these colonies to £22,000.[16]

Notwithstanding these issues, the scope of the RAC's interests continued to expand on both sides of the Atlantic, indicating that the

[15] James II, at RAC behest, proclaimed against interlopers and "their contempt for our royal prerogative"; 3 August 1685, T 70/169, ff. 31v–32v; Petition from the Royal African Company, 24 October 1683, and Petition from the Royal African Company, 12 August 1684, Orders of Council and Petitions and other Business at Court relating to the Royal African Company of England, 3 March 1681/2 to 22 September 1696, T 70/169, ff. 15v–16v, 23v.

[16] Petition of the Royal African Company regarding slaves, 19 April 1687, Orders of Council and Petitions and other Business at Court relating to the Royal African Company of England, 3 March 1681/2 to 22 September 1696, T 70/169, ff. 46v–47v.

company was enjoying at least some success. In December 1685, for instance, it sent one vessel with goods valued at £1906 7s 1d to the Gold Coast to trade for gold, ivory, and other "vendible" commodities in Europe. It was then to bring that cargo to Cabo Corso and collect 550 "Negroes, if they have them or expect them" for Jamaica or convey an alternate cargo if there were insufficient slaves at Cabo Corso. The following month, two RAC vessels went to the Gambia, one to collect 200 "Negroes" to bring to the Potomac River; the other to travel on to Cabo Corso with a cargo to exchange for gold, ivory, and malaguetta pepper, then head for Angola to acquire 450 "lusty and sound Negroes" for Barbados. In December 1688, the RAC sent a ship to Whydah to purchase 360 slaves at £3 per head; these slaves must be "sound and merchantable," between the ages of fifteen and forty and "the major part be males" as per agreement with Wyborne, now back in the company's good graces. The company further directed that "Negroes" should be "mustered" every fourteen days at this factory. Meanwhile, its authority to deliver slaves was officially extended to Virginia in 1687.[17]

The RAC also purchased the Danish factory at Frederiksborg in June 1688 after some intensive negotiations. Located on a hilltop that commanded Cabo Corso, which enabled it to "annoy" the English factory, Frederiksborg had been a source of corresponding concern and irritation since its construction in 1661. Although the company claimed a prior right to the site through an agreement allegedly made by Thomas Crispe, then an agent of the Guinea Company but now a member of the RAC, with the King of Fetu in 1649, "ye many changes of government & disturbances in England" had prevented the perfection of that arrangement. The Danes had taken over the site, but their situation had never been secure: by 1683, they were in "great streights," having had no

---

[17] So that the colony "may have a constant sufficient supply of merchantable Negroes at moderate rates in money or commodities," but the governor was to ensure that the company was paid and to stop interlopers and their associates; James II to Francis, Lord Howard of Effingham, 3 April 1687, Orders of Council and Petitions and other Business at Court relating to the Royal African Company of England, 3 March 1681/2 to 22 September 1696, T 70/169, f. 46. For the RAC's operations in this period, see, e.g., Instructions from the Royal African Company to Captain Thomas Woodfine, 10 December 1685, T 70/61, f. 3r; Instructions to Marmaduke Goodhand, 12 January 1685/6, T 70/61, f. 4r; Instructions to Peter Pickard, 12 January 1685/6, T 70/61, f. 4v; Instructions to Samuel Richard, 4 December 1688, T 70/61, f. 76.

supply from Denmark with "only one Danish Ship [calling] there in many years past." Thus, Frederiksborg had become a center of unlicensed trading, with its factors forced to rely for "shelter and trade" on interlopers "to the great damages of the English Company in their place of trade." The plight of the post raised the even worse prospect of the Danes selling out to another European rival. Thus, the company had, first, taken a mortgage on Frederiksborg and, when the Danish situation continued to deteriorate, bought the place in their own right. Christian V, though, objected that the RAC did not have the authority to purchase Danish territory, so the sale had to be completed by James II. This refusal of the Danish King to countenance the right of companies to engage in diplomacy reminds us of the limits to which seventeenth-century corporate power extended. Yet it also illustrates both the special relationship with James, both as Duke of York and as monarch, on which the company could draw in order to carry on its activities and, accordingly, its continuing vitality, notwithstanding its problems, before the Glorious Revolution drove its great patron from the scene.[18]

The seemingly inexorable increase in the volume of the slave trade during the seventeenth century also meant, notwithstanding the administrative separation of the Guinea and East Indian trades, that the importance of the commercial link between Asia and Africa correspondingly increased, since Asian textiles and cowries remained the primary commodities demanded by African suppliers of African goods and slaves. The Royal African Company and its competitors had to acquire the necessary calicoes, chintzes, and other Asian cloths in England whence they had been taken by the East India Company and then reexport them to Guinea. The EIC obtained these fabrics in the first instance through its contracts with Indian weavers, whereby it both recruited weavers to live under its authority but also – a less satisfactory method from the company's perspective – employed intermediaries, customarily, local merchants, to negotiate contracts with weavers living in areas outside its jurisdiction. This practice seems to have met EIC demand for fabric into the eighteenth century. The exponential rise of the slave trade after 1720 coupled with the increasing political role of the company in India after 1740, however, both further increased demand for Indian textiles and made it possible for the EIC to exercise greater control over the conditions by which it

---

[18] Royal African Company petition for the retention of Fort Frederiksborg, 7 January 1685/6, T 70/169, ff. 33v–36v. For the final sale of the fort, see T 70/169, f. 52v–53r.

employed weavers. This made it more difficult for workers, for instance, to cancel contracts and sell their wares to a higher bidder. Yet even into the later eighteenth century, when it became the political authority in Bengal, it seems "[c]onciliation rather than coercion appeared to be the Company's official watchword" in dealing with Indian weavers.[19]

The East India Company's ready access to Indian cloths enabled it to move from strength to strength commercially and politically despite its formal withdrawal from the Guinea trade in 1663. Between 1660 and 1689 its dividend rate rose from 20 to 50 percent, while the company reaped profits estimated at a very healthy £130,000 per annum, which more than offset the official £170,000 it paid to the government over this period.[20] Also, it was able to deal with domestic rivals relatively effectively, perhaps since none amassed the requisite wherewithal to conduct extensive Asian trade after the absorption of the Assada Adventurers. Moreover, its authority to seize and punish unauthorized traders received the imprimatur of a friendly House of Commons.[21]

The EIC also received reconfirmation of its chartered powers, which included the right to create governments under its corporate seal in 1687. This new grant clarified that the company served as the sole point of contact between the administration of English-governed areas of Asia and the Crown. It exercised this authority by creating a new municipal corporation for Madras, replete with Mayor, Mayor's Court, Aldermen, and Recorder. This brought the city more firmly under its jurisdiction but, even more important, encouraged local participation, even for non-English residents, in the local administration. That same year, the company moved its Arabian Sea presidency from Surat to Bombay, whose island now contained a diverse population of 60,000 inhabitants, although Bombay was not incorporated along the lines of Madras until 1726.[22]

The EIC did continue to suffer reverses, however, in the East Indies. In 1682, the Dutch took advantage of civil war in Bantam to intervene in that sultanate's politics. Their ensuing victory enabled them finally to

---

[19] Prakash, "From Negotiation to Coercion," 1339.

[20] Lawson, *The East India Company*, 44–5.

[21] The Case of the Jurisdiction of the House of Peers, between Thomas Skinner, Merchant, and the East India Company: 18 Charles II. A.D. 1666, Cobbett, *A Complete Collection of State Trials and Proceedings*, 6: 710–69.

[22] Shaw, *Charters Relating to the East India Company*, xi; Charter granted by the Governor and Company of Merchants, Trading into the East-Indies, to the Mayor, Aldermen, and Burgesses of Madras, 30 December 1687, ibid., 84–96.

expel the English from the factory they had occupied since 1613 and that had enjoyed unprecedented prosperity after 1669, even as Charles II and the company received ambassadors from the young Sultan of Bantam with a view to entering into an alliance. Yet the loss of this post, despite its historical significance and the final English abandonment of Java to the old enemy, did not constitute a comprehensive defeat, at least at first. Most of the pepper for which the EIC contracted (the price of which had risen by 2d per pound in March 1683) came from Sumatra where the company had cultivated good relations, although its Jambi factory on the east coast of Sumatra was sacked in 1679 at the end of that sultanate's war with its Malayan enemy Johor.[23]

Thus, instead of confronting Batavia over Java, EIC officials decided to move its Indies operations to the west coast of Sumatra, a location that was closer to Madras as well as to the friendly rulers of Aceh and further from hostile Malays. The Sultana of Aceh, Inayat Zakiatuddin Syah, did not want an English fort at her capital, which might have antagonized the Dutch, but she did agree to the establishment of one at Bencoolen (Bengkulu), so in 1685 the EIC began work on York Fort, importing slaves from Madagascar to build it. As with Madras, Bombay, and St. Helena, the company attempted a Batavia-style colony where its fortification defended a municipality inhabited primarily by Asian populations (although European migration was encouraged) with both indigenous and migratory elements and a surrounding area that could accommodate plantations.[24]

Bencoolen, though, proved yet another imperial disappointment for the English. First, the colony could not overcome the general decline of the Sumatran pepper trade due to the continuing warfare that beset the island's states from the mid-1660s. Thus, the new factory probably never handled the volume of pepper that had been transported from Bantam, and the costs of building and maintaining the fort there certainly exceeded those incurred by its predecessor. Moreover, the post provided a base for colonial-imperialist operations in Sumatra, undertaken in defiance of directives from London to avoid conflicts that could disrupt trade. As in Anglo-America, those pursuits fomented such strife that the costs of

---

[23] Lewis, "British Trade to Southeast Asia in the Seventeenth and Eighteenth Centuries Revisited."

[24] The Sultana of Jambi had made friendly overtures to the English as early as 1661; Queen of Acheh to Charles II, 12 October 1661, CO 77/8, f. 192; Locher-Scholten, *Sumatran Sultanate and Colonial State*, 39–40.

defending the colony regularly outpaced the revenues yielded from pepper. The endemic corruption of EIC officers on the ground aggravated the parlous situation of the factory.[25]

The grander plan for Bencoolen, in the mind of the East India Company directors, envisioned it as a terminus of trade with China, via its Taiwan factory that the EIC maintained from 1670 and 1699 and that became increasingly viable after the Qing Dynasty seized that island in 1683. The colony had a Chinese population when the English arrived, and the EIC tried, as their Anglo-American counterparts did with Europeans, to induce more Chinese to migrate there both to facilitate this intended China commerce as well as to grow plantation crops. Those who did migrate received a house, tax incentives, and other inducements to start businesses. In the end, however, these proved insufficient attractions, although a Chinese community did develop around the fort that was granted considerable powers of self-government. The numbers – and, thus, the economic contributions – of this community remained quite small, undoubtedly due to the poor quality of the soil, periodic outbreaks of smallpox and other epidemics, along with the regular outbreak of Malayan wars, some provoked by EIC servants, which nearly drove Bencoolen "to ruin" in the mid-1710s.[26]

One eighteenth-century Chinese colonist, Key Soon, did cultivate "a delightful garden designed to profit as well as pleasure" but at great cost to his purse and his person; he would have gone bankrupt reportedly "but for the assistance afforded him by the India Company."[27] Probably no more than one thousand Chinese people, who assumed the repairs of the fort, cultivated sugar plantations with slaves where they distilled arrack (the East Indian counterpart to rum), and developed a reputation among the English for industry, lived at Bencoolen in the 1730s. Notwithstanding its small size, the community and its cohabitation with Malays did set a precedent, as the most recent historian of this colony has noted, for the

---

[25] Farrington, "Bengkulu: An Anglo-Chinese Partnership"; Veevers, "'The Company as Their Lords and the Deputy as a Great Rajah.'" Local hostility compelled the evacuation of Bencoolen in 1719 for two years.

[26] Veevers, "The Company as Their Lords and the Deputy as a Great Rajah," 703–4; Stern, *The Company-State*, 74–6, 177–81. For the EIC's long interest in "Tywan," see, e.g., Francis Breton et al. from Swally to East India Company, 30 March 1646, IOR E3/20, ff. 2–8 at f. 6; Henry Dacres et al. to Surat, 4 August 1670, IOR E3/31, ff. 79r–79v; Bassett, "The Trade of the English East India Company in the Far East, 1623–84: Part I."

[27] Marsden, *The History of Sumatra*, 69.

development of Singapore after the English acquired that foothold at the outlet of the Straits of Malacca and the South China Sea in 1819.[28]

Meanwhile, the EIC's position in India now incurred a series of calamities, largely of its own doing. First, rebellions broke out at Bombay and St. Helena in 1684 in which disaffected colonists sought an end to EIC rule over those places. Their appeals for royal intervention against the "tyranny" of colonial administration echoed those made by near-contemporary rebels in Virginia (1676) and South Carolina (1719); Keigwin's Rebellion (Bombay) and Dennison's Insurrection (St. Helena) sought royalization of their colonies as the Carolinians later did but wound up at the gibbet rather than on the colonial council.[29]

While they suppressed these insurrections and perhaps due to overconfidence derived from the EIC's improved economic and political position in the early 1680s, the company, under the direction of Sir Josiah Child, pursued an increasingly aggressive policy against its Dutch and Portuguese adversaries on the subcontinent. They were also concerned with the potential effects of the endless wars of the Emperor Aurangzeb (reigned 1659–1707) on its trade. EIC officers undoubtedly recalled the destructive Maratha attack on Surat in 1664 during a prior conflict from which their operations had escaped unscathed, but would they be so fortunate again?

Thus, the company reorganized and centralized its organization in India, increased its army, and sought to expand its presence around the Bay of Bengal. In addition, Sir Josiah and his namesake, John, in command at Bombay until his death in February 1690, adopted a more belligerent approach in seeking a renewal of the EIC's *firman* from the Emperor. The resulting "Child's War," which began when a company fleet attacked Chittagong (in modern Bangladesh), brought only a humiliating reminder of the company's dependency on Indian goodwill: the Bengal attack was crushed and a Mughal army then devastated Bombay. As a result, the EIC had to submit to Aurangzeb and pay a fine of £15,000. It was, however, able to recover nicely: it received new *firmans* for Madras and Masulipatnam; was able to establish a new town, Calcutta, through a new license that it received to conduct trade at three adjacent villages at the mouth of the Hooghly River; and

---

[28] Batavia had an estimated Chinese population of 15,000 prior to massacre perpetrated by the colonial authorities in 1740 after a revolt; Farrington, "Bengkulu: An Anglo-Chinese Partnership," 115.

[29] Strachey, *Keigwin's Rebellion*, esp. 79–104; Grant, *Extracts from the Records of St. Helena*, 25–32.

retained its Bombay privileges. The EIC also began to support broader land ownership in that town, thereby fostering closer ties between the government and the inhabitants. Thus, it was reasonably well placed to survive – and then take advantage of – the precipitous decline of Mughal power, with which the English had nothing to do, after 1720.[30]

Back in England, the popularity of the fruits of overseas trade and colonization in the metropolis had created a serious dilemma for the Crown. The increasing availability of foreign products from textiles to tobacco over the course of the seventeenth century also greatly increased the customs revenue, which comprised a significant portion of the government's revenue, and, by 1675, overseas trade and colonies provided a significant portion of that customs revenue. This situation helped the Crown to "live off of its own." Thus, it did not need to summon Parliament, thereby depriving those who had concerns about royal policy and any undue exercise of the prerogative of a constitutional forum to air their grievances. In the 1620s and, even more haunting for Charles II and his brother, in the 1640s, the summoning of Parliament had given those opposed to Charles I's policies this opportunity with ultimately horrid results.[31]

Naturally, those with suspicions about the motives of the royal brothers after 1675 worked with equal feverishness, as their predecessors in the 1620s and 1640s had, to keep the parliamentary avenue open. The government's quandary over overseas activity arose from the demand that accompanied the supply of – or perhaps was triggered by the appearance of – overseas commodities. The desire for calicoes, cinnamon, coffee, and other once-exotic goods lowered their prices and enabled more people to afford them. At the same time, the pursuit of these "finer things" reflected, in a circular way, a new cultural sensibility that privileged the acquisition and consumption of such

---

[30] Stern, *The Company-State*, 61–99, 121–41; Lawton, *The East India Company*, 49–50; Pearson et al., "Symposium."

[31] For instance, imports of West Indian sugar into London more than doubled, from 148,000 hundredweight in 1663–9 to 371,000 hundredweight in 1699–1701; one-third of this sugar was reexported; Davis, "English Foreign Trade, 1660–1700." The EIC contributed £324,000 to the Crown between 1660 and 1684, a figure that does not include the payment of customs duties or less formal gratuities to other officials; Stern, *The Company-State*, 155. As Professor Aylmer has noted, in the reign of Charles II "over two-thirds of the customs revenue was collected in the port of London and its outports"; after 1671, this revenue was collected directly, not by farmers; Aylmer, *The Crown's Servants*, 32–3.

items. In addition to customs revenue, this quest for gentility provided more opportunities for sociability but also brought a backlash against the new preference for high living and luxury in the French style that allegedly drained specie from the realm through overseas trade.[32]

In particular, the popularity of coffee after the Restoration spawned a proliferation of coffeehouses. Here, those pursuing gentility eschewed alcohol and found environments, unlike public houses, where "refined" people could mix and discuss political issues with like-minded individuals, often with reference to pertinent publications made available by these establishments, as well as conduct business without concerns about engaging in unseemly behavior. The government, though, regarded the popularity of these venues with concern, as they provided locations for gatherings that it could not monitor satisfactorily. It made various efforts to regulate these establishments, although with a similar success, since banning these alleged hives of disaffection in order to curb unwanted public debate of government policy would have also deprived the King of the revenue produced by the coffee excise.[33]

Perhaps this scenario also illustrates the issues that arise in the application of the concept of "modernity" when considering the history of England. After all, it is one thing for governments to think about controlling matters to their satisfaction, as has been the case since the beginning of governments whatever the agendas of those involved may have been. These efforts, when they involve creating or increasing an apparatus for effecting state policy (which requires the acquisition and dissemination of state revenue), might be styled "centralization" or "state building." Yet reaches often exceed grasps – at least they did in the seventeenth century: political, personal, and structural obstacles invariably frustrated the full realization of governmental goals. Is it the pursuit of state power in the abstract, then, which constitutes a modernizing phenomenon? Or did the means – alleged, if not actual – that have

---

[32] Slack, "The Politics of Consumption and England's Happiness in the Later Seventeenth Century."

[33] Cowan, "The Rise of the Coffeehouse Reconsidered." The government also, of course, tried to orchestrate the production and dissemination of news; Raymond, "The Newspaper, Public Opinion, and the Public Sphere in the Seventeenth Century," 11–19. For Crown surveillance efforts of those officials deemed suspicious, another manifestation of increasing state capability that it inherited from the Protectorate, see, e.g., Information of Sir James Hay against Samuel Wilson, [October 1681], Stowe Ms. 186, f. 46; Sir James Hay to Secretary Jenkins, 19 September 1681, Stowe Ms. 186, f. 48; Tim Taylor to "Mr. Herne," 30 September 1681, f. 41, all BL.

been employed, both in the attempts to extend state power and in the responses to those attempts, create a modern sensibility?

Similar questions arise when considering those aspects of modernity that have less direct connections to state formation. What was actually modern about Restoration England? There was certainly novelty in terms of the distinctive aspects of sociability that became apparent, particularly in London, after 1660. Novelty is also apparent in that English people had developed a self-awareness that they lived in modern times: they were doing new things and pursuing the new ideas as they saw it. Accordingly, certain contemporaries celebrated the conception of these novelties and identified themselves as the progenitors of the new and improved.

The field of political arithmetic, which built on the careers of earlier thinkers such as Sir Francis Bacon and Samuel Hartlib, but became fully fledged during the reign of Charles II, exemplifies this phenomenon and its application to empire. A battery of authors, including Sir Charles Davenant, Gregory King, and Sir William Petty, composed an increasingly steady stream of studies of overseas topics that they submitted for governmental consideration. At the same time, Crown officials increasingly turned to the views of these observers in their quest to obtain clearer information on increasingly complex colonial situations. Although this body of work was customarily produced outside the government and was often grounded in the hothouse politics of the times, it provided the basis for the belief that accurate and neutral data could be compiled that would provide a rational basis for the implementation and conducting of state policy. This sensibility, in turn, fueled the twinned Western beliefs in progress and in Western civilization as the pinnacle of human achievement.[34]

Much of the wider contemporary sensibility that English people lived in new and exciting times accompanied the rise of a modern London after the Great Fire had reduced much of the medieval city to ashes. Coupled with

---

[34] E.g., Council of Foreign Trade and Plantations to Governor and Council of Barbados, 11 February 1660/1, CO 1/14, f. 149; same to Governor and Council of Virginia, 18 February 1660/1, CO 1/14, ff. 150v–152r. The Privy Council directed the customs farmers to appoint agents to conduct "an inspection" of the compliance of colonies with the Navigation Act, although this seems to have been ignored with the outbreak of the Dutch war, and ordered colonial governors to cooperate; Minutes of the Privy Council, 22 April 1664, PC 2/57, ff. 42v–43v at 42r–43v. For general discussions of what might be termed the first social scientists, see Glass, "Two Papers on Gregory King"; Slack, "Government and Information in Seventeenth-Century England"; Slack, "Progress and the Challenge of Affluence in Seventeenth-Century England."

improvements in agriculture, this demographic stabilization removed the threat of famine from the cycle of English life after 1623, lessened the impacts of bad harvests (a bane of preindustrial life), and generally lowered prices and raised wages. This comprehension, though, was restricted to those with the capability of making such observations, as many of those who migrated to the capital were preoccupied by coping with the wretched conditions in which they lived both within the city walls and in the ever-expanding hamlets outside them. The demographic situation in Stepney and its hamlets east of the Tower became unrecognizable from John Stow's time as the population of London well more than doubled during the seventeenth century, even though the population of England as a whole leveled off after 1650. Accordingly, the demands of Londoners for food, fuel, and other necessaries increased, and increasingly these were supplied by importation. Thus, social status, not to mention livelihood, became increasingly dependent on one's ability to acquire goods.[35]

Readier access to previously rare and unknown commodities that overseas trade conveyed to the metropolis furthered the emergence of this self-conscious modernism of late seventeenth-century England. But, again, did this situation, even with these developments, amount to the opening of a breach with the cultural, economic, and political comprehensions of the past? Of course, all historical phenomena have to begin sometime (and thus their initial appearance is, by definition, "unprecedented"). Did, though, the readier availability of printed matter and of venues to discuss matters (and, it would seem, a larger audience to avail themselves of these opportunities) constitute novelty in and of themselves, or did they rather resonate with constant human tendencies to seek and transmit knowledge (or gossip) and to exercise some control over one's life?[36]

---

[35] Gregory King's famous – and famously haphazard (notwithstanding its author's claims to objectivity) – survey of the social characteristics of England and Wales in 1688 (prepared in 1695) put their combined the population at 5.55 million living in 1.3 million households with a combined annual income of £43.5 million that translated into £7 18s per head. The virtues and limitations, including the author's comprehension of poverty, provided by King's analysis receive a thorough vetting in Arkell, "Illuminations and Distortions." Professor Harding estimates population of the City of London and its immediate environs to have mushroomed from some 200,000 in 1600 to over 500,000 in 1700. She comments that while Stow devoted "a few lines" to Stepney (for which see Chapter 1), the Rev. John Strype's 1720 edition of his "Survey" included a six-page description of the area stretching east of the Thames from the Tower; Harding, "City, Capital, and Metropolis," 117, 121–2.

[36] Cf. Houston and Pincus, "Introduction," esp. 10–11; Lake and Pincus, "Rethinking the Public Sphere in Early Modern England."

Returning to the particular subject of empire, the slavers and the East India Company were not the only ones to effect changes after 1675 in English overseas trade and colonization. The Society of Friends, a rather more morally palatable group – at least to modern observers – provided this alternate late seventeenth-century engine of empire. The most enduring of the sects that arose during the Civil Wars, "Quakers" attracted attention and opprobrium by eschewing important forms of the prevailing social order, which they blamed for the uproars of the 1640s and 1650s; they refused to swear oaths and opted for plain speech and attire. Even more controversially, their religious practice concentrated on the relationship of the Christian (viz., Friend) with her or his God with no need for the involvement of any sort of licensed clergy, as all authority, to their minds, came directly from God. Rather than focusing on ceremony or even sermons, every member cultivated the "inner light" provided by God through contemplation, prayer, and communing with Friends; attendees at their meetings spoke only when compelled to move by the spirit.[37]

Such beliefs were regarded as dangerously heretical, not to say anarchical, and as containing more than a whiff of sanctimonious hypocrisy by contemporaries. The apostolic efforts of early Friends, which included the eponymous quaking along with disrupting the services of others and other manifestations of disdain for more orthodox beliefs, did not contribute to their popularity among nonbelievers, although their evangelical fervor subsided. After the Restoration, the refusal of Friends to swear the Oath of Supremacy as required by statute exposed them to the draconian punishments prescribed for treason as well as those provided for their religious nonconformity; many of them suffered and died in the horrible conditions of the prisons of the day. William Penn, son of the fleet commander of the Western Design, was among the "weighty" Friends who took a lead in protesting the treatment accorded the members of the sect while trying to find a way for their radical views to meet mainstream minds.[38]

Quakers lived in and traveled to Anglo-America practically from the beginning of their movement. Some people, such as the former New England military leader John Underhill, had formed Quaker tendencies

---

[37] [Fox], *An Evident Demonstration to God's Elect*; [Fox], *This to the Clergy Who Are the Men That Goes about to Settle Religion.*
[38] [Penn], *England's Present Interest Discover'd*; [Penn], *The Continued Cry of the Oppressed for Justice.*

before the Society of Friends even existed. Others found the individual pursuit of their religious calling as a natural extension of godly behavior and readily responded to the appeals of missionaries who descended on America in the 1650s.[39]

The fertile soil that Friends found in Anglo-America, notwithstanding the opposition of colonial authorities, coupled with the fierce antipathy that their beliefs could generate among contemporaries in the metropolis, led to thoughts of a more general removal across the Atlantic. After the Treaty of Westminster confirmed the English acquisition of the former New Netherland, John Fenwick and Edward Byllynge purchased the western half of the New Jersey proprietorship. Despite the legal entanglements that immediately beset the colonization of West Jersey, Byllynge issued "Concessions" in 1676/7 that provided a written constitution for the colony along the lines that had been produced in Interregnum in England and for the contemporary Carolina colony as well as a settlement prospectus. Quakers then began settling the Delaware River Valley, which the Iroquois had helpfully begun to clear of the Susquehannocks, and Friends from New England joined a Scottish settlement in East Jersey at Perth Amboy.[40]

Quaker interest in Anglo-America, along with the entire scope of English overseas affairs not to mention English history in general, became enmeshed in the tumultuous political events of the latter part of the reign of Charles II that arose from the religious conversion of the Duke of York. The unfortunate inability of Queen Catherine to conceive a child left the Duke of York as the heir to the throne, a situation that enough English people found disquieting as to create a constitutional crisis over the question of whether a Roman Catholic should be King of England. As we saw in Chapter 8, during the Third Anglo-Dutch War a campaign began to bar York's accession to the throne or, at the least, to place his monarchy under constraints that would neutralize the allegedly inherent threat of his religion to the constitution and liberties of the kingdom.

The issue of religious toleration constituted a crucial element in all of the suspicion and confusion of this period. The King and Duke favored toleration but sought to include Catholics; hence, the Declaration of Indulgence that had brought outrage over this use of the prerogative that resulted in the Test. If, though, the royal brothers could attract enough Nonconformist support, they thought they could overcome fears that a prerogative grant

---

[39] Breen, *Transgressing the Bounds*, 249.
[40] Lurie, "The Long-Lived Proprietary," 328–33.

of toleration would "let in popery." This was not a far-fetched hope, as many English people in 1675–80 were sympathetic to an idea that had gained currency during the Interregnum. Independents, Baptists, and Presbyterians, including overseas merchants such as William Pennoyer, certainly did: Pennoyer was among the subscribers to the £40,000 loan made to Charles II to encourage his issuance of the Declaration.[41]

Other supporters of toleration included those, such as the Earl of Shaftesbury, who officially conformed to the Church of England but who had concerns about its religious primacy and the effects on the state of its corresponding closeness to the government. Indeed, Shaftesbury and his secretary-physician, John Locke, had made provision for a toleration while maintaining the statutory supremacy of the Church of England in the Fundamental Constitutions they prepared for Carolina in 1669 in order to encourage settlers to migrate there when the Earl took charge of the colony's proprietorship. This vehicle might have served in the metropolis for solving the religious question, just as it was envisioned as a possible sociopolitical blueprint, through its provisions for a titled aristocracy with attendant privileges to govern the colony as well as, seemingly oddly, voluntary serfdom.[42]

Crucially, though, the sympathy held by most Protestants for liberty of conscience did not extend to Roman Catholics, as it was firmly believed that a Roman Catholic sovereign would use their power to restore Catholicism as the established church and thus enslave their subjects to the Pope. The most fervent of the Whigs, as the opponents of James became known, including Shaftesbury and the republican Algernon Sidney, believed that York should be barred from the throne as his religion rendered him inherently tyrannical. There was substantial disagreement, though, as to what should be substituted when the natural legitimate heir was barred from succeeding to the throne: a republic, as Sidney but relatively few others, desired; some sort of regency council to govern on behalf of James; the legitimization of James, Duke of Monmouth, the King's eldest child; or a royal divorce and remarriage for Charles. Despite their disagreements over solutions, Whigs agreed on the precept that kingly power could be, if necessary, checked by the liberties of "the

---

[41] De Krey, *London and the Restoration*, 125–34.

[42] A unique attempt to address the labor problem of colonies, this device, often ridiculed as a vestige of feudalism, sought to formalize the manorial system that governed master–servant relations in England. The combination of insufficient migrants and the enduringly torrid South Carolina political scene meant that the Fundamental Constitutions only operated in the breach; Roper, "Conceiving an Anglo-American Proprietorship," 392–6.

people," a concept they defined generally as including independent men of property. The King and his supporters, who regarded monarchy as the center of liberty and order, adamantly opposed these ideas since they constituted tinkering with the prerogative, the essential component of kingly government: considerations of the succession, another bedrock precept of monarchy, invited additional insufferable inquiries into the exercise of royal power. The crucial questions for the English in 1681, as in 1641, were: to what extent – and on what bases – should the power of the Crown be limited?

The fierce struggle between the Whigs and the Crown and its supporters ("Tories") produced considerable heat. For many contemporaries the question of whether James would be monarch or not involved nothing less than the future of England, and the debate spun into an increasingly desperate series of plots and counterplots. For Royalists, it was imperative to avoid a repeat of the errors of the 1640s when pressure from London especially and other localities was brought to bear to the advantage of the Earl of Warwick and the other opponents of Charles I. The same scenario loomed forty years later through the pressure against the royal brothers brought by the Popish Plot, with Shaftesbury seemingly at the fore. The Crown's response to the emergence of the Whigs, which was often triggered by those keen to profess their loyalty to Charles II, increased its involvement in local – and overseas – matters to a new level as well as aggravating the conception of "Stuart tyranny."[43]

Requests for similar Crown intervention emanated from all sorts of quarters. If corporate behavior could be couched as violations of the prerogative and attacks on the position of the royal brothers, charters could even be voided, as in the case of the City of London; corporation memberships could also be cleared of those deemed to hold dangerous views in the heated political atmosphere of the last years of the reign of Charles II. This shift in approach, though, did not readily translate into an imperial situation in which the Crown now dictated policy or ran roughshod over the liberties of subjects.[44]

Indeed, the case of the Quakers and the creation of their Anglo-American colony, in conjunction with the contemporary eclipse of English aspirations in Morocco, illustrate how even after the Exclusion Crisis imperial administration remained ambiguous in terms of the nature of the

---

[43] For a sketch of the literature on the crisis of 1679–82, see De Krey, *London and the Restoration*, 169–73.
[44] Halliday, *Dismembering the Body Politic*, 149–236.

initiative and direct oversight the Crown could and did employ in its involvement in overseas trade and colonization. In 1678, the preposterous allegations of Titus Oates that a Jesuit conspiracy was afoot to raise rebellion in Scotland and Ireland, assassinate the King, burn London (as it was asserted the Jesuits had done in 1666), and lead a Catholic massacre of Protestants came to the King's attention. Oates's claims were referred for investigation to the respected magistrate Sir Edmund Berry Godfrey. It is quite likely that nothing would have come of it except that incriminating letters were found in the possession of Edward Coleman, the former secretary of the Duke of York, and Godfrey's mutilated body was found in a ditch several days after he had heard the evidence of Oates and his fellow perjurer, Israel Tonge. The ensuing tumult obliged Charles to send his brother out of the country and to appoint Shaftesbury as Lord President of a rejigged Privy Council. The murder of the Archbishop of St. Andrews by radical Covenanters in Scotland in 1677, who then rebelled in 1679, naturally brought to mind the events of forty years before, although this time the Scottish rebellion was quashed. Over the next two years the King and the Whigs fenced with parliaments called, prorogued, and dissolved; accusations hurled; trials conducted; and defendants executed often on dubious testimony or exonerated by packed juries. These machinations, in addition to driving York from England in 1680–1, brought the wholly innocent Roman Catholic Archbishop of Armagh, Oliver Plunkett, and other unfortunates, such as Coleman, to the block.

Meanwhile, the Crown waited for revenge until it had a solid case to bring against one of the perjured witnesses, whose unsuccessful attempts to prevent his own execution presented sufficient evidence for charging Shaftesbury with treason. To the fury of the King, though, a jury handpicked by the Whig officials of the London returned a verdict of *ignoramus* to great jubilation in the City. This series of events then provided the pretext for the intervention of Charles in London's next shrieval election to ensure the selection of his supporters to this office in 1682. When the election of the Crown's candidates caused rioting, the King used that tumult as the basis for initiating a *quo warranto* that obtained the recall and annulment of the City's charter. Shaftesbury, now fearing a retrial before a hostile jury, fled to Holland where he died in January 1683, incidentally depriving Carolina of its leading proprietary light.[45]

---

[45] De Krey, *London and the Restoration*, 221–71.

In the midst of this furor, Charles sought to exclude Sidney from Parliament. Thus, he saw the ratification of William Penn's application for a proprietary grant in America as a means of securing moderate support for the succession and the prerogative against the radicals. In exchange for Pennsylvania, the Quaker leader declined to support Sidney's candidacy for the House of Commons, and the republican was defeated in his bid for election. At the same time, the parliamentary opponents of the royal brothers pointed to Tangier – that constantly beleaguered and mismanaged drain of funds officered and garrisoned by Roman Catholics – as a prime example of the perils of "popish" government and refused to consider the Crown's requests for more money to maintain the place.[46]

The Pennsylvania grant passed the seals on 28 February 1681. As his fellow proprietors of New Jersey and Carolina did, Penn immediately began recruiting settlers and devised a "Frame of Government" and a "Charter of Liberties" for his province in accordance with the "public" responsibilities that their charters devolved on the recipients. Mary Geiter has rightly noted that Quakers were not undergoing general persecution at the particular time when the Pennsylvania charter was issued, as the King was trying to secure Nonconformist support against the Whigs in 1680; he succeeded in detaching Penn from his previous support of Sidney's candidacy for Parliament with this patent. Yet, as Penn and his co-religionists were well aware, persecution could resume at any time, from any governmental quarter, and without warning. The acquisition of this territory stretching west from the Delaware River provided a place where they established the frame of the colonial government and the local magistracy, thus providing Friends and other Nonconformists with a retreat from enthusiastic enforcement of the statutes against heterodox belief.[47]

Through the creation of this colony, the English now governed eastern North America between the St. Lawrence and Savannah Rivers, at least on paper. It is curious, though, that in this period of "Stuart absolutism" when the Crown was trying to extend its authority Charles II chartered yet another colonial proprietorship that devolved the

---

[46] Geiter, "The Restoration Crisis and the Launching of Pennsylvania"; Glickman, "Empire, 'Popery,' and the Fall of English Tangier."

[47] Frame of Government of Pennsylvania, 5 May 1682, http://avalon.law.yale.edu/17th_century/pa04.asp, amended by Frame of Government of Pennsylvania, 2 February 1682/3, http://avalon.law.yale.edu/17th_century/pa05.asp (accessed 29 August 2016).

responsibilities for recruiting settlers and governing the place on a private individual. The answer to this mystery may arise from the perennial issue of the Crown finances as well as the desire of the King to curry favor with the Quaker leadership: the administration of colonies was expensive and the task of recruiting inhabitants laborious, so it was best to devolve these responsibilities on a mustard-keen William Penn. The state of the royal purse, despite the payments made by Louis XIV to his cousin and the flourishing of overseas trade, remained the matter on which monarchy would stand or fall. Thus, when Tangier became so great a hemorrhage on the exchequer, Charles abandoned the Mediterranean experiment when the Moroccans resumed their siege after a truce of 1682 expired, another circumscription of English imperial aspirations.

On the other hand, Pennsylvania succeeded even if it did not exactly achieve its proprietor's vision of a peaceable kingdom. It not only survived, incorporating the remnants of the Swedish colony founded on the Delaware River forty-five years previously, but the combination of a relatively benign religious climate, Penn's associations with Continental groups who shared a theological affinity with Friends that provided the basis for recruitment of migrants, the fine harbor of Philadelphia, and a relatively healthy environment enabled the colony's population to thrive. Pennsylvania also managed to avoid the sort of devastating wars with its Indian neighbors that plagued its counterparts, such as King Philip's War and the Tuscarora and Yamasee Wars (1712–17) in the Carolinas, until the latter half of the eighteenth century.[48]

The sociopolitical development of "Penn's Woods," the first English colony to have been created since the acquisition of New York, on the face of things followed a track different from that of the customary English plantation. First, its geographical and commercial orientation did not connect automatically – or even readily – with the slave trade, even though the colony came into existence as the English continued to increase their involvement in the slave trade; metropolitan merchants did not play the prominent role in Pennsylvania's history as they did, for instance, in Jamaica. Then, the colony did attract relatively large numbers

---

[48] Wokeck, "German and Irish Immigration to Colonial Philadelphia." By 1693, ten years after the founding of the city, Philadelphia had 2,044 inhabitants, according to the most careful estimate. This figure doubled by 1720 to 4,883; Nash and Smith, "The Population of Eighteenth-Century Philadelphia," 366.

of European migrants, while the recruitment efforts for the hotter and more remote Jamaica largely failed to produce such a result.

Yet the lack of a ready association between the slave trade and Pennsylvania did not mean that slavery and the slave trade had nominal influence in the colony's socioeconomic development. For that matter, the inhabitants of "New Castle" had already subscribed to the prevailing Anglo-American view that "we cannot subsist" without slaves well before William Penn arrived on the scene, and Penn himself expressed a preference for using slave labor rather than servants. Thus, despite only one voyage recorded as having sailed from Guinea to Pennsylvania with 150 people between 1682 and 1720, Philadelphia had an estimated 630 inhabitants of African descent in 1710 (a number that decreased slightly to 611 by 1720). These enslaved people probably arrived via the intercolonial slave trade, and they came in numbers sufficient to provoke the same sort of concerns about African-European demographic ratios that were expressed in most of Anglo-America. These fears resulted in the enactment of a duty of £10 that was placed on each slave imported into the colony in 1761.[49]

Then, even though the economy of Pennsylvania may have had less metropolitan direction than its West Indian counterparts, migration to this colony – as with all of Anglo-America – was European-directed. Friends and like-minded Continental Europeans who migrated there may have sought to avoid the vagaries of religious politics that could turn exceedingly nasty, but many other Europeans who removed to Pennsylvania did so through the familiar vehicle of indentured servitude. If the 1750 account of the German organ-maker Gottfried Mittelberger can be credited, "this traffic in human flesh," if anything, increased in terms of the scope of number of buyers and sellers of labor contracts involved as well as in the number of people who entered into such contracts through the mid-eighteenth century: bound labor remained integral to life in Anglo-America until the independence of the United States.[50]

While Pennsylvania began to take root, the Crown recovered from the attacks of the Whigs. With the continuing support of the Sun King and the customs revenue continuing to flow, Charles felt free to ignore the statute

---

[49] McManus, *Black Bondage in the North*, 4–5. For the enslaved population of Pennsylvania, see Soderlund, "Black Importation and Migration into Southeastern Pennsylvania," 144–53; O'Malley, *Final Passages*, 106–7, 201–7.

[50] Eben, *Gottlieb Mittelberger's Journey to Pennsylvania*, 25–31; Fogelman, "Slaves, Convicts, and Servants to Free Passengers," 44.

requiring that Parliament be called every three years. Also, his opponents were in disarray: after Shaftesbury's death, the government uncovered the Rye House Plot to assassinate the royal brothers on their way from the Newmarket races. This provided the pretext to arrest and execute several leading Whigs, including Sidney; in broader terms, the discovery of the plot cast opprobrium on the "phanaticks" that enabled the reconfiguring of local institutions and left the Tories in command of the political field. Those who had hitched themselves to the Crown, such as Sir Josiah Child and the colonial governors Sir Edmund Andros and Edward Cranfield, gained ascendancy in overseas matters as did their counterparts in the metropolis. Those who had opposed the government left the scene through either death, as with Shaftesbury, or exile, as in the case of Locke.[51]

In one sense, those who triumphed in this Whig–Tory battle were clearly agents of the monarchy. Colonial administrators during the latter part of the reign of Charles II and the brief one of James II that followed, such as Andros, Sir Francis Nicholson, and Thomas Dongan (Governor of New York from 1682 to 1688, having previously served as Lieutenant-Governor at Tangier), tended to come from military backgrounds. Moreover, these "Restoration imperialists" were assisted by others, such as Edward Randolph, self-appointed enemy of "private" colonies, and William Blathwayt, the nephew of Thomas Povey, "England's first colonial civil servant," who might be styled governmental bureaucrats. These individuals made it their business to decry the "independent" behavior of Anglo-Americans, especially New Englanders: lines between "public" and "private" and between metropolis and colony might appear to have been drawn a bit more clearly in the administration of English overseas matters after 1675.[52]

Cranfield's experience, however, demonstrates the pitfalls of being an outsider with a view of government and subject that did not fit readily with that held by those whom he governed. It also demonstrates, however, the practical and philosophical limits under which "Restoration imperialism" operated. Following the seizure of New Netherland in 1664, royal commissioners had visited New England for the first time to

---

[51] The Royal African Company, with James remaining as its Governor from its beginnings until his departure, was a hotbed of prerogative supporters; De Krey, *London and the Restoration*, 317–25.

[52] Webb, "William Blathwayt, Imperial Fixer," 4; Hall, *Edward Randolph and the American Colonies*.

entertain the grievances of its inhabitants and relay them to the Crown with recommendations, as discussed in Chapter 8. Among those aggrieved was Robert Mason, the would-be proprietor of the area north of the Merrimack River whose family had been at loggerheads with Massachusetts over control of this territory for forty years. It took almost another fifteen years for the Crown to resolve this dispute by creating a new colony, New Hampshire, at the behest of Mason, who hoped that this move would secure his territorial claims while avoiding the costs of maintaining the province.[53]

As Owen Stanwood has shown, the creation of New Hampshire did not really constitute an example of expanding royal authority. Rather, it "was a classic public-private partnership, combining aspects of the older model of chartered or proprietary colonies with a new, royal vision." On the "public" side, the Crown appointed the governor – since Mason knew he would be unable to establish his proprietary authority over the inhabitants – but gave the rights to the soil to Mason. This move, though, cast land titles into doubt – always a chief concern among colonists – and prompted attendant alarm. Cranfield, who had achieved some success in overseeing the removal of the English settlers from Surinam at the end of the Third Anglo-Dutch War, sought to mediate, but his efforts only sparked a war of words (with the threat of worse) between a governor who came to regard many of this colony's inhabitants as dangerous fanatics (a loaded concept in the Anglophone world of 1682–3) and colonists who saw their governor as an agent of arbitrary government bent on suppressing their liberties. The colonists won the battle in the sense that Cranfield fled his government, surrendered his office, and earned an enduring historiographical label as a "grasping tyrant." None of that, though, helped resolve the land issues or the impoverished state of the province, which then became absorbed into the Dominion of New England, which was established in 1684.[54]

Moreover, being "prerogative men" did not render these officials, many of whom continued to serve in an imperial capacity after the Glorious Revolution, tyrannical or even insensitive to colonial concerns. As Stanwood's analysis reveals, even with their affinity for kingly government these officials largely – but, crucially, not entirely – shared an

---

[53] Unlike Pennsylvania, New Hampshire had a substantial number of European inhabitants at its creation, and the Crown could make the colony responsible for the cost of Cranfield's salary, a situation that did not help the governor's position.

[54] Stanwood, *The Empire Reformed*, 30–40.

approach to imperial relations with those they governed just as Anglo-Americans shared the general comprehension that the preferred governmental frame of *dominium politicum et regale* extended to colonies: Shaftesbury's Fundamental Constitutions of Carolina formally incorporated it, for instance. Thus, except for republicans, such as Sidney, and, at the other end of the spectrum, ultra-monarchists, such as Sidney's judge at his treason trial, Sir George Jeffreys, the denizens of the English political nation agreed that the prerogative of the Crown and the liberties of its subjects must be balanced. Where that balance might be best be achieved, though, proved a tricky issue to resolve and one all too easily enflamed by the pursuit of political agendas and attendant factional scheming and finger-pointing.[55]

Thus, Andros, who had a long overseas career, assumed the governorship of the new Dominion of New England, which his old commander James II established after he became King. The old charter of Massachusetts Bay was finally quashed in 1684, and that colony, along with New Hampshire, New York, Connecticut, Plymouth, and Rhode Island, was placed under one government headed by Andros in Boston, with Nicholson as his deputy in New York City. This maneuver, which might be regarded as a manifestation of "empire building" or even "Stuart tyranny," still reflected a meshing of metropolitan and colonial interests: Andros appointed the Massachusetts leader Joseph Dudley as the president of the new entity's council, and the Dominion slid into place with minimal fuss. Unfortunately for Andros, though, he was unable to allay fears of a Catholic–Indian conspiracy against New England that developed among his colonists in 1688. Failing to realize that the Massachusetts conception of the English Empire was a strictly Protestant one, his attempts to reassure them of royal protection foundered on the reality that the King himself was a papist and, thus, a part of the greater conspiracy. When news arrived in Boston that James had departed his throne, Bostonians seized the Governor, Randolph, Dudley, and other Dominion officials and awaited instructions from Whitehall. Yet although this imperial experiment ended, direct royal government of Massachusetts did not when the colony received a new charter from William and Mary in 1691.[56]

[55] Leng, "Shaftesbury's Aristocratic Empire"; Koenigsberger, "Monarchies and Parliaments in Early Modern Europe."
[56] Stanwood, *The Empire Reformed*, 40–81.

This coup, along with Leisler's Rebellion in New York and the revolt against the Calvert proprietorship in Maryland, was enabled by William of Orange's invasion of England in November 1688. Having been conveyed by a "Protestant wind" following the invitation of a group of leading Englishmen to intervene in the worsening relations between William's father-in-law James II and his subjects, the arrival of this force and the Dutchman's amazing success in attracting more supporters convinced James to abandon his three kingdoms. William and his wife, Mary, became joint monarchs in May 1689 after negotiations with Parliament. As part of their agreement, the "representatives of the people" now became a permanent part of the government. William's success also meant those of the King's opponents who had subsided in the early 1680s returned to prominence after 1688, including Locke, who joined the new Board of Trade in 1696. Yet those such as Andros, who had proven loyal servants of the Crown and were willing, as many were, to swear their allegiance to the new monarchs, were swiftly put to appropriate use: Sir Edmund became Governor of Virginia in 1692, Nicholson served as the first royal Governor of Maryland, and Andros's Boston chief councilor, the colonial Joseph Dudley, was Governor of Massachusetts and New Hampshire from 1702 to 1715. Moreover, the arch-Tory Sir Nathaniel Johnson, who resigned as Governor of the Leeward Islands and refused to accept any governmental post until the death of James II in 1701, accepted the proprietors' invitation to become Governor of South Carolina in 1702.[57]

The surprisingly limited personnel turnover in the aftermath of the Glorious Revolution raises questions as to the extent to which the overthrow of James II triggered fundamental changes in the character of English overseas affairs. Even so, recent reconsiderations of state power and mercantilism in the development of the English Empire have sought to align these phenomena with the events of 1688–9 and to stress the "revolution" in the Glorious Revolution. This view claims that the results that were achieved translated into a triumphant implementation of the

---

[57] Voorhees, "The 'Fervent Zeale' of Jacob Leisler." For Sir Nathaniel's loyal (and therefore controversial) service to the House of Stuart, see Roper, *Conceiving Carolina*, 57–61, 128–31. The Board of Trade, formed in 1696, provided a more bureaucratic clearinghouse for metropolitan consideration of colonial issues than the Lords of Foreign Trade and Plantation created under Charles II. As with its predecessors, though, it reported to the Privy Council and it included veterans of imperial affairs, notably Locke, among its members; Laslett, "John Locke, the Great Recoinage, and the Origins of the Board of Trade."

Whiggish vision of empire that had been curbed by the brief ascendancy of the Tories in the administration of the imperial state between 1678 and 1688. The Williamite victory also triggered a great debate over imperial policy that was grounded in "profound political and ideological differences in understanding the nature of value, the nature of property, and the proper economic aims of Britain," one in a series of such "contests between competing political economic strategies" that "took place in both the metropole and the periphery" that have been found to recur between the 1650s and the 1780s. Thus, the defeat of James meant the decline of views held by the likes of Sir Josiah Child that society largely derived its wealth from landed income and that the empire should be governed by royal prerogative. It also brought increasing objections to monopolies and proprietary grants, as violations of both the liberties of subjects and the newly institutionalized supremacy of parliamentary statute. From 1689, then, state policy increasingly promoted free trade (within the scope of the Staple Act) and the opening of colonial and foreign markets to English goods, while English people debated the best ways of promoting empire as well as the proper relationship between metropolis and colonies in their coffeehouses and in their newspapers.[58]

We should minimize neither the changes that occurred within metropolitan society and politics nor the extent of the debate over empire that took place in the press and other public forums, in both the metropolis and the colonies, after 1689. Indeed, it does not take a particular perspicacity to find that substantial differences existed between the England of Charles I and the Britain of Charles's grandnephew, George I (1714–27). Yet to what degree does a focus on the treatises and other publications (usually produced under government supervision) that articulated the apparently competing visions of reality emphasized by recent scholarship provide an especially helpful guide to understanding the history of the English Empire? The evidence gleaned from the correspondence, court minutes, and other unpublished documentation demonstrates that the nature of political behavior in the Anglophone world actually may not have been transformed between 1613 and 1688 or even after 1688: people forged and employed contacts and identified and pursued opportunities, often with unintended and

---

[58] Pincus, "Rethinking Mercantilism," 32; Pincus, "Reconfiguring the British Empire," in Pincus et al., "Forum," 63–70; Pettigrew, "Constitutional Change in England and the Diffusion of Regulatory Initiative, 1660–1714," 842–8.

undesired results, as they had always done even as the historical actors and their particular motives naturally changed over time.

We should, moreover, remain aware that monarchical power commanded considerable deference in the conduct of the English state even after May 1689; William and Mary and their successors ruled as well as reigned. At the same time, the post-invasion constitution of the English state amalgamated Crown and Parliament – even as a sort of shotgun wedding designed to defeat the machinations of Louis XIV – into a fiscal-military English state. This enabled the levying and collection of revenue and the application of that revenue through an increasingly recognizable bureaucracy with an unparalleled effectiveness. The formalization of the King-in-Parliament constitutional arrangement also ended the debates over the constitutional issues that had distracted and indeed convulsed the English state for the previous eighty years, and the government could now bring relative focus to the imperial issues it faced.[59]

These results differentiated the Glorious Revolution from the previous circumstances in which an English monarch had been deposed. In 1642, Charles I departed London for the north of his kingdom where he was able to rebuild his position to an extent that he was able to fight (albeit lose) a civil war. Meanwhile, the Parliamentarians readily filled the governmental void created by the withdrawal of the King from the capital and then used their new situation to advance both the parliamentary cause and their own interests; they became the English state. Forty-six years later, though, the rebels, so far from trying to assume control over the government, deployed a constitutional fig leaf (or, perhaps, figment) to maintain the institutional status quo: James was deemed to have abdicated and could be replaced by his elder daughter, Mary, and her husband, the Prince of Orange (the infant son of James and Mary of Modena having been deemed illegitimate).

The departure of James II to the protection of his French cousin meant there would be no recurrence of civil war in 1689. Since the principal threat to the victorious Williamites came from a powerful foreign enemy, rather than domestic ones as faced by those who ousted Charles I in the 1640s, the Glorious Revolution immediately became subsumed into the long struggle between Louis XIV and the Dutch Republic and its *stadhouder* – as intended by the Prince of Orange and the Estates-General. In order to make their post-1689 settlement permanent (and keep their

[59] Knights, "Fiscal-Military State."

heads), then, the English were obliged to contribute – and contribute substantially – to the Dutch conflict against the Sun King. Happily for the rebels of 1689, the pretext of legitimacy for their seizure of power meant that they could draw on state resources relatively seamlessly compared with the situation of Maurice Thompson and his cohort in the 1640s.[60]

The ensuing War of the League of Augsburg (a.k.a. King William's War) of 1689–97 confirmed the position of France as the new English imperial bogey; since English overseas interests had continued to expand, those interests naturally had assumed greater importance in this perception. The French fueled this sensibility with a vigorous pursuit of overseas trade and colonization after Louis XIV reached his majority, and especially after the appointment of Jean-Baptiste Colbert as his chief minister in 1665: they engaged in the Asian and African trades, invigorated the plantations in the Caribbean and the colony of New France, and sponsored explorations of the interior of North America that gave rise to claims over Louisiana and Hudson's Bay. They also seized the Gorée trading fort in Guinea from the Dutch in 1677 and established a factory at Pondichéry (Puducherry) on the Coromandel Coast south of Madras in 1674. Louis's continuing harassment of his Huguenot subjects as well of his sponsorship of his cousin's attempt to regain his throne via an invasion of Ireland confirmed the view, fervently nurtured by William and his ministers, of the French monarchy as the latest and most proximate incarnation of popish tyranny bent on enslaving the English nation (and, not coincidentally, restoring the unlamented James II).[61]

Whatever revolutionary effects the Glorious Revolution may have had in England, in imperial terms, the revamping of the English state that occurred in response to the Franco-Jacobite threat does not seem to have had immediate consequences. Most crucially, the prerogative, by which all colonial institutions had come into existence, remained the basis for imperial administration, with Parliament involved on only a very occasional basis. In Asia, the chartered East India Company, while keeping a nervous eye on its neighbors, reestablished its Chinese factory at Canton in 1700 and saw off the domestic attacks on its monopoly by 1709 as it carried on its commercial activities. It later began conveying opium to China in exchange for tea. The immense profits it derived from this

---

[60] Israel, "The Dutch Role in the Glorious Revolution."
[61] Wells and Wills, "Revolution, Restoration, and Debt Repudiation."

commerce enabled it to assume its deep and notorious influence on the politics, economy, and culture of Hanoverian Britain.[62]

Anglo-Americans for their part became even more enthusiastic participants in an empire that now involved a more formal participation of the metropolis but that still operated along familiar precepts with respect to the initiative and management of imperial matters and the corresponding efforts of colonists to maneuver themselves to their best advantage. Since securing a constant stream of "merchantable Negroes" at good prices constituted a consistently vital element of their world, prominent colonists readily enlisted in the ultimately successful campaigns against the attempts by the Royal African Company to enforce its patent and the subsequent efforts by the South Sea Company to divert substantial numbers of slaves to Spanish America pursuant to the license it had obtained in 1713.[63] They also sought the departure of inept or unpopular governors from office and the confirmation of colonial boundaries and land titles. The leadership of South Carolina, for instance, consistently turned to their patrons in their internecine fight over the Indian slave trade, in their successful effort to remove rice, the colony's staple, from the restrictions of the Navigation Act, and their equally successful orchestration of the removal of proprietary government in favor of direct Crown authority over their colony after their 1719 rebellion.[64]

Colonial-imperialists meanwhile continued to spearhead English territorial interests, using their powers of persuasion in pursuit of their agendas as they and previous generations had done ever since the future of Jamestown had been secured. Relations between the English colonies and their French neighbors, which had been punctuated with hostilities going back to Samuel Argall's 1613 attack on Acadia, did intensify, however, as Louis XIV's support for the Jacobite cause raised the geopolitical stakes throughout the Anglophone world. Yet the confirmation of the Protestant character of the English state and its Empire, a

---

[62] Bowen, "'No Longer Mere Traders,'" 23–7. The EIC mooted trading opium, one of the "natural products of this island," from Bombay as early as 1670; Gerald Aungier et al. to Company, 30 March 1670, IOR E/3/31, ff. 3–6 at 3.

[63] Pettigrew, *Freedom's Debt*, 127–38.

[64] Roper, *Conceiving Carolina*, 117–57. For general eighteenth-century Anglo-American enthusiasm for empire – as future Americans, including Benjamin Franklin, Henry Laurens, and Benjamin Rush, conceived of it – even into the mid-1770s, see Flavell, *When London Was Capital of America*, 1–5, 7–26, 189–234.

sentiment to which colonists wholeheartedly subscribed as Stanwood has demonstrated, only strengthened imperial ties.[65]

Indeed, Anglo-Americans readily joined – and even led – the fight against the new foe: a colonial force commanded by the New Englander and first post-Dominion Governor of Massachusetts Sir William Phips attacked Acadia (again) in 1690, and Virginia government dispatched the surveying expedition of George Washington to the Ohio Country, which triggered the French and Indian War/Seven Years War in 1754. Colonial interests also took the lead in the handful of instances in which parliamentary statutes governed imperial matters: in the case of the Molasses Act (1733), for example, West Indian planters invoked the navigation system to convince Parliament to preclude the practice of importing sugar by foreign middlemen into Britain via its colonies.[66]

These developments exemplify how entrenched the political and economic comprehension that had governed English overseas activities had become notwithstanding the many failures that had beset these endeavors. Moreover, the patronage and commercial ties – especially with respect to the ever-increasing trade in labor – that had devolved from this comprehension continued, in various ways, shapes, and forms, to provide the basis of empire from London to Bencoolen to Boston. Significant changes to this arrangement did not occur until after the worldwide victory of British arms against France was confirmed in 1763 – an imperial result pointedly quite different from that achieved by the English in their long struggle against the Dutch in the previous century.

The comprehensive scale of the global triumph brought a fiscal crisis of a similar scope, which, in accordance with the post-1689 constitutional understanding, drew the greater involvement of Parliament into imperial matters. In the Eastern Hemisphere, the Seven Years War drew the East India Company inextricably deeper into Indian politics. This proved incompatible with the company's autonomy; the costs it incurred in fighting the war, as well as the prominence achieved by its former factor-turned-nabob Robert Clive, obliged the

[65] Stanwood, "The Protestant Moment." The eschatological elements of this colonial sentiment, which regarded Bourbon France as the champion of the Beast as prophesied by the Book of Revelation, remained evident until the outbreak of the American War of Independence; Bloch, *Visionary Republic*, 22–50.

[66] Sheridan, "The Molasses Act and the Market Strategy of the British Sugar Planters"; Stanwood, *The Empire Reformed*, 156–9, 177–220.

governments of George III (1760–1820) to bring British interests in Asia increasingly under statutory authority from 1773.[67]

In Anglo-America, the ministry planned to generate funds through the direct taxation of colonial subjects, thereby bypassing an imperial system now regarded as obstructionist and cumbersome. The "representatives of the people" duly rubber-stamped this initiative, with famously calamitous effects: "Patriots" in thirteen of the colonies regarded these interventions both as dangerous novelties introduced by "evil counselors" and as a betrayal of the empire to which they had made and expected to continue to make substantial contributions. Their corresponding fears of "enslavement" resulted in a permanent breach between the United States of America and their former sovereign followed in turn by the comprehensive integration of Parliament into a revamped British Empire with a dedicated Colonial Office and a strengthened reconfiguration of hemispheric connections after 1783. Those who could not abandon a now suddenly old-fashioned political world found themselves in the wilderness in both actual and historiographical terms. Yet had the imperial culture that had formed during the seventeenth century functioned as it had done, even during the convulsions of the Interregnum, it is quite feasible to think that it could have similarly endured the post-1763 disputes and remained in place indefinitely.[68]

[67] Lawson, *The East India Company*, 103–25.

[68] For post-1783 connections between British Asia and Anglo-America, see McAleer, *Britain's Maritime Empire*, 1–37. For Anglo-American loyalists, see Bailyn, "Thomas Hutchinson"; Jasanoff, "The Other Side of Revolution."

Bibliography

Adams, Edward, *A Brief Relation of the Surprizing several English merchants Goods, by Dutch Men of Warre, their carrying them into Zealand, and there condemning them for Prize, upon no other score or account, but that they were English Mens* (London, 1664).

Adamson, John, *The Noble Revolt: The Overthrow of Charles I* (London: Weidenfeld & Nicolson, 2007).

"Agreement of Claiborne with Cloberry and Others for Trading to Virginia, May 24, 1631," *Maryland Historical Magazine* 4 (1909), 188–9.

Ames, Glenn J., "The Role of Religion in the Transfer and Rise of Bombay, c. 1661–1687," *HJ* 46 (2003), 317–40.

Amrith, Sunil S., "Tamil Diasporas across the Bay of Bengal," *AHR* 114 (2009), 547–72.

Anderson, Virginia DeJohn, *Creatures of Empire: How Domestic Animals Transformed Early America* (New York: Oxford University Press, 2006).

"New England in the Seventeenth Century," in Canny, *The Origins of Empire*, 193–217.

Andrews, Charles M., *British Committees, Commissions, and Councils of Trade and Plantations, 1622–1675* (Baltimore: Johns Hopkins University Press, 1908).

Andrews, Kenneth R., *Ships, Money and Politics: Seafaring and Naval Politics in the Reign of Charles I* (Cambridge: Cambridge University Press, 1991).

Trade, Plunder and Settlement: Maritime Enterprise and the Genesis of the British Empire, 1480–1630 (Cambridge: Cambridge University Press, 1984).

Anon., *A courante of newes from the East India. A true relation of the taking of the ilands of Lantore and Polaroone in the parts of Bande in the East Indies by the Hollanders, which ilands had yeelded themselves subject vnto the King of England* (London, 1622).

The Dutch drawn to Life (London, 1664).

The English and Dutch Affairs Displayed to the Life by a true Lover and Asserter of his Countries Honour (London, 1664).

The Hollanders declaration of the affaires of the East Indies. Or a true relation of that which passed in the Ilands of Banda, in the East Indies (London, 1622).

The Second Part of the Tragedy of Amboyna: Or, A True Relation of a Most Bloody, Treacherous, and Cruel Design of the Dutch in the New-Netherlands in America (London, 1653).

The Spanish pilgrime: or, An admirable discouery of a Romish Catholicke Shewing how necessary and important it is, for the Protestant kings, princes, and potentates of Europe, to make warre vpon the King of Spaines owne country (London, 1625).

A True Relation of the Unjust, Cruel, and Barbarous Proceedings against the English at Amboyna in the East-Indies by the Netherlandish Governour and Council there (London, 1651).

Appleby, John C., "'A Business of Much Difficulty': A London Slaving Voyage 1651–1654," *Mariner's Mirror* 81 (1995), 3–14.

"An Association for the West Indies? English Plans for a West India Company, 1621–1629," *JICH* 15 (1987), 213–41.

"English Settlement during War and Peace, 1603–1660," in Robert L. Paquette and Stanley L. Engerman (eds.), *The Lesser Antilles in the Age of European Expansion* (Gainesville: University Press of Florida, 1996), 88–103.

"A Guinea Venture, c. 1657: A Note on the Early English Slave Trade," *Mariner's Mirror* 79 (1993), 84–7.

Arena, Carolyn, "Indian Slaves from Guiana in Seventeenth-Century Barbados," *Ethnohistory* 64 (2017), 65–90.

Arkell, Tom, "Illuminations and Distortions: Gregory King's Scheme Calculated for the Year 1688 and the Social Structure of Later Stuart England," *Econ. HR* 59 (2006), 32–69.

Armitage, David, "The Cromwellian Protectorate and the Languages of Empire," *HJ* 35 (1992), 531–55.

The Ideological Origins of the British Empire (Cambridge: Cambridge University Press, 2000).

Articles of Agreements, made and concluded the 11th day of January 1651 (London, 1652).

Ashton, Robert, "Revenue Farming under the Early Stuarts," *Econ. HR* 8 (1956), 310–22.

Atherton, Ian, "Cathedrals, Laudianism, and the British Churches," *HJ* 53 (2010), 895–918.

Aylmer, G.E., *The Crown's Servants: Government and Crown Service under Charles II, 1660–1685* (Oxford: Oxford University Press, 2002).

The King's Servants: The Civil Service of Charles I, 1625–1641 (New York: Columbia University Press, 1961).

"Slavery under Charles II: The Mediterranean and Tangier," *EHR* 114 (1999), 378–88.

The State's Servants: The Civil Service of the English Republic, 1649–1660 (London: Routledge & Kegan Paul, 1973).

Baak, Paul E., "About Ex-Slaves, Uncaptured Contract Coolies and Unfreed Freedmen: Some Notes about 'Free' and 'Unfree' Labour in the Context of

Plantation Development in Southwest India, Early Sixteenth Century–Mid 1990s," *MAS* 33 (1999), 121–57.

Bailey, Mark, "Historiographical Essay: The Commercialisation of the English Economy, 1086–1500," *Journal of Medieval History* 24 (1998), 297–311.

Bailyn, Bernard, *The Barbarous Years: The Peopling of British North America: The Conflict of Civilizations, 1600–1675* (New York: Alfred A. Knopf, 2012).

The New England Merchants in the Seventeenth Century (New York: Harper & Row, 1964).

The Peopling of British North America: An Introduction (New York: Vintage, 1988).

"Thomas Hutchinson," in Bailyn, *Faces of Revolution: Personalities and Themes in the Struggle for American Independence* (New York: Vintage, 1992), 42–66.

Baird, Charles Washington, *History of the Huguenot Emigration to America*, 2 vols. (New York: Dodd, Mead, 1885).

Bangs, Jeremy Dupertuis, *Pilgrim Edward Winslow: New England's First International Diplomat* (Boston: New England Historic Genealogical Society, 2004).

Barber, Sarah, *The Disputatious Caribbean: The West Indies in the Seventeenth Century* (New York and Houndmills: Palgrave Macmillan, 2014).

"Power in the English Caribbean: The Proprietorship of Lord Willoughby of Parham," in Roper and Van Ruymbeke, *Constructing Early Modern Empires*, 189–212.

Barbour, Violet L., "Privateers and Pirates of the West Indies," *AHR* 16 (1911), 529–66.

Bard, Nelson P. (ed.), "The Earl of Warwick's Voyage of 1627," *The Naval Miscellany* 5 (Publications of the Naval Records Society, vol. 125, 1984), 15–93.

Bassett, D.K., "The 'Amboyna Massacre' of 1623," *Journal of Southeast Asian History* 1 (1960), 1–19.

"English Relations with Siam in the Seventeenth Century," *Journal of the Malayan Branch of the Royal Asiatic Society* 34 (1961), 90–105.

"English Trade in Celebes, 1613–1667," *Journal of the Malayan Branch of the Royal Asiatic Society* 31 (1958), 1–39.

"The Trade of the English East India Company in the Far East, 1623–84: Part I," *Journal of the Royal Asiatic Society of Great Britain and Ireland*, 1/2 (1960), 32–47.

Battick, John F., "Cromwell's Diplomatic Blunder: The Relationship between the Western Design of 1654–55 and the French Alliance of 1657," *Albion* 5 (1973), 279–98.

Beckles, Hilary McD., and Andrew Downes, "The Economics of Transition to the Black Labor System in Barbados, 1630–1680," *JIH* 18 (1987), 225–47.

Beeston, William, "A Journal Kept by Col. William Beeston, from His First Coming to Jamaica," in *Interesting Tracts Relating to the island of Jamaica* (St. Jago de la Vega: Lewis, Lunam, and Jones, 1800), 271–300.

Belcher, Gerald L., "Spain and the Anglo-Portuguese Alliance of 1661: A Reassessment of Charles II's Foreign Policy at the Restoration," *JBS* 15 (1975), 67–88.

[Berkeley, Sir William], *A Discourse and View of Virginia* (London, [1662]).

Bernhard, Virginia, "Beyond the Chesapeake: The Contrasting Status of Blacks in Bermuda, 1616–1663," *The Journal of Southern History* 54 (1988), 545–64.

  Slaves and Slaveholders in Bermuda, 1616–1782 (Columbia: University of Missouri Press, 1999).

Billings, Warren M., *Sir William Berkeley and the Forging of Colonial Virginia* (Baton Rouge: Louisiana State University Press, 2004).

  (ed.), *The Papers of Sir William Berkeley* (Richmond: Library of Virginia, 2007).

Black, Robert C. III, *The Younger John Winthrop* (New York: Columbia University Press, 1966).

Blake, John W., "The English Guinea Company, 1618–1660," *Proceedings and Reports of the Belfast Natural History and Philosophical Society*, 2nd ser., 3 (1945/6), 14–27.

  "Farm of the Guinea Trade," in H.A. Cronne, T.W. Moody, and D.B. Quinn (eds.), *Essays in British and Irish History in Honour of James Eadie Todd* (London: Frederick Muller, 1949), 86–107.

Blakemore, Richard J. "West Africa in the British Atlantic: Trade, Violence, and Empire in the 1640s," *Itinerario* 39 (2015), 299–327.

Bland, Edward, Abraham Wood, Sackford Brewster, and Elias Pennant, *The Discovery of New Brittaine* (London, 1650).

Bliesemann de Guevara, Berit, "State Formation," in *Oxford Bibliographies in Political Science*, available at www.oxfordbibliographies.com/view /document/obo-9780199756223/obo-9780199756223-0123.xml (accessed 21 January 2017).

Bliss, Robert M., *Revolution and Empire: English Politics and the American Colonies in the Seventeenth Century* (Manchester: Manchester University Press, 1990).

Bloch, Ruth, *Visionary Republic: Millennial Themes in American Thought, 1756–1800* (Cambridge and New York: Cambridge University Press, 1988).

Bonello, Julie, "The Development of Early Settler Identity in Southern Rhodesia, 1890–1914," *International Journal of African Studies* 43 (2010), 341–67.

Boomert, Arie, *The Indigenous People of Trinidad and Tobago from the First Settlers until Today* (Leiden: Sidestone Press, 2016).

Boothby, Richard, *A breife description of the most famous island of Madagascar or St. Laurence in Asia neare unto East India* (London, 1646).

Bottigheimer, Karl S., *English Money and Irish Land: The "Adventurers" in the Cromwellian Settlement of Ireland* (Oxford: Oxford University Press, 1971).

Bowen, H.V., "'No Longer Mere Traders': Continuities and Change in the Metropolitan Development of the East India Company, 1600–1834," in H.V. Bowen, Margarette Lincoln, and Nigel Rigby (eds.), *The Worlds of the East India Company* (Woodbridge and Rochester: Boydell & Brewer, 2002), 19–32.

Boxer, C.R., "Some Second Thoughts on the Third Anglo-Dutch War, 1672–1674," *Transactions of the Royal Historical Society*, 5th ser., 19 (1969), 67–94.

Bradburn, Douglas, and John C. Coombs (eds.), *Early Modern Virginia: Reconsidering the Old Dominion* (Charlottesville and London: University of Virginia Press, 2011).

Braddick, M.J., "Review: An English Military Revolution?," *HJ* 36 (1993), 965–75.

Braddick, Michael, *God's Fury, England's Fire: A New History of the English Civil Wars* (London: Penguin, 2009).

State Formation in Early Modern England, c. 1550–1700 (Cambridge: Cambridge University Press, 2000).

Bradford, William, *Bradford's History "Of Plimoth Plantation": From the Original Manuscript* (Boston: Wright & Palmer, 1928).

Breen, Louise A., *Transgressing the Bounds: Subversive Enterprises among the Puritan Elite in Massachusetts, 1630–1692* (New York: Oxford University Press, 2001).

Breen, T.H., and Stephen Foster, "Moving to the New World: The Character of Early Massachusetts Immigration," *WMQ* 30 (1973), 189–222.

Bremer, Francis J., *First Founders: American Puritans and Puritanism in an Atlantic World* (Durham: University of New Hampshire Press, 2012).

Building a New Jerusalem: John Davenport, a Puritan in Three Worlds (New Haven and London: Yale University Press, 2012).

"The English Context of New England's Seventeenth-Century History," *NEQ* 60 (1987), 323–35.

John Winthrop: America's Forgotten Founding Father (New York: Oxford University Press, 2003).

Brenner, Robert, *Merchants and Revolution: Commercial Change: Political Conflict, and London's Overseas Traders, 1550–1653* (London and New York: Verso, 2003).

Broeze, Frank, J.A., "Private Enterprise and the Peopling of Australasia, 1831–1850," *Econ. HR* 35 (1982), 235–53.

Brown, Christopher Leslie, *Moral Capital: Foundations of British Abolitionism* (Chapel Hill: University of North Carolina Press, 2006).

Brown, Elizabeth A.R., "The Tyranny of a Construct: Feudalism and Historians of Medieval Europe," *AHR* 79 (1974), 1063–88.

Browne, Thomas, *Vox Veritas or A Brief Abstract of the Case Between George Carew Esq.; Administrator of the goods and Chattells of Sir William Courten & Sir Paul Pyndar Knights deceased with their wills annexed and The East India Company of the Netherlands, with other Inhabitants of Amsterdam and Midleburgh* (London, 1683).

Burke, John, and John B. Burke, *A Genealogical and Historical History of the Extinct and Dormant Baronetcies of England, Ireland, and Scotland* (London: John Russell Smith, 1844).

Burnard, Trevor, "'Prodigious Riches': The Wealth of Jamaica before the American Revolution," *Econ. HR* 54 (2001), 506–24.

Calder, Irene M., *The New Haven Colony* (New Haven: Yale University Press, 1934).

Canny, Nicholas, "The Origins of Empire: An Introduction," in Canny, *The Origins of Empire*, 1–33.

  (ed.), *The Origins of Empire*, vol. 1, in Wm. Roger Louis (ed.), *The Oxford History of the British Empire* (Oxford: Oxford University Press, 1998).

Capp, Bernard, "*A Door of Hope* Re-opened: The Fifth Monarchy, King Charles and King Jesus," *Journal of Religious History* 32 (2008), 16–30.

Carew, George, *Lex talionis, or, the Law of marque or reprizals fully represented in the case of spoyls and depredations upon the ships, goods and factories of Sir William Courten and his partners in the East Indies, China and Japan* (London, 1682).

Carey, Daniel, "The Political Economy of Poison: The Kingdom of Makassar and the Royal Society," *Renaissance Studies* 17 (2003), 517–43.

Carlos, Ann M., "Bonding and the Agency Problem: Evidence from the Royal African Company, 1672–1691," *Explorations in Economic History* 31 (1994), 313–35.

Castell, William, *A Short Discoverie of the Coasts and Continents of America* (London, 1644).

Cave, Alfred A., *The Pequot War* (Amherst: University of Massachusetts Press, 1996).

Cell, Gillian T., "The Newfoundland Company: A Study of Subscribers to a Colonizing Venture," *WMQ* 22 (1965), 611–25.

Chancey, Karen, "The Amboyna Massacre in English Politics, 1624–1632," *Albion* 30 (1998), 583–98.

Chaudhuri, K.N., *The English East India Company: The Study of an Early Joint-Stock Company, 1600–1640* (London: Frank Cass & Co., 1965).

  The Trading World of Asia and the English East India Company: 1660–1760 (Cambridge: Cambridge University Press, 2006).

Cheves, Langdon III (ed.), *The Shaftesbury Papers* (Charleston: South Carolina Historical Society, 2000).

"Claiborne vs. Clobery et al. in the High Court of Admiralty," *Maryland Historical Magazine* 27 (1932), 17–28, 99–114, 191–214, 337–52; and 28 (1933), 26–43, 172–95, 257–65.

Clarendon, Edward, Earl of, *The Life of Edward Earl of Clarendon*, 2 vols. (Oxford: Clarendon Press, 1827).

Clark, G.N., and W.J.M. van Eysinga, *The Colonial Conferences between England and the Netherlands in 1613 and 1615*, 2 vols. (Leiden: E.J. Brill, 1940–51).

Clarke, Sir William, *The Clarke Papers. Selections from the Papers of William Clarke, Secretary to the Council of the Army, 1647–1649, and to General Monck and the Commanders of the Army in Scotland, 1651–1660*, C.H. Firth (ed.), 4 vols. (London: Longmans, Green, and Co., 1899).

Clulow, Adam, "The Art of Claiming: Possession and Resistance in Early Modern Asia," *AHR* 121 (2016), 17–38.

Cobbett, William (ed.), *A Complete Collection of State Trials and Proceedings for High Treason and Other Crimes and Misdemeanors from the Earliest Period to the Year 1783*, 34 vols. (London: Longman, Hurst, Rees, Orme and Brown, 1816–28).

Coffey, John, "Puritanism and Liberty Revisited: The Case for Toleration in the English Revolution," *HJ* 41 (1998), 961–85.

Cogswell, Thomas, "A Low Road to Extinction? Supply and Redress of Grievances in the Parliaments of the 1620s," *HJ* 33 (1990), 283–303.

"England and the Spanish Match," in Richard Cust and Ann Hughes (eds.), *Conflict in Early Stuart England, 1603–1642* (London: Longman Group, 1989), 107–33.

Coldham, Peter Wilson, *The Complete Book of Emigrants: 1607–1660* (Baltimore: Genealogical Publishing Co., 1987).

Collinson, Patrick, *Godly People: Essays on English Protestantism and Puritanism* (London: Bloomsbury Academic, 2003).

The Religion of Protestants: The Church in English Society, 1559–1625 (Oxford: Oxford University Press, 1984).

Como, David, "Secret Printing, the Crisis of 1640, and the Origins of Civil War Radicalism," *P&P*, no. 196 (2007), 37–82.

Coombs, John C., "Beyond the 'Origins Debate': Rethinking the Rise of Virginia Slavery," in Bradburn and Coombs, *Early Modern Virginia*, 239–78.

Cowan, Brian, "The Rise of the Coffeehouse Reconsidered," *HJ* 47 (2004), 21–46.

Craig, Alan K., "Logwood as a Factor in the Settlement of British Honduras," *Caribbean Studies* 9 (1969), 53–62.

Craven, Wesley Frank, "The Earl of Warwick, a Speculator in Piracy," *Hispanic American Historical Review* 10 (1930), 457–79.

"Indian Policy in Early Virginia," *WMQ* 1 (1944), 65–82.

Cray, Robert E. Jr., "'Weltering in Their Own Blood': Puritan Casualties in King Philip's War," *Historical Journal of Massachusetts* 37 (2009), 106–23.

Cressy, David, *Coming Over: Migration and Communication between England and New England in the Seventeenth Century* (Cambridge: Cambridge University Press, 1987).

"Revolutionary England, 1640–1642," *P&P*, no. 181 (2003), 35–71.

Crisp, Frederick Arthur, *Collections Relating to the Family of Crispe*, vol. 1 (p.p., 1882).

Cronon, William J., *Changes in the Land: Indians, Colonists, and the Ecology of New England* (New York: Hill & Wang, 1983).

Crouch, John, *Belgica Caracteristica. Or the Dutch Character. Being News from Holland. A Poem* (London, 1665).

Cust, Richard, *The Forced Loan and English Politics, 1626–28* (Oxford: Clarendon Press, 1987).

Charles I: A Political Life (New York: Longman, 2005).

Daaku, Kwame Yeboa, *Trade and Politics on the Gold Coast, 1600–1720* (Oxford: Clarendon Press, 1970).

Dalton, Heather, "'Into speyne to selle for slavys': English, Spanish, and Genoese Merchant Networks and Their Involvement with the 'Cost of Gwynea' Trade before 1550," in Toby Green (ed.), *Brokers of Change: Atlantic Commerce and Cultures in Precolonial Western Africa* (Oxford: Oxford University Press for the British Academy, 2012), 91–123.

D[arell], J[ohn], *Strange News from the Indies: Or, East-India Passages Further Discovered* (London, 1652).

Davenport, Frances Gardiner (ed.), *European Treaties Bearing on the History of the United States and Its Dependencies*, 2 vols. (Washington, D.C.: Carnegie Institution of Washington, 1929).

Davies, K.G., *The North Atlantic World in the Seventeenth Century* (St. Paul: University of Minnesota Press, 1974).

Davis, Nicholas Darnell, *The Cavaliers and Roundheads of Barbados, 1650–1652: With Some Account of the Early History of Barbados* (Georgetown: Argosy Press, 1887).

Davis, N. Darnell (ed.), "Papers Relating to the Early History of Barbados and St. Kitts," *Timehri* 6, n.s. (1892), 327–49.

Davis, Ralph, "English Foreign Trade, 1660–1700," *Econ. HR* 7 (1954), 150–66.

De Britaine, William, *The Dutch Usurpation: Or, A Brief View of the Behaviour of the States-General of the United Provinces towards the Kings of Great Britain* (London, 1672).

De Krey, Gary, *London and the Restoration, 1659–1683* (Cambridge: Cambridge University Press, 2005).

Deane, Charles (ed.), *A Discourse Concerning Western Planting Written in the Year 1584 by Richard Hakluyt* (Cambridge: John Wilson and Sons, 1877).

Debe, Demetri D., and Russell R. Menard, "The Transition to African Slavery in Maryland: A Note on the Barbados Connection," *Slavery & Abolition* 32 (2011), 129–41.

Dijk, Wil O., *Seventeenth-Century Burma and the Dutch East India Company, 1634–1680* (Singapore: Singapore University Press, 2005).

Donagan, Barbara, "The Clerical Patronage of Robert Rich, Second Earl of Warwick, 1619–1642," *Proceedings of the American Philosophical Society* 120 (1976), 388–419.

Donoghue, John, *Fire under the Ashes: An Atlantic History of the English Revolution* (Chicago and London: University of Chicago Press, 2013).

Drescher, Seymour, "White Atlantic? The Choice for African Slave Labor in the Plantation Americas," in David Eltis, Frank D. Lewis, and Kenneth L. Sokoloff (eds.), *Slavery in the Development of the Americas* (Cambridge: Cambridge University Press, 2005), 32–69.

Dunn, Richard S., "The Barbados Census of 1680: Profile of the Richest Colony in America," *WMQ* 26 (1969), 3–30.

"John Winthrop, Jr., Connecticut Expansionist: The Failure of His Designs on Long Island, 1663–1675," *NEQ* 29 (1956), 3–26.

"John Winthrop, Jr., and the Narragansett Country," *WMQ* 13 (1956), 68–86.

Sugar and Slaves: The Rise of the Planter Class in the English West Indies, 1624–1713 (Chapel Hill: University of North Carolina Press, 1972).

Eacott, Jonathan, *Selling Empire: India in the Making of Britain and America, 1600–1850* (Chapel Hill: University of North Carolina Press, 2016).

East London History Group, Population Studies Group, "The Population of Stepney in the Early Seventeenth Century: A Report on an Analysis of the Parish Registers of Stepney, 1606–1610," *Local Population Studies* 3 (1968), 39–52.

Eben, Carl Theo. (ed. and trans.), *Gottlieb Mittelberger's Journey to Pennsylvania in the Year 1750 and Return to Germany in the Year 1754* (Philadelphia: John Jos. McVey, 1898).

Elliott, J.H., *The Count-Duke Olivares: The Statesman in an Age of Decline* (New Haven and London: Yale University Press, 1986).

Eltis, David, "The Relative Importance of Slaves and Commodities in the Atlantic Trade of Seventeenth-Century Africa," *The Journal of African History* 35 (1994), 237–49.

Eltis, David, Frank D. Lewis, and Kimberly McIntyre, "Accounting for the Traffic in Africans: Transport Costs on Slaving Voyages," *JEH* 70 (2010), 940–63.

Enthoven, Victor, and Wim Klooster, "The Rise and Fall of the Virginia-Dutch Connection in the Seventeenth Century," in Bradburn and Coombs, *Early Modern Virginia*, 90–127.

Ethridge, Robbie, and Sheri M. Shuck-Hall (eds.), *Mapping the Mississippian Shatter Zone: The Colonial Indian Slave Trade and Regional Instability in the American South* (Lincoln: University of Nebraska Press, 2009).

Fage, J.D., "African Societies and the Atlantic Slave Trade," *P&P*, no. 125 (1989), 97–115.

Farnell, J.E., "The Navigation Act of 1651, the First Dutch War, and the London Merchant Community," *Econ. HR* 16 (1964), 439–54.

Farnell, James E., "The Usurpation of Honest London Householders: Barebone's Parliament," *EHR* 82 (1967), 24–46.

Farrington, Anthony, "Bengkulu: An Anglo-Chinese Partnership," in H.V. Bowen (ed.), *The Worlds of the East India Company* (Woodbridge: Boydell & Brewer, 2002), 111–17.

Fausz, J. Frederick, "Merging and Emerging Worlds: Anglo-Indian Interest Groups and the Development of the Seventeenth-Century Chesapeake," in Lois Green Carr, Philip Morgan, and Jean Russo (eds.), *Colonial Chesapeake Society* (Chapel Hill: University of North Carolina Press, 1989), 47–98.

Federowicz, J.K., *England's Baltic Trade in the Early Seventeenth Century Trade: A Study in Anglo-Polish Commercial Diplomacy* (Cambridge: Cambridge University Press, 1981).

Fickes, Michael L., "'They Could Not Endure That Yoke': The Captivity of Pequot Women and Children after the War of 1637," *NEQ* 73 (2000), 58–81.

Fideler, Paul A., "Impressions of a Century of Historiography," *Albion* 32 (2000), 381–407.

Firth, C.H. (ed.), *The Narrative of General Venables with an Appendix of Papers Relating to the Expedition to the West Indies and the Conquest of Jamaica* (London: Longmans, Green, 1900).

Fischer, David Hackett, *Albion's Seed: Four British Folkways in America* (New York: Oxford University Press, 1989).

Flavell, Julie, *When London Was Capital of America* (New Haven and London: Yale University Press, 2010).

Fogleman, Aaron Spencer, "From Slaves, Convicts, and Servants to Free Passengers: The Transformation of Immigration in the Era of the American Revolution," *The Journal of American History* 85 (1998), 43–76.

Foster, Nicholas, *A Briefe Relation of the Late Horrid Rebellion Acted in the Island of Barbadas in the West Indies* (London, 1650).

Foster, Stephen, *The Long Argument: English Puritanism and the Shaping of New England Culture, 1570–1700* (Chapel Hill: University of North Carolina Press, 1991).

Foster, William, "The Acquisition of St. Helena," *EHR* 34 (1919), 281–9.

   The Founding of Fort St. George, Madras (London: Eyre and Spottiswoode, 1902).

   (ed.), *The Embassy of Sir Thomas Roe to the Court of the Great Mogul, 1615–1619*, 2 vols. (London: Hakluyt Society, 1899).

   (ed.), *The English Factories in India, 1618–1621* (Oxford: Clarendon Press, 1906).

   (ed.), *The English Factories in India, 1618–1669: A Calendar of Documents in the India Office, the British Museum and the Public Record Office* (Oxford: Clarendon Press, 1914).

   (ed.), *The English Factories in India, 1642–1645: A Calendar of Documents in the India Office, Westminster* (Oxford: Clarendon Press, 1913).

   (ed.), *The English Factories in India, 1661–64* (Oxford: Clarendon Press, 1923).

[Fox, Margaret Askew Fell], *An Evident Demonstration to God's Elect* (London, 1660).

   This to the Clergy Who Are the Men That Goes about to Settle Religion (As they say) according to the Church of England (London, 1660).

Galenson, David W., *White Servitude in Colonial America: An Economic Analysis* (New York: Cambridge University Press, 1984).

Gallagher, John, and Ronald Robinson, "The Imperialism of Free Trade," *Econ. HR* 6 (1953–1954), 1–15.

Gallay, Alan, *The Indian Slave Trade: The Rise of the English Empire in the American South, 1670–1717* (New Haven and London: Yale University Press, 2002).

   (ed.), *Indian Slavery in Colonial America* (Lincoln: University of Nebraska Press, 2009).

Games, Alison, "Cohabitation, Suriname-Style: English Inhabitants in Dutch Suriname after 1667," *WMQ* 72 (2015), 195–242.

   "'The Sanctuarye of our Rebell Negroes': The Atlantic Context of Local Resistance on Providence Island, 1630–1641," *Slavery & Abolition* 19 (1998), 1–21.

   The Web of Empire: English Cosmopolitans in an Age of Expansion 1560–1660 (New York: Oxford University Press, 2008).

Gardiner, Samuel R., *History of England from the Accession of James I to the Outbreak of the Civil War, 1603–1642*, 10 vols. (London: Longmans, Green, 1884).

Gardiner, Samuel Rawson (ed.), *The Constitutional Documents of the Puritan Revolution, 1625–1660* (Oxford: Clarendon Press, 1906).

Gaskill, Malcolm, *Between Two Worlds: How the English Became Americans* (New York: Basic Books, 2014).

Geiter, Mary K., "The Restoration Crisis and the Launching of Pennsylvania, 1679–81," *EHR* 112 (1997), 300–18.

Gentles, Ian "The Politics of Fairfax' Army, 1645–9," in John Adamson (ed.), *The English Civil War: Conflict and Contexts, 1640–1649* (Basingstoke: Palgrave Macmillan, 2008), 186–94.

Glaisyer, Natasha, "Networking: Trade and Exchange in the Eighteenth-Century British Empire," *HJ* 47 (2004), 451–76.

Glass, D.V., "Two Papers on Gregory King," in D.V. Glass and D.E.C. Eversley (eds.), *Population in History: Essays in Historical Demography*, vol. 1: *General and Great Britain* (New Brunswick: Transaction Publishers, 2008), 159–220.

Glickman, Gabriel, "Empire, 'Popery,' and the Fall of English Tangier, 1662–1684," *The Journal of Modern History* 87 (2015), 247–80.

Goetz, Rebecca Anne, "Rethinking the 'Unthinking Decision': Old Questions and New Problems in the History of Slavery and Race in the Colonial South," *The Journal of Southern History* 75 (2009), 599–612.

Gough, Barry M., "Maori and Pakeha in New Zealand Historiography: Preoccupations and Progressions," *Albion* 15 (1983), 337–41.

Gould, J.D., "The Trade Depression of the Early 1620s," *Econ. HR* 7 (1954), 81–90.

Gragg, Larry, *Englishmen Transplanted: The English Colonization of Barbados, 1627–1660* (New York: Oxford University Press, 2003).

Gragg, Larry D., "A Puritan in the West Indies: The Career of Samuel Winthrop," *WMQ* 50 (1993), 768–86.

"'To Procure Negroes': The English Slave Trade to Barbados, 1627–60," *Slavery & Abolition* 16 (1995), 65–84.

Grant, Benjamin (ed.), *Extracts from the St. Helena Records Compiled by the Late Hudson Ralph Janisch, Esq., C.M.G., Governor of St. Helena* (St. Helena: B. Grant, 1885).

Graves, Edward, *A Brief Narrative and Deduction of the Several Remarkable Cases of Sir William Courten, and Sir Paul Pyndar, Knights; and William Courten Late of London Esquire, Deceased* (London, 1679).

Greaves, Richard L., *Deliver Us from Evil: The Radical Underground in Britain, 1660–1663* (Oxford: Oxford University Press, 1986).

Green, John (comp.), *A New and General Collection of Voyages and Travels*, 4 vols. (London, 1745–7).

Gritt, A.J., "The 'Survival' of Service in the English Agricultural Labour Force: Lessons from Lancashire, c. 1650–1851," *Ag. HR* 50 (2002), 25–50.

Groenveld, Simon, "The English Civil Wars as a Cause of the First Anglo-Dutch War," *HJ* 30 (1987), 541–66.

Grose, Clyde L., "The Anglo-Portuguese Marriage of 1662," *Hispanic American Historical Review* 10 (1930), 313–52.

Guasco, Michael, *Slaves and Englishmen: Human Bondage in the Early Modern Atlantic World* (Philadelphia: University of Pennsylvania Press, 2014).

Gura, Philip F., "'The Contagion of Corrupt Opinions' in Puritan Massachusetts: The Case of William Pynchon," *WMQ* 39 (1982), 469–91.

Hair, P.E.H., and Robin Law, "The English in Western Africa to 1700," in Canny, *The Origins of Empire*, 241–63.

Hall, David D., *A Reforming People: Puritanism and the Transformation of Public Life in New England* (New York: Alfred A. Knopf, 2011).

Hall, Louise, "New Englanders at Sea: Cape Fear before the Royal Charter of 24 March 1662/3," *The New England Historical and Genealogical Record* 102 (1970), 88–108.

Hall, Michael Garibaldi, *Edward Randolph and the American Colonies, 1676–1703* (Chapel Hill: University of North Carolina Press, 1960).

Hall, R., *The History of the Barbarous Cruelties and Massacres, Committed by the Dutch in the East-Indies* (London, 1712).

Halliday, Paul D., *Dismembering the Body Politic: Partisan Politics in English Towns, 1650–1730* (Cambridge, Mass.: Harvard University Press, 1998).

Hammer, Paul E.J., *The Polarization of English Politics: The Political Career of Robert Devereux, 2nd Earl of Essex* (Cambridge: Cambridge University Press, 1999).

Hamond, Walter, *A Paradox Prooving, that the Inhabitants of the Isle called Madagascar, or St. Lawrence, (In Temporall things) are the happiest People in the world* (London, 1640).

Handler, Jerome S., "The Amerindian Slave Population of Barbados in the Seventeenth and Early Eighteenth Centuries," *Caribbean Studies* 8 (1969), 38–64.

(ed.), "Father Antoine Biet's Visit to Barbados in 1654," *The Journal of the Barbados Museum and Historical Society* 32 (1967), 56–76.

Hanna, Mark G., *Pirate Nests and the Rise of the British Empire, 1570–1740* (Chapel Hill: University of North Carolina Press, 2015).

Harcourt, Robert, *A Relation of a Voyage to Guiana* (London, 1613).

Harding, Vanessa, ""City, Capital, and Metropolis: The Changing Shape of Seventeenth-Century London," in J.F. Merritt (ed.), *Imagining Early Modern London: Perceptions and Portrayals of the City from Stow to Strype* (Cambridge: Cambridge University Press, 2001), 117–43.

Harlow, Vincent T. (ed.), *The Voyages of Captain William Jackson (1642–1645)*, Camden Miscellany 13 (London: Camden Society, 1923), 1–39.

Hatcher, John, "Understanding the Population History of England, 1450 to 1750," *P&P*, no. 180 (2003), 83–130.

Hatfield, April Lee, *Atlantic Virginia: Intercolonial Relations in the Seventeenth Century* (Philadelphia: University of Pennsylvania Press, 2004).

Hecht, Irene W.D., "The Virginia Muster of 1624/5 as a Source for Demographic History," *WMQ* 30 (1973), 65–92.

Hening, William Waller (ed.), *The Statutes at Large; Being a Collection of All the Laws of Virginia from the First Session of the Legislature, in the Year 1619*, vol. 1 (New York: R. & W. & G. Bartow, 1823).

Henneton, Lauric, "The House of Hope in the Valley of Discord: Connecticut's Geopolitics beyond 'Anglo-Dutch' Relations (1613–1654)," in Jacobs and Roper, *The Worlds of the Seventeenth-Century Hudson Valley*, 169–96.

Henneton, Lauric, "Rumors, Uncertainty and Decision-Making in the Greater Long Island Sound (1652–1654)," in Lauric Henneton and L.H. Roper (eds.), *Fear and the Shaping of Early American Societies* (Leiden and Boston: Brill, 2016), 115–36.

Hervey, Mary Frederica Sophia, *The Life, Correspondence and Collections of Thomas Howard, Earl of Arundel* (Cambridge: Cambridge University Press, 1921).

Heywood, Linda M., and John K. Thornton, *Central Africans, Atlantic Creoles, and the Foundation of the Americas* (New York: Cambridge University Press, 2007).

Hickeringill, Edmund, *Jamaica Viewed: With All the Ports, Harbours, and their several Soundings, Towns, and Settlements thereunto belonging* (London, 1661).

Hill, G.W., and W.H. Frere (eds.), *Memorials of Stepney Parish* (Billing & Sons, 1890–1).

Hindle, Steve, "Hierarchy and Community in the Elizabethan Parish: The Swallowfield Articles of 1596," *HJ* 42 (September 1999), 835–51.

"Persuasion and Protest in the Caddington Common Enclosure Dispute, 1635–1639," *P&P*, no. 158 (February 1998), 37–78.

Hirst, Derek, "The Failure of Godly Rule in the English Republic," *P&P*, no. 132 (1991), 33–66.

"Locating the 1650s in England's Seventeenth Century," *History* 81 (1996), 359–83.

Hollis, Daniel W. III, "The Crown Lands and the Financial Dilemma in Stuart England," *Albion* 26 (1994), 419–42.

Holmes, Clive, *The Eastern Association in the English Civil War* (Cambridge: Cambridge University Press, 2007).

Horn, J.P.P., "Moving On in the New World: Migration and Out-Migration in the Seventeenth-Century Chesapeake," in Peter Clark and David Souden (eds.), *Migration and Society in Early Modern England* (Totowa: Barnes & Noble, 1988), 172–212.

Horn, James, "'To Parts beyond the Seas': Free Emigration to the Chesapeake in the Seventeenth Century," in Ida Altman and James Horn (eds.), *"To Make America": European Emigration in the Early Modern Period* (Berkeley and Los Angeles: University of California Press, 1991), 85–130.

(ed.), *Captain John Smith: Writings with Other Narratives of Roanoke, Jamestown, and the First Settlement of America* (New York: Library of America, 2007).

Horn, James, and Philip D. Morgan, "Settlers and Slaves: European and African Migrations to Early Modern British America," in Elizabeth Mancke and Carole Shammas (eds.), *The Creation of the British Atlantic World* (Baltimore: Johns Hopkins University Press, 2005), 19–44.

Hoskins, W.G., "Harvest Fluctuations and English Economic History, 1480–1619," *Ag. HR* 12, pt. 1 (1964), 28–46.

"Harvest Fluctuations and English Economic History, 1620–1759," *Ag. HR* 16, pt. 1 (1968), 15–31.

Hosmer, James Kendall (ed.), *Winthrop's Journal: "History of New England,"* 1630–1649, 2 vols. (New York: Charles Scribner's Sons, 1908).

Houston, Alan, and Steve Pincus, "Introduction: Modernity and Later-Seventeenth-Century England," in Alan Houston and Steve Pincus (eds.), *A Nation Transformed: England after the Restoration* (Cambridge: Cambridge University Press, 2011), 2–19.

Howe, Stephen, "British Worlds, Settler Worlds, World Systems, and Killing Fields," *JICH* 40 (2012), 691–725.

Hudson, Paul, "English Emigration to New Zealand, 1839–1850: Information Diffusion and Marketing a New World," *Econ. HR* 54 (2001), 680–98.

Hunt, Robert, *The Island of Assada Neere Madagascar Impartially Defined* (London, 1650).

Hunt, William, *The Puritan Moment: The Coming of Revolution in an English County* (Cambridge, Mass.: Harvard University Press, 1983).

Hutton, Ronald, "The Structure of the Royalist Party," *HJ* 24 (1981), 553–69.

Israel, Jonathan I., "The Dutch Role in the Glorious Revolution," in Jonathan I. Israel (ed.), *The Anglo-Dutch Moment: Essays on the Glorious Revolution and Its World Impact* (Cambridge: Cambridge University Press, 1991), 105–62.

"The Emerging Empire: The Continental Perspective, 1650–1713," in Canny, *The Origins of Empire*, 423–45.

Israel, Jonathan, "England, the Dutch Republic, and Europe in the Seventeenth Century," *HJ* 40 (1997), 1117–21.

Jacobs, Jaap, *The Colony of New Netherland: A Dutch Settlement in Seventeenth Century America* (Ithaca: Cornell University Press, 2009).

"The Hartford Treaty: A European Perspective on a New World Conflict," *de Halve Maen* 68 (1995), 74–9.

Jacobs, Jaap, and L.H. Roper (eds.), *The Worlds of the Seventeenth-Century Hudson Valley* (Albany: SUNY Press, 2014).

James, Sydney V., *John Clarke and His Legacies: Religion and Law in Colonial Rhode Island, 1638–1750*, Theodore Dwight Bozeman (ed.) (University Park: Pennsylvania State University Press, 1999).

Jansson, Maija (ed.), *Proceedings in Parliament, 1614 (House of Commons)* (Philadelphia: American Philosophical Society, 1988).

Jarvis, Michael J., *In the Eye of All Trade: Bermuda, Bermudians, and the Maritime Atlantic World* (Chapel Hill: University of North Carolina Press, 2010).

Jasanoff, Maya, "The Other Side of Revolution: Loyalists in the British Empire," *WMQ* 65 (2008), 207–32.

Jonson, Fredrik Albritton, "Natural History and Improvement: The Case of Tobacco," in Philip J. Stern and Carl Wennerlind (eds.), *Mercantilism Reimagined: Political Economy in Early Modern Britain and Its Empire* (Oxford: Oxford University Press, 2013), 117–33.

Judges, A.V., "Philip Burlamachi: A Financier of the Thirty Years' War," *Economica* 18 (1926), 285–300.

Kea, Ray A., *Settlements, Trade, and Politics in the Seventeenth-Century Gold Coast* (Baltimore and London: Johns Hopkins University Press, 1982).

Kelley, Donald R., *The Beginning of Ideology: Consciousness and Society in the French Reformation* (New York: Cambridge University Press, 1983).

Kennedy, Dane, "The Imperial History Wars," *JBS* 54 (2015), 5–22.

Kerrigan, Paul M., "Ireland in Naval Strategy, 1641–1691," in Pádraig Lenihan (ed.), *Conquest and Resistance: War in Seventeenth-Century Ireland* (Leiden and Boston: Brill, 2001), 151–76.

Kingsford, C.L. (ed.), *A Survey of London. Reprinted from the Text of 1603* (Oxford: Clarendon Press, 1908).

Klooster, Wim, "Anglo-Dutch Trade in the Seventeenth Century: An Atlantic Partnership?," in Allan Macinnes and Arthur H. Williamson (eds.), *Shaping the Stuart World, 1603–1714: The Atlantic Connection* (Leiden and Boston, 2006), 261–82.

The Dutch Moment: War, Trade, and Settlement in the Seventeenth-Century Atlantic World (Ithaca: Cornell University Press, 2016).

"Inter-imperial Smuggling in the Americas, 1600–1800," in Bernard Bailyn and Pat Denault (eds.), *Soundings in Atlantic History: Latent Structures and Intellectual Currents, 1500–1825* (Cambridge, Mass.: Harvard University Press), 141–80.

Knights, Mark, "Fiscal-Military State," in *Oxford Bibliographies* in Atlantic History, available at www.oxfordbibliographies.com/view/document/obo-9780199730414/obo-9780199730414-0073.xml (accessed 1 January 2017).

Koenigsberger, H.G., "Monarchies and Parliaments in Early Modern Europe: Dominium Regale or Dominium Politicum et Regale," *Theory and Society* 5 (1978), 191–217.

Kopperman, Paul E., "Profile of Failure: The Carolana Project, 1629–1640," *The North Carolina Historical Review* 59 (1982), 1–23.

Koot, Christian J., *Empire at the Periphery: British Colonists, Anglo-Dutch Trade, and the Development of the British Atlantic, 1621–1713* (New York: New York University Press, 2011).

Kupperman, Karen Ordahl, *Providence Island, 1630–1641: The Other Puritan Colony* (New York: Cambridge University Press, 1993).

"Puritan Colonization from Providence Island through the Western Design," *WMQ* 45 (1988), 70–99.

(ed.), *A True and Exact History of the Island of Barbados by Richard Ligon* (Indianapolis: Hackett Publishing, 2011).

Kussmaul, Ann, *Servants in Husbandry* (Cambridge: Cambridge University Press, 1981).

Lake, Peter, "Constitutional Consensus and the Puritan Opposition in the 1620s," *HJ* 25 (1982), 805–25.

Lake, Peter, and David Como, "'Orthodoxy' and Its Discontents: Dispute Settlement and the Production of 'Consensus' in the London (Puritan) Underground," *JBS* 39 (2000), 34–70.

Lake, Peter, and Steve Pincus, "Rethinking the Public Sphere in Early Modern England," *JBS* 45 (2006), 270–92.

Laslett, Peter, "John Locke, the Great Recoinage, and the Origins of the Board of Trade, 1695–1698," *WMQ* 14 (1957), 370–402.

Law, Robin, "The Slave Trade in Seventeenth-Century Allada: A Revision," *African Economic History* 22 (1994), 59–92.

Lawson, Philip, *The East India Company: A History* (New York and London: Longman, 1993).

LeFevre, Tate A., "Settler Colonialism," in *Oxford Bibliographies* in Anthropology, available at www.oxfordbibliographies.com/view/document/obo-9780199766567/obo-9780199766567-0125.xml (accessed 21 January 2017).

Leng, Thomas, "Shaftesbury's Aristocratic Empire," in John Spurr (ed.), *Anthony Ashley Cooper, 1621–1683* (Farnham: Ashgate, 2011), 101–25.

Lewis, Colin M., "Britain, the Argentine and Informal Empire: Rethinking the Role of Railway Companies," *Bulletin of Latin American Research* 27, Issue Supplement (2008), 99–123.

Lewis, Diane, "British Trade to Southeast Asia in the Seventeenth and Eighteenth Centuries Revisited," *The New Zealand Journal of Asian Studies* 11 (2009), 49–59.

Lindley, Keith, "Irish Adventurers and Godly Militants in the 1640s," *Irish Historical Studies* 29 (1994–5), 1–12.

Lipman, Andrew C., "Murder on the Saltwater Frontier: The Death of John Oldham," *Early American Studies* 9 (2011), 268–94.

The Saltwater Frontier: Indians and the Contest for the American Coast (New Haven and London: Yale University Press, 2015).

Lister, T.H. (ed.), *Life and Administration of Edward, Earl of Clarendon with Original Correspondence and Authentic Papers Never before Published*, 3 vols. (London: Longman, Orme, Brown, Green, and Longmans, 1837).

Locher-Scholten, Elsbeth, *Sumatran Sultanate and Colonial State: Jambi and the Rise of Dutch Imperialism, 1830–1907* (Ithaca: Cornell University Southeast Asia Program Publications, 2003).

Loth, Vincent C., "Armed Incidents and Unpaid Bills: Anglo-Dutch Rivalry in the Banda Islands in the Seventeenth Century," *MAS* 29 (1995), 705–40.

"Pioneers and Perkeniers: The Banda Islands in the 17th Century," *Cakalele* 6 (1995), 13–35.

Lurie, Maxine N., "The Long-Lived Proprietary," in Roper and Van Ruymbeke, *Constructing Early Modern Empires*, 327–55.

MacCormack, J.R., "The Irish Adventurers and the English Civil War," *Irish Historical Studies* 10 (1956–7), 21–58.

MacCormack, John R., "Irish Land and the English Civil War," Canadian Catholic Historical Association, *Report*, 25 (1958), 59–66.

MacMillan, Ken, *The Atlantic Imperial Constitution: Center and Periphery in the English Atlantic World* (New York and Houndmills: Palgrave Macmillan, 2011).

Sovereignty and Possession in the English New World: The Legal Foundations of Empire, 1576–1640 (Cambridge: Cambridge University Press, 2006).

Madley, Benjamin, "From Terror to Genocide: Britain's Tasmanian Penal Colony and Australia's History Wars," *JBS* 47 (2008), 77–106.

Makepeace, Margaret, "English Traders on the Gold Coast, 1657–1668: An Analysis of the East India Company Archive," *History in Africa* 16 (1989), 237–84.

Marsden, R.G. (ed.), *Documents Relating to the Law and Custom of the Sea*, 2 vols. (London: The Navy Records Society, 1916).

Marsden, William, *The History of Sumatra*, 2nd ed. (London, 1784).

Mayers, Ruth E., *1659: The Crisis of the Commonwealth* (Woodbridge and Rochester: Boydell & Brewer, 2004).

McAleer, John, *Britain's Maritime Empire: Southern Africa, the South Atlantic and the Indian Ocean, 1763–1820* (Cambridge: Cambridge University Press, 2017).

McCartney, Martha W., "An Early Virginia Census Reprised," *Archaeological Society of Virginia Quarterly Bulletin* 54 (1999), 178–96.

McCusker, John J., and Russell R. Menard, *The Economy of British America, 1607–1789* (Chapel Hill: University of North Carolina Press, 1991).

McManus, Edgar J., *Black Bondage in the North* (Syracuse: Syracuse University Press, 1973).

McPherson, Elizabeth Gregory, "Nathaniel Batts, Landholder on Pasquotank River," *The North Carolina Historical Review* 43 (1966), 66–81.

Menard, Russell R., "Making a 'Popular Slave Society' in Colonial British America," *JIH* 43 (2013), 377–95.

"Plantation Empire: How Sugar and Tobacco Planters Built Their Industries and Raised an Empire," *Agricultural History* 81 (2007), 309–32.

Sweet Negotiations: Sugar, Slavery, and Plantation Agriculture in Early Barbados (Charlottesville and London: University of Virginia Press, 2006).

Meuwese, Mark, "The Dutch Connection: New Netherland, the Pequots, and the Puritans in Southern New England, 1620–1638," *Early American Studies* 9 (2011), 295–323.

Mijers, Esther, "A Natural Partnership? Scotland and Zeeland in the Early Seventeenth Century," in Allan I. Macinnes and Arthur H. Williamson (eds.), *Shaping the Stuart World, 1603–1714: The Atlantic Connection* (Leiden and Boston: Brill, 2006), 233–60.

Miller, Aaron F., John D. Krugler, Barry C. Gaulton, and James I. Lyttleton, "'Over Shoes over Boots': Lord Baltimore's Final Days in Ferryland, Newfoundland," *The Journal of Early American History* 1 (2011), 167–82.

Miller, Perry, *The New England Mind: The Seventeenth Century* (Boston: Beacon Press, 1961).

Miller, W. Hubert, "The Colonization of the Bahamas, 1647–1670," *WMQ* 2 (1945), 33–46.

Morgan, Edmund S., *American Slavery, American Freedom: The Ordeal of Colonial Virginia* (New York: W.W. Norton, 1975).

The Puritan Dilemma: The Story of John Winthrop (Boston: Little, Brown, 1958).

Moore, Susan Hardman, *Pilgrims: New World Settlers and the Call of Home* (New Haven and London: Yale University Press, 2007).

Morrill, John, "Cromwell, Parliament, Ireland and a Commonwealth in Crisis: 1652 Revisited," *Parliamentary History* 30, pt. 2 (2011), 193–214.

The Nature of the English Revolution (London: Routledge: 2014).

"Rewriting Cromwell: A Case of Deafening Silences," *The Canadian Journal of History* 38 (2003), 553–78.

Morrill, John, and Phillip Baker, "Oliver Cromwell, the Regicide and the Sons of Zeruiah," in Jason Peacey (ed.), *The Regicides and the Execution of Charles I* (Basingstoke: Palgrave Macmillan, 2001), 14–35.

Moyer, Samuel, *The Humble Petition of Many Inhabitants in and about the City of London. Presented to the Parliament by Mr. Sam Moyer and others, 12 May 1659. Together with the Answer of the Parliament thereunto* (London, 1659).

Musselwhite, Paul P., "Bacon's Rebellion," in *Oxford Bibliographies* in Atlantic History, available at www.oxfordbibliographies.com/view/document/obo-9780199730414/obo-9780199730414-0269.xml (accessed 15 January 2017).

Nash, Gary B., and Billy G. Smith, "The Population of Eighteenth-Century Philadelphia," *The Pennsylvania Magazine of History and Biography* 99 (1975), 362–8.

Ndlovu-Gatsheni, Sabelo J., "Mapping Cultural and Colonial Encounters, 1880s–1930s," in Brian Raftopoulos and Alois Mlambo (eds.), *Becoming Zimbabwe: A History from the Pre-colonial Period to 2008* (Harare: Weaver Press and Johannesburg: Jacana Press, 2009), 39–74.

Neill, Edward D., *Virginia Carolorum: The Colony under the Rule of Charles the First and Second, A.D. 1625–A.D. 1685* (Albany: Joel Munsell's Sons, 1886).

Newell, Margaret Ellen, *Brethren by Nature: New England Indians, Colonists, and the Origins of American Slavery* (Ithaca: Cornell University Press, 2015).

Newman, Simon P., *A New World of Labor: The Development of Plantation Slavery in the British Atlantic* (Philadelphia: University of Pennsylvania Press, 2013).

Newton, Arthur Percival, *Colonising Activities of the English Puritans: The Last Phase of the Elizabethan Struggle with Spain* (New Haven: Yale University Press, 1914).

Nocentelli, Carmen, "The Dutch Black Legend," *Modern Language Quarterly* 75 (2014), 355–83.

Norton, Mary Beth, *Founding Mothers and Fathers: Gendered Power and the Forming of American Society* (New York: Alfred A. Knopf, 1996).

Nováky, György, "Small Company Trade and the Gold Coast: The Swedish Africa Company, 1650–1663," *Itinerario* 16 (1992), 57–76.

Okia, Opolot, "The Northey Forced Labor Crisis, 1920–1921: A Symptomatic Reading," *International Journal of African Historical Studies* 41 (2008), 263–93.

Okoye, Felix N.C., "Dingane and the Voortrekkers: A Note on South African Historiography," *The Journal of Negro History* 56 (1971), 135–40.

O'Malley, Gregory E., *Final Passages: The Intercolonial Slave Trade of British America, 1619–1807* (Chapel Hill: University of North Carolina Press, 2014).

Otto, Paul, "Henry Hudson, the Munsees, and the Wampum Revolution," in Jacobs and Roper, *The Worlds of the Seventeenth-Century Hudson Valley*, 85–102.

P., T., *The Low Dutch character'd, their Butter-box Opened, and their Juggles Apprehended and Reproved* (London, 1658).

Pagden, Anthony, *Lords of All the World: Ideologies of Empire in Spain, Britain and France, c. 1500–c. 1800* (New Haven and London: Yale University Press, 1995).

Parmenter, Jon, "After the Mourning Wars: The Iroquois as Allies in Colonial North American Campaigns, 1676–1760," *WMQ* 64 (2007), 39–76.

"Separate Vessels: Iroquois Engagements with the Dutch of New Netherland, c. 1613–1664," in Jacobs and Roper, *The Worlds of the Seventeenth-Century Hudson Valley*, 103–36.

Pearson, M.N., "Shivaji and the Decline of the Mughal Empire," *JAS* 35 (1976), 221–35.

Pearson, M.N., J.F. Richards, and P. Hardy, "Symposium: Decline of the Mughal Empire," *JAS* 35 (1976), 221–63.

[Penn, William], *The Continued Cry of the Oppressed for Justice* (London, 1675). *England's Present Interest Discover'd with Honour to the Prince, and Safety to the People* (London, 1675).

Pepys, Samuel, *Diary and correspondence of Samuel Pepys, F.R.S.: secretary to the Admiralty in the reign of Charles II and James II* (London: J.B. Lippincott & Co., 1855).

Pestana, Carla Gardina, "Early English Jamaica without Pirates," *WMQ* 71 (2014), 321–60.

The English Atlantic in an Age of Revolution, 1640–1661 (Cambridge, Mass., and London: Harvard University Press, 2004).

"English Character and the Fiasco of the Western Design," *Early American Studies* 3 (2005), 1–31.

Protestant Empire: Religion and the Making of the British Atlantic World (Philadelphia: University of Pennsylvania Press, 2009).

Pettigrew, William A., "Constitutional Change in England and the Diffusion of Regulatory Initiative, 1660–1714," *History* 99 (2014), 839–63.

Freedom's Debt: The Royal African Company and the Politics of the Atlantic Slave Trade, 1672–1752 (Chapel Hill: University of North Carolina Press, 2013).

Pincus, Steven C.A., "From Butterboxes to Wooden Shoes: The Shift in English Popular Sentiment from Anti-Dutch to Anti-French in the 1670s," *HJ* 38 (1995), 333–61.

"Popery, Trade and Universal Monarchy: The Ideological Context of the Outbreak of the English Civil War," *EHR* 107 (1992), 1–29.

Protestantism and Patriotism: Ideologies and the Making of English Foreign Policy, 1650–1668 (Cambridge: Cambridge University Press, 1996).

Pincus, Steve, *1688: The First Modern Revolution* (New Haven and London: Yale University Press, 2009).

"Rethinking Mercantilism: Political Economy, the British Empire, and the Atlantic World in the Seventeenth and Eighteenth Centuries," *WMQ* 69 (2012), 3–34.

Pincus, Steve, Cathy Matson, Christian J. Koot, Susan D. Amussen, Trevor Burnard, and Margaret Ellen Newell, "Forum: Rethinking Mercantilism," *WMQ* 69 (2012), 3–70.

Pope, Peter E., *Fish into Wine: The Newfoundland Plantation in the Seventeenth Century* (Chapel Hill: University of North Carolina Press, 2004).

Porter, R., "The Crispe Family and the African Trade in the Seventeenth Century," *The Journal of African History* 9 (1968), 57–77.

Power, M.J., "East London Housing in the Seventeenth Century," in Peter Clark and Paul Slack (eds.), *Crisis and Order in English Towns* (London: Routledge & Kegan Paul, 1972), 237–62.

Prakash, Om, *The Dutch East India Company and the Economy of Bengal, 1630–1720* (Princeton: Princeton University Press, 1985).

"The Dutch and English East India Company's Trade in Indian Textiles in the Seventeenth and the Eighteenth Century: A Comparative View," in Maxine Berg, Felicia Gottman, Hanna Hodacs, and Chris Nierstrasz (eds.), *Goods from the East, 1600–1800: Trading Eurasia* (Houndmills and New York: Palgrave Macmillan, 2015), 183–94.

"From Negotiation to Coercion: Textile Manufacturing in India in the Eighteenth Century," *MAS* 41 (2007), 1331–68.

Prestwich, Menna, "Diplomacy and Trade in the Protectorate," *The Journal of Modern History* 22 (1950), 103–21.

Prynne, William, *A fresh discovery of some prodigious new wandring-blasing stars, & firebrands, stiling themselves new-lights, firing our church and state into new combustions. Divided into ten sections, comprising severall most libellous, scandalous, seditious, insolent, uncharitable, (and some blasphemous) passages* (London, 1645).

Puckrein, Gary A., *Little England: Plantation Society and Anglo-Barbadian Politics, 1627–1700* (New York and London: New York University Press, 1984).

Questier, Michael, "Catholic Loyalism in Early Stuart England," *EHR* 123 (2008), 1132–65.

Ratelband, K. (ed.), *Vijf dagregisters van het kasteel São Jorge da Mina (Elmina) aan de Goudkost, 1645–1647* ('s-Gravenhage: Martinus Nijhoff, 1953).

Rawley, James A., and Stephen D. Behrendt, *The Transatlantic Slave Trade: A History* (Lincoln: University of Nebraska Press, 2005).

Raymond, Joad, "The Newspaper, Public Opinion, and the Public Sphere in the Seventeenth Century," *Prose Studies* 21 (1998), 109–36.

Records of the Town of Newark, New Jersey: From Its Settlement in 1666 to Its Incorporation as a City in 1836 (Newark: For the New Jersey Historical Society, 1864).

Refai, G.Z., "Sir George Oxinden and Bombay, 1662–1669," *EHR* 92 (1977), 573–81.

Richter, Daniel K., *Before the Revolution: America's Ancient Pasts* (Cambridge, Mass.: Harvard University Press, 2011).

Ritchie, Robert C., *The Duke's Province: A Study of New York Politics and Society, 1664–1691* (Chapel Hill: University of North Carolina Press, 1977).

Roberts, Justin, "Surrendering Surinam: The Barbadian Diaspora and the Expansion of the English Sugar Frontier, 1650–1675," *WMQ* 73 (2016), 225–56.

Robertson, James, "Making Jamaica English: Priorities and Processes," in L.H. Roper (ed.), *The Torrid Zone: Colonization and Cultural Interaction in the*

Seventeenth-Century Caribbean (Columbia: University of South Carolina Press, forthcoming).

Rommelse, Gijs, "The Role of Mercantilism in Anglo-Dutch Political Relations, 1650–1674," *Econ. HR* 63 (2010), 591–611.

The Second Anglo-Dutch War (1665–1667): Raison d'état, Mercantilism and Maritime Strife (Hilversum: Uitgeverij Verloren, 2006).

Roper, L.H., "The 1701 'Act for the Better Ordering of Slaves': Reconsidering the History of Slavery in Proprietary South Carolina," *WMQ* 64 (2007), 395–418.

"Charles I, Virginia, and the Idea of Atlantic History," *Itinerario* 30 (2006), 33–53.

"Conceiving an Anglo-American Proprietorship: Early South Carolina History in Perspective," in Roper and Van Ruymbeke, *Constructing Early Modern Empires*, 389–409.

Conceiving Carolina: Proprietors, Planters, and Plots, 1662–1729 (New York and Houndmills: Palgrave Macmillan, 2004).

The English Empire in America, 1602–1658: Beyond Jamestown (London: Pickering & Chatto, 2009).

"The Fall of New Netherland and Seventeenth-Century Anglo-American Imperial Formation, 1652–1676," *NEQ* 87 (2014), 666–708.

"The Ties That Bound: The Conception of Anglo-America, 1617–1667," *The Journal of Early American History* 1 (2011), 142–66.

Roper, L.H., and B. Van Ruymbeke (eds.), *Constructing Early Modern Empires: Proprietary Ventures in the Atlantic World, 1500–1750* (Leiden and Boston: Brill, 2007).

Rorke, Martin, "English and Scottish Overseas Trade, 1300–1600," *Econ. HR* 59 (2006), 265–88.

Rose-Troup, Frances, *The Massachusetts Bay Company and Its Predecessors* (New York: Grafton Press, 1930).

Routh, E.M.G., *Tangier: England's Lost Atlantic Outpost, 1661–1684* (London: John Murray, 1912).

Roy, Thirthankar, "Sardars, Jobbers, Kanganies: The Labour Contractor and Indian Economic History," *MAS* 42 (2008), 971–88.

Russell, Conrad, *Parliaments and English Politics, 1621–29* (Oxford: Oxford University Press, 1979).

Salley, Alexander S. Jr. (ed.), *Narratives of Early Carolina, 1650–1708* (New York: Barnes & Noble, 1967).

Schomburgk, Sir Robert S., *The History of Barbados* (London: Longman, Brown, Green, and Longmans, 1848).

Scott, W.R. *The Constitution and Finance of English, Scottish and Irish Joint Stock Companies to 1720*, 3 vols. (Cambridge: Cambridge University Press, 1912).

Seaver, Paul S., *Wallington's World: A Puritan Artisan in Seventeenth-Century London* (Stanford: Stanford University Press, 1985).

Settle, Elkanah, *Insignia Batavia, or, the Dutch trophies display'd being exact relations of the unjust, horrid, and most barbarous proceedings of the Dutch against the English in the East-Indies* (London, 1688).

Shadle, Brett L., *The Souls of White Folk: White Settlers in Kenya, 1900s–1920s* (Manchester: Manchester University Press, 2015).

Shankman, Andrew, "A Synthesis Useful and Compelling: Anglicization and the Achievement of John M. Murrin," in Ignacio Gallup-Diaz, Andrew Shankman, and David J. Silverman (eds.), *Anglicizing America: Empire, Revolution, Republic* (Philadelphia: University of Pennsylvania Press, 2015), 20–56.

Shaw, John (ed.), *Charters Relating to the East India Company from 1600 to 1761: Reprinted from a Former Collection with Some Additions and a Preface for the Government of Madras* (Madras: R. Hill, 1887).

Shaw-Taylor, Leigh, "The Rise of Agrarian Capitalism and the Decline of Family Farming in England," *Econ. HR* 65 (2012), 26–60.

Shephard, Robert, "Court Factions in Early Modern England," *The Journal of Modern History* 64 (1992), 721–45.

Sheridan, Richard B., "The Molasses Act and the Market Strategy of the British Sugar Planters," *JEH* 17 (1957), 62–83.

Sugar and Slavery: An Economic History of the British West Indies, 1623–1775 (Kingston: Canoe Press, 1994).

Siminoff, Faren R., *Crossing the Sound: The Rise of Atlantic American Communities in Seventeenth-Century Eastern Long Island* (New York: New York University Press, 2004).

Slack, Paul, "Government and Information in Seventeenth-Century England," *P&P*, no. 184 (2004), 33–68.

"Material Progress and the Challenge of Affluence in Seventeenth-Century England," *Econ. HR* 62 (2009), 576–603.

"The Politics of Consumption and England's Happiness in the Later Seventeenth Century," *EHR* 122 (2007), 609–31.

Smith, David L., "Diplomacy and the Religious Question: Mazarin, Cromwell and the Treaties of 1655 and 1657," *E-rea* 11, no. 2; available at http://erea.revues.org/3745, DOI: 10.4000/erea.3745.

"Oliver Cromwell and the Protectorate Parliaments," in Patrick Little (ed.), *The Cromwellian Protectorate* (Woodbridge and Rochester: Boydell Press, 2007), 14–31.

Smith, Edmond J., "'Canaanising Madagascar': Africa in English Imperial Imagination, 1635–1650," *Itinerario* 39 (2015), 277–98.

Smuts, R.M., "The Puritan Followers of Henrietta Maria in the 1630s," *EHR* 93 (1978), 26–45.

Soderlund, Jean R., "Black Importation and Migration into Southeastern Pennsylvania, 1682–1810," *Proceedings of the American Philosophical Society* 133 (1989), 144–53.

Solana, Ana Crespo, "A Network-Based Merchant Empire: Dutch Trade in the Hispanic Atlantic," in Gert Oostindie and Jessica V. Roitman (eds.), *Dutch Atlantic Connections, 1680–1800: Linking Empires, Bridging Borders* (Leiden and Boston: Brill, 2014), 139–58.

Souden, David, "'Rogues, Whores and Vagabonds'? Indentured Servant Emigration to North America and the Case of Mid Seventeenth-Century Bristol," in

Peter Clark and David Souden (eds.), *Migration and Society in Early Modern England* (Totowa: Barnes & Noble, 1988), 150–71.

"Speech of Sir William Berkeley, and Declaration of the Assembly, March 1651," *VMHB* 1 (1893), 75–81.

Stanwood, Owen, *An Empire Reformed: English America in the Age of the Glorious Revolution* (Philadelphia: University of Pennsylvania Press, 2011).

"The Protestant Moment: Antipopery, the Revolution of 1688–1689, and the Making of an Anglo-American Empire," *JBS* 46 (2007), 481–508.

Starn, Randolph, "Review Article: The Early Modern Muddle," *The Journal of Early Modern History* 6 (2002), 296–307.

Starna, William A., and José A. Brandão, "From the Mohawk-Mahican War to the Beaver Wars," *Ethnohistory* 51 (2004), 725–50.

Steckley, G.F. (ed.), *The Letters of John Paige, London Merchant, 1648–58* (London: London Record Society, 1984).

Stein, Tristan, "Tangier in the Restoration Empire," *HJ* 54 (2011), 985–1011.

Stern, Philip J., "'A Politie of Civill & Military Power': Political Thought and the Late Seventeenth-Century Foundations of the East India Company-State," *JBS* 47 (2008), 253–83.

The Company-State: Corporate Sovereignty and the Early Modern Foundations of the British Empire in India (New York: Oxford University Press, 2011).

"Politics and Ideology in the Early East India Company-State: The Case of St. Helena, 1673–1709," *JICH* 35 (2007), 1–23.

Stone, Lawrence, *The Causes of the English Revolution, 1529–1642* (London: Routledge and Kegan Paul, 1972).

Strachey, Ray, and Oliver Strachey, *Keigwin's Rebellion (1683–4): An Episode in the History of Bombay* (Oxford: Clarendon Press, 1916).

Stradling, R.A., *Philip IV and the Government of Spain, 1621–1665* (Cambridge: Cambridge University Press, 1988).

Sturman, Rachel, "Indian Indentured Labor and the History of International Rights Regimes," *AHR* 119 (2014), 1439–65.

Subrahmanyam, Sanjay, *The Political Economy of Commerce: Southern India, 1500–1650* (Cambridge: Cambridge University Press, 2002).

Swingen, Abigail L., *Competing Visions of Empire: Labor, Slavery, and the Origins of the British Atlantic Empire* (New Haven and London: Yale University Press, 2015).

Taylor, Alan, *American Colonies: The Settling of North America*, vol. 1 (New York: Penguin, 2002).

Temple, Richard C. (ed.), *The Travels of Peter Mundy, in Europe and Asia, 1608–1667*, 5 vols. (London: Hakluyt Society, 1919).

Thompson, Andrew, "Informal Empire? An Exploration in the History of Anglo-Argentine Relations, 1800–1914," *Journal of Latin American Studies* 24 (1992), 419–36.

Thompson, Christopher, *Parliamentary History in the 1620s: In or Out of Perspective?* (Wivenhoe, U.K.: p.p., 1986).

Thompson, Edward Maunde (ed.), *Correspondence of the Family of Hatton*, vol. 1 (London: Camden Society, 1878).

Thorndale, William, "The Virginia Census of 1619," *The Magazine of Virginia Genealogy* 33 (1995), 155–70.

Trigger, Bruce G., "The Mohawk-Mahican War: The Establishment of a Pattern," *The Canadian Historical Review* 52 (1971), 276–86.

Trumbull, Benjamin, *A Complete History of Connecticut, Civil and Ecclesiastical from the Emigration of the First Planters*, 2 vols. (New Haven: Maltby, Goldsmith, 1818).

Turner, Frederick Jackson, "The Significance of the Frontier in American History," in Frederick Jackson Turner (ed.), *The Frontier in American History* (New York: Henry Holt, 1921), 1–38.

Tyacke, Nicholas, *Anti-Calvinists: The Rise of English Arminianism, c. 1590–1640* (Oxford: Oxford University Press, 1990).

"The Puritan Paradigm of English Politics, 1558–1642," *HJ* 53 (2010), 527–50.

"The Rise of Arminianism Reconsidered," *P&P*, no. 115 (1987), 201–16.

Underdown, David, *Fire from Heaven: Life in an English Town in the Seventeenth Century* (New Haven and London: Yale University Press, 1992).

Ungerer, Gustav, *The Mediterranean Apprenticeship of British Slavery* (Madrid: Editorial Verlum, 2008).

Van Ittersum, Martine Julia, "Debating Natural Law in the Banda Islands: A Case Study in Anglo-Dutch Imperial Competition in the East Indies," *History of European Ideas* 42 (2016), 459–501.

"The Long Goodbye: Hugo Grotius' Justification of Dutch Expansion Overseas, 1615–1645," *History of European Ideas* 36 (2010), 386–411.

Van Ruymbeke, Bertrand, "Judith Giton: From Southern France to the South Carolina Lowcountry," in Marjorie Julian Spruill, Joan Marie Johnson, and Valinda W. Littlefield (eds.), *South Carolina Women: Their Lives and Times* (Athens: University of Georgia Press, 2010), 26–39.

Veevers, David, "'The Company as Their Lords and the Deputy as a Great Rajah': Imperial Expansion and the English East India Company on the West Coast of Sumatra, 1685–1730," *JICH* 41 (2013), 687–709.

Veracini, Lorenzo, "Settler Colonialism: Career of a Concept," *JICH* 41 (2013), 313–33.

Voorhees, David William, "The 'Fervent Zeale' of Jacob Leisler," *WMQ* 51 (1994), 447–72.

Wallace, Brodie, "Governing England through the Manor Courts, 1550–1850," *HJ* 55 (2012), 275–315.

Vidal, Cécile, "French Louisiana in the Age of the Companies, 1712–1731," in Roper and Van Ruymbeke, *Constructing Early Modern Empires*, 133–61.

"Virginia in 1632–33–34," *VMHB* 8 (1900), 147–61.

"Virginia in 1637: Harvey's Second Administration," *VMHB* 9 (1901), 170–81.

"Virginia in 1641–1649," *VMHB* 17 (1909), 14–33.

"Virginia in 1650," *VMHB* 17 (1909), 133–46.

W., E., *Severall Remarkable Passages concerning the Hollanders ... with the Continuation of the Case between Sir William Courten His Heires and Assigns and The East-India Company of the Netherlands* (London, 1673).

W., W., *The English and Dutch Affairs Displayed to the Life* (London, 1664).

Waldegrave, Powle, *An Answer to Mr. Boothbies Book of the Description of the Island of Madagascar in Vindication of the Honorable Society of Merchants trading to East-India from the many Aspersions laid upon them by the said Boothbie* (London, 1649).

Wall, Robert Emmet Jr., *Massachusetts Bay: The Crucial Decade, 1640–1650* (New Haven and London: Yale University Press, 1972).

Walsh, Lorena S., *Motives of Honor, Pleasure, and Profit* (Chapel Hill: University of North Carolina Press, 2010).

Warren, Wendy, *New England Bound: Slavery and Colonization in Early America* (New York: W.W. Norton, 2016).

Waters, Henry Fitz-Gilbert (ed.), *Genealogical Gleanings in England*, 2 vols. (Boston: New England Historic Genealogical Society, 1901).

Watson, I. Bruce, "The Establishment of English Commerce in North-Western India in the Early Seventeenth Century," *The Indian Economic and Social History Review* 13 (1976), 375–91.

"Fortifications and the 'Idea' of Force in Early English East India Company Relations with India," *P&P*, no. 88 (1980), 70–87.

Webb, Stephen Saunders, *1676: The End of American Independence* (New York: Alfred A. Knopf, 1984).

"William Blathwayt, Imperial Fixer: From Popish Plot to Glorious Revolution," *WMQ* 25 (1968), 3–21.

Wells, John, and Douglas Wills, "Revolution, Restoration, and Debt Repudiation: The Jacobite Threat to England's Institutions and Economic Growth," *JEH* 60 (2000), 418–41.

Wenzlhuemer, Roland, "Indian Labour Immigration and British Labour Policy in Nineteenth-Century Ceylon," *MAS* 41 (2007), 575–602.

Weslager, C.A., *The English on the Delaware, 1610–1682* (New Brunswick: Rutgers University Press, 1967).

Willan, T.S., *The Early History of the Russia Company, 1553–1603* (Manchester: Manchester University Press, 1956).

The Muscovy Merchants of 1555 (Manchester: Manchester University Press, 1953).

Williams, Eric, *Capitalism and Slavery* (Chapel Hill: University of North Carolina Press, 1944).

Wilson, Peter, *The Thirty Years War: Europe's Tragedy* (Cambridge. Mass.: Harvard University Press, 2009).

Wilson, Samuel, *An Account of the Province of Carolina in America* (London, 1682).

Winn, Phillip, "Slavery and Cultural Creativity in the Banda Islands," *The Journal of Southeast Asian Studies* 41 (2010), 365–89.

Wokeck, Marianne S., "German and Irish Immigration to Colonial Philadelphia," *Proceedings of the American Philosophical Society* 133 (1989), 128–43.

Wolfe, Patrick, "History and Imperialism: A Century of Theory, from Marx to Postcolonialism," *AHR* 102 (1997), 388–420.

Wood, Alfred C., *A History of the Levant Company* (Oxford: Oxford University Press, 1935).

Woodward, Donald, "Early Modern Servants Revisited," *Ag. HR* 48 (2000), 41–50.

Woofe, Abraham, *The Tyranny of the Dutch against the English* (London, 1660).

Woolrych, Austin, *Britain in Revolution: 1625–1660* (Oxford: Oxford University Press, 2002).

   Commonwealth to Protectorate (London: Phoenix Press, 1982).

Worden, Blair, *God's Instruments: Political Conduct in the England of Oliver Cromwell* (Oxford: Oxford University Press, 2012).

   "Providence and Politics in Cromwellian England," *P&P*, no. 109 (1985), 55–99.

[Worsley, Benjamin], *The Advocate: or, A Narrative of the state and condition of things between the English and Dutch Nations, in relation to Trade, and the consequences depending thereupon, to either Common-wealth* (London, 1651).

Wright, Irene A., "The Spanish Resistance to the English Occupation of Jamaica, 1655–1660," *Transactions of the Royal Historical Society*, 4th ser., 13 (1930), 117–47.

Wright, J. Leitch Jr., *The Only Land They Knew: American Indians in the Old South* (Lincoln: University of Nebraska Press, 1999).

Wrigley, E.A., and R.S. Schofield, *The Population History of England, 1541–1871: A Reconstruction* (Cambridge: Cambridge University Press, 1989).

Zagorin, Perez, *Rebels and Rulers, 1500–1660*, 2 vols. (Cambridge: Cambridge University Press, 1982).

Zahedieh, Nuala, "The Merchants of Port Royal, Jamaica, and the Spanish Contraband Trade," *WMQ* 43 (1986), 570–93.

   "Trade, Plunder, and Economic Development in Early English Jamaica, 1655–89," *Econ. HR* 39 (1986), 205–22.

Zook, George Frederick, "The Company of Royal Adventurers of England Trading into Africa, 1660–1672," *The Journal of Negro History* 4 (1919), 134–231.

Index